Site Analysis

Site Analysis

A Contextual Approach
to Sustainable Land Planning
and Site Design

Second Edition

James A. LaGro Jr.

John Wiley & Sons, Inc.

This book is printed on acid-free paper. ⊗

Copyright © 2008 by John Wiley & Sons, Inc. All rights reserved

Published by John Wiley & Sons, Inc., Hoboken, New Jersey

Published simultaneously in Canada

Wiley Bicentennial Logo: Richard J. Pacifico.

For general information about our other products and services, please contact our Customer Care Department within the United States at (800) 762-2974, outside the United States at (317) 572-3993 or fax (317) 572-4002.

Wiley also publishes its books in a variety of electronic formats. Some content that appears in print may not be available in electronic books. For more information about Wiley products, visit our web site at www.wiley.com.

Library of Congress Cataloging-in-Publication Data:

LaGro, James A.
  Site analysis : a contextual approach to sustainable land planning and site design / James A. LaGro, Jr.—2nd ed.
      p. cm.
  First ed. published 2001.
  Includes bibliographical references and index.
  ISBN 978-0-471-79798-2 (cloth)
  1. Building sites—Planning. 2. Building sites—Environmental aspects.
  3. Land use—Planning. 4. Land use—Environmental aspects. I. Title.
    NA2540.5.L34 2008
    720.28—dc22   2007010270

Printed in the United States of America

10 9 8 7 6 5 4 3 2 1

Contents

Contents

Preface

CONTEXT

A context-sensitive approach to sustainable planning and development helps to protect public health, safety, and welfare. By avoiding inherent site problems, or constraints, and by capitalizing on inherent site assets, or opportunities, site planners can limit long-term maintenance costs and, more important, reduce the risks to life and property from natural hazards. The careful analysis of sites—and the site's context—can lead to better development proposals and, ultimately, to higher-quality built environments.

Qualified site planners and designers are vital to this process. Proposals for carefully sited projects may receive faster approvals and permitting, improved marketability, and rent and sales premiums (Bookout, 1994). The emphasis of the second edition, like the first, is on the site planning process and the organization, analysis, and communication of information throughout this process. This second edition keeps the same structure and format as the first but delves into greater depth within each phase of the site planning process.

WHAT'S NEW

New content has been added to every chapter of this second edition. Substantial revisions were made to Chapter 1 (Shaping the Built Environment), Chapter 2 (Visualization of Spatial Information), Chapter 3 (Site Selection), Chapter 6 (Site Inventory: Biological Attributes), Chapter 7 (Site Inventory: Cultural Attributes), Chapter 8 (Site Analysis: Integration and Synthesis), Chapter 9 (Conceptual Design), Chapter 10 (Design Development), and Chapter 11 (Project Implementation). Chapter 10 from the first edition was divided and expanded to create Chapters 10 and 11 in the second edition. This revised edition explores in more detail the linkages between site conditions and ecologically sustainable development—and redevelopment—of the built environment. More attention is also given to finer-scale site and building design issues and to the development regulations and design review processes that influence the shaping of the built environment.

ORGANIZATION OF THE BOOK

This book is divided into four parts. Part I, Process and Tools, contains Chapter 1 (Shaping the Built Environment) and Chapter 2 (Visualization of Spatial Information). The first chapter summarizes the site planning and design process and places site planning and design in the broader context of sustainable planning and development. The second chapter addresses the basic principles of mapping and graphic communication in site planning and design.

Part II, Site Selection and Programming, also has two chapters. Chapter 3 (Site Selection) examines the goals and methods of site suitability analysis leading to the comparison and selection of sites. Chapter 4 (Programming) focuses on programming methods such as user surveys, focus groups, and market analyses.

Part III, Site Inventory and Analysis, is the core of the book. Chapter 5 (Site Inventory: Physical Attributes) and Chapter 6 (Site Inventory: Biological Attributes) cover a wide array of physical and biological attributes that, depending on the unique features of the site and the program, may be analyzed during the site planning and design process. Chapter 7 (Site Inventory: Cultural Attributes) concentrates on documenting relevant cultural, historic, and regulatory attributes. Chapter 8 (Site Analysis: Integration and Synthesis) describes how site opportunities and constraints for specific project programs are identified and documented in support of the subsequent phases of the site planning and design process.

The last three chapters of the book are in Part IV, Design and Implementation. Chapter 9 (Conceptual Design) addresses the spatial organization of the programmed uses and activities on the site. Chapter 10 (Design Development) addresses the spatial articulation of the organizational framework established in the conceptual design phase. This chapter explores design theory and "form-based" development regulations, which communities are increasingly employing to guide development and shape changes to the built environment. Chapter 11 (Project Implementation), the book's final chapter, addresses the permitting and approval processes, techniques for mitigating development impacts, and construction documentation and contract administration. The book concludes with an Appendix and a Glossary. The Appendix lists both commercial, non-profit, and government resources for data and other relevant planning and design information.

EDUCATIONAL USES

The Council of Landscape Architectural Registration Boards (CLARB) conducted a task analysis of the profession of landscape architecture in North America in 1998. One goal of the survey was to document the types of work performed by practicing landscape architects. The respondents were asked to identify their work tasks and rank them in terms of each

TABLE I-1 Partial results of a survey of more than 2000 landscape architects. Self-assessment of work tasks (by rank) that affect public health, safety, and welfare.

Rank	Task
2	Identify relevant laws, rules, and regulations governing the project.
3	Evaluate natural site conditions and ecosystems (for example, slopes, wetlands, soils, vegetation, climate).
6	Identify required regulatory approvals.
10	Evaluate the capability of the site and the existing infrastructure to support the program requirements.
11	Elicit user's intentions and determine needs.
15	Determine the opportunities and constraints of the site.

Source: CLARB, 1998, p. 7.

activity's perceived contribution to the protection of public health, safety, and welfare. This is an important question because state licensing laws for landscape architects, architects, and other professions are explicitly intended to protect public health, safety, and welfare. Completed surveys were received from a randomly selected sample of more than 2000 landscape architects. Six of the fifteen most important tasks listed in the CLARB survey—including two of the top three—involve either site selection or site analysis (Table I-1).

This second edition of *Site Analysis* is intended for students in introductory design studios and site inventory/analysis courses in landscape architecture and students in site planning courses in architecture and urban planning. These include both graduate and undergraduate courses taught in universities throughout North America and, to a more limited extent, in Europe, Central and South America, Africa, and Asia. This book is also intended for practitioners studying for professional licensing exams in landscape architecture, architecture, or planning. Although the book is most relevant to professional practice in North America, the text also should have utility in Europe, Asia, and other developed and developing areas. Finally, this book also can serve as a resource to elected local officials and citizens in the United States who serve on local boards and commissions charged with reviewing site plans and land development proposals.

Acknowledgments

Maps and other project graphics for the first edition were generously provided by: Paul Kissinger (Edward D. Stone, Jr., and Associates); Jim Fetterman (The HOK Planning Group); Jack Scholl (Environmental Planning & Design); Fran Hegeler (Wallace, Roberts & Todd, LLC); Meg Connolley (Land Design); and Bob Thorpe (R. J. Thorpe and Associates).

Several educators provided insightful reviews of an early outline and synopsis of the book's first edition. Constructive critiques were received from Jack Ahern (University of Massachusetts); Gary Clay (California Polytechnic State University, San Luis Obispo); Randy Gimblett (Arizona State University); Paul Hsu (Oklahoma State University); David Hulse (University of Oregon); Nate Perkins (University of Guelph); Rob Ribe (University of Oregon); and Peter Trowbridge (Cornell University). Additional assistance was provided by Rosi LaGro and David LaGro.

For the second edition, generous contributions of additional maps and project graphics were made by Jim Fetterman (The HOK Planning Group); Fran Hegeler and Jim Stickley (Wallace, Roberts & Todd); and Paul Moyer (EDAW, Alexandria). The revision process was aided by several published reviews of the first edition and by constructive suggestions from three anonymous reviewers of the author's second edition proposal to the publisher. David LaGro also provided helpful comments on the proposal. Bridget Lang advised, cajoled, and offered thoughtful and constructive reviews of the entire draft manuscript.

Margaret Cummins, acquisitions editor at John Wiley and Sons, facilitated the production of both the first and second editions. Additional assistance from the publisher was provided by Jennifer Mazurkie, James Harper, Kim Aleski, Lauren Poplawski, Amy Zarkos, and copyeditor Elizabeth Marotta.

part I

Process and Tools

Site planning occurs within an environmental and cultural context. As human populations have grown, society's impacts on the earth's ecosystems have increased. Sustainable approaches to site planning attempt to minimize development impacts both on the site and off-site. Vital environmental processes must be protected and, where feasible, degraded ecosystems restored.

Part I of this book summarizes a contextual approach to site planning and design. The first chapter addresses important design goals that can help shape better, and more sustainable, built environments. The second chapter addresses the important role of mapping and other forms of graphic communication in the site planning and design process.

chapter 1

Shaping the Built Environment

Sustainable design balances human needs (rather than human wants) with the carrying capacity of the natural and cultural environments. It minimizes environmental impacts, and it minimizes importation of goods and energy as well as the generation of waste.

U.S. National Park Service

1.1 INTRODUCTION

1.1.1 Functions of Nature

Landscapes have long been settled, cultivated, and in other ways modified by humans. Yet our ability to alter the earth's atmosphere, oceans, and landscapes has exceeded our current capacity to mitigate the impacts of these changes to our environment. Advances in telecommunications technologies, combined with extensive transportation networks and sprawl-inducing land use regulations, continue to loosen the geographic constraints on land development spatial patterns.

"Economic constraints on locational behavior are relaxing rapidly, and, as they do, the geography of necessity gives way to a geography of choice. Transportation costs, markets, and raw materials no longer determine the location of economic activities. We have developed an information-based economy in which dominant economic activities and the people engaged in them enjoy unparalleled locational flexibility. In this spatial context, amenity and ecological considerations are more important locational factors than in the past.

TABLE 1-1 Landscapes encompass natural environmental systems that directly benefit humans.

Function	Goods or Services
Production	Oxygen
	Water
	Food and fiber
	Fuel and energy
	Medicinal resources
Regulation	Storage and recycling of organic matter
	Decomposition and recycling of human waste
	Regulation of local and global climate
Carrier	Space for settlements
	Space for agriculture
	Space for recreation
Information	Aesthetic resources
	Historic (heritage) information
	Scientific and educational information

Source: Adapted from deGroot, 1992, Table 2.0–1.

Cities located in amenity regions of North America are growing more rapidly than others and such trends will intensify as society becomes more footloose" (Abler et al., 1975, p. 301).

The earth's environmental systems perform a wide array of functions that are essential to human health and welfare. For example, nature's "infrastructure" helps protect the quality of the air we breathe and the water we drink, and it provides many other environmental "goods and services." In *Functions of Nature*, deGroot (1992) organizes nature's beneficial services into four functional categories: production, regulation, carrier, and information (Table 1-1). These services sustain life on the planet.

The following indicators reveal, however, that human activities are degrading the environment and imposing serious impacts on the earth's capacity to sustain life:

- Tropical forests are shrinking

- Topsoil losses exceed new soil formation

- New deserts are formed annually

- Lakes are dying or drying up

- Groundwater tables are falling as water demand exceeds aquifer recharge rates

- Rates of plant and animal species extinction are increasing

- Groundwater continues to be contaminated with pesticides and other contaminants

- Global climate change and warming (mean temperature is projected to rise)

□ Sea level is projected to rise between 1.4 meter and 2.2 meters by 2100

□ Growing hole in the ozone layer over Antarctica

Source: http://earthtrends.wri.org/

Additionally, hurricanes, floods, and other natural hazards increasingly threaten human health, safety, and welfare. According to the National Science Foundation (NSF), since 1989 natural hazards have accounted for an average of about $1 billion in losses per week in the United States. Many disasters causing the loss of life and property can be prevented, or at least mitigated, by proactive decisions to reduce these risks (H. John Heinz, III, Center for Science, Economics, and the Environment, 2000). Mileti (1999), who led the 132 experts, concludes the following:

The really big catastrophes are getting large and will continue to get larger, partly because of things we've done in the past to reduce risk.... Many of the accepted methods for coping with hazards have been based on the idea that people can use technology to control nature to make them safe.

There are, in fact, practical limits to growth, and some locations are far more suitable for development than others. For example, loss of life and property from natural hazards can be avoided, or at least minimized, if the development of the built environment respects nature's patterns and processes.

1.2 TOWARD SUSTAINABLE BUILT ENVIRONMENTS

1.2.1 Community Sustainability

The United Nations Environment Programme (2003) defines *sustainability* as "meeting the needs of current and future generations through integration of environmental protection, social advancement, and economic prosperity." In Ottawa, Canada, as part of the process for developing the city's Official Plan ("A Vision for Ottawa"), citizens agreed to the following set of community sustainability principles. A sustainable community

□ minimizes harm to the natural environment, recognizes that growth occurs within some limits, and is ultimately limited by the environment's carrying capacity;

□ respects other life forms and supports biodiversity;

□ uses renewable and reliable sources of energy and fosters activities that use materials in continuous cycles;

□ does not compromise either the sustainability of other communities by its activities (a geographic perspective) or the sustainability of future generations (a temporal perspective);

□ values cultural diversity;

□ employs ecological decision making (for example, integration of environmental criteria into all municipal government, business, and personal decision-making processes);

□ makes decisions and plans in a balanced, open, and flexible manner that includes the perspectives from the community's social, health, economic, and environmental sectors;

□ has shared values within the community (promoted through sustainability education) and makes the best use of local efforts and resources (nurtures solutions at the local level).

Source: www.web.net/ortee/scrp/20/23vision.html

Public policy plays a significant role in shaping the built environment (Ben-Joseph and Szold, 2005). For example, zoning codes in the United States emerged in the early twentieth century to protect public health, safety, and welfare (Platt, 2004). These land use controls were effective in separating new residential areas from polluting industries and ensuring that new housing construction met basic health and safety standards. Separating incompatible land uses has long been justified in the United States as a legitimate "police power" of local government (Platt, 2004). Some land use combinations, such as heavy industry and housing, are inherently incompatible. However, zoning codes routinely separate residential development from shops, restaurants, and other commercial uses, often with detrimental consequences for the built environment and public health.

This approach to land use planning typically weakens community identity by facilitating low-density suburban sprawl. In combination with transportation policy and planning decisions, many zoning codes in the United States not only encourage sprawl but also inhibit more sustainable forms of development. Although some communities have made significant strides toward sustainable growth and pedestrian-friendly development, there is a significant need in the United States for land use planning and regulatory reforms (Schilling and Linton, 2005).

1.2.2 Community Resources

A vital step toward developing a sustainable community is to first identify the community's natural and cultural assets. The conservation of natural and cultural resources is a fundamental site planning concern (Figure 1-1). Diamond and Noonan (1996, p. xix) call for recognition of a broad set of community resources:

A constituency for better land use is needed based on new partnerships that reach beyond traditional alliances to bring together conservationists, social justice advocates, and economic development interests. These partnerships can be mobilized around natural and cultural resources that people value.

According to Arendt (1999), there are nine fundamental types of natural and cultural resources that should be inventoried at the community level:

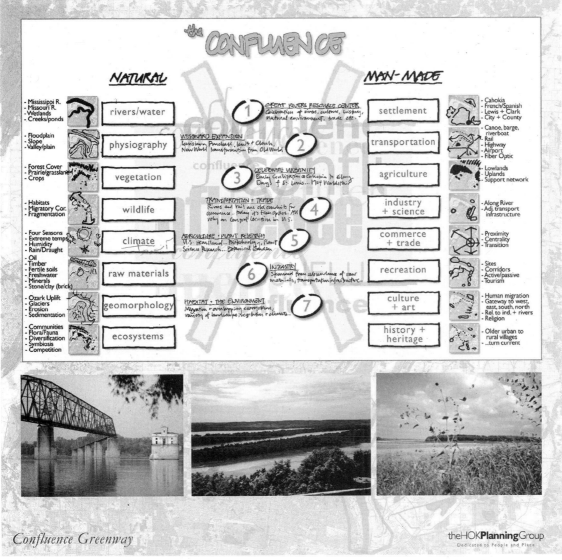

Figure 1-1 Natural and man-made factors influencing a greenway planning project along the Mississippi River in St. Louis, Missouri, USA. Source: The HOK Planning Group.

- Wetlands and wetland buffers
- Floodways and floodplains
- Moderate and steep slopes
- Groundwater resources and aquifer recharge areas

- Woodlands
- Productive farmland
- Significant wildlife habitats
- Historic, archaeological, and cultural features
- Scenic viewsheds from public roads

Collectively, these resources form a unique mosaic or "signature" that defines a community's sense of place to residents and visitors alike. Given their ecological, economic, and psychological importance within the built environment, these natural and cultural resources should be primary determinants of urban form, from the regional to the site scale (Figure 1-2).

1.2.3 Planning Better Communities

The City of Portland, Oregon, has an Office of Sustainable Development whose mission is "to provide leadership and contribute practical solutions to ensure a prosperous community where people and nature thrive, now and in the future" (www.portlandonline.com/osd).

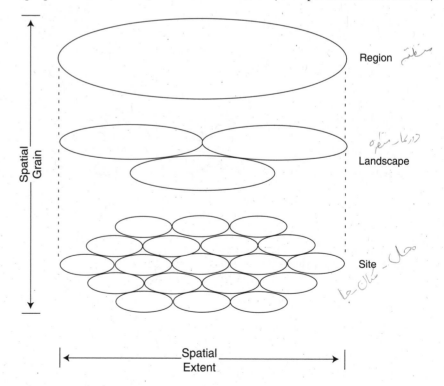

Figure 1-2 Spatial hierarchy—regions, landscapes, sites.

Through outreach, technical assistance, policy and research, the Office of Sustainable Development works to do the following:

- Increase the use of renewable energy and resources

- Reduce solid waste and conserve energy and natural resources

- Prevent pollution and improve personal and community health

Making the built environment more sustainable involves creating more transportation options, more housing choices, and more pedestrian-friendly, mixed-use neighborhoods. Smart Growth principles, endorsed by the American Planning Association and the U.S. Environmental Protection Agency, are practical goals for shaping—and reshaping—the built environment. These principles, guiding both public and private sector decision making, are summarized below.

Smart Growth Planning Goals

- Foster distinctive, attractive communities with a strong sense of place

- Preserve open space, farmland, natural beauty, and critical environmental areas

- Strengthen and direct development toward existing communities

- Mix land uses

- Foster compact building design

- Create a range of housing opportunities and choices

- Create walkable neighborhoods

- Provide a variety of transportation choices

Smart Growth Process Goals

- Make development decisions predictable, fair, and cost effective

- Encourage community and stakeholder collaboration in development decisions

Source: www.smartgrowth.org

Smart growth and sustainable design are complementary paradigms for shaping the built environment. Both approaches encourage the development of pedestrian-friendly communities that not only conserve but celebrate local cultural and natural resources.

1.2.4   Sustainable Site Design

Most communities grow incrementally through a continual process of development and redevelopment. Typically, most of this growth occurs through projects at the site scale. Each

Figure 1-3 Suitability for sustainable development is determined by existing patterns of natural and cultural resources, as well as by the patterns of physical and socioeconomic attributes.

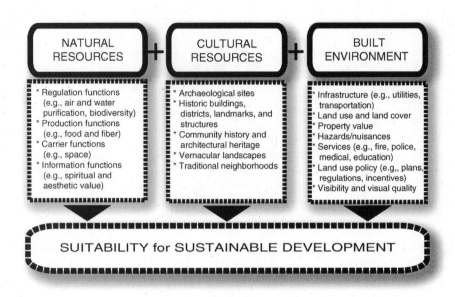

site's carrying capacity is a measure of the type and density of development that can be supported without detrimental effects to society, the economy, or the environment (Figure 1-3). The development of unsuitable sites—or poorly designed development on otherwise suitable sites—can have many negative impacts.

Development impacts vary widely and affect a broad array of natural and cultural resources (Sanford and Farley, 2004). On-site impacts may diminish visual quality and reduce habitat for native vegetation and wildlife. Off-site impacts may include traffic congestion, flooding, or pollution of local surface waters. In *Guiding Principles of Sustainable Design*, for example, the U.S. National Park Service (1993) assesses the potential environmental impacts of new park facility construction by seeking answers to these questions:

- What inputs (energy, material, labor, products, and so on) are necessary to support a development option and are the required inputs available?

- Can waste outputs (solid waste, sewage effluent, exhaust emissions, and so on) be dealt with at acceptable environmental costs?

- Can development impacts be minimized?

A sustainable approach to site planning pays close attention to development intensity and location and considers the initial benefits and impacts of development, as well as the project's life cycle costs. Site planning that is responsive to inherent environmental constraints reduces construction costs, allows the continuation of critical environmental processes, and protects intrinsic natural and cultural amenities. Sustainable site planning is context-sensitive, therefore, minimizing negative development impacts by respecting the

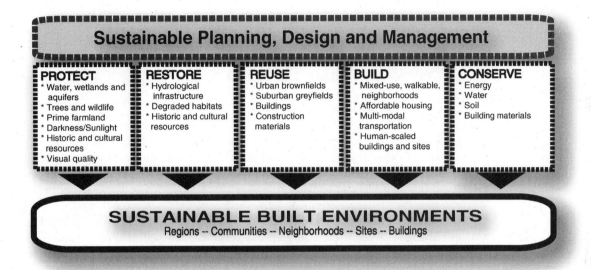

Figure 1-4 Sustainable planning, design, and management is a holistic approach to creating environmentally sensitive development and mitigating environmental degradation.

landscape's natural patterns and processes (Figure 1-4). In *Fostering Living Landscapes* (1997, p. 275), Carol Franklin writes:

> It is the growing realization of the interconnectedness of development and environmental processes worldwide and within our communities that drives the evolution of sustainable design. At every scale, sustainable design is fundamentally about integrating the natural structure of the site with the built environment.

The U.S. Green Building Council's Leadership in Energy and Environmental Design (LEED) rating systems for buildings, sites, and neighborhoods are voluntary guidelines that are incrementally improving the sustainability of the built environment. Green buildings enhance employee job satisfaction and productivity (Rocky Mountain Institute) and cost substantially less to operate and maintain than conventional buildings. Careful choices of construction materials and the use of energy and water conserving technologies also reduce development impacts on the environment. Increased productivity, of course, can enhance business profitability (Russell, 1997, pp. 54–55; Stein, 1997, pp. 54–55). Sustainable development is good for business in other ways as well, such as improving market competitiveness by creating favorable "experiences" that enhance customer satisfaction. According to Pine and Gilmore (1999), customer "experiences" are the foundation for future economic growth. Because unsustainable business practices can reduce profitability and competitiveness, sustainability is an issue that is now commonly addressed in a business school education (Burch, 2001).

1.3   THE POWER OF PLACE, THE ROLE OF DESIGN

1.3.1   Good Design Makes a Difference

Mayors, bankers, real estate developers, and many others involved in urban affairs contribute to the "design" or spatial configuration of the built environment. Some designs, however, are far better than others. The arrangement and articulation of streets, buildings, and all other site elements are "design decisions" that—for better or worse—shape the built environment. Design professionals, such as architects and landscape architects, are trained to base these decisions on fundamental design principles, ethical standards, and a thorough understanding of social and environmental context.

The average citizen may think that good design is a frill, or that it simply costs too much to justify the expense. There are many reasons, however, to justify the expense of investing in competent site planning and design. In *Designing the City: A Guide for Advocates and Public Officials*, interviews with mayors, real estate developers, and other individuals expressed strong opinions about the value of good design in the built environment (Bacow, 1995), as follows:

- "Good design promotes public health, safety, and welfare."

- "Good design makes a city work better, not just look better."

- "Good design attracts people to a city, and those people help pay for essentials that help instill pride and satisfaction in what citizens get for their taxes."

- "Well-designed (real estate) products will succeed in tight markets where poorly designed products will not."

Public investment in physical amenities, including historic districts, parks, and waterfront areas, are important community assets that can spur economic growth and serve as catalysts for additional development. These kinds of amenities may also attract companies and individuals seeking to relocate to areas that can provide a high quality of life.

Quality of life is dependent on many factors, including our safety and sense of security, individual freedom, our physical and mental health, leisure and recreation, and opportunities for self-expression as individuals (Kaplan and Kivy-Rosenberg, 1973). Most, if not all, of these factors are affected by the spatial organization and articulation of the built environment. Single-use, sprawling development patterns tend to reduce people's housing choices and limit opportunities for healthier, active living (Frumkin, 2002; Transportation Research Board, 2005).

TABLE 1-2   **Benefits of context-sensitive, sustainable site planning and design.**

SOCIETY	Pedestrian/bicyclist safety
	Opportunities for active living
	Sense of community
	Attractive surroundings
	Safe neighborhoods
	Proximity to public services
	Minimizes negative impacts on surrounding properties
	Protects cultural and historic resources
ECONOMY	Attracts investment
	Attracts visitors and tourists
	Adds property value
	Creates marketable "experiences"
	Quicker real estate sales and rentals in tight markets
	Attracts high-skilled employees and employers
	Less time spent commuting
	Uses land efficiently
ENVIRONMENT	Conserves energy
	Protects biodiversity
	Reduces air and water pollution, and urban heat islands)
	Protects natural processes and sensitive natural areas

Good design that is *sustainable* can reduce the long-term life-cycle costs of operating and maintaining buildings, infrastructure, and sites within the built environment. According to Joseph Romm (1995), up-front building and design costs may represent only a fraction of the building's life-cycle costs. When just 1 percent of a project's up-front costs are spent, up to 70 percent of its life-cycle costs may already be committed; when 7 percent of project costs are spent, up to 85 percent of life-cycle costs have been committed. Consequently, sustainable design benefits society, the economy, and the environment (Table 1-2).

1.4   SITE-PLANNING PROCESS

Site planning is a multiphased process (Figure 1-5). Kevin Lynch (1971, pp.3–4) defined site planning as follows:

> Site planning is the art of arranging the external physical environment to support human behavior. It lies along the boundaries of architecture, engineering, landscape architecture, and city planning, and it is practiced by members of all these professions. Site plans locate structures and activities in three-dimensional space and, when appropriate, in time.

Figure 1-5 Site planning and design process.

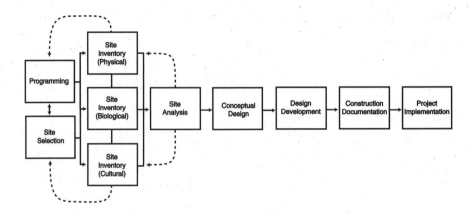

Equally important, site planning also involves choices about where not to build. Site planning must be informed, therefore, by a thorough understanding of the site's character and context. Sustainable site planning protects and restores degraded natural and cultural resources and minimizes detrimental impacts of development on the environment.

1.4.1 Preproject (or Predesign) Phases

Clients initiate site-planning projects. Clients may be private individuals; partnerships; corporations; nonprofit organizations; or federal, state, or local governments. In some cases, a client may simply choose a firm that it has worked with in the past. Or the firm may be chosen for its reputation, specializations, or proximity to the client or site. In other cases, a client—especially if it is a government agency—may solicit firms with a Request for Qualifications (RFQ) or a Request for Proposals (RFP). Once the firm is selected, a contract for professional services typically defines the work that will be completed on the project. This contract includes a scope of services, a schedule for delivering the services, and a budget and payment schedule.

Programming

Site-planning projects vary not only in site areas and locations within the urban-rural continuum but also in prospective site uses. One project might involve the construction of roads, buildings, and other infrastructure. Another project might not have any new construction but focuses instead on the conservation, restoration, and management of natural areas or cultural resources. Programming defines the project's objectives and functional requirements, including the proposed activities, area allocated for each activity, and the functional or spatial relationships among those activities.

TABLE 1-3 Example of program elements for an affordable housing project.

Building height	Unit Density	Number of units (by type)			
Three-story	20 DU/AC	Studio	1BR	2BR	3BR
		10	30	50	10
Five-story	30 DU/AC	Studio	1BR	2BR	3BR
		15	45	75	15

Source: Adapted from Affordable Housing Design Advisor. (www.designadvisor.org)

The program focuses the subsequent analysis and design activities. The program for a multifamily housing project, for example, might include the number, type, and density of housing units that will be constructed on the site (Table 1-3).

The program may be developed by the client alone, or with the assistance of consultants with programming expertise. Programming often includes market analyses, or user demand studies, and the analysis of relevant precedents. Client objectives and preferences for the project are also considered, including the desired uses, special features, design styles, budgets for various project components, and maintenance concerns. An in-depth discussion of programming can be found in Chapter 4.

1.4.2   Site Assessment Phases

Site Selection

Land development typically occurs in one of two ways: clients have a site and choose a program to develop on that site, or clients have a program of intended uses and need a site for those uses. Across the urban–rural continuum, parcels of land vary greatly in size, shape, character, and context. Site selection involves identifying and evaluating alternative sites and selecting the best location for the intended program. More details on the site selection process can be found in Chapter 3.

Site Inventory

Collectively, the features of the site and its surroundings, in conjunction with the project's program, determine the attribute data that are collected for the site inventory. Site inventories map important physical, biological, and social or cultural attributes (Table 1-4). These may include circulation patterns and traffic volumes, existing utility systems, or architectural character within the surrounding built environment. On large projects, attribute mapping and analysis are particularly well suited for applications of geographic information systems. Ecologists, hydrologists, anthropologists, and other experts may participate in collecting, mapping, and analyzing site and contextual attribute data. Yet for any given program and site, there are always attributes that can be ignored to make the process more efficient. The project's program—or intended uses of the site—helps limit the scope of this data collection effort. Chapters 5, 6, and 7 examine the site inventory processes in greater detail.

TABLE 1-4 Examples of physical, biological, and cultural attributes that may be mapped at the site scale.

Categories	Subcategories	Attributes
Physical	Soils	Bearing capacity
		Porosity
		Stability
		Erodibility
		Fertility
		Acidity (pH)
	Topography	Elevation
		Slope
		Aspect
	Hydrology	Surface drainage
		Water chemistry (e.g., salinity nitrates or phosphates)
		Depth to seasonal water table
		Aquifer recharge areas
		Seeps and springs
	Geology	Landforms
		Seismic hazards
		Depth to bedrock
	Climate	Solar access
		Winds (i.e., prevailing or winter)
		Fog pockets
Biological	Vegetation	Plant communities
		Specimen trees
		Exotic invasive species
	Wildlife	Habitats for endangered or threatened species
Cultural	Land use	Prior land use
		Land use on adjoining properties
	Legal	Political boundaries
		Land ownership
		Land use regulations
		Easements and deed restrictions
	Utilities	Sanitary sewer
		Storm sewer
		Electric
		Gas
		Water
		Telecommunications
	Circulation	Street function (e.g., arterial or collector)
		Traffic volume
	Historic	Buildings and landmarks
		Archaeological sites
	Sensory	Visibility
		Visual quality
		Noise
		Odors

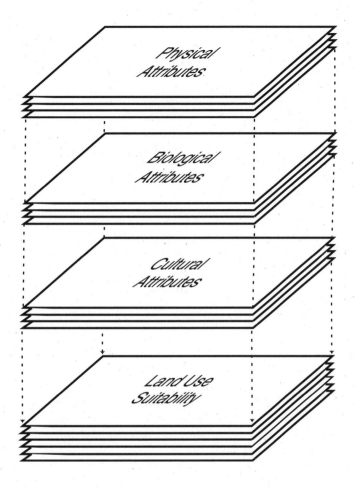

Figure 1-6 Relationship between attribute mapping and land use suitability analysis.

Site Analysis

The site analysis summarizes the site's suitability for the programmed uses. A variety of physical, biological, and cultural attributes can influence the site's suitability for the project under consideration. Information contained in the site's inventory maps can be synthesized to create one or more maps of the site's suitability for development, generally, or its suitability for specific program objectives (Figure 1-6).

Site suitability for a *specific* project is a function of the site's assets and liabilities—or opportunities and constraints. The assets (opportunities) associated with a site may be unique natural or cultural resources that warrant protection. These assets may enhance the site's aesthetic quality and contribute to the site's sense of place within the community or region. Many sites include degraded natural areas that should be restored or enhanced in conjunction with the site's development. Site constraints include chemical contamination from prior commercial or industrial uses. The site analysis may assess whether environmental remediation is needed, what action should be taken to protect adjacent properties from contamination, and what buildings and infrastructures can be used or recycled (Platt

TABLE 1-5   Hazards, constraints, or nuisances that may influence site selection and development

Categories	Hazards	Constraints	Nuisances
Physical	Flooding	Shallow bedrock	
	Storm surge	Shallow water table	
	Hurricane	Erosion susceptibility	
	Earthquake	Hardpan soils	
	Landslide	Expansive clay soils	
	Volcano	Open water	
	Avalanche	Wetlands	
		Aquifer recharge areas	
		Springs and seeps	
		Steep slopes	
Biological	Wildfire	Endangered Species	Insects
Cultural	Toxic waste	Wellheads	Harsh views
	Unstable fill	Historic sites	Odors
		Archaeological sites	Noise

and Curran, 2003). The site analysis also considers regulatory constraints such as zoning and other land use controls.

Mapping the site's opportunities and constraints is essential for sustainable land planning and design (Table 1-5). Providing an understanding of the site within its biophysical and socio-cultural context, the site analysis can be useful to allied professions engaged in the land development and impact mitigation process (see Figure 1-7). More detailed information on this process is available in Chapter 8.

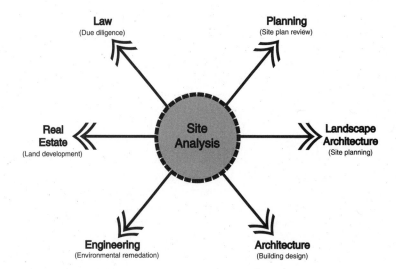

Figure 1-7 Information from the site analysis is utilized by many professions engaged in the land development process.

A site inventory—mapping the site's physical, biological, and cultural attributes—is not a site analysis. A vegetation map, for example, may show the site's existing conditions for a single attribute—the locations of plant communities and also, perhaps, individual specimen trees. This map, like other inventory maps, is valid for any use that might be considered for that site. The fate of the existing vegetation depends on the decisions made in subsequent phases of the site-planning process.

1.4.3   Design Phases

Conceptual Design

Site design is an iterative process transitioning from the general to the more specific. Concept development, the process of adapting the program to the site, flows directly from the site analysis. Sustainable site design adapts the project's program elements to the unique features of the site. Topography, climate, and hydrology, for example, are important environmental factors that shape the design of the built environment. Cultural attributes, including local history and architecture, are also important design determinants.

Concept plans spatially organize the project's proposed elements and on-site improvements. If the program is unrealistic, the design concept and, potentially, budget estimates should reveal those deficiencies, resulting either in a revision of the program and concept, or the selection of a different site. Creating two or more concept plans is particularly useful when seeking consensus from a diverse set of stakeholders. If one concept is clearly superior to the others, then the evidence supporting the better alternative is made more persuasive by comparing it to feasible, but less desirable, alternatives. Frequently, the best concept will be a hybrid plan that is created by merging ideas from two or more alternative concepts. Examples of concept plans, and a more detailed discussion of conceptual design, can be found in Chapter 9.

Design Development

On a concept plan, major program elements—and important existing conditions—are drawn diagrammatically. Circulation pathways are often portrayed as "arrows," for example, and major uses or activity zones are portrayed as "bubbles." The design development process refines, or spatially articulates, these diagrammatic elements of the concept plan. Regardless of the project's program, design development involves documenting—with plans, sections, elevations, and three-dimensional perspectives—how the plan's components will appear and relate to one another functionally. Subsequent design iterations define and articulate the buildings, walls, parking lots, pathways, and other "hard" and "soft" spaces within each of the general land use areas.

Construction Documentation

The construction drawings (that is, plans, elevations, sections, and details) together with the written construction specifications comprise the construction documents (C.D.s). The C.D.s are prepared to ensure that the implementation of the project accurately reflects the approved designs. Once this documentation is complete and the necessary financing and approvals are acquired, the project can be implemented.

1.4.4   Implementation Phase

Depending on the location and scope of the project, approvals and permits may be required from government agencies at the local, state or provincial, and national levels. Local government, especially, plays a significant role in shaping the built environment through the site plan and development review process. More detailed information on this process can be found in Chapter 11.

1.5   KNOWLEDGE, SKILLS, AND VALUES

Site planning is a location-specific, problem-solving endeavor. Unique combinations of site and program create design problems that may have dozens of potentially satisfactory solutions. Some of these solutions, however, are better than others. A satisfactory solution meets the program's functional requirements, while also creating a sustainable and livable place within the built environment.

Site-planning projects typically fall into three basic types:

☐ Projects with no buildings

☐ Projects with one building

☐ Projects with two or more buildings

Projects with no buildings include parks, greenways, and other active and/or passive recreation or nature conservation areas. These are an important but relatively small percentage of professional site planning. Projects involving the siting of one or more commercial or residential building, for example, are much more common. Ideally, the design of the site's building is integrally linked with the planning and design of the site. This typically requires close coordination—particularly during the design-development phase—between the project's architects and landscape architects. Projects involving the siting of several buildings offer opportunities to arrange the buildings in connected sequences of carefully designed outdoor space.

Good site planning requires not only a broad set of skills and knowledge but also the ethics and values to protect critical environmental areas and create sustainable and livable places. Poor site planning may create a variety of unintended consequences. A poorly designed site may, for example, create a vehicle-dominated development that ignores pedestrian needs. Poor design may also create vehicle circulation conflicts, increase human exposure to natural hazards, or degrade environmental quality.

The site planning and design process is far from trivial, as evidenced by professional licensing examinations for architects and landscape architects (NCARB, 2005; CLARB,

2006). According to the National Council of Architectural Registration Boards (NCARB, 2005, p.36), the Architect Registration Exam (ARE) expects registered architects to integrate: "human behavior, historic precedent, and design theory in the selection of systems, materials, and methods related to site design and construction." The ARE also tests for the ability to

> delineate areas suitable for the construction of buildings and other site improvements responding to regulatory restrictions and programmatic requirements... and define a site profile and maximum buildable envelope based on zoning regulations and environmental constraints.

Both the ARE and the Landscape Architect Registration Exam (LARE) recognize the complexity of site planning, and test for competence in relevant areas. The LARE's "site design" section, for example, states:

> Landscape architects are expected to develop site or land use plans that take into consideration the off-site and on-site influences to development. Landscape architects must consider various codes, consultant studies, and principles of sustainability when creating a site design.

Furthermore, the Comprehensive Planning Examination administered by the American Institute of Certified Planners (AICP) also expects planners to be familiar with site-planning issues. The exam's "Plan Implementation" section, for example, includes material on "Plan and development project review (including maps, site plans, and design review)."

1.6   CONCLUSION

Development suitability is not uniformly distributed across the landscape. A comprehensive understanding of the site and its context is an essential precursor to "fitting" a project's program to the site. Each site has a unique set of physical, biological, and cultural attributes, and some of these attributes substantially limit the site's suitability for certain uses. If the site's existing conditions are poorly understood, the site's development can result in detrimental environmental, social, and economic impacts.

Site planning by qualified professionals is a multiphased activity to ensure that land is utilized in ways that are functionally efficient, aesthetically pleasing, and environmentally sustainable. In addition to the construction of buildings, walkways, or other structures, sustainable site development often involves the restoration and enhancement of the site's ecological infrastructure.

Visualization of Spatial Information

2.1 INTRODUCTION

Visual or graphic imagery are an effective and efficient way to communicate both abstract and concrete ideas (Ackoff, 1989, pp. 3–9). Adapting the project's program to the unique conditions of the site requires information—typically, derived from an analysis of the site and its immediate surroundings. Transforming this data into spatially explicit information (for example, maps) is an essential part of the site planning and design process.

This chapter addresses the visualization of spatial information in site planning. It summarizes important principles of cartography—or mapmaking—describes the components of a geographic information system (GIS), and explores some of the ways that this information technology can facilitate the site inventory and analysis process. Sources of spatial data, including aerial photographs, LIDAR, and global positioning systems (GPS), are discussed. This chapter also examines fundamental principles of graphic communication for planning and design.

2.2 GRAPHIC COMMUNICATION

2.2.1 Communication Theory

The site planning and design process is a series of activities that involves the visualization of diverse spatial information. Communicating this information graphically helps clients, consultants, and other stakeholders understand—and participate in—the planning and design process. Maps, models, and other illustrative materials play an important role in effective communication about the project objectives, existing conditions of the site and its context, and ideas for the site's design.

Systems theorists speculate that the content of the human mind can be classified into the following five categories (Ackoff, 1989, pp. 3–9; Bellinger et al., 2004):

- Data

- Information

- Knowledge

- Understanding

- Wisdom

The first four categories concern what is or has been known about the present or the past. *Information*, for example, answers the questions of "who," "what," "where," and "when"; *knowledge* answers the question of "how"; and *understanding* provides an appreciation of the question "why" (Ackoff, 1989, pp. 3–9). The fifth category, *wisdom*, concerns the future, enabling the application of knowledge, understanding, and the utilization of information to design and visualize alternative futures.

Site planners must understand a site's past and present, within its spatial and temporal context, to effectively design the site's sustainable future. Design, therefore, is an expression of wisdom—building on and synthesizing information, knowledge, and understanding of the natural and built environments (Figure 2-1).

Symbols are used alone and in combination to convey information about existing site and contextual conditions. Important features of a site and its surroundings may be graphically depicted as points, lines, or polygons. In some instances, individual elements are portrayed by a combination of two or more symbols. Whether drawn by hand or with the aid of a computer, symbols convey information about both existing and proposed site elements. This information includes site hazards and constraints. It also includes site assets, amenities, and opportunities to accommodate the project program and add value— aesthetically, ecologically, and/or economically.

Figure 2-1 Information, knowledge, understanding, and wisdom. *Source:* Reprinted from "The Futurist" with permission from the artist, Tom Chalkley.

Effective diagrams and other graphics simplify reality and reveal significant patterns and processes. Edward T. White (1983, p.1) comments:

> We designers are often more comfortable and skilled at drawing plans, elevations, sections, and perspectives than at diagramming project needs, issues, and requirements. We sometimes seem overly anxious to draw the architectural answers to ill-defined project questions and reluctant to invest in graphic techniques that help us better understand the project needs and that stimulate responsive and creative design concepts.

Diagramming is also an effective way to communicate information about the proposed design of a project. Diagrams may convey information, for example, about the desired relationships among existing and proposed site elements. Without this supporting evidence, why should public sector reviewers believe that a land development proposal is appropriate for the site? And how can they or other community stakeholders offer suggestions for possible improvements to the plan?

When preparing to communicate project information graphically, five factors should be considered: message, medium, audience, setting, and time (Wester, 1990).

Message

Efforts to communicate graphically may have one of three results: the message is received as sent; the message is not received; or a message is received, but the message is not what was intended. The message will vary from one phase of the planning and design process to the next, of course, and from one site to another. During the site inventory, for example, essential information will include the locations of significant constraints such as steep slopes, shallow bedrock, or wetlands. During concept development, however, essential information includes the locations of proposed buildings and pedestrian and vehicular circulation systems, including the physical linkages among them.

Medium

Because the messages vary throughout the site planning and design process, the techniques for communicating this diverse information must also vary. Construction drawings, for example, are not only technical but also legal documents that are part of the contract for a project's implementation. These drawings must be precisely drafted—whether by hand or with a computer. In contrast, concept plans may be simple "bubble" diagrams. The concept plan is a diagram showing the future spatial organization of the site. This is relatively informal and is often drawn—not drafted—in a "loose" graphic style (Linn, 1993). Clarity is achieved by simplifying the message and by omitting extraneous information. Too much precision may convey to reviewers that the plan is already "etched in stone." Consequently, a highly refined concept plan may inhibit "buy in" of stakeholders and limit constructive dialogue on potential improvements to the plan.

Audience

Project graphics should help orient and inform the intended audience. In site planning and design, graphic communication is often intended for multiple audiences. On many projects, the audience includes the client, design team, government officials, planning commissions, and other community stakeholders. An audience's expertise and familiarity with planning and design should determine what—and how—project information is conveyed. This often requires emphasizing the most important information and omitting less important and potentially distracting information.

Setting

The setting for communicating project information should be considered when preparing and organizing graphic information. If a presentation will occur in a large public meeting room, digital photographs and illustrations may be projected with a laptop computer and video projector in a Microsoft PowerPoint presentation. In a smaller setting, like a conference room, drawings mounted on foam-core presentation boards may be more appropriate. Displaying the full array of drawings can help facilitate a more productive dialogue with the audience.

Time

The amount of time available to prepare and present the graphic materials determines, in part, which graphic techniques to employ. A "quick and dirty" tracing paper presentation may be appropriate for discussing alternative concepts with the client and other members of the design team. Whether the images will be available to the audience for subsequent review is also a consideration. If the audience has the opportunity to study the work, then more information can be conveyed with detailed labels, notes, and—if appropriate—tables and graphs.

2.3   MAPPING FUNDAMENTALS

2.3.1   What Is a Map?

A map is a graphic representation, or model, of a geographic setting (Robinson et al., 1995). Maps are an efficient way to graphically portray important physical, biological, and cultural conditions of the site and adjacent areas. Jenks (1976, p. 19) states:

> Maps are created to provide information about spatial relationships. No other medium communicates distance, directional, and areal pattern relationships as well.

To make a map, the following three basic elements must be known (Fisher, 1982, p. 5):

- ☐ Study space

- ☐ Information or values to be displayed

- ☐ Locations, within the space, to which the information applies

Throughout human history, maps have been drawn or printed on cloth, paper, mylar, and other surfaces. Today, site planners increasingly rely on computer-generated digital maps—or hard-copy maps plotted from digital data. Regardless of the medium by which

TABLE 2-1 Two common ways of expressing a map's scale.

Ratio	Equation
1:24,000	1 inch = 24,000 inches, or 1 inch = 2,000 feet
1:10,000	1 centimeter = 10,000 centimeters, or 1 centimeter = 10 meters

maps are presented, several issues must be considered, including map scale, measurement scale, and map projection.

2.3.2   Map Scale

Map scale defines the spatial relationship between mapped features and the actual dimensions represented on the map. The map scale is the ratio of the distance on the map to the distance on the surface portrayed by the map. Map scale, therefore, is commonly expressed as a reduction ratio (e.g., 1:24,000). A map of the world, for example, would have a very large unit of surface measurement (e.g., 1:12,000,000), whereas a map of a city would have a much smaller unit of surface measurement (e.g., 1:5000). Small map ratios (with large units of surface measurement) correspond to large map scales. In other words, a map's scale gets larger as the map's unit of measurement becomes closer in size to the geographic unit of measurement. As a rule of thumb, large-scale maps have reduction ratios of 1:50,000 or less; small-scale maps have reduction ratios of 1:500,000 or more (Robinson et al., 1995).

Map scale also may be expressed in actual units of distance measure. In the United States, where businesses and governments still employ the English measurement system, map scale is often expressed in inches and feet (e.g., 1 inch = 200 feet). This is especially common in site planning. Converting map scale from a ratio to an equation is straightforward (Table 2-1). Converting linear or area measurements between English and metric scales also may be necessary (Table 2-2).

TABLE 2-2 Conversion of length and area between metric and English units of measurement.

Measure	Unit (English)	Unit (Metric)
Length	1 foot = 12 inches	0.3048 meter
	1 yard = 3 feet	0.914 meter
	1 mile = 1,760 yards	1.61 kilometers
	0.39 inches	1 centimeter
	3.28 feet = 1.09 yards	1 meter = 100 centimeters
	0.62 miles	1 kilometer = 1,000 meters
Area	1 square yard	0.84 square meters
	1 acre = 43,560 square feet	0.40 hectares
	1 square mile	2.59 square kilometers
	1.20 square yards	1 square meter
	2.47 acres	1 hectare = 10,000 square meters
	0.39 square miles	1 square kilometer

TABLE 2-3   Common measurement scales and examples of site attributes expressed in each scale.

Scale	Site Attributes
Nominal	Land use
	Plant communities
	Slope aspect
Ordinal	Soil drainage capability
	Visual quality
Interval	Terrain elevation
Ratio	Slope gradient

2.3.3   Measurement Scale

Attribute values may be mapped as either absolute or derived values, but these values are typically expressed in one of the following four measurement scales (Table 2-3):

□ Nominal

□ Ordinal

□ Interval

□ Ratio

Each of these measurement scales can be useful in site planning.

Nominal Scale

Attribute values that do not imply rank or order are expressed as nominal categories. Land use, for example, is an attribute that is expressed in this way. Land use classes include residential, commercial, and industrial uses. Although these land uses differ in many ways, land use is not an attribute that implies rank or quantity. Land cover is another attribute that can be mapped and displayed on a nominal scale.

Ordinal Scale

The ordinal scale of measurement conveys a gradation or ranking of elements. For example, the U.S. Natural Resources Conservation Service (NRCS) ranks soils by the limitations they present to various types of agriculture, recreation, and construction. Site limitations for excavations to construct building foundations range from no significant constraints at one end of the gradient to severe constraints at the other end.

Interval Scale

The interval scale of measurement applies to attributes with continuous spatial distributions. This measurement scale has equal increments between units, but zero does not have to be included within the range of interval values. Topographic elevation is an example of a continuously distributed attribute measured on an interval scale. Development intensity—measured by the percentage of a parcel's area covered by buildings and other impervious surfaces—is another attribute that can be expressed on an interval scale.

Ratio Scale

The ratio scale of measurement divides one attribute value by another. Topographic slope, for example, is an attribute measured on the ratio scale. Gradient values are computed by dividing the slope's vertical change in elevation by the slope's horizontal length. Slope values may be expressed as either a ratio (e.g., 3:1) or a percentage (e.g., 33 percent). A slope expressed as a percentage value is the angle of the slope relative to a horizontal, or flat, surface. Percentages are typically used to quantify the slope gradient of hillsides and unpaved site surfaces. Ratio values are commonly used in the building industry to quantify roof slopes, or pitches.

2.3.4   Map Types

Maps are classified by scale, function, or subject matter (Robinson et al., 1995). Three basic map types, distinguished by function, are as follows:

- □ Reference maps

- □ Thematic maps

- □ Charts

Although serving different purposes, each map type may have features occurring in one of the other types. Reference maps and thematic maps are particularly useful in planning and design (Table 2-4).

TABLE 2-4   Examples of reference maps, thematic maps, and navigational charts.

Class	Information Conveyed
Reference maps	Topography Flooding hazards Bathymetry
Thematic maps	Elevation ranges Land use types Vegetation communities Soil suitability for building construction
Charts	Aeronautical routes and airports Nautical routes and hazards Streets and highways

Figure 2-2 Parcel map for
Washington County,
Washington. Source: Roger
Livingston, Washington County,
Washington.

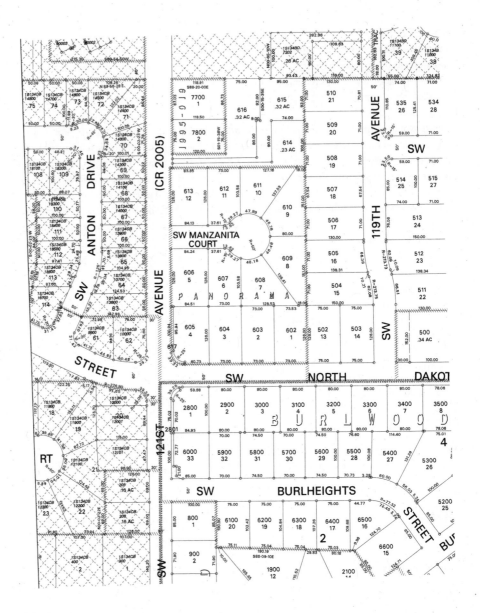

Reference Maps

Reference maps convey information about a variety of natural and cultural phenomena. Plat maps (Figure 2-2), for example, portray land ownership by showing the individual land parcels delimited by ownership boundaries. A plat map is a planimetric reference map, portraying only the horizontal positions of features (in two–dimensional space). A topographic map is another common form of reference map. These maps show natural and built features and the terrain's relief. Landforms are graphically portrayed with contours—isolines that link points of equal elevation—and some topographic maps use shading and color. Typically, these maps also show buildings, utility corridors, and roads. Other potentially useful reference maps include street and utility maps, flood hazard maps, and wetland maps (see Appendix).

Old reference maps may be valuable sources of information to learn about the historic uses of a site. These historic maps can be particularly useful when a site's prior land uses suggest that hazardous wastes may exist on the site (American Society of Civil Engineers, 1996). Sanborn maps of cities in the United States were created between 1867 and 1970 to assist fire insurance companies in assessing the risks of insuring properties (Environmental Data Resources, Inc., www.edrnet.com). A collection of more than 1.2 million Sanborn maps document the history of approximately 12,000 cities and towns. These maps are available online at most university libraries, major public libraries, and at the U.S. Library of Congress.

Thematic Maps

Thematic maps express information about a single, spatially distributed attribute. Biophysical as well as cultural site attributes can be portrayed with two types of thematic maps:

- Chloropleth maps

- Isopleth maps

A chloropleth map expresses attribute data as discrete classes or categories. Classification, a form of generalization or spatial aggregation, partitions the range of attribute data values into intervals. Each of these intervals, or classes, is represented on the chloropleth map by a single color or texture (Muller, 1976, pp. 169–175).

Chloropleth maps are effective ways of visually expressing important site attributes, such as soil type, slope gradient, and land use suitability (Figure 2-3). Land use—a cultural attribute—can be classified into many different categories. A land use classification system developed by the U.S. Geological Survey (Anderson et al., 1976) has three classification levels. Categories are arranged within a nested hierarchy, ranging from the general (Level I) to the specific (Level III). For example, the "urban" land use class is a Level I category. Level II subcategories of the urban class include residential, commercial, and industrial uses.

An isopleth map, in contrast to a chloropleth map, displays the locations and numerical values of a single attribute. For example, an isopleth map of topographic

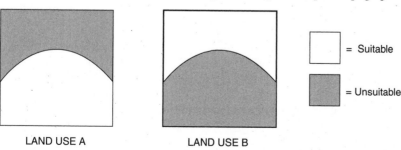

LAND USE A   LAND USE B $\square$ = Suitable

$\blacksquare$ = Unsuitable

Figure 2-3 Schematic examples of a two-class chloropleth map of a site's suitability for two different land uses.

elevation partitions the entire range of elevations within the mapped area into equal increments. An isopleth map of elevation might show several elevation classes, each of which represents the locations where elevations fall within equal increments (e.g., 10 meters). Therefore, each elevation class is simply a subset of all the elevations within the mapped area.

An important decision in thematic mapping is choosing the number of classes to map. Research on human cognition suggests that seven (plus or minus two) is the maximum number of objects that most individuals can compare without becoming confused (Miller, 1956; Saaty and Vargas, 1982). Therefore, the number of map classes within a theme should be kept as small as practicable. Additional information is usually included on a thematic map to help the user understand the context of the mapped area. Typically, this information includes property boundaries; adjacent roads or streets; and streams, lakes, or other significant natural features.

Charts

A chart is a type of map created to aid transportation. Charts include road maps, aeronautical charts, and navigational charts. Road maps can be useful, particularly early in the planning and design process, when a general understanding of the site's context is still being formulated.

2.4 PRINCIPLES OF EFFECTIVE GRAPHIC COMMUNICATION

2.4.1 Hierarchy

Information hierarchies play an important organizing role in graphic and nongraphic communication. Hierarchies place greater emphasis on the most important information to convey the intended messages more effectively. In written communication, for example, letters of the alphabet are symbols that are combined to form words, which are organized into sentences and paragraphs. Graphic communication for planning and design also employs symbols—points, lines, and polygons—which convey information individually and in combination.

In site planning, hierarchies are created by decisions regarding the design and arrangement of the elements on each sheet. These elements include the following:

- Illustrations (maps, photos, plans, sections, elevations, and perspectives)

- Text (title information for the entire sheet and for individual sheet components; labels and notes associated with individual images or the entire project)

- Tables and graphs (summarize important data concerning existing or proposed site attributes)

Attention may be drawn to more important information by emphasizing the size; font; placement; line weight; or color of certain text or the lines and polygons within certain images. Contrast—making any one of these elements stand out in relation to the other nearby elements—implies that the accentuated elements have greater importance.

Layout Hierarchy

Layout is the spatial arrangement of images, text, and other elements on a sheet or slide. The placement of elements on the sheet, or other two-dimensional medium, affects the clarity of the intended message. The size and proportions of the presentation medium (or sheet) influence the arrangement of the elements on that medium. A common approach is to divide the sheet into halves, thirds, or quarters (Samara, 2003). The resulting spaces can be columns or rows running the entire sheet length and width. Or the sheet can be subdivided horizontally and vertically, creating a grid cell framework that can help in organizing the images and text on the sheet. Central placement of an element on a sheet or presentation slide helps to accentuate that information.

Line Weight Hierarchy

Line weight is a combination of line width and value, or darkness. Effective diagramming, especially in the site analysis and conceptual design phases, employs a range—or hierarchy—of line weights to clearly communicate information and ideas. Greater line weight implies greater importance.

Lettering Hierarchy

Titles and subtitles serve as visual signposts that facilitate "way finding" among the information conveyed about a project. Legibility is increased when important parts of the message are emphasized through increased letter size, line weight, style, or color. Effective labeling is concise and informative. Labels may be in "bullet" form, a type of shorthand that conveys essential information succinctly, rather than in full sentences. Labels supplement the information represented in diagrams, plans, and other illustrations.

Not all information on a map or drawing deserves equal weight; a lettering hierarchy helps draw attention to the more important information. Larger letters are typically used for the project and individual sheet titles. Other title information typically includes a designer's or firm's name, other team members, the month, the date, north arrow, and graphic scale. Legibility is a fundamental concern, and some fonts – such as Helvetica — are easier to read than others. Text with lowercase lettering also tends to be easier to read than text with all capital letters.

Graphs and Tables

In each phase of the planning and design process, it may be appropriate to communicate statistics about the program, the existing site, or the proposed plan. Tables and graphs are efficient ways of summarizing relatively large quantities of data. They are particularly useful when classifying data and showing relationships among attributes or variables. The area or percentage of a site devoted to various proposed land uses, for example, can be easily summarized with a pie chart or other type of graph. Analytic graphs are an under-utilized tool, in site planning and design, for summarizing important information.

2.5   BASE MAPS

A project base map provides a common structure or framework for each phase of the land planning and design process. The base map contains key information about the site's existing conditions, including the locations of the following:

- □ Property boundaries

- □ Public rights-of-way and easements

- □ Topography

- □ Existing buildings

- □ Existing streets and utility lines (above and below ground)

- □ Adjacent property uses and owners

The base map serves as the template for organizing and displaying the site inventory and analysis, as well as the design concepts and site plan. The size and orientation of the base map depends largely on the size and shape of the site, the complexity of the program, and the importance of nearby off-site factors. If the site is an unusual shape, then fitting a site base map on a single sheet may require unconventional sheet dimensions. Ideally, a single size and orientation is used consistently for the entire set of illustrative materials.

The size of the base map is also a function of the map's scale. A land-use planning project for a relatively large area (e.g., several hundred acres or hectares) could conceivably have a relatively small-scale base map (e.g., 1:200 or 1:400). Conversely, a site-planning project for a residential or commercial building on a much smaller area (e.g., one acre or hectare) could have a relatively large-scale base map (e.g., 1:20 or 1:40). Ancillary information that is often included on the base map includes the following:

- □ Site location map (a small-scale map showing the site within its community context)

- □ Title information (for example, project name, location, designer, consultants)

- □ North arrow

- □ Graphic map scale

- □ Data sources (date of site boundary survey, name of surveyor, and other source data)

A title "block" is a common feature of construction drawings, which include layout plans, grading plans, and planting plans. But title information can be presented in a less structured format, too. For example, the inventory and analysis maps created early in the site-planning process can be relatively informal in appearance. A site analysis map or a conceptual land use plan may even be drawn freehand.

2.5.1   Remote Sensing

Remote sensing is the process of collecting and analyzing data about the earth's environment from a distance, usually from an aircraft or satellite. Digital sensors aboard airplanes and satellites record both visible and invisible electromagnetic energy reflected from the earth's surface. The major commercial satellite-based sensors record data in several wavelength bands. Multiple sensors, with different spectral sensitivities, facilitate image processing and analysis using different combinations of remotely sensed data. These digital images support research and monitoring in geology, engineering, agriculture, and other fields. Aerial photography, perhaps the most common form of remote sensing, is particularly useful for land planning.

Aerial Photography

Military reconnaissance was one of the earliest applications for aerial photographs. Aerial photographs have also been used in the assessment of land suitability for agriculture. Most agricultural areas in the United States were photographed, or "flown," in the 1930s and subsequently at various intervals by the U.S. Department of Agriculture (USDA). These photographs, in conjunction with soils data acquired through field sampling, facilitated the mapping of soils throughout most of the United States.

Airborne cameras capture either oblique or vertical images of the earth's surface. Oblique aerial photographs can provide synoptic views of the site from a relatively low viewing angle. These photos are often acquired to get an overall sense of the site that cannot be easily attained from the ground. Vertical aerial photos are taken with the surface of the camera lens parallel to the earth's surface. These can be very useful in analyzing a site, but vertical photographs are not maps. These aerial photos have both vertical and horizontal distortion that, unless corrected, precludes accurate measurements of surface distance directly from the photos (Lillesand and Kiefer, 2000).

Horizontal distortion results from the physical properties of the camera lens. The horizontal scale of an uncorrected aerial photograph actually varies over the photo's surface. At the edges of the photograph, the distance depicted is greater than the same distance depicted closer to the photo's center. Horizontal distortion can be corrected through digital photogrammetry, using specialized software and a rectification process called "rubber sheeting."

In contrast to horizontal distortion, variation in the distance between the camera and the earth's surface causes vertical distortion. Vertical distortion is especially significant in photographs of landscapes with large elevation changes, as in hilly or mountainous terrain. Vertical distortion is not a significant problem in photographs of terrain where there is relatively little variation in elevation.

Three basic film types are commonly used in aerial photography for land planning purposes. These films are as follows:

- Color

- Black and white (panchromatic)

- Color infrared

Color infrared film is sensitive to visible light and to portions of the electro-magnetic spectrum that are invisible to the human eye. Sensitive to near-infrared light, this film is particularly useful in monitoring vegetation growth and vigor. Color infrared photographs are regularly used to detect the spread of oak wilt blight, the progression of gypsy moth dispersal and damage, and other tree diseases and insect infestations.

Aerial photos can be used for land use and land cover inventories and to gain a synoptic view of the site within its environmental and cultural context (Paine and Kiser, 2003). On very large sites, and for community-wide planning, digital orthophotographs can prove very useful. These digital images are easily incorporated within geographic information systems. They also can serve as bases images for annotation overlays.

LIDAR

LIght **D**etection **A**nd **R**anging (LIDAR) is a relatively new laser-scanning technology that is proving to be very useful in creating remotely-sensed topographic surveys. Similar to radar, a lidar instrument mounted on a low-flying aircraft transmits light to the landscape below. Some of this light is reflected or scattered back to the instrument where it is recorded or imaged. The time for the light to travel out to the target and back to the lidar, and the properties of that reflected light, is used to determine the range to the target as well as its general properties (www.ghcc.msfc.nasa.gov/sparcle/spar-cle_tutorial.html).

Because LIDAR can "see" through vegetation to detect subtle topographic variation below tree and shrub canopies, these data can provide more accurate topographic information than aerial photography and at a lower cost and within a shorter period than a field survey (Triad Associates, 2005). The resulting digital elevation models are particularly useful in the early stages of development projects involving site selection and the suitability analysis of multiple sites. High-resolution, public-domain topographic data for western Washington, for example, is available through the Puget Sound Lidar Consortium (www.pugetsound).

2.5.2   Global Positioning Systems (GPS)

The GPS is a worldwide navigation and positioning system created for both military and civilian use. Developed by the U.S. Department of Defense, a network of 24 satellites serve as spatial reference points, enabling receivers on the ground to compute their geographic position. The GPS identifies geographic position in three basic steps (Hurn, 1993, pp. 7–9), as follows:

Step 1: Satellites are the reference points

The orbital motion—and exact positions—of 24 GPS satellites are continuously monitored by ground tracking stations.

Step 2: Signal travel time gives distance

Special-coded messages, or signals, are regularly transmitted by satellite. A receiver on the ground calculates its distance to the satellite by multiplying the signal travel time by the speed of light.

Step 3: Three distances give position

Using trigonometry, the ground receiver uses the distances to the three satellites to "triangulate," or locate the receiver's position on the earth's surface.

GPS is particularly useful for the inventory and analysis of natural and cultural features on large sites. Handheld GPS receivers can be used to map individual specimen trees, wetlands and other plant communities, and other site features.

2.6 GEOGRAPHIC INFORMATION SYSTEMS (GIS)

A GIS consists of computer hardware and software, data on locations and attributes, and data about the data—or metadata. Rapid advances in computer hardware and software have vastly improved the mapping and spatial analysis capabilities of commercially available GIS technology. Improvements in software interfaces have made formerly tedious mapping and spatial analysis tasks accessible to a broad audience.

Advances in information technology during the last two decades have made GIS powerful and cost-effective tools for land analysis, planning, and management. The advantages of using a digital GIS include the following (Arlinghaus, 1994):

- □ Ease and speed of map revision and map scale changes

- □ Inexpensive production of short-run special purpose maps

- □ Potentially greater mapping accuracy

- □ Changes in the database are immediately reflected in digital maps

- □ Spatial analysis

Digital spatial data are available in two forms: raster or vector. Raster data are grid-cell surfaces composed of hundreds, thousands, or—with large data sets—millions of cells. Vector data, in contrast, consist of arcs, nodes, and polygons. Both types of spatial data are linked to tabular databases that store attribute information about the locations delineated by each grid cell or arc, node, and polygon. The choice of GIS data models, or forms, depends on the intended purpose of the data.

Raster data are widely used for environmental modeling and natural resource management. Site gradients, such as elevation, are effectively expressed in a raster format. Vector data, in contrast, are well suited for mapping cultural features such as roads and land parcel boundaries.

Massachusetts GIS (MassGIS) is a state-level government initiative providing a central source of large-scale georeferenced data. These and other digital data are potentially useful for planning applications at the municipality, neighborhood, and site scales. Vector data layers that are, or will be, available in the MassGIS library include the following:

- ▫ Administrative boundaries (for example, municipal zoning and regional planning agencies)

- ▫ Infrastructure (for example, state roads, transmission lines, rail trails)

- ▫ Topography and physical resources (for example, surficial geology, soils)

- ▫ Water-related features (for example, wetlands and streams, aquifers, barrier beaches)

- ▫ Cultural resources (for example, state register of historic places and landmarks)

- ▫ Regulated areas (for example, underground storage tanks and wellhead protection areas)

Digital orthophotos for the entire state are available on compact disc (CD) or through the Internet at www.state.ma.us/mgis. Black-and-white orthophotos are available in four resolutions (0.5, 1.0, 2.0, and 5.0 meters). Digital terrain models (DTMs) are also available with 3-meter contours. These images meet or exceed the National Map Accuracy Standards (Box 2-1). The source of the data, the scale of the data, and how and when it was collected can affect data accuracy and, of course, the reliability of analyses based on these data. Therefore, the accuracy at which the data was developed should determine the maximum scale at which the data are displayed and overlayed. Disregarding the scale of the source material can introduce errors when attempting to register (or overlay) multiple data layers.

2.6.1 Georeferencing

Maps are georeferenced to coordinate systems or mathematical projections. According to Fisher (1982, p. 20), "A map projection is the transformation of coordinates measured on the earth's surface (spherical coordinates or latitude and longitude) to coordinates measured on a flat surface (planar or x and y coordinates)."

Many different coordinate systems are used in mapmaking. An in-depth review of coordinate systems is beyond the scope of this book, but a few of the more widely adopted systems are briefly summarized. Among the coordinate systems used in the United States, the Universal Transverse Mercator (UTM) grid system is widely used for topographic maps, natural resource maps, and satellite imagery. The UTM grid system divides the area of the earth between 84-degrees north and 80-degrees south latitude into cells that are 6 degrees of longitude (east–west dimension) and 8 degrees of latitude (north–south dimension). Each 6-degree-by-8-degree cell, or quadrilateral, is divided into a nested system of squares. The sizes of these square grid cells (for example, 10,000 meters or 1,000 meters) depend on the scale of the map.

Other coordinate systems that are widely used in United States, and in similar forms in other countries, are the State Plane Coordinate (SPC) system and the Public Land Survey System (PLSS). The SPC system, a rectangular grid structure linked to locations within the national geodetic survey system, has four times the accuracy of the UTM system (Robinson et al., 1995). The PLSS is a much older coordinate system. First implemented in 1785, this grid structure was used to map about three-fourths of the land area of the United States (Robinson et al., 1995). The primary units of this nested grid system are townships (six-by-six-mile squares), sections (one-by-one-mile squares), and quarter sections (160 acres).

2.7 CONCLUSION

Graphic communication, or visualization, of spatial information is an essential part of contemporary professional practice. Spatial information about the site and its surroundings is essential for context-sensitive, sustainable site planning and design. Advances in geographic information systems and three-dimensional visualization technologies, combined with the commercial availability of an increasingly large inventory of digital maps, have substantially broadened the analytical and communication capacities of site planners.

BOX 2.1   United States National Map Accuracy Standards

With a view to the utmost economy and expedition in producing maps that fulfill not only the broad needs for standard or principal maps, but also the reasonable particular needs of individual agencies, standards of accuracy for published maps are defined as follows:

1. Horizontal accuracy. For maps on publication scales larger than 1:20,000, not more than 10 percent of the points tested shall be in error by more than 1/30 inch, measured on the publication scale; for maps on publication scales of 1:20,000 or smaller, 1/50 inch. These limits of accuracy shall apply in all cases to positions of well-defined points only. Well-defined points are those that are easily visible or recoverable on the ground, such as the following: monuments or markers, such as bench marks and property boundary monuments; intersections of roads, railroads, etc.; corners of large buildings or structures (or center points of small buildings); etc. In general, what is well defined will be determined by what is plottable on the scale of the map within 1/100 inch. Thus, whereas the intersection of two road or property lines meeting at right angles would come within a sensible interpretation, identification of the intersection of such lines meeting at an acute angle would obviously not be practicable within 1/100 inch. Similarly, features not identifiable on the ground within close limits are not to be considered as test points within the limits quoted, even though their positions may be scaled closely on the map. In this class would come timber lines, soil boundaries, etc.

2. Vertical accuracy, as applied to contour maps on all publication scales, shall be such that not more than 10 percent of the elevations tested shall be in error more than one-half the contour interval. In checking elevations taken from the map, the apparent vertical error may be decreased by assuming a horizontal displacement within the permissible horizontal error for a map of that scale.

3. The accuracy of any map may be tested by comparing the positions of points whose locations or elevations are shown on it with corresponding positions as determined by surveys of a higher accuracy. Tests shall be made by the producing agency, which shall also determine which of its maps are to be tested and the extent of the testing.

BOX 2.1   United States National Map Accuracy Standards (continued)

4. Published maps meeting these accuracy requirements shall note this fact on their legends, as follows: "This map complies with National Map Accuracy Standards."
5. Published maps whose errors exceed those stated above shall omit from their legends all mention of standard accuracy.
6. When a published map is a considerable enlargement of a map drawing (manuscript) or of a published map, that fact shall be stated in the legend. For example, "This map is an enlargement of a 1:20,000-scale map drawing," or "This map is an enlargement of a 1:24,000-scale published map."
7. To facilitate ready interchange and use of basic information for map construction among all federal mapmaking agencies, manuscript maps and published maps, wherever economically feasible and consistent with the uses to which the map is to be put, shall conform to latitude and longitude boundaries, being 15 minutes of latitude and longitude, or 7.5 minutes, or 3¾ minutes in size.

Source: Issued June 10, 1941 by the U.S. Bureau of the Budget. Revised April 26, 1943 and June 17, 1947.

part II

Site Selection and Programming

The next two chapters address site selection and programming—two closely related phases of the site-planning process. The order of these chapters reflects the sequence of activities that occurs on many site-planning projects. Often, a client already owns a site, and then a detailed program is developed for that site. In other cases, however, the client has a set of objectives, and then a search is made for a site that can best accommodate those objectives.

Regardless of the sequence of events (programming before site selection or site selection before programming), the site planner must ultimately adapt the project's program to the selected site. Sustainable and context-sensitive site planning requires a thorough understanding of the site's suitability for the proposed program. This analytical and creative process often begins with site selection and programming.

chapter 3

Site Selection

3.1 INTRODUCTION

Site selection plays an important role in sustainable development. Using land efficiently—and in accordance with the site's suitability for the intended purposes—is a fundamental precept of "smart" growth, or sustainable development. Development that is sustainable requires fewer inputs of energy and materials and generates fewer negative outputs such as water and air pollutants.

The U.S. Green Building Council's LEED certification program considers the site's context and previous land use history in evaluating developments for possible certification as Platinum, Gold, or Silver "green" projects (www.usgbc.org/LEED). Choosing to build on an urban infill site, especially if it is previously developed land, helps to minimize urban sprawl and reduce the development's "ecological footprint" (Wackernagel and Rees, 1996). Urban infill is development that occurs on "vacant or remnant lands passed over by previous development"; urban redevelopment involves the "replacement, remodeling, or reuse of existing structures to accommodate new development" (Otak, 1999, p.1).

Many urban and suburban infill sites have excellent access to both public transportation and existing utility systems. Infill and redevelopment projects on these sites contribute to important local and regional planning objectives, including the following (Otak, 1999, p.2):

- Revitalization of downtown and close-in neighborhoods

- Housing development near employment and services

- Neighborhood preservation and enhancement

- Walkable neighborhoods and, where appropriate, transit-supportive development

- Decreased commuter traffic congestion

- Efficient use of existing urban services and facilities

□ Economic development and improved tax base

□ Energy conservation through reduced reliance on the automobile

□ Creating community centers

Especially in lower density suburbs, redevelopment of "greyfield" sites has many social and economic benefits. These are alluded to in a report summarizing the results of a survey of leading real estate investors, developers, and analysts (Pricewaterhouse Coopers and Lend Lease Real Estate Investments, 1999, p. 14), as follows:

Suburbs struggle because they have let developers run amok, oblivious to traffic growth, sewer system capacity or even recreational needs. . . . Increasingly, better suburban centers are starting to look like smaller versions of traditional cities, featuring attractive neighborhoods, easily accessible retail and office districts, and mass transportation alternatives to the car.

Greyfields Into Goldfields, a publication by the Congress for the New Urbanism, features twelve case studies of successful redevelopment projects that converted "dead malls" into "living neighborhoods" (Sobel et al., 2002). Greyfields are previously developed sites that have minor and relatively easily mitigated environmental contamination. These sites include strip malls, regional malls, and other low-density shopping malls, typically with one-story, flat-roofed buildings surrounded by large surface parking lots. With thousands of architecturally bland, vehicle-centric malls in the United States especially, these sites present a tremendous opportunity to significantly improve the built environment through infill and redevelopment.

Mixed-use development, combining residential and commercial uses, can create pedestrian-friendly neighborhoods where residents and workers are less dependent on automobiles for at least some of their daily trips. Compact, mixed-use development also helps to diminish commuting times, lower energy consumption, and reduce air pollution (Platt and Curran, 2003).

Urban infill and redevelopment may face significant obstacles. For example, development costs can be higher on urban infill sites than on suburban fringe sites. Another challenge is the effects of rigid zoning codes that prohibit higher-density, mixed-use development.

Some state and local governments are taking steps to encourage sustainable redevelopment and infill, including revising inflexible zoning codes that mandate rigid building setbacks, lot size minimums, and other building standards that, in effect, legislate low-density, sprawling development. Additional strategies include the reduction of public incentives and subsidies for "greenfield" development on the suburban fringe. One component of this strategy is to target capital investments for public infrastructure in areas that are suitable for redevelopment.

The public cost savings of urban infill and redevelopment can be substantial. A study in New Jersey compared the costs of accommodating 908,000 new residents for more than 20 years in two different ways: sprawl versus a more compact form of development. The study found that the compact development pattern would save as much as $2.3 billion in public facility capital construction costs and over the next 20 years as much as $160 million annually in operation and maintenance costs (Burchell and Mukherji, 2000).

3.2   SITE SELECTION SCOPE

The scope or breadth of a site selection study is a function of project objectives, project requirements, and spatial extent of the search. These are discussed in more detail in the following sections.

3.2.1   Project Objectives

Site selection is an activity conducted for many purposes. Although the range of project objectives is broad, site selection studies can be categorized, on the basis of proposed land uses or activities, into a relatively small number of groups (Table 3-1). Real estate development projects result in the construction of buildings and site facilities serving residential, commercial, and other related purposes. Yet, site selection studies are conducted for purposes other than land development, including habitat restoration, farmland protection, and public open space acquisition.

3.2.2   Project Requirements

Each project program generates site requirements that must be met. These may include minimum parcel size, proximity to transportation and utilities, suitable soils, and many

TABLE 3-1   Typology of site selection goals and selected project outcomes.

Goals	Project Outcomes (Examples)
Habitat restoration and enhancement	Wetland, prairie, riparian area, forest
Protection and conservation of natural resources	Public open space, farmland
Construction of public and quasi-public facilities	Affordable housing School Jail or prison Park Infrastructure (highways, airports)
Business expansion, relocation, and establishment	Manufacturing facility Restaurant Bank Corporate headquarters
Real estate development	Housing (apartments, condominiums) Mixed-use (retail, housing)

other parameters. Once the site selection criteria are established, alternative sites can be identified, evaluated, and compared before selecting the preferred site.

An important factor that influences the scope of a site selection study is the context within the urban–rural continuum. A variety of physical and legal attributes associated with the built environment tend to vary along a landscape continuum from most rural to most urban. Land use regulations and land value are two of the many attributes that vary, spatially, within the built environment. These cultural and biophysical attributes are "design determinants" that should influence the location and character of new development.

3.2.3 Spatial Extent of the Search

Site-planning projects come about in one of two ways: A client may already own one or more sites and the future uses of the land have yet to be determined, or the project objectives have been determined and a site must be found to accommodate those objectives. Depending on the client's goals, potential sites may be widely dispersed geographically (Box 3-1); however, they might all be located within one large, contiguous parcel under the same ownership. Consequently, site selection involves one of two courses of action: selecting a site from two or more noncontiguous sites or selecting a site from within a larger, contiguous parcel—possibly already owned by the client.

Noncontiguous, Stand-alone Sites

Potential sites are either selected or rejected based on each site's suitability for the intended uses. This screening process may span a range of spatial scales, involving the analysis of not only the sites but also the communities in which the sites are located. In today's global economy, businesses that are expanding or relocating may evaluate sites in several countries.

Location analysis is a fundamental component of the site selection process. Sixty percent of the member firms within the International Development Research Council (IDRC) include "location analysis" among their offered services (Table 3-2).

Site selection decisions at the national and regional scales are driven by coarse-scale data aggregated for large geographic areas, such as states and provinces, counties, and municipalities. When a small number of suitable communities have been identified, additional data are collected on potential sites within each area.

Sites Within a Larger, Contiguous Property

Site selection may involve the evaluation of sites within a larger, contiguous parcel that is under a single ownership. This commonly occurs on projects initiated by public or private institutions that have relatively large land holdings. Colleges and universities, for example, are often faced with renovating and, in many cases, expanding their campus facilities (Box 3-2). Campus expansion or redevelopment may involve the construction of new student housing, parking structures, research or classroom space, or facilities for recreational and intercollegiate athletics.

Many college and university campuses are several hundred acres (or hectares) in area, and several potential building sites may be available for any given project. Yet, these sites can vary dramatically in their suitability for the proposed site uses. On a hilly site, for example,

TABLE 3-2 Selected real estate services provided by associate member firms of the International Development Research Council (IDRC).

Service	Percentage of Firms
Location analysis	60
Economic development	45
Project management	39
Real estate development	31
Brokerage	30
Strategic planning	29
Corporate real estate management	26
Construction	25
Property management	25
Financial services	24
Land use planning	22
Management consulting	20
Architectural design	19
Engineering	15
Appraisal	14
Environment assessment	11
Legal	4
Title	1

Source: Site Selection (1999, Jan., p.1122).

development constraints for a proposed dormitory might include the soil's high susceptibility to erosion or the site's poor accessibility to the disabled. On a relatively flat site, in contrast, constraints might include poor drainage and susceptibility to flooding. These are just some of the physical attributes that can potentially influence the siting, design, and—ultimately—the function of either a new building or an outdoor facility.

3.3 THE SITE SELECTION PROCESS

3.3.1 Evaluating Site Suitability

Selecting the most suitable site available for a development or redevelopment project has potential benefits that include the following:

☐ Improved function of the proposed land uses

☐ Greater convenience for the site's users

☐ Enhanced aesthetics

☐ Fewer negative environmental impacts

☐ Reduced construction, operation, and maintenance costs

Chapters 4, 5, and 6 examine the site inventory process that documents the key biological, physical, and cultural attributes of the site and its immediate surroundings. These mapped inventories yield critical information that supports detailed site planning and architectural design. Nevertheless, several site and contextual attributes are commonly considered, though usually in far less detail, during the site selection process. These attributes include the intrinsic (on-site) as well as extrinsic (off-site) factors that fundamentally determine the site's suitability for the intended project.

The site selection process has seven discrete steps.

Preplanning

1. Clarify project objectives and requirements

2. Determine the site selection criteria

Data Collection and Analysis

3. Identify potential sites

4. Evaluate each site's suitability

5. Rank the alternative sites

6. Select the best site and document the results

7. Test project feasibility

These steps are discussed in more detail over the next several pages and are summarized, diagrammatically, in Figure 3-1.

#1 Clarify Project Objectives and Requirements

The client initiates the project and the site selection process. Clients include public agencies, nongovernment organizations, and private businesses. Project objectives among these different clients can vary widely.

Public sector projects usually engage multiple stakeholders in a participatory site selection process. Public agencies engage in site selection for purposes that promote the public interest. Two common objectives are conserving public resources and encouraging economic development. These may be achieved by directing public investment to locations where it will be used most efficiently and where new development will not negatively impact critical environmental and cultural resources.

Businesses—whether owned by individuals, partnerships, or corporations—initiate site selection studies to relocate existing business activities or to expand businesses into new markets. Virtually any type of business may engage in site selection, ranging from small retail and service sector operations to large international corporations involved in manufacturing or natural resource extraction and processing.

Real estate development is another business activity that regularly involves site selection. Location, location, location—as the old adage goes—are the three most important factors

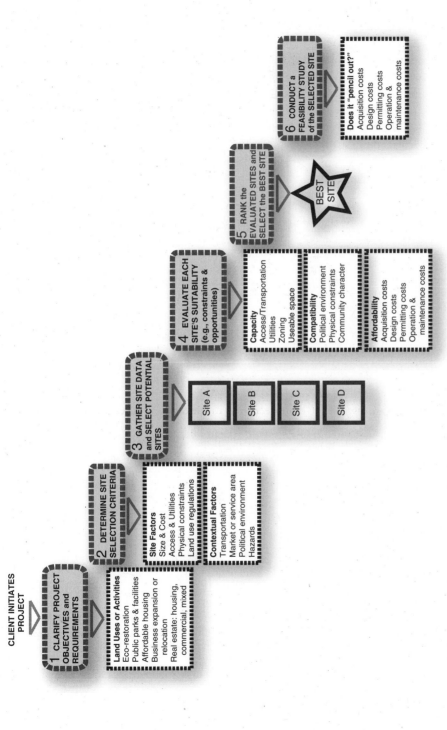

Figure 3-1 Site selection process diagram.

in real estate development. And, for this reason, careful site selection is a critical part of the real estate development process.

#2 Determine the Site Selection Criteria

Site suitability is a function of site conditions, contextual factors, and projected costs (Table 3–3). Site selection criteria focus the task of choosing an appropriate and, ideally, the best site. Carefully chosen selection criteria can efficiently screen the set of potential sites. Site suitability is largely a function of the site's capacity to provide the conditions necessary for the proposed uses. The capacity of the site to sustain the proposed uses or activities includes the following:

◻ Physical conditions (for example, adequate site area, solar access, soils, trees and other natural amenities, access to utilities and transportation)

◻ Legal conditions (for example, easements, zoning, development regulations)

TABLE 3-3   **Generalized typology of site selection considerations.**

Site Conditions	Biophysical (topography, soils, geology, vegetation, hazards)
	Legal and regulatory (easements, zoning)

Capacity: Does the site provide adequate conditions/substrate for the project?

Contextual Factors	Market or service area
	Physical conditions (access to utilities: energy, water, waste treatment) (access to services: police, fire, schools, recreation) (access to transportation) (visibility/visual quality) (absence of hazards)
	Regulatory "climate"

Compatibility: Is the proposed project compatible with the surroundings?

Project Costs and Benefits	Evaluation, acquisition, and holding costs
	Design and engineering costs
	Permitting and approval costs
	Construction and mitigation costs
	Operation and maintenance costs

Affordability: Does the project's benefits outweigh it's costs?

Yet, site suitability is a function of the compatibility of the proposed uses with the site's social, regulatory, and environment context. This compatibility is determined by the area's physical conditions (for example, the scale and architectural character of the surrounding neighborhood).

And, finally, it is a function of the proposed project's affordability at that site. The affordability of completing the proposed project on the site includes the following:

- Site acquisition and holding costs

- Site design and engineering costs

- Mitigation costs

- Operation and maintenance costs

Many different social, economic, and environmental factors may influence the success of a land development, redevelopment, or restoration project. Choosing an appropriate set of selection criteria will narrow the search and streamline the process of evaluating and comparing potential sites and, ultimately, selecting the best site.

Site suitability is evaluated by analyzing key site and contextual attributes, or "threshold" criteria, that help efficiently focus the site selection study. The attributes considered are a reflection of the intended uses of the site and the context of the sites that are likely to be considered. Frequently, a relatively small number of attributes will have a disproportionately large influence on the site selection process. These could be essential site or contextual attributes that, if absent, exclude sites from further consideration. Conversely, these could be undesirable site or contextual attributes that, if present, would make the project infeasible.

Site Conditions

Physical constraints are important considerations in the site selection process. Shallow depths to groundwater, for example, reduce a site's suitability for the construction of buildings, underground utilities, and associated infrastructure. The suitability of the soil for on-site wastewater treatment systems is also a primary site selection criterion for proposed housing in rural areas without access to municipal sewer service. And, in some regions, depth to bedrock may be a key criterion in selecting sites for the construction of buildings with deep foundations.

Urban sites can present complications for development, but many of these sites offer excellent redevelopment opportunities. Typically, urban brownfield sites have easy access to a full range of public services and utilities. Moreover, federal, state, and local brownfield programs now help facilitate the redevelopment of these sites. In the state of Wisconsin, for example, a "Land Recycling Law" (WiscAct 453) had two major objectives, as follows:

- Encourage local governments to take title to environmentally contaminated land and restore the sites to productive use

- Exempt municipalities from responsibility for remedial action, if the property is acquired through a tax delinquency proceeding or by order of a bankruptcy court

TABLE 3-4   Site area standards for selecting public school sites in the state of Alaska.

School Type	Minimum Site Area
Elementary School	10 acres + 1 acre for each 100 students
Middle School	20 acres + 1 acre for each 100 students
High School	30 acres + 1 acre for each 100 students
K-12 School	20 acres + 1 acre for each 100 students

Source: Alaska Department of Education (1997. p.5)

Public sector redevelopment programs reduce financial risks and allow remediation—in certain situations—to conditions that are less than pristine. Instead of requiring complete waste removal on every contaminated site, certain types and quantities of wastes are allowed to remain underground, if steps are taken to prevent storm water infiltration of the contaminated soils. Impervious barriers, such as compacted clay layers, control leaching and inhibit the movement of contaminants into the groundwater.

The area of the site is an important factor in many site selection studies. For example, site area is a threshold criterion in evaluating sites for public schools in the state of Alaska (United States). Moreover, the preferred land area for a public school site varies with the type of school that will be constructed (Table 3-4).

Different site attributes are important in selecting sites for other uses. For example, the American Society of Golf Course Architects (2000) suggests that sites selected for golf course development should have the following:

- A visually interesting landscape (for example, rolling hills and mature vegetation), which will minimize earthmoving operations and reduce construction costs;

- adequate soil drainage and quality topsoil, which is essential for growing fine turf;

- sufficient utility availability (for example, electricity and potable water);

- convenient access to transportation infrastructures, which is necessary to attract golfers at various skill levels.

Contextual Factors

Physical access to transportation infrastructure remains an important site selection factor for most land uses. A site's access to adequate utility service capacity is another important consideration. These services include the delivery of potable water, electricity, and natural gas, as well as the collection and treatment of wastewater. Telecommunication technologies greatly expand the range of suitable locations for many commercial activities. Yet, access to high-speed telecommunications is not ubiquitously available and may be, therefore, an important site selection criterion for certain uses.

Visibility to a site from adjacent streets or other off-site locations may be an asset or a liability, depending on the purposes for which the site is being considered. Visual quality may also influence site selection decisions. Natural and cultural amenities often enhance property values and contribute to a site's unique sense of place. Major water bodies, forests, and mountainous or hilly terrain are natural amenities that add significant value to nearby properties, especially those with unobstructed views of the amenity. Context-sensitive, sustainable design ensures that these positive site features are well protected from development impacts.

A contextual approach to site selection considers the compatibility of proposed uses with the existing uses of the area surrounding the site. Evaluating a site's suitability for the intended uses may involve demographic and economic data for households within a specified distance of potential sites. For example, criteria for selecting prison sites in the United States encompass physical conditions of potential sites as well as the site's social context. These criteria include (Ammons et al., 1992) the following:

- Proximity to the communities from which most inmates come

- Areas capable of providing or attracting qualified professional staff of racial and ethnic origins compatible with the inmate population

- Areas with adequate social services, hospitals, schools, universities, and employment opportunities to support the correctional goals

Other off-site factors include the site's visibility from adjacent roads and highways and the ease with which views to a new prison can be screened (Krasnow, 1998).

Government permitting and approval processes may also influence the site selection decision. The permitting and approval process for new development is intended to protect the public health, safety, and welfare. Neighborhood concerns about vehicle traffic, building height, and development density can lead to project delays and modifications of the project's objectives.

If all relevant site and contextual factors could be measured in quantitative terms, the process of evaluating criteria and selecting the best available site would be relatively straightforward. Most site selection decisions, however, involve financial as well as social, environmental, and ethical considerations. The client, the design team, future project users, and other stakeholders may hold very different values and, therefore, priorities regarding the site selection criteria. Any conflicts or inconsistencies among potential selection criteria should be resolved early in the site selection process.

#3 Identify Potential Sites

On some projects, the client may provide a list of potential sites for evaluation. In other cases, the potential sites must be identified (Figure 3-2). Sources of site data that are useful in identifying potential sites include the following:

- Multiple listing services (MLS) for property that is for sale or rent

- Maps of vacant, infill, and redevelopable land prepared by local municipalities during comprehensive plan updates and neighborhood studies

- Street and highway maps

The identification of potential sites is a form of spatial analysis that lends itself to applications of geographic information systems (Castle, 1998).

Figure 3-2 Oblique aerial photograph with potential project sites delineated. Source: Wallace, Roberts & Todd, LLC.

Local governments, especially, are increasingly supportive of development and redevelopment that adds jobs and contributes to local property and sales tax revenues. In addition to providing maps of available infill and redevelopment sites, local governments may also provide data that are useful for site selection, including site area, available utilities, and applicable development regulations.

#4 Evaluate Each Site's Suitability
Once potential sites have been identified, additional data are needed to assess each site's suitability for the proposed project. Some common data sources include the following:

- ☐ Aerial photographs (for example, Google Earth)
- ☐ Parcel boundary and tax assessor data
- ☐ Highway maps
- ☐ Utility maps

□ Topographic maps

□ Soils maps

□ Ground-level photographs showing views on- and off-site

A boundary survey, showing property boundaries, is commonly required for the sale of a property. These are often readily available for sites under consideration. Because of the costs and time involved in acquiring a topographic survey, this more detailed information is usually not available until after a site has been selected.

Evaluating site suitability for a proposed land use or ecological restoration activity typically involves the analysis of both quantitative and qualitative data. For example, public investment in schools and park facilities are important policy decisions that have significant impacts on the fiscal and natural resources of the involved communities (Figure 3-3). To conserve these resources, investments in new facilities should be preceded by rigorous site evaluation. The importance and challenge of site selection is reflected in the following quote from the Alaska Department of Education (1997, p.2):

The perfect school site can be envisioned as generally level with some topographic interest, having complete utilities, stable, well-drained soils, excellent road and pedestrian access, protection from excessive weather patterns, [and] with ample space for school facilities, playground, and sports fields. The site would be accessible to present and future populations and be free of any natural or environmental hazards. It would be removed from undesirable business, industry and traffic hazards but convenient to important facilities and recreational/outdoor learning areas. In most communities, however, the perfect site is elusive and difficult to find.

The City of San Francisco, for example, adds to its extensive public open space system through a selection process that prioritizes sites meeting the following criteria (City and County of San Francisco Recreation and Park Department, 2006, p.3):

□ Open spaces, facilities, and other real property in neighborhoods that are designated as follows: "high-need areas" in the Recreation and Open Space Element of the City's General Plan

□ Open spaces, facilities, and other real property in neighborhoods that are experiencing a significant increase in residential population and that have few open spaces or recreational resources

□ Significant natural areas that are not otherwise protected from degradation or development.

The process of evaluating sites for potential open space acquisition in San Francisco employs an extensive set of suitability criteria (Box 3-3).

Typically, site suitability is evaluated using a predetermined scale for rating the selection criteria. A qualitative rating scale, for example, may be as simple as three rating categories:

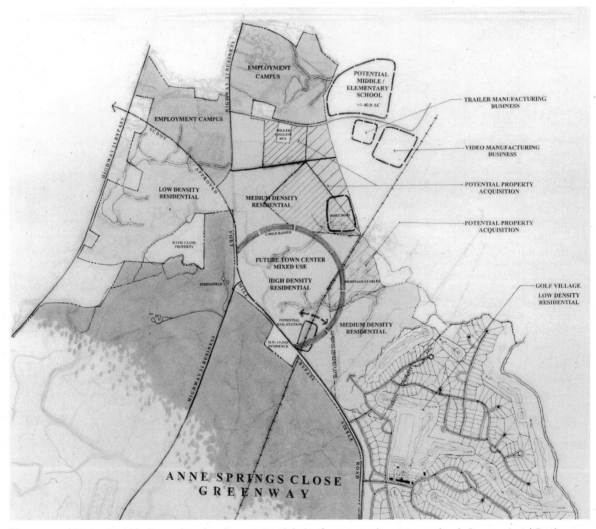

Figure 3-3 Conceptual land use plan showing a potential site for a new elementary school. Source: Land Design.

acceptable, somewhat acceptable, and unacceptable. A quantitative scale, in contrast, assigns a numerical value to each rating class. Examples of rating scales for evaluating site selection criteria include the following:

Qualitative or nominal rating scale with three classes

- ☐ Acceptable
- ☐ Somewhat acceptable
- ☐ Unacceptable

Quantitative rating scale with three classes

+1 Favorable (meets the objective)

0 Neutral

−1 Unfavorable (fails to meet the objective)

Quantitative rating scale with five classes

4 = excellent (most desirable/most cost effective)

3 = good

2 = fair

1 = poor

0 = unacceptable (least desirable/least cost effective)

By using threshold criteria that reflect the most important site or contextual attributes, a large number of potential sites can be initially screened. If the threshold criteria are adequately met by one or more sites, the process can proceed to consider other selection criteria. Conversely, if a site does not satisfy all of the threshold criteria, then that site is eliminated from further consideration. This initial screening process effectively reduces the number of potential sites to a manageable "short list," usually between three and ten sites. This process conserves the time and resources available to collect additional data and compare candidate sites.

Threshold criteria can be physical, economic, or legal attributes of the site or its context. For example, flooding potential from nearby water bodies is considered in the siting of public schools in Alaska. The guidelines for evaluating this selection criterion are as follows:

Once a site or a small number of potential sites have been chosen, more detailed studies of site suitability can assess the "fit" between each site and the intended program. The goal of this comparative site evaluation is to identify the best site for the project under consideration.

Flooding Potential	*Score*
Site is not in floodplain; no nearby water bodies	4
Site is in proximity to water bodies but well above floodplain	3
Site is in close proximity to flood prone areas	2
Site is within floodplain boundaries	1
Site floods routinely	0

Source: Alaska Department of Education.

When sites are being evaluated for multiple proposed uses, the site selection process becomes more complex. Different land uses may require different types of sites. One approach in evaluating site suitability is to prioritize the proposed land uses, then "solve" the site selection "problem" for the most important land use. When a small number of sites have been identified for the primary land use, then the process can continue with choosing the next most important land use, and so on. Once a site is selected, the site planning process involves a more detailed site analysis.

3.3.2 Comparing the Suitability of Alternative Sites

#5 Rank the Alternative Sites

Site suitability ratings are summarized in a matrix as either numerical or graphical values for each selection criterion. The site evaluation matrix is simply a table that lists the potential sites and the evaluations of each site selection criterion (Figure 3-4). There are no inherent limits on either the number of selection criteria or sites that can be evaluated. There are practical limits, however, dictated by the time and resources available, as well as by the risks of selecting a poorly suited site.

One approach is to complete the site evaluation matrix by rating each criterion without attempting to condense these ratings into one or more summary indices. When criteria are rated on a quantitative scale, the scores may be combined into a single site suitability index that is either "weighted" or "unweighted." Simply adding the suitability scores for all

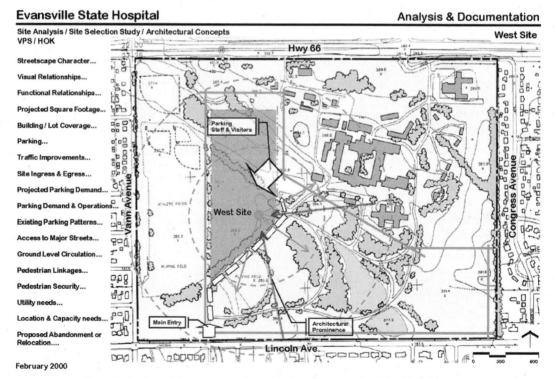

Figure 3-4 Potential site (west) for a new medical building. Source: The HOK Planning Group.

selection criteria is one approach, yielding a total "unweighted" suitability score for each site, as follows:

$$\text{Site suitability score (unweighted)} = X_1 + X_2 + X_3 \ldots X_n$$

where X_1, $X_2 \ldots X_n$ are suitability scores for the selection criteria

While this approach is attractive for its simplicity, combining the ratings for a diverse set of selection criteria may mask important information about the sites' suitability for the intended project. Site conditions, cost factors, and contextual factors are all lumped together in one total score. Moreover, the unweighted approach gives equal importance to each selection criterion. A potentially significant limitation of this approach is that some criteria are, in fact, more important than others.

A refinement of the unweighted approach is to "weight" each criterion according to each factor's influence on site suitability. These weights are assigned on the basis of each attribute's perceived importance to suitability of a site for the proposed uses. The algorithm for a weighted site evaluation is as follows:

$$\text{Site suitability score (unweighted)} = X_1(W_1) + X_2(W_2) + X_3(W_3) \ldots X_n(Wn)$$

where X_1, $X_2 \ldots X_n$ are suitability scores for the selection criteria, and

where W_1, $W_2 \ldots W_n$ are criteria weights

An example of a weighting scheme, with five levels or weights, is shown in Table 3-5. The weighted approach gives the most important selection criteria a greater influence on the results of the site selection study. Because the scheme for weighting the selection criteria can dramatically influence the results of the evaluation, the weights must be chosen carefully. On public sector projects, especially, this often requires negotiation among the various stakeholders.

A fourth approach recognizes the complexity inherent in the site selection process and calculates separate indices for categories or groupings of selection criteria. Rather than relying on a single index to summarize the complex effects of site and cultural factors on the proposed uses, the site selection decision is based on consideration of suitability indices for different attribute categories.

TABLE 3-5 Sample weighting scheme for site selection criteria

Weight	Importance to Project
5	Essential
4	Very important
3	Important
2	Somewhat important
1	Not very important

Source: Alaska Department of Education (1997, p. 3).

Regardless of which approach is taken, the sites must be ranked or at least divided into groups of sites with similar suitability ratings. In a study of potential sites for the Hood Canal Bridge, for example, the Washington State Department of Transportation (2005) analyzed 18 sites but did not weight the suitability criteria or compute a summary score for each site. All of the 18 sites were evaluated and placed in one of the following four categories:

- □ Preferred sites

- □ Acceptable sites

- □ High-risk sites

- □ Least reasonable sites

The candidate sites were mapped, and the site evaluation matrix included graphic symbols to convey the suitability of each site.

#6 Select the Best Site and Document the Results

The type of client and project determines who has decision-making authority to select sites for further study. For example, this may be an individual, a committee, or a board or commission. Public projects usually have a site selection process that encourages public participation. A site evaluation report is often prepared to summarize the site selection process and the results (Box 3-4). The objective, once the best site is selected, is to secure the site and there is often an option to purchase the land.

3.3.3 Project Feasibility

#7 Testing Project Feasibility

Once the best site has been selected, the project's feasibility may be studied in more detail before the site is purchased and the project moves to subsequent phases of the site-planning process. Whether a private sector or public sector project, feasibility studies typically examine the proposed project's costs and benefits. A project's financial feasibility is determined, in part, by the physical characteristics of the site and by contextual factors, including the market for potential customers, competing projects in the area, and regulatory constraints, as well as the community's expectations and attitudes concerning land development. Feasibility studies may include the following four parts:

- □ Market analysis (private sector projects)

- □ Assessment of site- and context-specific constraints and opportunities (for example, risk assessment)

- □ *Pro forma* financial statements (private sector development), or capital budget/ funding (public sector project)

- □ Design concepts (for example, concept plans and 3-D simulations)

On a real estate development project, a feasibility study must determine if the selected site will "pencil out," or yield the expected return on investment (ROI). A discounted cash flow analysis estimates projected costs and revenues. The pro forma is the spreadsheet that summarizes the project's anticipated cash flow, showing expenses, revenues, and profits (Peiser, 1992). The pro forma also estimates the project's anticipated ROI.

A typical residential development project may involve other activities such as obtaining a mortgage financing commitment and analyzing risks associated with the proposed development. A common objective in testing a project's feasibility is to determine those areas on the site that are suitable for the intended uses. This preliminary site analysis may identify developable as well as nondevelopable site areas. The site feasibility study shows the "envelope" or area of the site that is suitable for development. The feasibility study may also include a conceptual site plan, showing the spatial arrangement of the program elements on the site. The approximate "footprints" or areas of the program elements may then be organized, diagrammatically, on the base map's developable areas to determine if the proposed program will "fit" on the site.

There are usually many different ways, however, to organize or arrange program elements on a site. And among those alternative arrangements, or site plans, there can be significant variability in design quality, social and environmental impacts, and financial cost.

A feasibility study provides critical information, including: a) how much of the site can be developed (for example, physical and regulatory constraints limit the developable area, to some extent, on most sites); b) what regulatory permits and approvals are needed to develop the site; and c) estimates of the time and political obstacles or incentives that can be expected (Triad Associates, 2001). If the site has not yet been purchased, the client may then decide to purchase it. In some situations, the client may be advised to acquire adjacent parcels of land to assemble a larger site with greater potential and project flexibility. If the constraints for the proposed project are formidable, however, the client may be advised to forgo purchasing the site.

Site Evaluation, Acquisition, and Holding Costs

For sites with a history of previous commercial or industrial uses, considerable time and effort may be devoted to acquiring site information before purchasing the property. Land acquisition costs include consultants' fees for site evaluation and selection. The purpose of this investigation, or "due diligence," is to ensure that all potential risks and costs have been anticipated before acquiring the property. An option to purchase a site is one way that a prospective buyer can reduce the initial costs and financial risks. If the client decides not to buy, the financial "exposure" on the project is limited.

After a site is purchased, land holding costs accrue as the development process continues. These include financing or opportunity costs of the investment and the real estate taxes on the property. Property taxes on privately owned land, buildings, and other site improvements are an important source of revenue for local governments in the United States (Kmitch and Baker, 2000). Property taxes provide general revenue to fund a variety of public facilities, including parks, schools, and public services such as fire and police protection.

Site Design and Engineering Costs

During most of the nineteenth and twentieth centuries, urban growth and development in the United States occurred in waves or stages, beginning in the urban core and moving outward to the rural fringe. Land parcels that were "passed over during the first wave of development tend to be developed later, at higher densities" (Peiser, 1992, p. 48). These sites may have remained undeveloped for a variety of reasons. A landowner may have simply held on to the land for speculative purposes, in anticipation of the property increasing in value. In other cases, however, these sites are undeveloped because they have significant development constraints.

Difficult sites are more costly to develop for several reasons. Rugged topography, unstable soils, or shallow bedrock are just a few of the physiographic constraints that make design and construction more complex and, therefore, more expensive. These vacant parcels are often attractive for development because they are well served by existing public infrastructure and are often located in areas convenient to shopping, cultural, and educational facilities.

Although most sites can be modified to accommodate the construction of buildings, roads, and related infrastructure, the development of environmentally sensitive sites can have negative on-site and off-site consequences. The potential impacts include degraded terrestrial and aquatic ecosystems, due to the fragmentation and destruction of wildlife habitat. Life safety risks to humans may also result from site disturbances that increase the likelihood of landslides or other environmental hazards. Developing difficult sites may substantially increase the complexity and cost of project design and permitting.

Permitting and Approval Costs

Not all project costs can be quantified in monetary terms. Environmental degradation from proposed land development may impose costs to society, rather than to the responsible parties. These negative environmental impacts are externalities—the result of what economists call market failures. A fundamental role of local government is to protect public health, safety, and welfare by minimizing negative externalities. Development impact fees are one way in which the government attempts to assign these costs to responsible parties.

To be legally upheld—or deemed constitutional—land use controls in the United States must protect public health, safety, and welfare. As more has been learned about the built environment's impacts on ecosystem function and public health, public scrutiny of development proposals has increased. Yet, attitudes toward new development vary widely among communities, leading to differing attitudes concerning where, when, and how development will be allowed to proceed.

A site's location may determine whether a proposed development project receives the community's support. Objections to development or redevelopment proposals often rest on concerns about the projects' off-site impacts. These impacts may affect local environmental quality, the community's fiscal well being, or neighboring residents' quality of life. Logically, then, the site selection process should consider the project's potential off-site impacts. Neighborhood concerns can prevent a project from being approved or result in substantial revisions to the project's scope.

The complexity of the project design and permitting process is greatly influenced by the site's physical and cultural attributes, context and, therefore, it's suitability for development. Exactions are payments to either the local or county government to mitigate development impacts. Frequently, exactions compensate communities for the increased costs of providing public services for new development (Altshuler and Gomez-Ibanez, 1993). On residential subdivision projects, for example, exactions often include payments for off-site infrastructure costs, such as street intersection improvements, installation of new traffic signals, and utility system extensions. Exactions also include impact fees—or dedication of land in lieu of payments—for public schools, neighborhood parks, or other public facilities. Typically, exactions must be paid before any lots can be legally sold.

Construction and Mitigation Costs

The site selection process may consider the costs of implementing the project. Site preparation costs typically include excavation and site grading, storm water management, installation of site utilities, building construction, and landscaping. Physical site constraints may substantially increase these costs, particularly if development is planned for areas that are poorly suited for construction. These constraints range from poor soil drainage or shallow depths to bedrock to the potentially life-threatening hazards of flooding and landslides. Development of poorly suited sites, or development of unsuitable areas on otherwise suitable sites, can significantly increase construction costs for site grading and storm water management, vehicle and pedestrian circulation systems, site utilities, and building construction.

Ian McHarg's credo (1969), "design with nature," remains a compelling and sensible site-planning objective. Designing with nature reduces development impacts on the complex web of biophysical systems that functionally link land, water, and biota. Moreover, the conservation of a site's natural resources can make the development site a more desirable place to reside, work, and play.

Mitigation of the project's impacts may be required as a condition of project permitting and approval. Mitigation requirements may include wetland restoration or banking and extensive storm water management. Many development projects increase demands on public services and facilities. These impacts are a function of the project's proposed land uses and the density of the new development. Expected increases in vehicular traffic, for example, may require mitigation fees, or exactions, to pay for improvements in the transportation infrastructure. Intersection improvements, including new traffic signals, are common forms of mitigation. Impact fees for public services such as fire and police protection are also quite common, regardless of the type of project.

School district impact fees, however, are targeted at residential or housing development. Depending on the municipality in which the project is located, these fees can amount to several thousand dollars per dwelling unit. For example, according to a 2005 survey of jurisdictions in King County, Washington State (United States), school district impact fees for a new single-family home ranged from none in the Seattle district to more than $5000 in parts of the Auburn district (Triad Associates, 2005). Impact fees were generally lower for multifamily dwellings.

On industrial projects, however, the impacts and mitigation requirements may be quite different. In a study of potential heavy industrial sites in Teller County, Colorado, the potential impacts evaluated for each site included the following:

- Impacts on sensitive natural resources (for example, slopes, habitats, wildlife migration corridors)

- Traffic impacts (for example, level of service, traffic conflicts)

- Infrastructure impacts

- Visual impacts

- Air quality impacts (for example, dust, odors)

- Noise

- Blowing materials

- Introduction of pests

- Light pollution

- Water quality impacts (for example, storm water, flooding)

Recommended mitigation measures were assessed for each site and each potential area of impact. Chapter 11 includes further discussion of project implementation issues.

Operation and Maintenance Costs and Benefits

Maintenance, management, and other operational costs are influenced by the site's location and setting. "Life cycle" costs are associated with buildings as well as a site's grounds. Building heating and cooling costs, for example, are not only affected by the building's design and construction but also by the building's siting. When continuing costs are considered in development decisions, then sustainable or "green" development may be more cost efficient than conventional, resource intensive alternatives. Other initial and ongoing costs concern the provision of transportation and access and storm water management.

Sites that are subject to natural hazards may be subject to significant additional costs. If hazard insurance is available, premiums will be higher than for comparable property that is not within a hazard area. Wind, water, and storm surges increase the risks of property damage and destruction. Other environmental factors that influence maintenance and operating costs include: site drainage, flooding, site erosion, and proximity to other natural hazards (Alaska Department of Education, 1997).

Some businesses in today's global economy conduct international searches for sites where they may locate new facilities. The selection of the site—in some cases from among a regional, national, or international set of alternatives—can impact many facets of a company's operations, including the company's profitability. For a heavy-manufacturing facility, proximity to sources of essential raw materials may be the most important criterion in the site selection decision. This is particularly true if the raw materials are bulky and expensive to transport. In contrast, for a firm that manufactures precision instruments, a location near an available supply of skilled labor—such as tool and die makers—could be critically important. Other commonly considered attributes include corporate tax rates, quantity and quality of the available workforce, and utility capacities and rates.

Real estate development projects "market" properties to prospective buyers or renters. Market studies provide information on the competition selling or renting residential or commercial properties. Rental and sales prices within an area are influenced by the quality and quantity of competing real estate. The value of commercial real estate, especially, is strongly influenced by its accessibility.

According to *Site Selection* magazine's annual survey of developers, owners, managers, and promoters of office parks, proximity to an interstate highway interchange is a key contextual attribute. The demand for office park visibility and easy highway access is reflected in office park site costs (O'Connor, 1996), as follows:

> Our survey results show that with increasing distance from the interstate there is a steady decline in the average price per acre of prepared sites. For sites less than one mile from the interstate, the average price per acre is $53,000. For sites between one and five miles from the interstate, the average asking price drops to $45,000 per acre, and for sites between five and 10 miles from the interstate, the average price dips to $31,000 per acre.

Preferences for residential locations vary widely among different segments of society. Different clientele, or housing "markets," are largely defined by age, occupation, education level, income, and family status. For younger couples with children, for example, housing preferences may be influenced by the proximity and quality of primary and secondary schools, public health and human services, or outdoor recreational opportunities.

Development Incentives

Economic development incentives play a substantial role in shaping commercial and industrial development patterns in the United States. According to the International Economic Development Council, the main goal of economic development is to improve "the economic well being of a community through efforts that entail job creation, job retention, tax base enhancements and quality of life" (www.iedconline.org). The rationale for development incentives rests on the economic benefits that may accrue to the state, county, or municipality offering the assistance. These benefits include job creation and capital investment, which often increase public revenues from income taxes and property and sales taxes.

Development incentives may play a significant role in the site selection process. State, county, and local incentives include tax abatements, fee waivers, low-interest loans, and off-site improvements to public infrastructure (Haresign, 1999, pp. 1118–1120). These development subsidies are usually based on the expected economic benefits from the new business. Economic benefits are typically measured by easily quantified metrics such as the number of jobs created, the expected payroll, or the revenue generated by selling a publicly owned facility (Moore, 1999, pp. 804–819).

Tax Increment Financing (TIF) may be offered to stimulate economic development in neighborhoods with relatively high levels of unemployment. In TIF districts, property assessments, which determine property taxes in most communities, are temporarily frozen at predevelopment levels. Economic development subsidies may include site preparation costs, assistance with the site plan review and permitting process, and site selection services.

Financial incentives are offered with the assumption that these investments have substantial economic multiplier effects. For example, the State of Iowa provided $54.9 million in incentives to entice Wells Fargo Home Mortgage to develop an office campus in the Greater Des Moines metropolitan area. *Site Selection* magazine recognized this as one of the 10 largest economic development transactions in the United States in 2003. The project's first phase consists of 960,000 square feet of new office space on 160 acres. The projected economic benefits are more than $400 million, including the creation or retention of 5300 jobs in the Des Moines area.

Economic development programs in the United States create jobs and stimulate capital investment, yet these programs often facilitate the relocation and expansion of businesses from one community to another. Competition for new businesses pits states against states and cities against cities. The extensive use of economic incentives is fueling a "war" among states to attract new businesses (Guskind, 1989; Buss, 2001). Moreover, these "business-friendly" policies pay little or no attention to the environmental or public health implications of the resulting development. For example, most suburban office "parks" in America are single-use developments accessible only by private vehicle.

Suburban office parks tend to have large, surface parking lots and minimal pedestrian infrastructure. Not only do distant office parks reduce workers' opportunities for active living and good health, these large developments also limit access by potential employees who do not own vehicles. In Anoka, Minnesota (a Minneapolis suburb), more than 20 businesses relocated from an urban site to a distant suburban office park that had no access to public transportation (Libby et al., 2000).

3.4 CONCLUSION

Site selection is a process for identifying suitable parcels of land for specific purposes. Site selection typically involves the collection and analysis of a wide array of site and contextual data. A site's location can have a fundamental influence on the complexity and cost of a project's planning and implementation. Land use regulations, cultural, economic, and biophysical attributes all influence—to varying degrees—the ability of a site to successfully accommodate a particular project program. Determining which site and contextual attributes to evaluate depends largely on the intended uses of the site.

BOX 3-1   In Practice

SUMMARY OF A NATIONAL-SCALE SITE SELECTION PROCESS FOR LOCATING A NEW BUSINESS FACILITY

1. Pre-project Planning
   a. Form a site selection team (skills needed include finance, marketing, manufacturing operations, human resources, transportation/distribution, engineering, law, and environment).
   b. Identify goals and objectives of the new facility (for example, lowering operating costs, entering new markets).
   c. Develop a budget and analyze the feasibility of building a new facility (for example, design and engineering concepts, facility requirements, market research, and financial feasibility).
   d. Identify critical site evaluation criteria (for example, quality and quantity of the workforce, transportation and utilities, and site and building characteristics).
   e. Determine which site evaluation factors are necessities and which are desirable but less critical.
   f. Collect and analyze data for these factors (if available from national sources).
   g. Identify a geographical area for the site search (typically between 5 and 10 states).

2. Narrowing the Search
   a. Collect more detailed data on the communities (typically between 15 and 20) that are being considered. State and local development organizations can usually provide needed data (for example, higher education resources, payroll costs, average salaries, transportation, quality of life).
   b. Using the community data and the site evaluation criteria, narrow the number of potential sites to five or six.

3. Community Fieldwork and Site Visits
   a. Visit each community to meet with major employers and local leaders and collect additional community information (for example, labor costs and availability, transportation and utility service capacity, neighborhood and housing conditions).
   b. Visit each site and any accompanying buildings to collect additional information (for example, available site utilities, utility service capacity, construction date of buildings).
   c. Using the additional community and site data, narrow the number of remaining sites to two or three.
   d. Prepare a report on the results of the work for review by company management. Identify, for each site, the projected facility costs (for example, land costs, site development costs, utility extension costs, construction costs). Also identify available community financial assistance or development incentives.
   e. Once the best site is selected, additional site data should be collected to identify potential sources of unusual development costs (for example, severe soil conditions, hazardous contamination).

   Source: www.siteseekers.org.

BOX 3–2   In Practice

Site Selection Study
Evansville State Hospital
Evansville, Illinois (United States)

Consultants
The HOK Planning Group, St. Louis, Missouri (United States)

Overview
The new Evansville State Hospital is a 228-bed replacement facility. The hospital is a mental health center for the state of Illinois. This new facility is located in a parklike setting on property adjacent to the existing hospital (Figures 3–4 and 3–5). It provides housing and treatment facilities that meet current standards for the care of patients and the efficient use of staff.

Selection Process
The HOK Planning Group created a series of illustrations that graphically document the factors that were considered in selecting the site for the new hospital building. Two potential sites were identified. Both sites, east and west, were near the old hospital on a single, large parcel of land owned by the state of Illinois. Site selection criteria for this project included the following: potential site development costs, site accessibility (Figure 3-6), and proximity to existing facilities (Figure 3-7). Other criteria included access to existing utilities (Figure 3-8) and existing drainage patterns (Figure 3-9). The site selection matrix (Figure 3-10) summarizes the evaluation of these criteria.

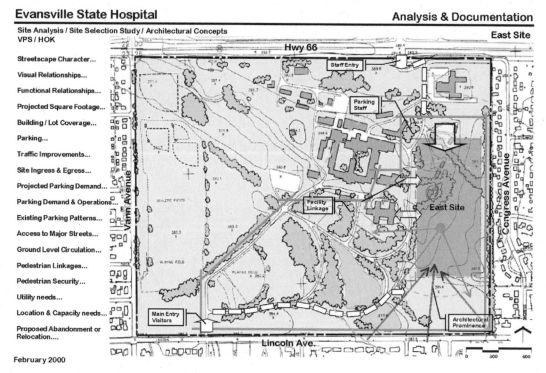

Figure 3-5   Potential site (east) for the new medical building. *Source:* The HOK Planning Group.

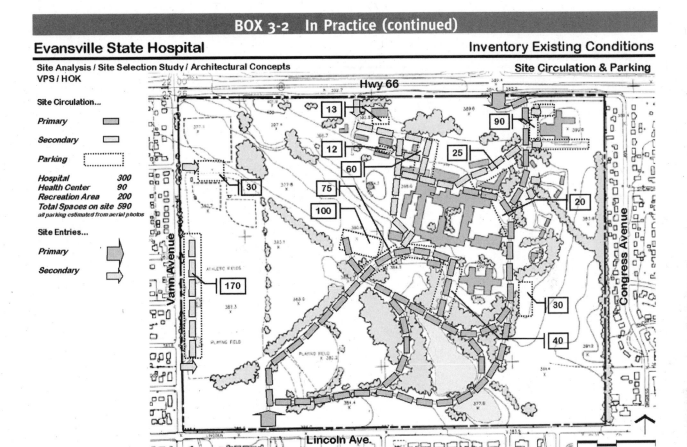

Evansville State Hospital

Inventory Existing Conditions

Site Analysis / Site Selection Study / Architectural Concepts
VPS / HOK

Site Circulation & Parking

Site Circulation...

Primary

Secondary

Parking

Hospital	300
Health Center	90
Recreation Area	200
Total Spaces on site	590

all parking estimated from aerial photos

Site Entries...

Primary

Secondary

February 2000

Figure 3-6   Existing vehicle circulation and parking. Source: The HOK Planning Group.

BOX 3-2 In Practice (continued)

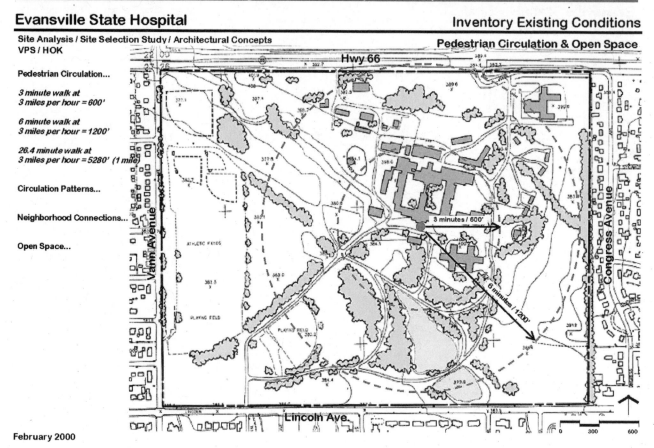

Evansville State Hospital

Inventory Existing Conditions

Site Analysis / Site Selection Study / Architectural Concepts
VPS / HOK

Pedestrian Circulation & Open Space

Pedestrian Circulation...

3 minute walk at
3 miles per hour = 600'

6 minute walk at
3 miles per hour = 1200'

26.4 minute walk at
3 miles per hour = 5280' (1 mile)

Circulation Patterns...

Neighborhood Connections...

Open Space...

February 2000

Figure 3-7 Existing pedestrian circulation. Source: The HOK Planning Group.

BOX 3-2   In Practice (continued)

Evansville State Hospital

Inventory Existing Conditions

Site Analysis / Site Selection Study / Architectural Concepts
VPS / HOK

Infrastructure

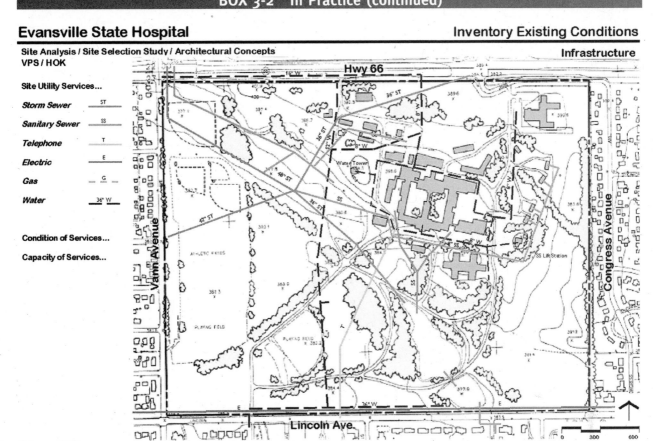

February 2000

Figure 3-8   Existing utility systems. Source: The HOK Planning Group.

BOX 3-2   In Practice (continued)

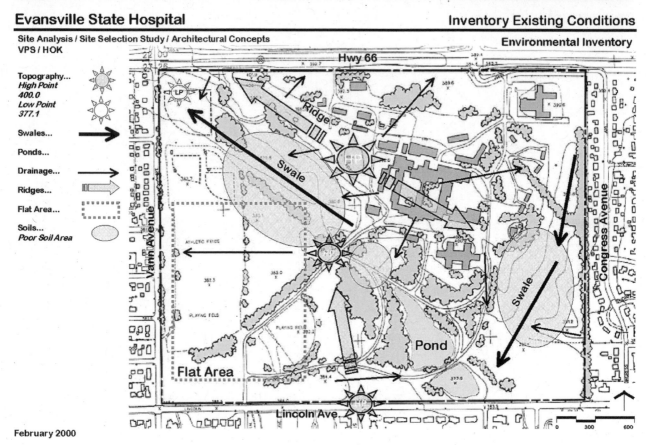

February 2000

Figure 3-9   Inventory of existing environmental conditions. Source: The HOK Planning Group.

BOX 3-2   In Practice (continued)

Evansville State Hospital   Site Selection Criteria

Site Analysis / Site Selection Study / Architectural Concepts
VPS / HOK

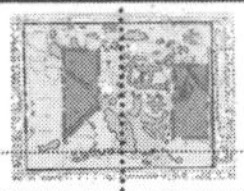

Issue	West	East
1. Cost of Site Development		
A. Topography (Leveling the Site)		
B. Soils		
C. Sewer Connection	+	✓
D. Utilities	✓	✓
- Water		
- Gas	✓	✓
- Telephone		
- Electric		
E. Demolition	+	—
2. Construction Area of Site	✓	☆
3. Proximity to Existing Facilities	—	☆
4. Existing Tree Damage	—	☆
5. Site Access		
A. Public	+	+
B. Service	✓	+
6. Site Buffers		
A. Street	+	+
B. Neighbors	+	—
C. Existing Buildings	+	+ —

☆ Very Good   + Good   ✓ Acceptable   — Negative

February 2000

Figure 3-10 Site selection matrix comparing criteria ratings for the two alternative sites. Source: The HOK Planning Group.

BOX 3-3   In Practice

Site Selection Study (2006)
Public Open Space and Natural Areas
City and County of San Francisco, California (United States of America)

This site selection process is used for the continuing acquisition of open space for new parks and public recreation areas.

I. Minimum Criteria
All sites must meet all of the "base" or threshold criteria to be considered for further evaluation. This step ensures that the sites meet at least the minimum standards for site size, maximum slope, absence of unstable soils or other hazardous or toxic conditions, adequate sunlight, and pedestrian access. More detailed evaluation of sites for potential acquisition employs an extensive set of suitability criteria.

II. Site Suitability Criteria (425 Points)

Base criteria (175 points)
Size (20 points)

     0.5–1.0 acre = 5 points

     1.0–4.0 acres = 10 points

     more than 4.0 acres = 20 points

BOX 3-3 In Practice (continued)

more than 4.0 acres = 20 points

Threatened by development (10 points)
Green space not zoned open space = 10 points
If site requires eminent domain, subtract 25 points.

Slope (15 points)

Flat (less than 2 percent slope over 75 percent of site) = 15 points
Sloped (less than 8.3 percent slope over 75 percent of site) = 10 points

Sunlight (15 points)

Site adjacent on all sides to zoning district(s) with land use controls limiting height over 40 feet (15 points)

Views (25 points)

Site offers view of the ocean or bay = 10 points
Viewshed protection = 15 points
If freeway or highway is within 200 feet, subtract 10 points.

Site Access and Accessibility (70 points)

Bus stop within 2 blocks of site = 10 points
More than 1 side of site entry = 10 points
Accessible for the disabled = 30 points
Site is adjacent to the bay trail, bay ridge trail, or coastal trail = 15 points
Site is adjacent to a numbered routed on the Official San Francisco Bike Route = 5 points

Health and Safety (20 points)

Adjacent average daily traffic is below 2000 = 10 points
Adjacent average daily traffic is below 3000 = 5 points
No prior development on site (green space) = 10 points
If adjacent to polluting facility, subtract 15 points.

Bonus Criteria (250 points)
Natural Resource Areas and Cultural Resources (Bonus up to 70 points)

Historic or cultural resources on site = 15 points
Relatively undisturbed sites supporting significant and diverse plant and wildlife habitat = 15 points

BOX 3-3   In Practice (continued)

Healthy trees = 15 points

Over a historic creek (requires site investigation, if justified by historic records) = 10 points

Adjacency and Gaps (Bonus up to 180 points)

Within a high-need area = 100 points

Outside the service area of all existing open space property = 30 points

Open space as part of an approved planning document leading to higher residential densities = 50 points

BOX 3-4   The Site Evaluation Report

The site evaluation report typically includes the following elements (adapted from Alaska Department of Education,1997, and Wike and Bowers, 1995):

☐ **Title page**

☐ **Table of Contents**

☐ **Executive Summary**
[Summarizes the purpose and scope of the study, including the type and size of the planned facilities; briefly describes the sites; indicates which site was selected and the rationale for choosing the selected site.]

☐ **Introduction**
[Describes the purpose and scope of the study.]

☐ **Site selection process**
[Explains the site selection criteria and the criteria rating and weighting schemes.
Graphics: context map showing each site and its immediate surroundings; location map showing all of the sites that were considered and key landmarks or reference points such as major streets or highways, or municipal boundaries; property boundary surveys; aerial photograph of each site, site cross-sections, and photographic panoramas.]

☐ **Comparative evaluation of candidate sites**
[Describes the strengths and weaknesses of each individual site.
Graphics: site evaluation matrix; tabulated data summarizing the individual site evaluations, and allowing comparison among the alternative sites.]

☐ **Conclusions**
[Briefly summarizes the study's conclusions]

☐ **References**

☐ **Appendices**

Programming

4.1 INTRODUCTION

Once a site is selected for development or redevelopment, its future uses can be determined—or programmed—in more detail. This preliminary program is revised and refined as more information is acquired about the site and the future users' needs and preferences. The program is typically expressed in terms of the quantity and quality of spaces needed to meet anticipated future needs. Programming also occurs over a range of spatial scales, from the entire site down to individual buildings on the site.

Client objectives vary widely among the private corporate sector, the private nonprofit sector, and the public sector. Programmers help clients set project priorities and sometimes make difficult choices among conflicting development or redevelopment options. According to Tusler et al. (1993, p. 233), a successful programmer:

- □ communicates the proposed process to all involved;

- □ does not lock in preconceived solutions;

- □ reconciles subcomponent needs with overall organizational goals and resources;

- □ frequently tests and reviews design concepts, as functional and space models are explored.

Programming for new buildings, especially, has developed into a recognized professional specialization, separate from the field of architecture. These specialists are particularly active in programming for hospitals, schools, prisons, and other similar facilities, which have a clearly defined public purpose.

Tusler et al. (1993) identify four reasons for the development of a programming profession whose members do not necessarily have formal educations in architecture. In their opinion, a major reason for this separation stems from contemporary expectations for professional architectural services. Clients may not associate project programming with the architectural profession. Other reasons for the separation involve the culture of the architecture profession itself. According to Tusler et al. (1993, p. 228–229), these self-imposed factors include:

◻ perceived conflicts of interest in defining the scope of work and also providing subsequent professional design services;

◻ bias in the professional design schools against specialization;

◻ limited education of designers in psychology, communications, finance, statistics, and other skills necessary for effective programming.

Whether architects should be responsible for both programming and design is an issue on which there are widely differing opinions. However, there is consensus on the importance of programming in the facilities development process.

Site planning is also a problem-solving process, and for each and every project site planners are faced with a unique set of problems to solve. These problems may not be explicitly articulated, initially, but they nevertheless influence the scope and direction of the subsequent inventory, analysis, and design phases.

Programming for site-planning projects is currently a less institutionalized process than programming for public buildings and other institutional facilities. Programming at the site scale requires knowledge and a set of skills that is more often taught in either business schools or planning programs than in architectural landscape, architectural, or engineering programs. Yet programming is an increasingly important activity within the site planning and design process.

Increasingly, the planning and design of the built environment has become a multi-disciplinary team effort. Professional competence in one area requires an expanding combination of knowledge and skills. Architects, engineers, and landscape architects not only provide programming, analysis, and design services but also advise clients during the administration of the contracts for project construction. Typically, however, a team leader must coordinate communication among all involved parties and ensure that the information generated by each team member is adequately considered and synthesized.

Maxwell and Brown (1993, p. 260) comment on the role of the programmer: "The programmer must be [an] expert not only at synthesizing disparate—and often seemingly unrelated—user data but also at translating these data into practical, 'designer-friendly' information." The separation of programming and design responsibility reduces the potential for biased program analysis and prevents inappropriate design solutions caused by preconceptions or misconceptions about the design problem to be solved (Brown and Scarborough, 1993).

Programming in isolation from the project designers, however, can potentially overlook important site issues. Commenting on trends in health care architecture, Tusler et al. (1993, p. 242) conclude:

What is necessary is for both disciplines, design and programming, to be involved simultaneously in the very early, formative stages of project conception. There also needs to be mutual respect for each other's specialization and a close working relationship as an integrated team.

4.2   PROGRAMMING METHODS

4.2.1   Goal Setting

According to Goldman and Peatross (1993), project programming entails four basic steps, as follows:

- Initiate the project

- Develop the project mission and objectives

- Determine the project's operational and physical requirements

- Document and present the program to the client

Establishing a list of program goals and objectives is an important step in the site planning and design process (Figure 4-1). In addition to determining the project's operational and physical requirements, programmers—in consultation with the client and other stakeholders—must clarify quality-level expectations.

4.2.2   Data Collection

The program is a function of several related factors, including client goals, market demand, legal context, project budget, and existing site conditions. Appropriate responses to these factors require the analysis of a diverse set of data. Based on a survey of 74 professional programmers, Preiser (1985, p.11) found that the most common methods of gathering program data were by rank, as follows:

- Interviews

- Surveys

- Document analysis

- Behavioral observation

- Visiting a state-of-the-art project

- Literature search

- Other (for example, interactive group techniques such as charrettes, workshops, and discussions)

These data-gathering activities focus on three areas: site and context, user needs and preferences, and design precedents. These are discussed in the following section.

Site and Context

Site visits in the programming phase provide information about the site and contextual attributes that are most likely to either facilitate or hinder the desired uses of the site

Figure 4-1 Project goals, objectives, and program elements conveyed graphically and verbally in a clearly organized poster format. Note that each goal begins with an action verb. Source: The HOK Planning Group.

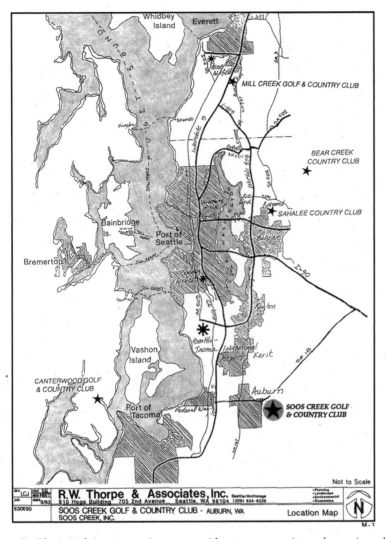

Figure 4-2 Programming considers market context for commercial projects. This map shows the locations of other major golf courses in the vicinity of a proposed golf course community (Soos Creek) near Seattle, Washington
Source: R. W. Thorpe and Associates.

(Figure 4-2). The initial site reconnaissance provides an opportunity to determine which of the site attributes should be inventoried and analyzed as the planning and design process continues. A client may have unrealistic expectations for the development of a site, and any potential site limitations should be addressed early in this process. The attributes, when considered in the context of program objectives, allow an initial evaluation of the site's opportunities and constraints.

The initial site reconnaissance should be aided by relevant supporting information, including the following:

☐ Historic and current aerial photographs

☐ Zoning maps

- ◻ Road maps

- ◻ County soil survey maps

- ◻ Flood hazard maps

- ◻ Tax assessment maps

Some of these documents are readily available from local and state governments (see Appendix). Although the scale of these maps is generally too coarse to support detailed site-planning decisions, these documents can provide information that is useful in narrowing the scope of the subsequent site inventory and analysis. More detailed site maps may be available from the property owner.

User Needs and Preferences

One of the primary goals of programming is to reach agreement with the client and other stakeholders about the expectations for the project. Therefore, one of the first steps in programming is to identify the decision makers and to define the decision-making process (Goldman and Peatross, 1993). Public sector projects, such as affordable housing or a new park, typically involve a large and diverse group of stakeholders. According to Goldman and Peatross (1993, p. 362), these may include the following:

- ◻ Elected officials

- ◻ Appointed officials

- ◻ Facility operators

- ◻ Funding managers and analysts

- ◻ Public works and building maintenance staff

- ◻ Citizen groups representing taxpayers

There may be diversity among stakeholders and multiple levels of decision makers that must be consulted directly, or indirectly through their representatives, before important programming decisions can be finalized. To make this process most efficient, the programming team might want to establish two committees: "a policy committee composed of upper-level administrators and officials and a working committee composed of managers and operators" (Goldman and Peatross, 1993, p. 363).

Transportation planning is an area where stakeholders are commonly involved in the resolution of potentially contentious public sector decisions. The modified Multiattribute Utility Analysis (MUA) is one approach that has been used to reach consensus on highway construction projects in California (Schwartz and Eichhorn, 1997, pp. 142–148). The nine-step process used in the modified MUA is as follows:

- ◻ Select the stakeholder group

- ◻ Agree on problems or need

- ☐ Identify issues and concerns

- ☐ Develop evaluation criteria

- ☐ Develop alternatives

- ☐ Select and collect impact data for each alternative

- ☐ Weigh evaluation criteria

- ☐ Measure evaluation criteria

- ☐ Rank alternatives and conduct sensitivity analysis

With private-sector projects, surveys, focus groups, and other means of soliciting consumer preferences can help projects meet the demands of specific market sectors. These sectors, or demographic groups, include young single professionals; families with school-aged children; older couples whose children no longer reside with them (for example, empty nesters); and the retired elderly. Learning more about consumer preferences prior to construction and marketing can help site planners adapt the program to the site and its setting. By soliciting consumer preferences, market analysts can gain valuable insights concerning important project attributes that should be considered in the programming and site selection processes. For example, a variety of locational factors typically influence consumers' decisions in selecting their dwelling locations. Depending on the demographic profile of the household, preferences may be influenced by the following:

- ☐ Proximity to workplace

- ☐ Quality of nearby schools

- ☐ Neighborhood safety

- ☐ Proximity to restaurants, grocery stores, and other shopping opportunities

- ☐ Nearby recreational facilities

These and other factors may not be important to every household, but collectively, they reflect the concerns of a substantial market segment.

Visual preference surveys (VPS) are another useful way to solicit stakeholder opinions concerning future development, redevelopment, or restoration alternatives (Nelessen, 1994). Ewing (2001, p.271) writes:

> VPS helps citizens and community leaders envision design alternatives in ways that words, maps, and other communications media cannot. This makes it ideal for "visioning" projects, design charrettes, and other physical planning activities with public involvement.

Visual preference surveys are particularly useful in helping communities and neighborhoods determine how they would like their community or neighborhood to look in the future. This process can be focused on the key design issues that impact the quality of the built environment. These include the following:

□ Building scale and massing (for example, height and shape)

□ Building articulation (for example, façade, signs, roof)

□ Building placement (for example, relationship to street, site entrances)

□ Open space (for example, lighting and landscaping)

□ Vehicle parking (for example, screening and relationship to street)

Most visual preference surveys use the following approach (Ewing, 2001, p.271–273):

□ Fifty to one hundred participants are shown photographs or slides of scenes.

□ Viewing time per scene is a half minute or less.

□ Scenes may be evaluated in any of three ways: a) rating on a Likert scale, such as 1 to 5 (1 = least preferred, 5 = most preferred); b) ordinal ranking of scenes; and c) forced choice between scenes in paired comparisons.

□ Statistical analysis of the preference ratings considers means, medians, and variance to help explain preferences and differences across scenes.

□ Viewers may be asked to explain their preferences, which can enhance the interpretation of the results.

Visual preference surveys also have educational value. They help participants become more aware of how the design of the built environment influences community attractiveness and function.

Design Precedents

Relatively high population densities, long periods of intensive urban development, and a strong public policy interest in the design of the built environment make European countries living laboratories for architects, landscape architects, and urban designers. Nivola (1999) suggests that one major difference between European and American cities is the vast amount of space that is available in the United States compared to Europe. The abundance of land in the United States have indirectly led to the development of vehicle-oriented cities and suburbs that are, consequently, inhospitable environments for pedestrians and bicyclists.

For decades, North American architects and landscape architects have traveled abroad to enrich their understanding of urban design and to supplement their formal design training (Fabos et al., 1968; Schulze, 1994). European cathedrals, plazas, parks, and waterfronts continue to be among the special places sought out by foreign educated designers. This process of expanding and refining one's design vocabulary through travel is enhanced by careful observation— often by keeping a sketchbook of notes and drawings, including perspective sketches, sections, elevations, and design details. Perhaps the most important reason to keep a sketchbook, at least early in one's design training, is that this activity nurtures critical observation—or the ability to "read" the built environment. Once acquired, every environment—elegant or mundane—can be assessed with a discerning eye.

Post-occupancy evaluations are on-site investigations of both the structure and function of the built environment. Preiser et al. (1988, p. 3) define this activity:

> Post-occupancy evaluation is the process of evaluating buildings in a systematic and rigorous manner after they have been built and occupied for some time. POEs focus on building occupants and their needs, and, thus, they provide insights into the consequences of past design decisions and the resulting building performance. This knowledge forms a sound basis for creating better buildings in the future.

Post-occupancy evaluations of outdoor spaces such as parks, plazas, and campuses are less common. Yet this type of precedent analysis is an important, but still underutilized, method of advancing site planning and design practice and ultimately improving the quality of the built environment.

Behavioral observation is an important part of post-occupancy evaluation. Human behavior at outdoor sites varies significantly with changes in the day of the week, the time of day, the weather, and other factors such as scheduled activities or special events (Whyte, 1980). These factors can dramatically alter the use of a site over the course of a day, a week, or a year. The behavior of site users may also vary considerably with differences in age, gender, and other demographic factors.

Systematic and carefully planned post-occupancy evaluations can yield important information about a myriad of issues relevant to land planning and design. Zube (Miller, 1997, p.68) comments:

> We do not invest an adequate amount of resources studying our design/planning successes and failures from an aesthetic, ecological, and functional perspective. We could learn much of benefit to both teaching and practice.

Post-occupancy evaluations can improve site planning and design practice by identifying successful models that can be adapted to local circumstances. These analyses can also reveal design mistakes, or missed opportunities, that could be avoided in future projects. In the now classic *Learning from Las Vegas,* Robert Venturi and colleagues document a post-occupancy evaluation of the Las Vegas "Strip" during the 1960s (Venturi et al., 1972). The authors analyze and cleverly explain the architectural and spatial qualities along this highway corridor.

Precedent studies, of which post-occupancy evaluations are one type, are focused efforts to learn from prior experience. Precedent studies—or case studies—are vital tools for advancing many fields of endeavor, from medicine to urban design, site planning, and architecture (Clark and Pause, 2005). A contemporary example of precedents influencing urban design is the New Urbanism movement's reliance on earlier, more traditional forms of development (Duany, Plater-Zyberk, and Speck, 2001). New urbanism, or traditional neighborhood development (TND), advocates a return to mixed-use, human-scale development, which is a design paradigm that is firmly rooted in the past.

Knowledge of relevant planning and design precedents can help inform programming and design decisions. Design successes—or failures—and comparisons among alternative design approaches can yield valuable lessons or "best practices" that can then be incorporated in future projects. Site planning precedent studies may collect information such as:

- programmed uses and requirements, including the needs of special user groups (for example, children, the chronically ill, the elderly);

- spatial organization and articulation of buildings, circulation systems, and open space;

- design responses to site and contextual factors;

- techniques for protecting and restoring environmental and cultural resources;

- construction and operational costs.

Precedent studies of completed projects provide examples—or models—that can be reinterpreted and adapted to solve design problems involving a similar combination of program, site, and context. The ability to interpret and evaluate existing built environments is also an invaluable skill for public sector staff who are responsible for evaluating land development proposals.

4.3 PROGRAM DOCUMENTATION

4.3.1 Project Objectives

A program may specify the amount of space required for the proposed activities, the desired adjacency relationships among the activities, and the phasing of future implementation (Figure 4-3). The program may also specify the expected quality of the spaces and structures within the project. These program expectations can be expressed on several levels. Programmers must initially identify the general types of land uses, activities, or facilities that will occur on the site. But there are many possibilities, and the best mix of uses depends on the client's goals as well as on the size, character, and location of the site. Once the types of uses or facilities have been identified, the quantity and quality of these can be determined (Box 4-1). For example, one of the land uses included in a development program might be multifamily housing. But additional information concerning the quantity and quality of this use must be determined. This could include the desired number of dwelling units, the number of bedrooms in each dwelling type, and the amenities to be included in each unit.

Open space is also a program element. *Meaningful* open space facilitates groundwater infiltration, provides visual amenities and recreational opportunities, and protects wildlife habitats. The benefits of open space are compounded, in most cases, when the open spaces comprise a contiguous network (United States Environmental Protection Agency, 2001).

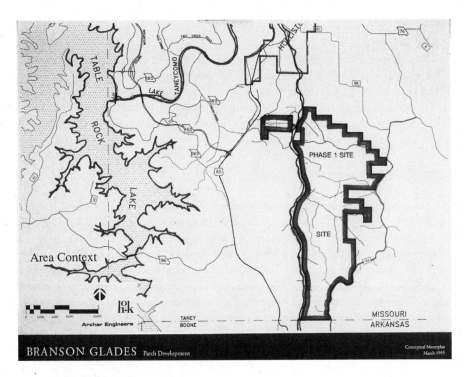

Figure 4-3 Programming may also involve phasing of future development activities
Source: The HOK Planning Group.

4.3.2   Functional Relationships

Development programs may include activities or uses that are relatively incompatible. Community facilities for wastewater treatment, for example, are typically considered incompatible with residential and commercial uses. Consequently, these incompatible land uses are separated spatially. Conversely, other site activities or uses may need to be physically adjacent to one another.

The desired spatial relationships among programmed uses may be determined from client surveys, reviews of the literature, and other sources. These spatial relationships fall into one of four categories, as follows:

- ☐ Adjacency is essential

- ☐ Adjacency is desirable but not essential

- ☐ Adjacency is unimportant

- ☐ Adjacency should be avoided

An adjacency matrix is a useful tool for summarizing and evaluating the desired spatial relationships among program elements. The spatial relationships among programmed uses may entail more than simple physical proximity. Adjacent land uses may be connected functionally (for example, pedestrian circulation), or visually, or both. Whether adjacent uses are functionally and/or visually linked is an important design issue that should be identified in the programming phase.

When programs are complex, the assessment of spatial relationships among program elements can be difficult to interpret from an adjacency matrix. This problem can be alleviated, somewhat, by creating spatial relationships diagrams. Each plan-view "bubble" diagram portrays the desired spatial or functional relationships between a targeted land use, at the center of the diagram, and other programmed uses arranged around this central element.

4.3.3   Design Guidelines

The programming process can go well beyond the simple compilation of lists describing expected uses and the land area or facilities needed for each use. The development of design guidelines, for example, is an extension of the programming process. Design guidelines are not site-specific solutions to a project's design problems. Yet, they typically portray the desired qualities of design solutions. Design guidelines may address a variety of site components that have significant effects on a project's economic success and environmental impact. These include stormwater drainage and infiltration techniques, street dimensions and parking lot configurations, building proportions and setbacks, and site furniture and signage.

Municipalities may use a design review process, in conjunction with design guidelines, to enhance or maintain the visual quality of neighborhoods, business districts, and other areas (Table 4-1). Design guidelines can be communicated with text and numbers, but

TABLE 4-1   Municipal development regulations typically establish design requirements that significantly influence the character of the built environment.

Site Element	Attribute (Minimum and/or Maximum may be Specified)
Streets	Width Intersection corner radius Cul-de-sac length
Lots (parcels)	Area Width Depth
Buildings	Dwelling unit density Building coverage (percentage of lot area) Building height Building placement (i.e., front yard, side yard, backyard setbacks)
Parking areas	Number of parking spaces, by land use Location of parking areas Number of access driveways
Plantings	Number, size, and species of street trees Parking area landscaping and screening

graphic representations are far more effective. Guidelines may specify desired building facade articulation along a commercial block of a downtown redevelopment district, for example, or the preferred sizes, colors, and styles of benches or light fixtures along the district's streetscapes.

Large public institutions and corporations are especially sensitive to physical design issues. Creating or maintaining a particular "image" or "brand" is typically a high-priority issue. Design guidelines can also help ensure that new development is appropriate for the site's physical and social context. Zeisel and Maxwell (1993, p.168) see the need for explicit guidelines, as follows:

> In order to translate a facilities program into a physical environment for a work-place, designers need more than numbers and diagrams. They need planning and design principles that respond to the organization's style—its culture.

This is especially important on university campuses and other large sites where development is phased and implemented by different designers and builders.

A visually unified built environment is achieved through the repetition of individual design elements. Repeating similar colors, shapes, and textures, for example, can create a harmonious, or visually unified, environment. Although visual quality is an important concern of design guidelines, this is not the only objective. The maintenance and replacement of worn-out or damaged site furniture, for example, is more expensive if there is not consistency in the types and manufacturers of furniture installed on a site.

4.4   CONCLUSION

Programming is an integral part of any site planning and design project. The programming process requires information about user needs, the site and its context, and both successful and unsuccessful design precedents. Depending on project objectives and site conditions, programs may vary in specificity. A project program may be simply a list of desired project elements, but the expected qualities of programmed uses are usually articulated—often in the form of design guidelines.

BOX 4-1   Facility Programming and Site Suitability Analysis

Arlington County, Virginia (United States of America)

Site Planning
EDAW, Inc.
Alexandria, Virginia

Architecture
Rummel, Klepper & Kahl, LLP
Baltimore, Maryland

BOX 4-1   Facility Programming and Site Suitability Analysis (continued)

Background
The U.S. Congress initiated this study to assess the potential for siting a boathouse (rowing facility) within Arlington County along the Potomac River. The facility would be located along the Virginia side of the river on public lands managed by the National Park Service. Four sites along the Potomac River were considered (Figure 4-4).

Project Scope
This study included the development of a minimum and a maximum program for the potential boathouse. These two programs were used to analyze the feasibility of each study site. The criteria used to assess each site's suitability for the Arlington County Boathouse addressed physical conditions, visual/cultural resources, environmental impacts, economics, and operational issues.

Program/Project Requirements
Developing the program for the boathouse involved several information gathering steps, including:

☐ review of a study prepared by Arlington County's Water-Based Recreational Facility Task Force in 1995;

☐ interviews with crew coaches at the three Arlington County public high schools;

☐ precedent studies of three area boathouses and one area boat club.

Based on this information, the minimum boathouse program included:

☐ the existing boat storage needs and immediate expansion plans of the crew teams at three Arlington County public high schools;

☐ exercise areas, lockers, showers and storage space for the three schools;

☐ boat-repair area;

☐ minimal office space;

☐ access for trailers, school buses, and emergency vehicles;

☐ gas storage area;

☐ outdoor rigging areas.

The maximum boathouse program included all of the above requirements along with additional boat storage area for other high school crew teams in the area, individual rowers, and other community rowing programs (Figure 4-5).

Facility and Site Analysis
The analysis of four sites included assessments of site constraints, conditions of the river for rowing, transportation access, required infrastructure improvements, and potential visual impacts (Figure 4-6, 4-7, and 4-8). Schematic site plans were prepared for a minimum program and a maximum program for each site. Improvements necessary to accommodate each program on the sites were identified, including a new access drive, drop-off area, and parking lot (Figure 4-9). Photos

BOX 4-1   Facility Programming and Site Suitability Analysis (continued)

of the existing conditions at each site were compared with photosimulations of the proposed buildings on each site to assess the potential visual impacts (Figure 4-10 and 4-11).

Synopsis of Public Comments Received

Public comments received during the planning process helped identify the various concerns associated with locating a boathouse along the Potomac River. Comments regarding the sites under consideration relate to rowing conditions, proximity to the public high schools, transportation access, environmental issues, aesthetic concerns, and cultural/historical factors.

Comparison Between Sites

Figure 4-12 compares the programs, improvements required at each site, and the potential impacts of each site and program alternative.

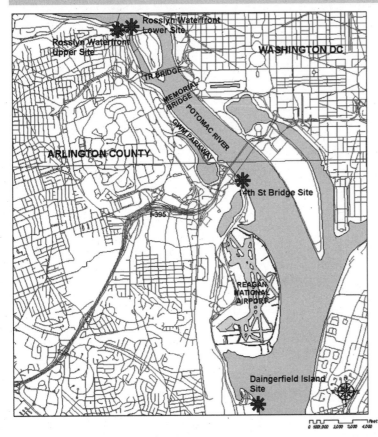

Figure 4-4   Map showing the locations of sites considered for the proposed boathouse on the Potomac River. Source: EDAW, Inc.

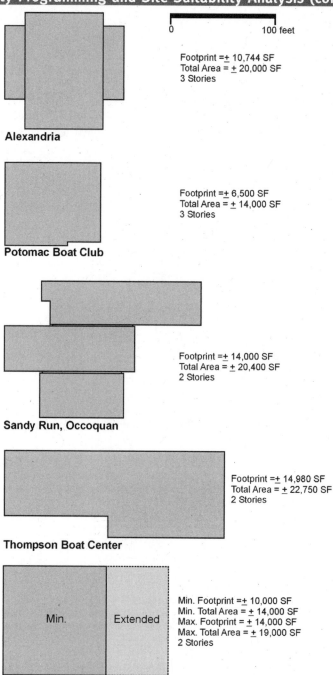

0   100 feet

Footprint =± 10,744 SF
Total Area = ± 20,000 SF
3 Stories

Alexandria

Footprint =± 6,500 SF
Total Area = ± 14,000 SF
3 Stories

Potomac Boat Club

Footprint =± 14,000 SF
Total Area = ± 20,400 SF
2 Stories

Sandy Run, Occoquan

Footprint =± 14,980 SF
Total Area = ± 22,750 SF
2 Stories

Thompson Boat Center

Min. Footprint =± 10,000 SF
Min. Total Area = ± 14,000 SF
Max. Footprint = ± 14,000 SF
Max. Total Area = ± 19,000 SF
2 Stories

Min.   Extended

Proposed Arlington County Boathouse

Figure 4-5 Building footprints for existing boathouse precedents and the minimum and maximum proposed boathouse programs.

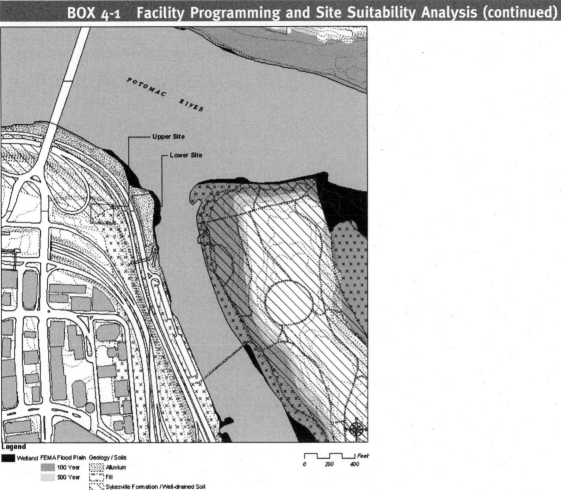

Figure 4-6   Inventory map of floodplains and soils at the Rosslyn waterfront sites. Source: EDAW, Inc.

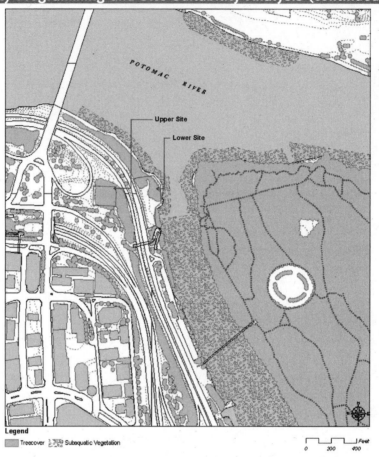

Figure 4-7   Inventory map of tree cover and subaquatic vegetation at the Rosslyn waterfront sites. Source: EDAW, Inc.

BOX 4-1   Facility Programming and Site Suitability Analysis (continued)

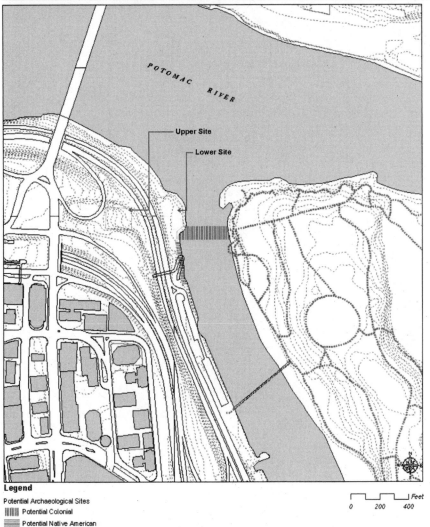

POTOMAC RIVER

Upper Site

Lower Site

Legend

Potential Archaeological Sites

|||||| Potential Colonial

≡≡≡ Potential Native American

Feet
0   200   400

Figure 4-8   Inventory map of potential archaeological sites at the Rossylyn waterfront sites. Source: EDAW, Inc.

BOX 4-1   Facility Programming and Site Suitability Analysis (continued)

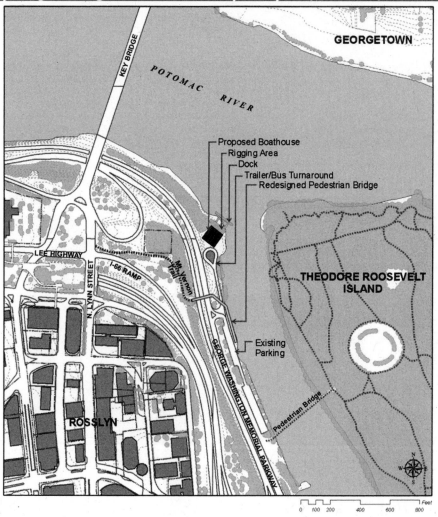

Figure 4-9   Schematic site plan for the lower Rossyln waterfront site. Source: EDAW, Inc.

BOX 4-1   Facility Programming and Site Suitability Analysis (continued)

Figure 4-10 Photograph of the existing view of the site from the Potomac River. Source: EDAW, Inc.

Figure 4-11 Photosimulation of the potential view of the site with the proposed boathouse from the Potomac River. Source: EDAW, Inc.

BOX 4-1 Facility Programming and Site Suitability Analysis (continued)

Table ES.1: Alternative Site Comparison

	ROSSLYN WATERFRONT (LOWER SITE)		ROSSLYN WATERFRONT (UPPER SITE)		14TH STREET RAILROAD BRIDGE AREA		DAINGERFIELD ISLAND SITE	
	MINIMUM PROGRAM	MAXIMUM PROGRAM	MINIMUM PROGRAM	MAXIMUM PROGRAM	MINIMUM PROGRAM	MAXIMUM* PROGRAM	MINIMUM PROGRAM	MAXIMUM PROGRAM
Rowing Conditions								
Depth of Water	Shallow close to the shore / may require minimal dredging				Sufficient Depth		Sufficient depth	
Potential Conflicts	Established 'no-wake' zone reduces potential for conflicts				No established 'no-wake' zone		Proximity to sail boats / no established 'no-wake' zone	
Potential Practice Days Lost due to Weather	Less than one day per week during Spring months				Two to three days per week during Spring months		Two to three days per week during Spring months	
Potential Significant Environmental Impacts								
Approx. Area of Disturbance	1.02 acres	1.23 acres	1.38 acres	1.46 acres	2.08 acres	2.07 acres	0.83 acres	0.98 acres
Approx. Area of Vegetation Impacted (treed area)	20, 200 SF	28,700 SF	39,000 SF	41,300 SF	11,500 SF	9,600 SF	35,400 SF	42,100 SF
Topography (Approx. Amount of Required Cut)	20,000 cu.ft.	28,000 cu.ft.	35,000 cu.ft.	63,000 cu.ft.	-	-	-	-
Approx. Areas of Wetlands Disturbed	5,400 SF	8,300 SF	7,800 SF	7,800 SF	7,600 SF	7,700 SF	5,500 SF	5,900 SF
Transportation								
Average Travel Times from the Three Schools (Depart Schools at 3:15 PM)	15 minutes		14 minutes		17 minutes		17 minutes	
Average Travel Times to the Three Schools (Depart Sites at 6:00 PM)	15 minutes		16 minutes		15 minutes		18 minutes	
Transit Access	Rosslyn Metro about 0.33 miles from the site		Rosslyn Metro about 0.25 miles from the site		Metro not easily accessible		Metro not easily accessible	
Infrastructure Improvements								
Water Service	Approx. 100 feet of new service		Approx. 100 feet of new service		Approx. 2,400 feet of service**		Approx. 900 feet of new service	
Sewer Service	Approx. 900 feet of new service		Approx. 500 feet of new service		Approx. 2,400 feet of service**		Approx. 1,000 feet of new service	
Electrical Service	Approx. 100 feet of new service		Approx. 450 feet of new service		Approx. 2,400 feet of service**		Approx. 1,000 feet of new service	
Access	Realignment of pedestrian bridge, new access road (±770 feet in length)		Construction of a new pedestrian bridge and trail, new access road (±575 feet)		Construction of new access road (±1,825 feet), relocation of MV Trail (±600 feet)		Construction of new access road (±440 feet)	
Cost of Development (Order of Magnitude)	± $6.2 million	± $7.4 million	±$6.0 million	±$7.1 million	±$5.7 million	±$6.8 million	±$5.0 million	±$6.2 million

Other resources that were examined for potential impacts include wildlife, historical, cultural and visual resources.
*The maximum plan is located slightly south of the minimum plan to provide a comparison of sites within the 14th Street Bridge area.
** The new service is identified from a Comfort Station proposed to be constructed close to Gravelly Point parking area.

Figure 4-12 Table comparing alternative sites and programs. Source: EDAW, Inc.

part III

Site Inventory and Analysis

Context-sensitive site planning requires an understanding of relevant site and contextual attributes. One set of attribute data may be useful for siting one particular activity or land use; whereas, a different set of attributes may be useful for siting other uses. In some cases, a single site attribute will determine the suitability—or feasibility—of a site for a particular use. Deciding which attributes to map and analyze, and which attributes to ignore, requires consideration of at least four factors, as follows:

☐ Proposed site uses (for example, project program)

☐ Existing on-site and off-site conditions

☐ Requirements for permitting and approvals

☐ Costs of data collection and analysis

Collectively, these four factors dictate the scope of the site inventory and analysis.

chapter 5

Site Inventory:
Physical Attributes

*Sustainable design, sustainable development, design with nature, environmentally
sensitive design, holistic resource management—regardless of what it's called,
"sustainability," the capability of natural and cultural systems being continued over
time, is key.*

—U.S. National Park Service

5.1 INTRODUCTION

Every site is embedded within a landscape. The site inventory is an essential step in
understanding the character of the site and the physical, biological, and cultural linkages
between the site and the surrounding landscape. Land development, restoration, and
management require a broad knowledge of, and appreciation for, environmental and
cultural systems. Both basic and applied research has contributed to our understanding of
physical, biological, and cultural phenomena. This knowledge base is the foundation for
land planning, design, and management theory. The *American Heritage Dictionary of the
English Language*, 3rd edition, defines *theory* as follows:

1. A system of assumptions, accepted principles, and rules of procedure devised to analyze,
   predict, or otherwise explain the nature or behavior of a specified set of phenomena.

2. A belief that guides action or assists comprehension or judgment.

The field of medicine is a good example of the synergistic relationship between theory
and application, or—put another way— between research and practice. Research on heart
function, blood chemistry, and many other aspects of human physiology inform the

medical practitioners (for example, surgeons, cardiologists, nurses) about health care. The natural and social sciences similarly provide the theoretical underpinnings of efforts to modify, restore, and manage land.

Decisions to develop or restore a parcel of land require an understanding of the site as well as the surrounding landscape. Because site planning and design involve decisions about future uses of land, an understanding of human behavior, attitudes, and preferences is also necessary. Yet the site inventory is a focused process of collecting and mapping essential attribute data. It is not a "fishing expedition," or an open-ended investigation of all biophysical or cultural phenomena that occur on or near the site. If this data-gathering activity is not well focused, the site inventory can consume vast amounts of time, money, and professional expertise. The goals of the inventory must be predefined, therefore, to narrow the scope of the data collection effort. The project program, although subject to revision, helps to focus this inventory.

The site inventory may be completed in stages by a team of specialists. The first stage of any inventory involves site reconnaissance. This relatively quick site assessment identifies potentially significant site assets and liabilities. After the initial reconnaissance, one of the first tasks is to develop a base map. The base map serves as the template for attribute mapping and analysis, as well as for subsequent land planning and design (see Chapter 2). If a topographic survey of the site is available, the base map could include project boundaries and other key site information (Table 5-1). If the site reconnaissance includes an aerial inspection, oblique aerial photos of the site can provide useful contextual information (Figure 5-1).

TABLE 5-1 Site data that may be conveyed on a topographic survey.

Category	Locational Data
Legal	Property lines (angles and distances) Easements and building setback lines Site area
Topography	Elevation contours Spot elevations for high points and low points
Vegetation	Wooded areas Isolated trees (species and diameter at breast height)
Soils/Geology	Boreholes
Hydrology	Surface water Wetlands 100-year floodways and flood fringe
Utilities	Type (e.g., sanitary sewer, electric, gas, telephone) Size of line Manholes, hydrants, and other fixtures
Structures	Buildings
Circulation	Streets and rights-of-way Curbs and gutters Parking areas

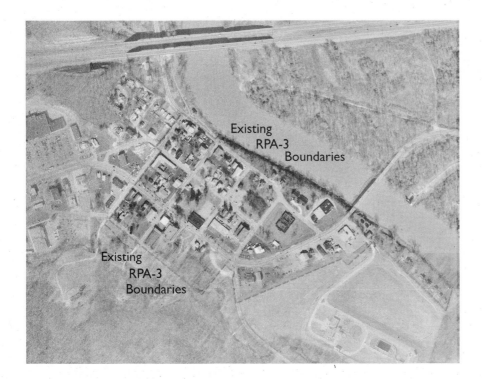

Figure 5-1 Vertical aerial photograph with project boundaries superimposed. Source: The HOK Planning Group.

Many site attributes, such as vegetation or slope, are unevenly distributed over the landscape. However, some attributes, such as average seasonal temperatures and precipitation, show very little spatial variation at the site scale. Attributes such as temperature and precipitation can vary dramatically, of course, throughout the year. This temporal variation may substantially influence the uses of the site from season to season. Consequently, it may be appropriate that site inventory maps document the spatial distribution of a particular attribute at more than one time of the year. Site attributes that vary seasonally include wildlife distributions, wind direction and speed, and seasonal high water table.

5.2   PARCEL SIZE AND SHAPE

Land development—and redevelopment—occur over a range of site scales. For example, many single-use commercial projects require relatively small sites of less than one acre (0.4 hectares). In contrast, large-scale residential and mixed-use developments may require sites of 10 or more acres (4.05 hectares). Sometimes, two or more contiguous parcels of land are combined to create one larger parcel under a single ownership.

Parcel size or area is an inherent constraint on a site's development potential. If all other factors are equal, larger sites can accommodate more extensive and more diverse development than smaller sites. Local zoning regulations, for example, may limit site development by restricting building height, building site coverage, and housing density. Housing density is

Figure 5-2 Relationship between parcel shape and edge-to-interior ratio for two parcels of equal area.

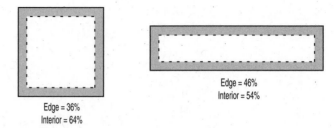

Edge = 36%
Interior = 64%

Edge = 46%
Interior = 54%

commonly expressed as the number of dwelling units allowed per unit area (acre or hectare). The "yield" of housing units increases, therefore, as the site area increases.

On smaller sites, external factors are more likely to directly impact the potential uses of the site. Larger sites, therefore, may allow greater flexibility in accessing the site and in accommodating program elements on the site. Additional site areas also allow for the integration of open space, including natural areas and buffer zones to separate incompatible land uses and to screen undesirable views off site.

The shape of the site can have an impact on reducing development potential and design flexibility. This is especially true on smaller sites and on narrow, linear sites that have a higher edge-to-interior ratio than properties that are more compact in shape (Figure 5-2). The greater proportion of "edge" increases the site's exposure to the surrounding landscape. If the site is adjacent to a busy highway or other nuisance land use, for example, a linear or small site will substantially limit the site planner's ability to buffer the undesirable noises and visual impacts. However, if the site is adjacent to a natural amenity, a parcel with a relatively high edge-to-interior ratio will benefit from this proximity, particularly if the amenity is likely to persist well into the near future (Figure 5-3).

In combination, the size and shape of a site can significantly affect its suitability for potential development. Municipal zoning regulations, for example, may impose building "setbacks" from front, side, and back property boundaries. These or other development restrictions can occupy a relatively large percentage of a linear site's total area and potentially render the site infeasible for development from a financial perspective. In addition to on-site constraints, the immediate surroundings of potential sites are also important considerations in the site inventory. Context is particularly important when evaluating small or linear sites for uses that are potentially incompatible with the surrounding land uses.

5.3   TOPOGRAPHY

Topography is an important factor in most land planning decisions. Consequently, having a topographic survey of the site is often essential. The U.S. Geological Survey (USGS) makes topographic maps at several scales (for example, 1:250,000, 1:24,000). These maps provide information on the biophysical and cultural context of a community or region. Site topographic surveys, in contrast, are much larger in scale and are usually completed by a licensed land surveyor in accordance with specifications tailored to the program and the site. Three key attribute maps can be derived from a topographic survey. These maps graphically depict elevation, slope, and aspect — three fundamental landform components.

Figure 5-3   Water is an amenity that can significantly increase

5.3.1   Elevation

Spatial variation in elevation produces slopes that have both a gradient and an orientation—or aspect. Each of these three attributes can have a substantial influence on site planning and design decisions. Site elevations, for example, affect both drainage patterns and visibility. Variation of elevation on a site and the surrounding landscape determines the size and spatial configuration of local viewsheds. Visible areas may encompass portions of the site, or the entire site, and they may extend into the surrounding landscape.

Mapping

Elevation data are typically portrayed as contour lines on topographic maps. For site planning purposes, however, an effective way to visualize topographic relief is to create a chloropleth map of elevation. To limit the visual complexity of the map and make it easy to understand, the map should have relatively few (five to nine) classes of elevation. The range of existing elevations on and adjacent to a site determines the range of each elevation class. For example, if the highest elevation on the site is 1327 feet above a local benchmark, and the lowest elevation is 832 feet, the map must show a range of elevation of at least 495 feet (1327–832 = 495). To limit the map's visual complexity, 495 can be divided by 6 classes for a result of 82.5 feet. To create elevation classes of equal increments, 82.5 can be rounded up to 100. Each "layer" is then shaded or colored—typically with a spectrum ranging from cool colors (low elevations) to warm colors (high elevations)—to enhance the map's effectiveness (Figure 5-4).

Figure 5-4 Chloropleth map showing six elevation classes. Each class represents a range of one hundred feet of elevation change. Source: The HOK Planning Group.

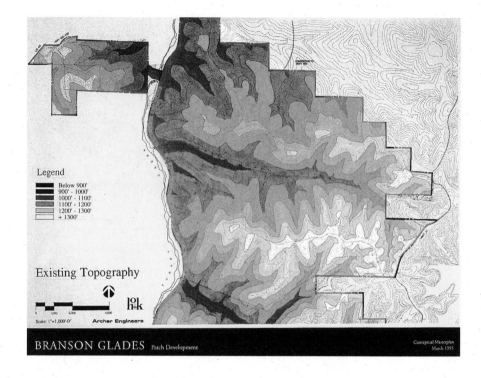

Legend

Below 900'
900' - 1000'
1000' - 1100'
1100' - 1200'
1200' - 1300'
+ 1300'

Existing Topography

Scale: 1"=1,000'-0"   Archer Engineers

BRANSON GLADES   Patch Development

Conceptual Masterplan
March 1995

5.3.2 Slope

Differences in soil parent materials and weathering account for characteristic landforms or landscape "signatures." Landforms and, therefore, slopes, are the result of constructional processes (for example, deposition) and destructional processes (for example, erosion) acting on geologic structures (Bloom, 1978). Moreover, the slopes of undeveloped sites reflect the local area's surficial geology.

A site's suitability for roads, walkways, buildings, and other structures is, in part, a function of the existing slopes on the site. In Hong Kong and San Francisco, for example, development frequently occurs on sites with steep slopes. But these cities have relatively warm climates. In locations with freezing winter temperatures, steep slopes are a significant safety concern when designing vehicle and pedestrian circulation systems. Gradients must be relatively low to prevent slipping on icy surfaces.

Mapping

Slope gradients can be computed with most GIS and CAD software and easily mapped. Different colors are typically used to identify different slope classes (Figure 5-5). The range of each mapped slope class depends on the intended uses of the site and the specific site and contextual conditions, including soil characteristics, vegetative cover, and applicable regulatory requirements. For example, to prevent significant environmental and aesthetic impacts from new development, municipalities or other regulatory agencies may prohibit

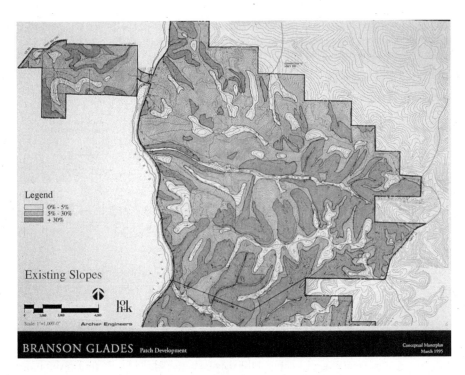

Figure 5-5 Chloropleth map of slope gradient. Source: The HOK Planning Group.

construction on very steep slopes (for example, greater than 25 percent) and require special design and construction methods on moderate to steep slopes (for example, 8 to 15 percent or 15 to 25 percent). Conversely, sites that are essentially flat (for example, less than 1 percent slope) may be poorly drained. Each of these different slope conditions warrants mapping, because these locations must be considered in the planning of the site.

5.3.3 Aspect

A slope's orientation, or aspect, is simply the direction that the slope faces. Aspect is typically identified, therefore, by compass direction (for example, north or northeast). Variation in slope and aspect influence the amount of solar radiation received by the site on a daily and seasonal basis. For example, in the Northern Hemisphere, north-facing, ten-degree slopes will receive less solar radiation than south-facing slopes of the same gradient. In the winter, the sun's highest point above the horizon is an acute angle. The north-facing slopes, when exposed to direct sunlight, receive less solar radiation per unit surface area than do the south-facing slopes. Because the slope faces away from the sun, the solar radiation striking a north-facing slope hits the surface at a shallow, or acute, angle. Consequently, sunlight strikes the slope in a more diffuse pattern, delivering to the surface less solar energy per unit area (Figure 5-6).

As with other physical attributes, the importance of a slope's aspect depends, partly, on the proposed uses of the site. At higher northern latitudes, for example, south-facing slopes

Figure 5-6 Influence of slope aspect on the intensity of solar radiation striking the slope surface. Source: Marsh, *Landscape Planning, Third Ed., copyright © 1998, p. 289, Figure 15.1. Reprinted by permission of John Wiley & Sons, Inc.*

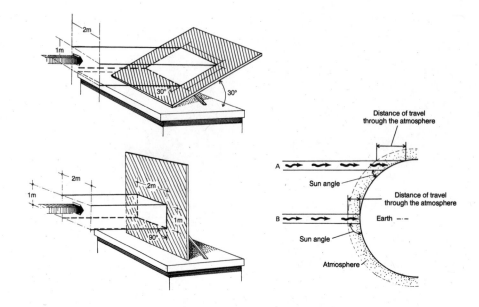

are better suited for siting buildings that will incorporate active and/or passive solar heating. A project that involves siting downhill skiing slopes will certainly consider slope, elevation, and aspect. Conversely, a north-facing slope may be better suited for ski trail development in areas with relatively mild winters, to limit the melting of snow from direct solar radiation.

Mapping

Slope aspect, like slope gradient, can be mapped manually or with commercially available GIS software. Typically, aspect is classified using eight categories: north, northeast, east, southeast, south, southwest, west, and northwest. These are portrayed graphically by either shading or color. Aspect influences microclimate by affecting the level of solar radiation that strikes the site. Therefore, more shaded northern slopes (in the Northern Hemisphere) are rendered with cooler colors or heavier hatching than are the other slopes with greater solar exposure.

5.4 GEOLOGY

Elevation and slope are good examples of quantitatively expressed landform attributes. Landform classification describes significant physiographic features of terrestrial, riparian, and aquatic environments. For example, eskers, kames, and moraines are the distinct signatures of prior glaciation. Landform classification is useful in site or regional inventories and analyses, particularly for characterizing difficult-to-quantify attributes like scenic beauty, sense of place, and landscape character. Landforms, in conjunction with vegetation, define viewsheds, or visibility on a site, and can create visual interest. Landforms also influence microclimate, stormwater runoff and infiltration, and the distribution of plant and animal species.

Surficial geology is, concerned with the structure, composition, and stability of the materials beneath and—in some locations—at the earth's surface. In some landscapes, bedrock is buried many yards or meters below the ground surface. Bedrock geology has a persistent effect on landforms, due to the different rates of weathering that occurs on the soil parent materials. Soil formation, soil erosion, and soil deposition are natural processes that involve rock fragmentation and weathering. Weathering occurs unevenly because of variations in the bedrock's chemical composition and structure.

An important attribute of surficial geology is the depth-to-bedrock. If excavation is planned for building foundations or for other site structures, the depth to bedrock should be investigated. If excavation is planned for a site with shallow bedrock or glacial eratics (boulders), blasting or other special methods of removal may be necessary. The cost of excavating a cubic yard or meter of rock is many times greater than the cost of excavating the same volume of soil. Consequently, these difficult subsurface conditions can significantly increase the costs of construction.

Mapping

A geologic map shows the age and distribution of rock layers and other geologic materials. These attributes influence a site's suitability for excavation and grading, wastewater disposal, groundwater supply, pond construction, and other common land development objectives (Way, 1978). Geologic maps also show locations that are susceptible to earthquakes, landslides, and other hazards.

A geologic map usually includes information on topography and cultural elements, such as roads to help orient the map user. Colors and letter symbols identify each kind of geologic unit at, or near, the Earth's surface. A volume of rock of a specific type and age range is considered a geologic unit. Therefore, a sandstone of one age might be shown as one color, for example, while a sandstone of a different age might be shown as a different color. (For more information on geologic maps, see: http://www2.nature.nps.gov/geology/usgsnps/gmap/gmap1.html)

A searchable catalog of paper and digital geologic maps is available on the Internet through the United States Geological Survey (http://ngmdb.usgs.gov/ngmdb/ngm_catalog.ora.html). Several map themes in the database are potentially useful in site planning and design (Table 5-2).

In addition to the more generalized maps, which are available from public sources, detailed site-scale data may be acquired for site planning and design. In this case, a site's subsurface conditions are typically assessed in conjunction with the topographic survey. Data on depth-to-bedrock are collected by drilling bore holes with a mechanical driller. These samples provide information about the site's soil and surficial geology (Joyce, 1982). The spacing and number of bore-holes depends on the conditions of the site and the purposes of the investigation. Sites with great variability in soil and geologic conditions may require more intensive subsurface investigation. Similarly, when large buildings will be constructed on a site, the area and depth of the subsurface investigation will be greater than if the project did not include these structures. This investigation usually requires the services of a geotechnical engineer.

Volcanic activity and earthquakes are relatively common events in some parts of the world. These geological disturbances are potentially devastating hazards that must be

TABLE 5-2 Selected map themes of the National Geologic Map Database.

Category	Theme
Geology	General (e.g., rocks and sediment at or near the Earth's surface)
	Structure (e.g., thickness of buried rock units)
	Engineering (e.g., engineering properties of soils)
	Coastal (e.g., areas of coastal zone erosion or sedimentation)
Natural Resources	Nonmetallic resources (e.g., sand and gravel)
	Water (e.g., groundwater aquifers and water quality)
	Other (e.g., geothermal resources)
Hazards	Earthquake hazards (e.g., faults and earthquake zones)
	Volcano hazards (e.g., eruption history)
	Landslides (e.g, existing landslides and landslide potential)

Source: United States Geological Survey, 2000.

considered when planning new development in these areas In some landscapes, especially those impacted by deforestation, landslides are also common. The locations of potential natural hazards can be documented in the site inventory (Figure 5-7).

5.5 HYDROLOGY

Water circulates in the environment through precipitation, overland flow, infiltration, storage, and evapotranspiration. Groundwater moves by capillary action through the porous spaces between unconsolidated sand, gravel, and rock, and between the fractures and faults in the underlying bedrock. The upper surface of the saturated area, the water table, generally mirrors the surface terrain. In landscapes where groundwater is the source of local or municipal wells, groundwater pumping can have substantial impacts on the depth of the water table.

Topographic relief creates drainage patterns, which, in turn, influence vegetation associations and distributions. The spatial correlation between vegetation associations and site drainage patterns is particularly strong in arid and semiarid landscapes where water is often the primary limiting factor on plant growth and distribution. Although the groundwater–vegetation linkage is more subtle in less arid environments, the continuous— or seasonal saturation of soils creates suitable conditions for wetland vegetation. In coastal environments, brackish or saline surface and groundwater result in the development of salt marshes and other distinct wetland communities.

Without mitigation, urban development can have significant impacts on local and regional hydrology, including the following (United States Environmental Protection Agency, 1993):

    □ Increased volumes and rates of runoff discharges

    □ Reduced time needed for runoff to reach surface waters

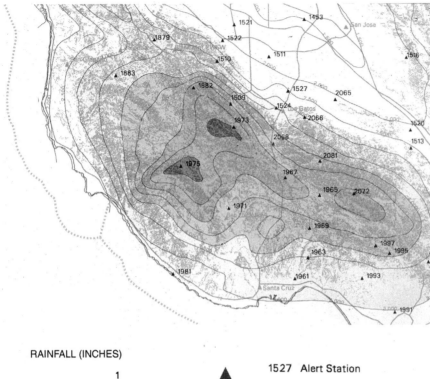

Figure 5-7 Inventory map of landslide hazard susceptibility in the San Francisco Bay region. Source: Wilson, R. C., and Jayko, A. S., 1997. Preliminary maps showing rainfall thresholds for debris-flow activity, San Francisco Bay region, California. U.S. Geological Survey Open-File Report 97–945 F, in Ramsey and others, 1999. Landslide hazard susceptibility maps for the San Francisco Bay region. Tools for emergency planning during 1997–98. El Niño: ESRI Map Book, v. 14, p. 18–19.

- ☐ Increased frequency and severity of flooding

- ☐ Reduced streamflow during prolonged periods of dry weather

Land development usually involves the construction of buildings and paved surfaces that are impervious or nearly impervious. Any site-disturbing activities can increase the risks of flooding, erosion, and other ecological impacts to properties "downstream." For this reason, stormwater management is an increasingly regulated component of the land development process.

Figure 5-8   To protect the quality of potable water supplies, land use controls limit development in areas near community wells. Source: Marsh, Landscape Planning, Third Ed., copyright © 1998, p. 142, Figure 7.11. Reprinted by permission of John Wiley & Sons, Inc.

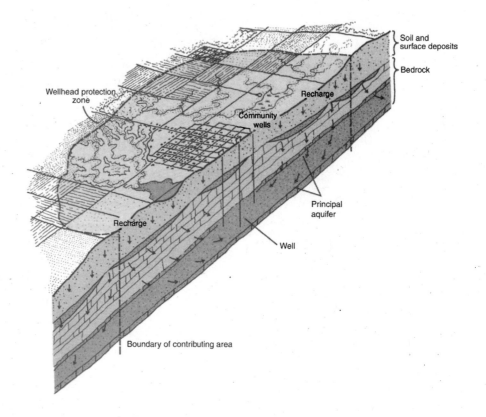

Land use changes may also negatively impact water quality. Contamination may result, for example, from erosion and sedimentation, chemicals, or microorganisms. Surface water pollution associated with stormwater runoff can negatively impact ecosystems and reduce the aesthetic and recreational value of rivers, lakes, and other water bodies. Groundwater pollution from septic tank effluent can also limit an area's suitability for wells.

When local groundwater is the source of a community's potable water, efforts must be made to ensure that on-site wastewater treatment systems and stormwater runoff do not contaminate local wells (Figure 5-8). For the past few decades, siting requirements for on-site wastewater treatment systems have used soil conditions as the primary siting criterion. As treatment technologies continue to evolve, more highly engineered on-site wastewater treatment systems are being constructed in many formerly unsuitable locations (LaGro, 1996). These include areas with bedrock and/or water table as shallow as 20cm below the ground surface.

Mapping

Water movement, infiltration, storage, and discharge should be considered in the site inventory of physical attributes. This assessment of hydrologic conditions requires consideration of the site's surface and subsurface features. Characterizing surface conditions involves the analysis of topography, vegetation, surface water distribution, land use, climate, and soil-forming processes and deposits (Kolm, 1996). Hydrologic maps may also locate the primary paths of groundwater flow and the locations of groundwater discharge to the surface. Hydrologists or geological engineers assess aquifer permeability, thickness, and discontinuities. Characterizing the three-dimensional subsurface geologic structure involves the analysis of stratigraphy, lithology, and structural and geomorphologic discontinuities (Kolm, 1996).

Maps of groundwater and local geological conditions are particularly important in land use planning for rural and urban fringe areas (Figure 5-9). Detailed site data can help in determining an area's potential sources of potable groundwater (Figure 5-10). Surface drainage also should be mapped (Figure 5-11), as well as potential flood hazard areas (Figure 5-12). Aquifer recharge areas are also particularly important locations to identify and protect from development.

5.6 SOILS

Physical, biological, and often cultural factors influence soil genesis and morphology. Climate, parent material, and landform position are key physical factors. Biological factors include the growth, death, and decomposition of vegetation, microorganisms, and other biota living above ground or within the soil itself. Soil properties are also affected by previous land use (Ferguson, 1999).

Depending on the site's location and the intended program, soil attributes that an inventory may consider include the following:

- □ Acidity/alkalinity (pH)
- □ Permeability
- □ Erosion potential
- □ Depth to seasonally high-water table
- □ Depth-to-bedrock

Subsurface conditions affect not only the complexity of excavation and construction but also the design of new structures. A new building or structure must be designed and constructed to ensure that the integrity of the structure is not compromised. For structures in higher northern latitudes, for example, foundations must be constructed to a depth below the lowest frost level. This depth may be three or more feet (about one meter) below the ground surface. For large multistory buildings, foundations are constructed to considerably greater depths.

Soils vary widely in texture, fertility, permeability, and other attributes that influence plant growth and development. A soil medium favorable for plant health reduces the impact of pests and diseases. Erosion frequently occurs when vegetation cover is either removed or substantially damaged during site clearing and construction. Topsoil losses from prior agricultural activities or other erosive forces increase the costs of reestablishing vegetation on a site after construction.

Generalized Groundwater Elevation Contour and Geologic Map

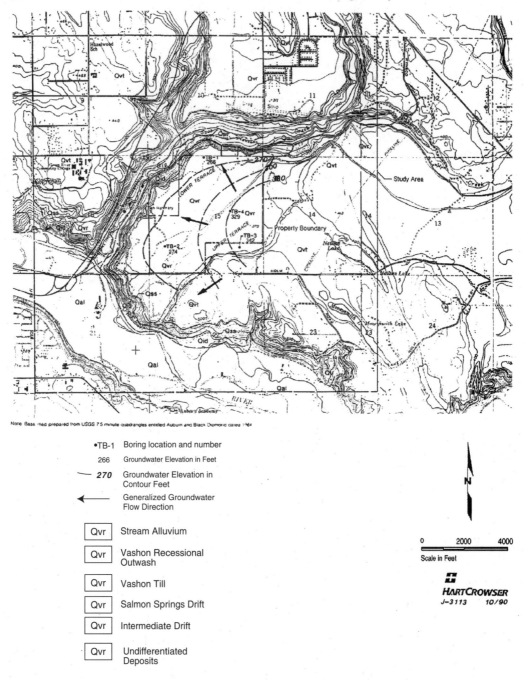

Note: Base map prepared from USGS 7.5 minute quadrangles entitled Auburn and Black Diamond dated 1984.

•TB-1	Boring location and number
266	Groundwater Elevation in Feet
— 270	Groundwater Elevation in Contour Feet
←	Generalized Groundwater Flow Direction
Qvr	Stream Alluvium
Qvr	Vashon Recessional Outwash
Qvr	Vashon Till
Qvr	Salmon Springs Drift
Qvr	Intermediate Drift
Qvr	Undifferentiated Deposits

N

0   2000   4000
Scale in Feet

HARTCROWSER
J–3113   10/90

Figure 5-9   Map of groundwater elevation and surficial geology. Source: R. W. Thorpe and Associates.

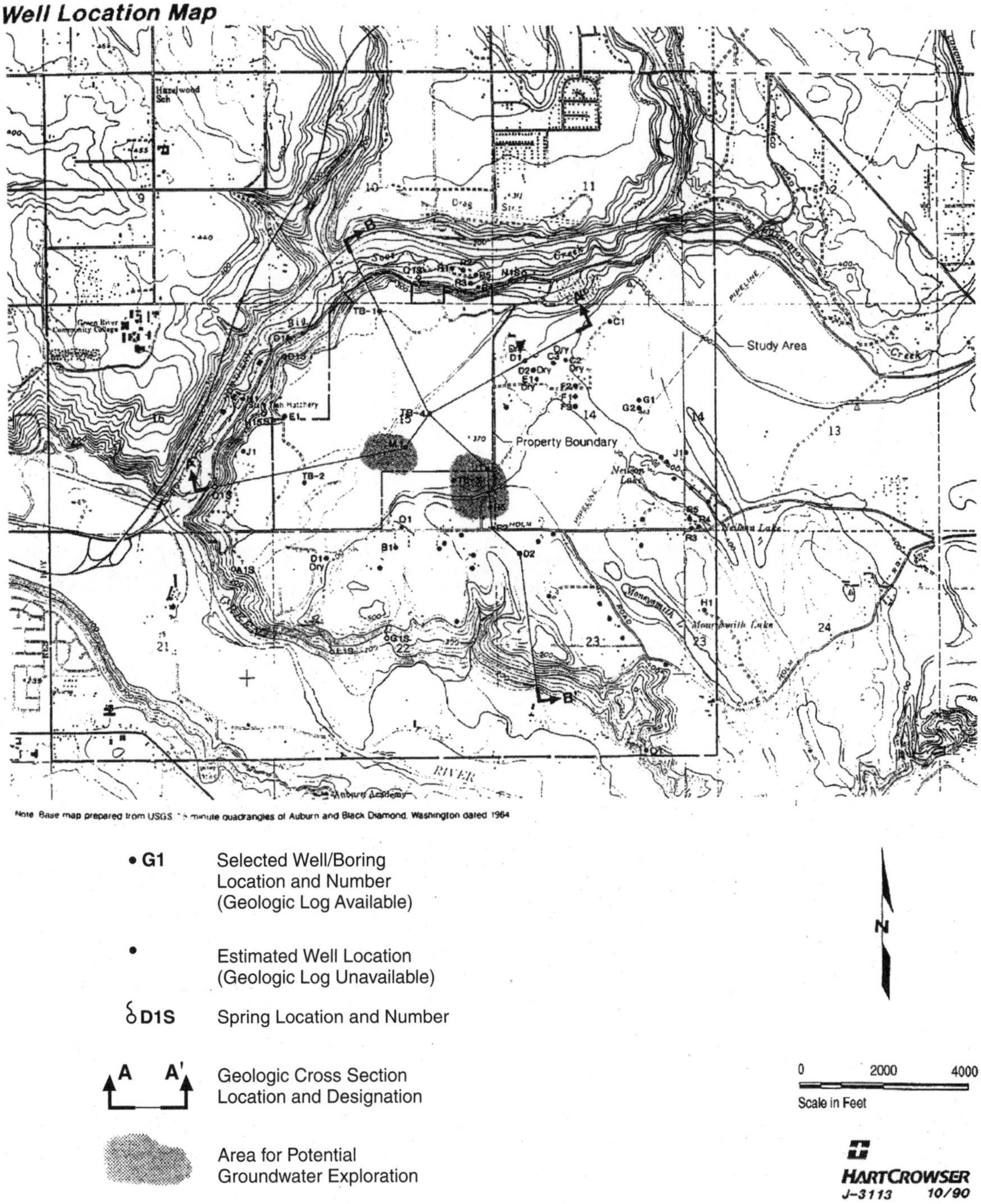
Well Location Map
Study Area
Property Boundary
Creek
Nelson Lake
Mountsmith Lake
RIVER
Auburn Academy
PIPELINE
Note: Base map prepared from USGS 7.5 minute quadrangles of Auburn and Black Diamond, Washington dated 1964
• G1 Selected Well/Boring Location and Number (Geologic Log Available)
• Estimated Well Location (Geologic Log Unavailable)
D1S Spring Location and Number
A A' Geologic Cross Section Location and Designation
Area for Potential Groundwater Exploration
N
0 2000 4000
Scale in Feet
HARTCROWSER
J-3113 10/90

Figure 5-10 Map of potential well locations. Source: R. W. Thorpe and Associates.

Figure 5-11 Inventory map showing watershed boundaries (ridges) and major drainage patterns (valleys). Source: The HOK Planning Group.

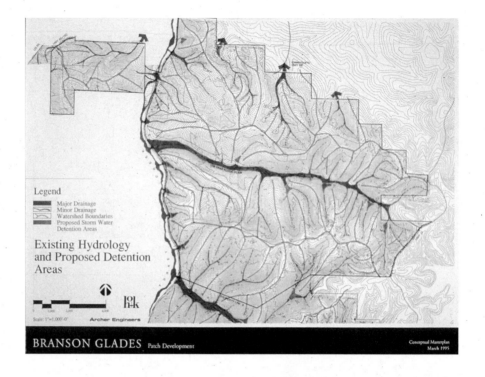

Figure 5-12 Map showing floodway and 100-year flood zone along a river in the Midwest. Source: The HOK Planning Group.

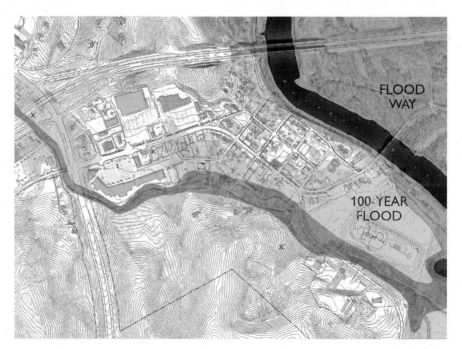

Where on-site wastewater treatment systems will be installed, soils must be evaluated for their permeability and capacity to remove chemical and pathogen contaminants from wastewater effluent. Bacteria and other microbes in the soil perform this natural treatment function. Very rapidly draining soils, typically those with high sand and gravel content, may be poorly suited for on-site wastewater treatment. Similarly, impervious soils, such as hardpan, are also constraints that limit on-site wastewater treatment. If hazardous wastes are present on the site, the costs of remediation can be significant. Sites with a history of previous industrial or commercial activities may be contaminated with a variety of hazardous substances, and investigation of a site's subsurface conditions is warranted.

Mapping

In the United States, most landscapes outside of urbanized areas have had soils inventoried and mapped. The U.S. Department of Agriculture's Soil Survey maps are spatially coarse (for example, 1:15,840 scale) and are generally inappropriate for making detailed site planning decisions. These maps do not capture the fine-scale variability that occurs in the depth to bedrock, depth to water table, and other key attributes. However, the general suitability of different soil types, for the proposed site uses, can be portrayed with chloropleth maps (Figure 5-13).

5.7 CLIMATE

Atmospheric conditions that may influence site planning and design decisions include precipitation, air temperature, solar incidence, wind direction, and wind speed. These attributes vary annually, seasonally, and daily. Seasonal and monthly climate data are available from national weather services (for example, in Australia, at www.bom.gov.au/climate). Local weather records can provide additional information about the daily weather conditions that can be expected each season. Collectively, these data include the following:

- Temperature (maximum, minimum, and day/night temperature variation)

- Humidity (high, low, and averages)

- Wind (maximum, average velocity, and direction)

- Rainfall (monthly total and maximum for any one day)

- Snowfall (monthly total and maximum for any one day)

- Solar radiation (monthly average)

- Potential natural hazards

The U.S. Department of Agriculture (USDA) Plant Hardiness Zone map shows the locations where different average annual minimum temperatures can be expected each year in the United States, Canada, and Mexico. The United States National Arboretum "web version" of the map depicts eleven zones (Table 5-3), each of which represents a different

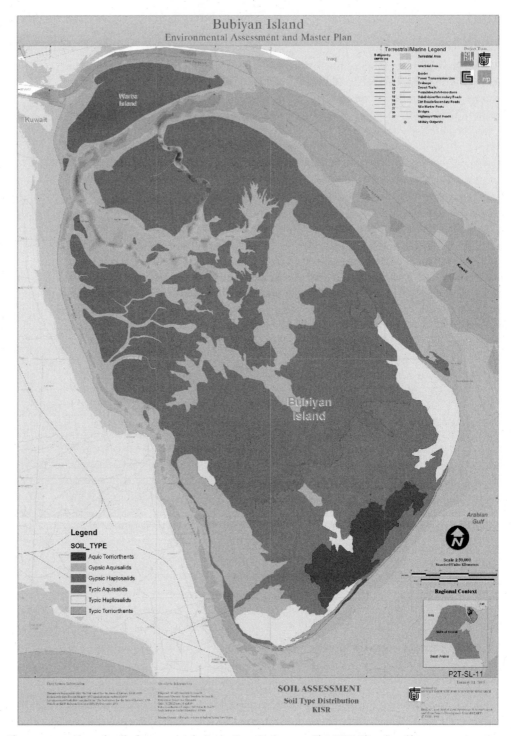

Figure 5-13   Map of soils for a coastal site in Kuwait. Source: The HOK Planning Group.

TABLE 5-3 Plant hardiness zones, average annual minimum temperature ranges, and representative cities or states in each climatic zone of North America.

Zone	Temperature Range	City or State
1	Below −50 F (−45.6 C)	Fairbanks, Alaska
2a	−50 to −45 F (−45.5 to −42.8 C)	Flin Flon, Manitoba (Canada)
2b	−45 to −40 F (−42.7 to −40.0 C)	Unalakleet, Alaska
3a	−40 to −35 F (−39.9 to −37.3 C)	International Falls, Minnesota
3b	−35 to −30 F (−37.2 to −34.5 C)	Tomahawk, Wisconsin
4a	−30 to −25 F (−34.4 to −31.7 C)	Minneapolis/St.Paul, Minnesota
4b	−25 to −20 F (−31.6 to −28.9 C)	Nebraska
5a	−20 to −15 F (−28.8 to −26.2 C)	Illinois
5b	−15 to −10 F (−26.1 to −23.4 C)	Mansfield, Pennsylvania
6a	−10 to −5 F (−23.3 to −20.6 C)	St. Louis, Missouri
6b	−5 to 0 F (−20.5 to −17.8 C)	McMinnville, Tennessee
7a	0 to 5 F (−17.7 to −15.0 C)	Oklahoma City, Oklahoma
7b	5 to 10 F (−14.9 to −12.3 C)	Griffin, Georgia
8a	10 to 15 F (−12.2 to −9.5 C)	Dallas, Texas
8b	15 to 20 F (−9.4 to −6.7 C)	Gainesville, Florida
9a	20 to 25 F (−6.6 to −3.9 C)	Houston, Texas
9b	25 to 30 F (−3.8 to −1.2 C)	Fort Pierce, Florida
10a	30 to 35 F (−1.1 to 1.6 C)	Barstow, California
10b	35 to 40 F (4.4 to 1.7 C)	Miami, Florida
11	above 40 F (above 4.5 C)	Mazatlán (Mexico)

Source: United States Department of Agriculture, 1990.

set of winter conditions for plants (United States Department of Agriculture, 1990). This map provides a guide to regional climatic conditions, but it cannot account for local variations in microclimate within each zone.

Microclimate is modified by vegetation in several ways. Shade trees, for example, intercept the solar radiation that would otherwise strike pavement, rooftops, and other inorganic surfaces. These surfaces, especially if they are dark in color, absorb and subsequently reradiate more heat energy than vegetation. Leaves of plants also tend to cool air temperatures through evapotranspiration. In addition to moderating air temperature and humidity, plants can improve air quality by removing certain chemical pollutants and, as a result of photosynthesis, add oxygen to the atmosphere. Depending on the height of the tree, or any other vertical element, shadows of varying lengths will be cast during the course of a day. Shadow length also varies due to seasonal variations in the earth's relationship to the sun (Figure 5-14). Slope and aspect also influence surface temperatures through their effect on the amount of solar radiation striking the site's surface.

Microclimate has a particularly important effect on two aspects of the built environment: energy consumption for the heating and cooling of buildings, and the comfort of people in outdoor settings. Both energy consumption and microclimate are influenced, however, by the spatial organization and orientation of buildings, structures, and outdoor spaces. Energy consumption for heating and cooling buildings can be reduced through

Figure 5-14 Diagram of
seasonal changes in the
maximum daily sun angle for a
mid-latitude location in the
Northern Hemisphere.
Source: Marsh, *Landscape
Planning,* Third Ed., copyright
© 1998, p. 290, Figure 15.3.
Reprinted by permission of John

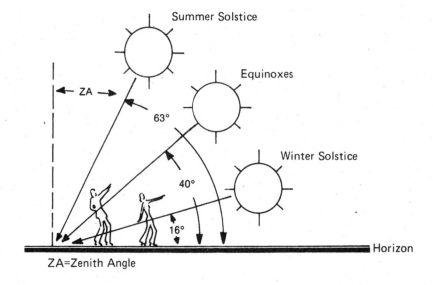

both passive and active solar designs. Greater energy efficiency can be achieved by moderating the solar radiation striking and entering a building, and by moderating winds and breezes near the building. In environments where winds are strong and persistent, significant modifications of building forms may be necessary.

Winter winds can be buffered somewhat with windbreaks, and land uses can be arranged to reduce the negative effects of winds on outdoor activities. A person is thermally comfortable when there is a balance between the body's heat losses and heat gains. Metabolic energy (generated within the body) and radiation (from the sun and from the earth) are the main sources of energy available to heat a person. Energy can be lost from a person's body mainly through evaporation of perspiration, convection from wind, and radiation. In outdoor environments, solar radiation and wind are the microclimatic factors that can be most easily modified by design (Brown and Gillespie, 1995).

Ambient air temperatures in outdoor areas depend, in part, on whether the space is exposed to full sunshine. Surface materials and vegetation within the space also affect air temperatures. Paving materials like brick and stone absorb solar radiation, reradiate the energy as heat, and, thereby, raise the air temperature immediately above the paved surfaces. Direct sunlight warms people when it hits either their clothing or skin. The heat index is an estimate of "apparent temperature"—the temperature that one feels because of the interaction between air temperature and relative humidity. Direct sunlight can raise heat index values by as much as 15 degrees Fahrenheit (United States National Oceanic and Atmospheric Agency, 2000).

In a classic study of the relationships between environment and human behavior, William H. Whyte (1980) used time-lapse photography to document the locations of people in Seagram's Plaza in New York City. The rooftop of an adjacent building was his vantage point for viewing the plaza below. On a relatively cool spring day, plaza users either sat or stood in locations that were exposed to direct sunlight. As shadows swept across this

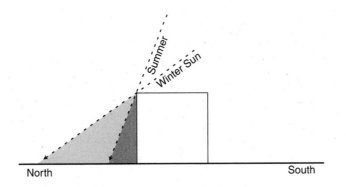

Figure 5-15 Schematic diagram of the seasonal variation in shade cast by a building in the northern hemisphere. Solar exposure in outdoor spaces near a building varies not only with weather conditions but also with time of day, day of year, and location of the space in relation to both the building and the sun.

outdoor plaza, people came and went, but the majority of users at any one time were in the sun. In effect, the users moved across the space in synchronization with the movement of the area exposed to full sunlight.

Buildings, trees, walls, and other vertical elements cast shadows that influence site microclimate. Understanding sun and shade patterns adjacent to both existing and proposed construction is especially essential in site planning and design for urban sites (Figure 5-15).

Mapping

Microclimate can vary greatly over short distances and over short time spans. Brown and Gillespie (1995) recommend a process for mapping site microclimate that identifies the site's exposure to both solar radiation and wind. A solar radiation map, which could be a digital layer in a GIS, can be created by overlaying and combining these three attribute layers: slope gradient, slope aspect, and vegetation (deciduous and coniferous trees, primarily). There are many possible combinations of slope, aspect, and tree cover, so the resulting map can be very complex. One possible map class, for example, would represent all site areas with less than 10 percent south-facing slopes and no tree cover. Another class would represent all areas with greater than 10 percent north-facing slopes and coniferous tree cover. In the northern latitudes, these two areas would receive markedly different levels of solar radiation during the winter months.

The complexity of the solar radiation map depends on the number of classes in each input layer. If each of these three layers has several classes, the potential number of combinations would be relatively high. For example, the slope gradient map could have three classes (0–10 percent, 10–20 percent, and greater than 20 percent); the slope aspect map could have eight classes (for the eight compass points); and the tree cover map could have four classes (no tree cover, deciduous trees, coniferous trees, and mixed deciduous/coniferous trees). If these three layers were combined, the resulting map of all slope, aspect, and tree cover combinations could have 96 classes (3 classes multiplied by 8 classes multiplied by 4 classes). Although useful as an intermediate layer, this map would be difficult to interpret. Within a GIS, however, this map could be reclassified, or recoded, to yield a much smaller number of classes that more clearly convey the site's microclimate. One possibility would be to aggregate each of the various slope, aspect, and vegetation combinations into one of the following four classes (Beer, 1990):

□ Very warm areas

□ Warm areas

□ Cool areas

□ Very cool areas

This recoding would have to consider the site's exposure to solar radiation and seasonal winds. These two factors will depend, of course, on the regional climate (for example, hot-arid or warm-humid). They will also depend on the site's terrain and vegetation patterns.

Prevailing summer breezes and winter winds are typically shown as arrows on a site inventory map. Because wind is highly variable in both speed and direction, it may be graphically depicted with "wind roses." These diagrams show the frequency distribution of the wind direction, velocity, and duration at a specific location. Solar access is another important microclimatic factor that warrants documentation. Particularly in urban settings, where buildings may be either immediately adjacent to the site or on the site itself, shade diagrams should be evaluated. Combined with seasonal changes in the position of the sun above the horizon, a variety of sun, shade, and wind patterns can occur on a site (Figure 5-16). When the development program includes outdoor spaces for seating, eating, and other activities, then shade diagrams should be evaluated. Because the position of the sun above the horizon changes daily from sunrise to sunset, these diagrams are typically created for several times of the day and year. These diagrams coincide with the times of day and year when the programmed outdoor spaces (such as plazas and terraces) are most likely to be occupied with people. Shade diagrams may be appropriate, for example, for these four times of the day:

□ Midmorning (10 a.m.)

□ Noon (12 p.m)

□ Midafternoon (2 p.m.)

□ Late afternoon (4 p.m.)

Variation in solar access—and shadows—during the course of the year depends largely on the latitude of the site. In higher latitudes, especially in areas where cold winter temperatures are the norm, the use of outdoor space is strongly influenced by microclimate. Shade diagrams are typically prepared for these days of the year:

□ Midsummer (summer solstice)

□ Midwinter (winter solstice)

□ Equinox (vernal or autumnal)

The summer and winter solstices occur on about June 21 and December 22. The equinox occurs each year on about March 21 and September 22. Day and night are equal in length on the equinox.

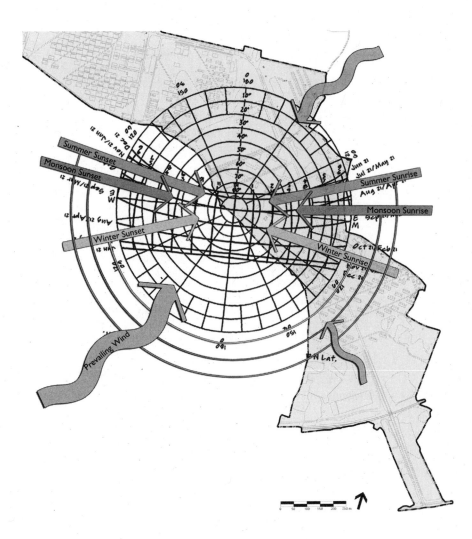

Figure 5-16 Climate analysis for a coastal land-planning project in India. Source: The HOK Planning Group.

5.8   NATURAL HAZARDS

Natural hazards include atmospheric, hydrologic, geologic, and wildfire events that, because of their location, severity, and frequency, have the potential to adversely impact humans, their structures, or their activities (Organization of American States, 1990). These natural phenomena present significant risks to human life and property. Typically, little can be done to control these potentially destructive forces. The most practical solution, therefore, is to avoid development of areas that are most at risk.

The cost of damage attributable to natural hazards in the United States has been estimated at an average of $1 billion per week (Mileti, 1999). Until the late 1990s, the U.S. government routinely allowed the reconstruction of destroyed homes and other buildings

TABLE 5-4 Selected physical factors to consider in site planning and design.

Category	Attribute	Land Use Significance
Hydrology	Depth to water table	Suitability for building foundation excavations Suitability for on-site wastewater treatment
	Drainage patterns	Flooding hazards Stormwater management Groundwater recharge
Geology	Depth to bedrock	Suitability for building foundation excavations Suitability for on-site wastewater treatment
	Fault lines	Earthquake hazards Landslide hazards
Soils	pH Porosity Structure and texture	Plant selection and growth Suitability for on-site wastewater treatment Erosion potential
Topography	Slope gradient	Circulation system safety Building design and construction complexity Erosion potential Stormwater management
	Slope aspect	Microclimate Suitability for solar architecture
	Elevation	Visibility and visual quality Drainage patterns
Climate	Wind direction	Location of outdoor activities Windbreak location
	Solar access	Building design and placement Location of outdoor activities

on sites that were repeatedly struck by floods and other natural disasters. With wider recognition of global warming, the environmental, economic, and human impacts of natural hazards—particularly hurricanes—have become an important public policy concern. Global vulnerability to hurricanes is substantial, because a large proportion of the world's population lives near the oceanic coasts.

The Year 2000 Building Code marks a substantial shift in public policy regarding construction in areas prone to natural hazards. In an attempt to reduce continued rebuilding in floodplains and other hazardous areas, the federal government has purchased some of the more vulnerable properties. The U.S. Geological Survey has also created a series of maps that inventory the risks of various natural hazards in the United States. These are potentially useful information sources for site planning projects in areas subject to life-threatening natural hazards.

5.9 CONCLUSION

A site inventory of physical attributes is driven by both the project's program and the characteristics of the site itself. Physical attributes on a site can have a broad impact on how a site is developed (Table 5-4). Potential data sources include aerial photographs, subsurface borings, and a wide variety of reference maps. Although not always possible due to budgetary constraints, visiting a site at different times of the year can yield a much more comprehensive understanding of local site conditions, especially drainage patterns, wind patterns, and microclimate.

chapter 6

Site Inventory:
Biological Attributes

6.1 INTRODUCTION

The site inventory process is divided into three parts in this book—each covered in a separate chapter. This separation is a useful, but artificial, division. In site planning practice, distinctions between these three activities are less pronounced. Landscapes have both biotic and abiotic components, and their structure and ecological function are influenced by the complex interplay of biological, cultural, and physical factors. For example, landscape corridors of cultural origin may be barriers to the movement of ground-dwelling animals, or serve as conduits for pathogens and invasive exotic species. Roads, utility corridors, and other built, linear features—may isolate endemic populations of plant and animal species, and ultimately doom those species to extinction at the local level, and possibly at broader spatial scales.

6.2 ECOLOGICAL COMMUNITIES

An ecological community is an aggregation of interacting species living together in the same place. Complex interactions among climate, soils, topography, natural disturbances, and the organisms themselves influence the composition and spatial distribution of ecological communities (Sadava et al., 2006). Communities are often named for the dominant plant species, which may be dominant because of either its physical size or abundance. Two examples of North American communities are the beech-maple-hemlock and the oak savanna communities (Carpenter et al., 1975). Ecotones—the spatial boundaries of communities—are especially important areas, biologically. Animals that are mobile may find shelter in one ecotone but more abundant food in another.

6.2.1 Habitat Fragmentation

Human activities such as agriculture, forestry, and urban development have dramatically altered the structure and ecological function of many, if not most, of the landscapes in Europe and heavily civilized parts of other continents. Continuing land use changes may destroy some habitats but also fragment and functionally disconnect others. Fragmentation of ecological corridors and other habitats is a global environmental concern.

Natural corridors in the landscape facilitate the movement of organisms between habitats. Existing corridors, therefore, are particularly important elements in most landscapes and require protection to help maintain biodiversity and ecosystem connectivity. Identifying gaps in these corridors is also important because these can be targets for restoration (Hilty et al., 2006).

Large, contiguous natural areas, especially riparian corridors, should be given the highest priority for protection from development. But simply leaving natural areas untouched may not be enough to ensure their continued biodiversity. Small, isolated patches of forest, for example, may lose indigenous animal species because of the barriers created by adjacent development. Many animal species need more than one habitat type for different life cycle stages, such as reproduction and migration. The daily activities of seeking food and water, for example, also may be hindered by the habitat's surroundings.

Mapping
Land cover information for the United States is available through the U.S. Geological Survey's Land Cover Institute (http://www.landcover.usgs.gov/). A 30-meter resolution National Land Cover Dataset (NLCD) is available in digital format. The 31-volume compact disc (CD) set contains 21 categories of land cover, percent tree canopy, and percent urban imperviousness derived from 30-meter resolution Landsat imagery.

Large-scale (for example, 1:1,200) aerial photographs can facilitate even more detailed land cover mapping. Color infrared photographs are helpful, for example, in identifying differences in vegetation health and vigor. Detailed information concerning the community's composition of native and exotic species, as well as the abundance and health of those species, is usually confirmed by visiting the site (Figure 6-1). A chloropleth map can show the locations of significant site vegetation (Figure 6-2). In areas where plant communities have evolved under a fire regime, the frequency of wildfires—a natural hazard for any nearby development—may also be mapped (Figure 6-3).

6.2.2 Exotic Species

For thousands of years, plant and animal species have been adapting to habitats altered by human activities. Coincident with European settlement of North America, many introduced species became naturalized. Centuries of global trade, migration, and settlement have introduced thousands of non-native or exotic species to new environments.

Figure 6-1 Landscape architect assessing vegetation type and quality in southwest Florida. Note desiccation of the cypress trees (*Taxodium distichum*) caused by regional drainage canals excavated during the mid–twentieth century.

These exotic—and sometimes invasive—species include megafauna, like horses and pigs. They also include megaflora, like the eucalyptus and melaleuca trees. Examples of other exotic plants include vines (kudzu) and shrubs (Brazilian pepper).

Within the United States, an estimated 50,000 species of exotic plants, animals, and microbes cause significant ecological changes in both managed and natural ecosystems (Myers, 1979; Pimentel et al., 2000, pp. 53–65). Nearly half of the species listed as threatened or endangered under the federal Endangered Species Act are at risk primarily because of predation by, or competition with, invasive nonnative species (Wilcove et al., 1998, pp. 607–615). Exotic species also have substantial economic impacts. Annual expenditures for the control of nonindigenous species are estimated to exceed $6 billion per year in the United States alone (Pimentel et al., 2000, pp. 53–65).

Carried by ships, trucks, and airplanes, both large and small species have been introduced into new habitats. Exotic species are particularly successful colonizers when

Figure 6-2 Map showing three densities of vegetative cover. Source: The HOK Planning Group.

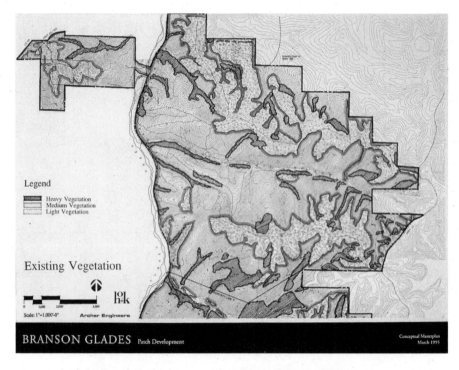

Figure 6-3 Map of fire frequency in the Santa Monica mountains of California. Map categories reflect the number of times the land has burned. Source: © 1999 James A. Woods.

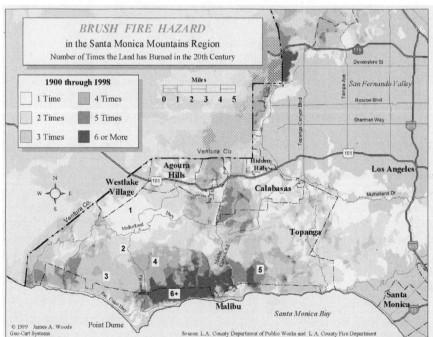

the new habitats present minimal constraints to their development and reproduction. Typically, these competitive controls limit the populations of each species in their home territories. One type of competitive control is predation. A potentially invasive species may be limited in its native habitat by grazing (in the case of plants) or predation (in the case of animals). Other species may compete for the same resources, such as food and space. Competition for the same ecological "niche" helps hold in check the populations of the competing species. William E. Odum (1959), in the classic *Fundamentals of Ecology*, writes:

> The habitat of an organism is the place where it lives or the place where one would go to find it. The ecological niche, however, is the position or status of an organism within its community and ecosystem resulting from the organism's structural adaptations, physiological responses, and specific behaviors (inherited and/or learned.) The ecological niche of an organism depends not only on where it lives but also on what it does. By analogy, it may be said that the habitat is the organism's "address," and the niche is its "profession," biologically speaking.

Many exotic species have been intentionally transported to—and, in fact, distributed within—new habitats. For example, the Melaleuca tree, now one of the most invasive tree species in the Florida Everglades, was intentionally seeded by airplanes in the mid–twentieth century (Davis and Ogden, 1994). Without understanding the potential impacts of the plant on the Everglades ecology, the seeds were dispersed in an effort to dry the wetlands and create new land for agriculture and urban development. Similarly, the eucalyptus tree was imported to California from Australia and planted widely as a new source of timber. In the benign California climate, and with little competition and no significant natural controls, the eucalyptus subsequently colonized many of the state's native oak forests and savannas (Santos, 1997).

There are many practical reasons to protect native plant and animal habitats. Riparian areas and wetlands, for example, also serve important hydrologic functions. In addition to the intrinsic ecological benefits of biodiversity (Wilson, 1988), natural areas are open spaces that may also serve important cultural functions, such as providing aesthetic amenity and outdoor "laboratories" for natural science education (deGroot, 1992).

Mapping

On sites with significant natural areas, consideration should be given to mapping the distributions of invasive exotic species. This information can be used in developing a targeted plan for eradicating invasive exotic species and restoring degraded native communities. Depending on the land use program and the site's context, restoration of wetlands, prairies, and/or woodlands may be feasible. Maps of the site's soils, hydrology, and vegetation can help in identifying the most suitable locations for these eradication and restoration activities.

6.2.3 Wetlands

Since the beginning of European settlement in the early 1600s, the area that is now the coterminous United States has lost—through agriculture, urban development, and other land uses—more than half the area's original wetland acreage (Dahl, 1990). In the United States, the federal agencies involved in wetland regulation define wetlands on the basis of hydrology, vegetation, and soils. Most states have also developed regulatory definitions of wetlands, but these definitions tend to emphasize the presence of certain vegetation, rather than the area's soils and hydrology. Wetlands classified on the basis of plant and soil conditions generally fall into one of the following three categories (Tiner, 1997; United States Fish and Wildlife Service, 2000):

- Areas with hydrophytes and hydric soils (marshes, swamps, and bogs)

- Areas without soils but with hydrophytes (aquatic beds and seaweed-covered rocky shores)

- Areas without soil and without hydrophytes (gravel beaches and tidal flats) that are periodically flooded

The federal Fish and Wildlife Service's wetland classification scheme has five general classes and several subclasses, as follows (Cowardin et al., 1979):

- Marine (open ocean and its associated coastline)

- Estuarine (tidal waters of coastal rivers and embayments, salty tidal marshes, mangrove swamps, and tidal flats)

- Riverine (rivers and streams)

- Lacustrine (lakes, reservoirs, and large ponds)

- Palustrine (marshes, wet meadows, fens, playas, potholes, pocosins, bogs, swamps, and small shallow ponds)

A large majority of the wetlands in the United States are in the palustrine system; most of the remaining wetlands are in the estuarine system.

Wetlands perform a myriad of important functions that directly benefit humans. Coastal wetlands, for example, are nursery grounds for shellfish and other commercial sport fish (Figure 6-4). Other species, such as migratory birds, spend stages of their life cycle in these habitats. Wetlands serve as storage areas for stormwater runoff and are the interface for water movement above and below ground. This movement may occur in either direction— that is, from above to below (aquifer recharge) or from below to above (springs).

Wetland restoration and "banking" are allowed in some jurisdictions for mitigation purposes. Consequently, new wetlands are created in anticipation that existing wetlands will be destroyed. Yet, this practice is not without criticism. Constructed wetlands do not typically have the biodiversity of indigenous natural wetlands. Another concern involves the location of both the destroyed and created wetlands. Unless the new wetlands are near the destroyed wetlands, wetland banking may alter local hydrologic regimes and contribute to flooding.

Figure 6-4 Salt marsh—a grassy coastal wetland that is rich in marine life. Amelia Island, Florida.

Mapping

The National Wetlands Inventory (NWI), administered by the United States Fish and Wildlife Service, includes information about the extent, characteristics, and status of wetlands in the United States. The NWI now includes an online, digital wetlands database for the entire United States (http://wetlandsfws.er.usgs.gov/NWI/). These maps, although relatively coarse in scale, are an important source of land planning data. Yet these mapping programs are not intended to record the location of small and ephemeral wetlands. Ephemeral wetlands are those in which soils are saturated for a relatively brief period each year or, in more arid landscapes, even less frequently. These wetlands can be critical habitats for some species of migratory birds. Field assessments are usually needed to identify and map all significant site wetlands (Figure 6-5).

6.3 TREES

Trees on a site are assets that can yield multiple ecological, economic, and social benefits. Trees provide shade and can reduce heating and cooling costs of nearby buildings. By providing a significant natural amenity, trees also can increase the value of real estate by as much as 15 percent (National Association of Home Builders, 1991). The International Society of Arboriculture, a nonprofit organization dedicated to research and education, identifies four factors to consider in evaluating the economic value of trees (Perry, 1999):

☐ Tree size

☐ Tree species (hardy, well-adapted species are worth most)

Figure 6-5 Wetland map prepared in planning a land development project in the state of Washington. Source: R. W. Thorpe and Associates.

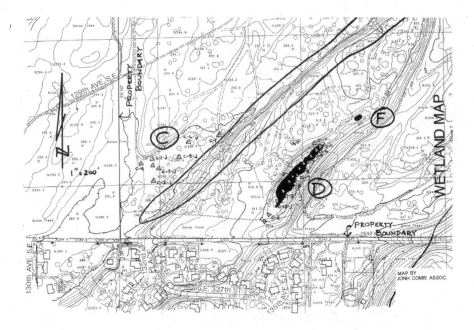

- □ Tree condition or health (for example, roots, trunks, branches, leaves)

- □ Tree location (functional and aesthetic values)

Trees serve multiple design functions that directly benefit people. For example, they provide shade, screen undesirable views, and serve as wind breaks (Figure 6-6). Trees also have significant aesthetic value. They may provide a focal point or visual amenity, or provide spatial enclosure for an "outdoor room" (Figure 6-7). Consequently, a tree standing alone is usually worth more—from an economic perspective—than one that is growing in a group.

During the construction of buildings, utilities, and other site structures, existing trees on a site require protection. Common, yet easily avoided, construction damage may kill trees outright or lead to their slow demise. Typical construction impacts include soil compaction of the root zone, scraping the bark from trunks and branches, and grading (that is, cutting or filling) within the root zone. Many species of trees have a fine-meshed mat of feeder roots within the top 12 inches (30.48 cm) of soil. Therefore, construction disturbances should not occur within the "drip line" of a tree's canopy, at the very least. Increasingly common are municipal tree preservation ordinances that require the protection of trees throughout the development process (Arendt, 1999).

Mapping

Sustainable or "green" development respects the natural environment and ensures, for example, that trees are protected and incorporated into the site plan (Petit et al., 2004). Tree inventories commonly record information on the size, species, and location of the site's significant trees. Tree size is measured by the diameter of the trunk at breast height (dbh). Site surveys completed by licensed surveyors will typically include the locations of trees

Figure 6-6 Palm trees providing shade in a Mediterranean coastal community in Nice, France.

larger than a specified size (for example, dbh = 4 inches/10.16 cm). Global positioning systems (GPS) provide another way to map communities and individual specimen trees. With a handheld GPS receiver, a botanist or other individual who can identify the local flora walks the site and digitally records the boundaries of each major plant community. Taking a color aerial photograph into the field can help orient the analyst and make the digital mapping process more efficient.

Figure 6-7 Large, deciduous canopy tree provides shade and spatial enclosure in Geneva, Switzerland.

6.4 WILDLIFE

Populations of most wildlife species are naturally discontinuous. That is, the entire population consists of groups of subpopulations, called metapopulations (McCullough, 1996). For example, separated wooded patches may be home to colonies of birds, mammals, and other animals. Local-scale extinctions of metapopulations are not unusual and often are a natural part of ecosystem dynamics. This is a natural process involving local extinctions, migration and colonization, and reproduction. It is essential, however, that the area in which a local extinction occurs remains viable as a habitat for future colonization and repopulation of the species. If the habitat is destroyed or degraded, or made inaccessible by intervening barriers, then the geographic range of the species is permanently reduced.

Conserving wildlife habitats within our built environments has many benefits. For example, many bird species are prolific consumers of insects—particularly insects that are pests to humans. Birds also have significant aesthetic value, bringing satisfaction to avid bird watchers and casual observers alike.

Increasing numbers of bird species are endangered or threatened for extinction. The most effective method for protecting any bird species—whether they are an endangered and threatened species—is to protect their natural habitats (Figure 6-8).

Mapping

The intent of the federal Endangered Species Act (ESA) is to prevent local as well as regional extinctions of species. The United States Fish and Wildlife Service maps the spatial distributions of endangered and threatened species in the United States. Other governments around the world do so, as well (Figure 6-9). These maps typically show the geographic range where the habitats and individuals of these species are likely to be present.

Figure 6-8 Crab plover (*Dromas ardeola*), a protected migratory bird species in Kuwait. Source: The HOK Planning Group.

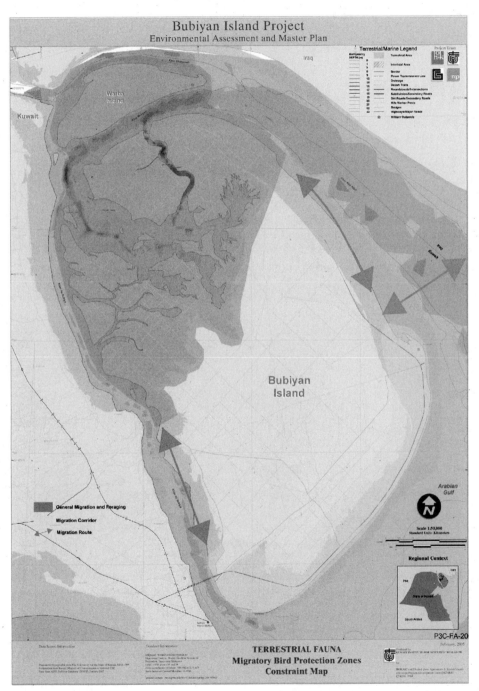

Figure 6-9   Migratory bird protection zones in an area of Kuwait. Source: The HOK Planning Group.

Site level data on wildlife distributions are typically acquired through field studies by qualified biologists.

6.5 CONCLUSION

Landscape ecology, an interdisciplinary environmental science, provides a valuable conceptual framework for studying landscapes and making environmental planning, restoration, and management decisions (Naveh and Lieberman, 1984; Forman and Godron, 1986). These scientists are continually learning more about the structure and function of landscapes, and the impacts of human activities on the environment (Turner et al., 2001).

The general public is also gaining a greater awareness of the linkages between environmental quality and human health and welfare. Heightened concern for environmental quality has led to increasing demands for accountability—and therefore documentation—of the potential impacts of land development proposals. Protecting existing native vegetation and wildlife is not only good for the environment, but it also contributes to the site's unique sense of place.

Mapping a site's key biological attributes is an important part of the site inventory. Identifying these resources helps to protect the ecological integrity of the site during and after the plan's implementation. Which attributes to map and evaluate depends, as with physical and cultural attributes, on the future uses of the site.

Site Inventory:
Cultural Attributes

The concept of public welfare is broad and inclusive. . .the values it represents are
spiritual as well as physical, aesthetic as well as monetary. It is within the power of
the legislature to determine that the community should be beautiful as well as
healthy, spacious, [and] clean.

—William O. Douglas, U.S. Supreme Court Justice, *Berman v. Parker,* 1954

7.1   INTRODUCTION

All land use changes occur within a cultural context. For the purposes of this book, cultural context encompasses the historical, legal, aesthetic, and other socially significant attributes associated with land and landscapes. Creating, or maintaining, a "sense of place" hinges on understanding and responding to site context (Hough, 1990, Beatley and Manning, 1997). For example, by adopting forms and materials that are common in the region or community, sense of place can be strengthened. Development that "fits" the site is adapted to the site's unique character and context. And both character and context are defined by physical, biological, and cultural attributes.

An inventory of relevant cultural attributes typically addresses a wide range of social, economic, and legal factors. The built environment is a complex array of buildings, streets, and other structures that evolves incrementally, resulting in a mosaic of physical elements and jurisdictional boundaries that vary in age and origin. Cultural features— whether historical, aesthetic, legal, or perceptual—create opportunities and constraints for development.

7.2   LAND USE AND TENURE

7.2.1   Prior and Current Land Use

Prior land use on a site may influence development suitability in a variety of ways. Knowledge that a site was previously used for industrial or commercial uses, for example, could indicate that chemicals and other toxic wastes remain on the site, either above or below ground.

Prior to the 1960s, commercial and industrial sites in the United States were often used as dumping grounds for a variety of chemical wastes. In other cases, poorly maintained storage tanks led to unintended leaks of chemicals into the soil and groundwater. Heavy metals and other highly toxic compounds pose serious health risks, particularly to children. In the 1970s, toxic chemicals found oozing from the ground within a housing development in Love Canal, a neighborhood of Niagara Falls, New York, was a landmark event in the development of hazardous waste policy in the United States (Beck, 1979). Federal legislation was subsequently adopted to redress the nation's toxic waste problem.

The U.S. Environmental Protection Agency (EPA) was charged, in 1980, with administering the resulting Superfund Program (www.epa.gov/earthday/history.htm). Although created to clean up contaminated sites, this program had dramatic, yet unintended, consequences on the nation's cities. Liability for the cleanup costs of contaminated sites could be assigned to a property's new owners even if they were not responsible for—or even aware of—the original pollution. In addition, Superfund regulations held these property owners liable for the remediation costs of restoring the sites to precontamination conditions.

The enormous costs of even small toxic waste cleanups had a chilling effect on the redevelopment of commercial and industrial sites. The significant legal and financial risks of purchasing and attempting to develop these contaminated, or "brownfield," sites effectively encouraged urban "sprawl" by redirecting new development to "greenfield" sites on the urban periphery. Especially in the industrial districts of older cities, vacant brownfield sites inhibited economic investment in the surrounding neighborhoods, thereby, worsening the economic and social impacts of the environmental pollution. Finally, during the 1990s, a major shift in public policy began significantly reducing financial risks—and creating new incentives—for the redevelopment of contaminated brownfield sites (National Governors Association, 2000).

When considering brownfield sites for redevelopment, the sites should be carefully assessed prior to purchase and detailed planning and design. In the United States, this entails an ASTM Phase One Environmental Site Assessment (ESA). An environmental site assessment requires the services of legal, environmental, and engineering professionals with expertise in regulatory compliance and project permitting (American Society of Civil Engineers, 1996). The ESA summarizes the site's ownership and land use history, in addition to current soil and groundwater conditions. All buildings and other structures on the site are also evaluated and mapped. The cost of an ASTM Phase One site assessment in the late 1990s ranged from $60,000 to $200,000, depending on the size of the parcel, the complexity of the existing site structures, and the types of contaminants found on the site

(Talarico, 1998). Permanent deed restrictions may be required to ensure that the contaminated areas remain sealed from infiltrating storm water.

Prior agricultural uses on a site may create other environmental challenges. Historically, farming in the United States was often practiced with little concern for soil conservation and management. Consequently, many farms were subjected to extensive topsoil losses from soil erosion.

Current nearby land uses may have either positive or negative impacts on the proposed uses of the site. In assessing a site's land use context, attributes that might be documented include the following:

☐ Land use types (for example, residential, commercial, industrial)

☐ Land use intensities (for example, building heights or number of stories, dwelling units per acre/hectare, average daily vehicle traffic)

7.2.2 Land Ownership

Information on land ownership or "tenure" is commonly available in publicly accessible databases (e.g., county-level Register of Deeds). These records may include a certified survey map of the parcel boundaries, a history of land ownership, and any deed restrictions or covenants associated with the property. Digital parcel data are becoming increasingly common.

Mapping

Digital maps and associated "metadata" comprise a *cadastre*. Many digital databases are available commercially or, in some cases, through government departments or agencies. In the United States, for example, one company sells digital topographic data models that are viewable as either two- or three-dimensional images (www.delorme.com). This company also offers detailed digital maps of streets, trails, unique natural features, and historic sites. Other digital data, such as vertical and oblique color infrared aerial photographs, are increasingly available for downloading through government sources (for example, federal Upper Midwest Environmental Sciences Center, www.umesc.usgs.gov). The vertical aerial photographs, in particular, provide a relatively detailed resource for interpretating land use and land cover over large planning areas.

7.3 LAND-USE REGULATION

A site inventory must consider the legal context for site planning and design decisions. Yet legal context varies widely at the local, the state or regional, and—especially—the national scale. Moreover, laws and public policies change over time. The approach taken in this book is to focus on concepts and principles (such as, endangered species protection, stormwater management) and to provide some examples of major laws, policies, and permitting procedures from the United States. One limitation of this approach, of course, is that the legal context in the United States may be quite different from that in Australia, Britain, Canada, or New Zealand. However, development regulations in these and other nations address many of the same themes—namely, the protection of the environment and public health, safety, and welfare.

7.3.1 Federal and State Regulations

Although land use control is generally considered a local government issue in the United States, cumulative land use changes often have regional and even national implications. Consequently, federal and state laws and policies have been enacted to protect environmental quality and preserve historic and other cultural resources. The National Environmental Policy Act (1969) was the first in a series of major federal legislation with broad influences on land use in the United States. In addition, several other federal laws and polices are designed to protect cultural resources or enhance quality of life. The Americans with Disabilities Act (ADA), for example, also has important site development implications that are addressed in later chapters of this book.

Federal regulations typically establish standards or administrative rules that are implemented at the state and local levels. The National Coastal Zone Management (CZM) Program (http://coastalmanagement.noaa.gov), for example, is a voluntary partnership between the federal government and U.S. coastal states and territories. Authorized by the Coastal Zone Management Act, the purpose of the program is to (United States National Oceanic and Atmospheric Agency, 2000b):

☐ preserve, protect, develop and—where possible—restore and enhance the resources of the Nation's coastal zone for this and succeeding generations;

☐ encourage and assist the states to exercise their responsibilities effectively in the coastal zone to achieve wise use of land and water resources of the coastal zone, giving full consideration to ecological, cultural, historic, and aesthetic values as well as the needs for compatible economic development;

☐ encourage the preparation of special area management plans to provide increased specificity in protecting significant natural resources, reasonable coastal-dependent economic growth, improved protection of life and property in hazardous areas, and improved predictability in governmental decision-making;

☐ encourage the participation, cooperation, and coordination of the public, federal, state, local, interstate and regional agencies, and governments affecting the coastal zone.

The Coastal Nonpoint Pollution Control Program is an important component of coastal management in the United States. This program requires states and territories with approved coastal zone management programs to develop and implement methods for coastal nonpoint pollution control. Techniques to limit the addition of pollution to coastal waters have been developed by the EPA for five source categories of nonpoint pollution: agricultural runoff, urban runoff, forestry runoff, marinas, and hydromodification. As human population continues to increase, and the built environment covers an increasingly larger portion of the United States, state-level growth management programs are becoming more common (Gale, 1992, 425–439).

7.3.2 Local Plans and Regulations

In the United States, the power to regulate land use is granted to local governments through state-level enabling legislation. Land use regulations are a subset of the community's "police powers" for protecting the public health, safety, and welfare. Local governments influence the pace, location, and character of new development with comprehensive plans, zoning codes, and related public policies (Nivola, 1999).

Comprehensive Plans

Comprehensive plans are community level "vision" statements about how a community intends to grow and develop, typically over a twenty- to thirty-year period (Becker and Kelly, 2000). With growing support for "smart growth" policies, many municipalities across the nation are involved in comprehensive planning. Wisconsin's "smart growth" legislation (Wisconsin Act 9, adopted in 1999) requires that all local governments have a comprehensive plan by January 1, 2010, if they engage in programs or actions that affect land use (Ohm, 1999). The act also requires that comprehensive plans address a wide range of objectives, policies, and programs to guide future development and redevelopment.

A comprehensive plan addresses several issues that are relevant to sustainable site planning, including housing, transportation, utilities, natural and cultural resources, and economic development. Each theme includes specific goals, such as the following (City of Madison, 2006, p.3):

- □ Promote the redevelopment of lands with existing infrastructure and public services and the maintenance and rehabilitation of existing residential, commercial, and industrial structures.

- □ Encourage neighborhood designs that support a range of transportation choices.

- □ Protect natural areas, including wetlands, wildlife habitats, lakes, woodlands, open spaces, and groundwater resources.

- □ Protect economically productive areas including farmland and forests.

- □ Encourage land uses, densities, and regulations that promote efficient development patterns and relatively low municipal, state governmental, and utility costs.

- □ Preserve cultural, historic, and archaeological sites.

- □ Build community identity by revitalizing main streets and enforcing design standards.

- □ Provide an adequate supply of affordable housing for individuals of all income levels throughout each community.

- Provide adequate infrastructure and public services and an adequate supply of developable land to meet existing and future market demand for residential, commercial, and industrial uses.

- Balance individual property rights with community interests and goals.

- Plan and develop land uses that create or preserve varied and unique urban and rural communities.

- Provide an integrated, efficient, and economical transportation system that affords mobility, convenience, and safety and meets the needs of all citizens, including transit-dependent and disabled citizens.

Zoning Codes

Zoning codes are a common form of land use regulation at the local level. A zoning map may have hundreds of districts in which certain uses are permitted and other uses are prohibited (Figure 7-1). Zoning codes in the United States have been the target of justified criticism (Kunstler, 1993, 1998). Conventional or "Euclidean" zoning contributes to urban sprawl by rigidly separating residential uses from non-residential uses, and by fostering land consumptive development patterns that make transportation by walking or public transit virtually impractical.

Local zoning codes allow variances from the code requirements under certain conditions. Increasingly common variations on zoning variances are the planned unit development (PUD) or planned development districts (PDD). These rezoned districts may be permitted to allow the consolidation of multiple parcels into a single master-planned project, often for mixed-use development. The PUD or PDD provides greater flexibility in meeting the density and land use requirements for the site as a whole.

Local land use regulations also include subdivision ordinances. The subdivision of a parcel of land into several smaller parcels is a key step in many residential development projects. Subdivision ordinances typically set minimum requirements for parcel size. These ordinances may also limit the number and location of curb cuts, or street access points, allowed to a property. They often establish building setbacks from adjacent properties.

The revision of zoning codes and subdivision ordinances is a growing trend in North America, Australia, and other regions. Progressive communities are rewriting these development regulations to encourage "smart growth" through form-based zoning codes, design guidelines, and rigorous design review. Attempting to mitigate decades of sprawl-inducing public policy, municipalities are increasingly focusing on both the function and "character" of new development.

The site inventory documents the legal constraints that limit or, in other ways, influence the future uses of the site. Legal issues that should be investigated for each site include the following (White, 1983, and Garvin, 1996):

- Zoning classification (permitted land uses and densities)

- Easements, covenants, and other deed restrictions

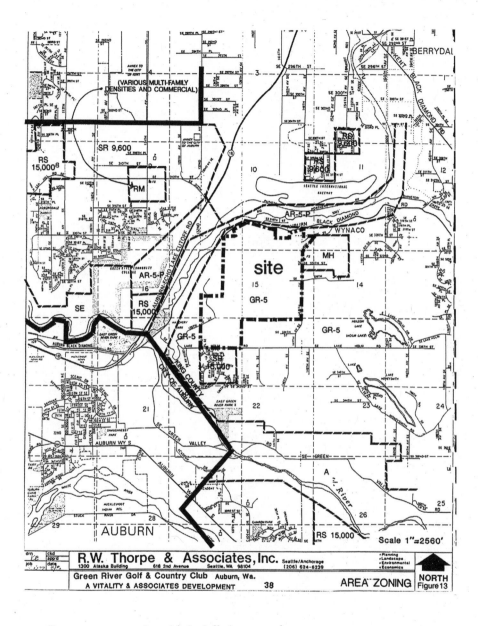

Figure 7-1 Zoning map for the area surrounding a site planned for a new golf course community near Seattle, Washington. Source: R. W. Thorpe and Associates.

☐ Government agencies with jurisdiction over the property

☐ Building placement requirements (required front-, back-, and side-yard setbacks from property boundaries)

☐ Allowable buildable area

☐ Building height, bulk, floor-area ratio, or footprint restrictions

□ Parking and driveway requirements

□ Minimum requirements for open space (public and private)

□ On-site recreation or environmental requirements

□ Stormwater management and erosion control requirements

□ Landscaping requirements

□ Required special permits, regulations, and planning procedures (for example, variances, design review, public hearings, environmental tests/data)

The maximum allowable building envelope, as prescribed by local zoning codes, can be illustrated, graphically, with three-dimensional computer modeling software. One currently popular program that makes this task relatively easy is *Google Sketchup* (http://sketchup.google.com/).

7.4 PROPERTY VALUE

Banks and other lending institutions routinely require property appraisals before financing real estate purchases. Property appraisers consider the attributes of the site itself and the improvements made to the site, such as buildings and other structures. They also consider the effects of site context, such as the value of nearby properties, adjacent street traffic, and scenic off-site views of the built or natural environments.

Real estate appraisal in the United States attempts to predict the probable selling price of a property by modeling, as closely as possible, the influence of site and contextual factors on buyers' and sellers' decisions. In general, appraisal theory approaches the concept of value by synthesizing three different models of economic behavior. These three models are called *approaches to value* and are referred to as the cost approach, the sales comparison approach, and the income approach (Castle, 1998, p. 87).

Each of these three appraisal methods estimate property value based on the "highest and best use" of the site. Yet highest and best use reflects the property owner's objectives—not the community's. Real estate projects with high financial returns but significant environmental impacts will be valued more favorably, of course, in appraisals that ignore these externalities.

Context also plays a crucial role in property value. Environmental amenities are not evenly distributed over the landscape, for example, and sites vary widely in proximity and access to those amenities. Moreover, the presence or absence of these amenities can influence a site's suitability for different uses. Scenic views of lakes, rivers, or other environmental features may contribute significantly to a site's desirability for residential uses and for some commercial uses, such as restaurants, where patrons may seek the ambience of a beautiful natural setting (Figure 7-2).

Environmental amenities and cultural or built amenities such as parks and golf courses, enhance property values. The positive influence of amenities on property value is reflected in the price disparity among housing lots in resort communities. Beachfront parcels, for

Figure 7-2 Surrounding scenic views are amenities that increase property values. Basel, Switzerland.

example, sell at a premium compared to nearby and otherwise comparable lots that are not immediately adjacent to the amenity. If the beachfront sites were used for some industrial purpose, the scenic waterfront views would play little or no role in the value of the products manufactured there. Consequently, the concept of "highest and best use" suggests that the qualities of a site and its surroundings should determine, at least in part, the purposes for which the land is used.

Property ownership entails both rights and responsibilities. The "bundle" of development rights accompanying a property depends upon the parcel's location and physical, biological, and cultural attributes. Regulations that exceed the basic functions of protecting public health, safety, and welfare have been challenged in the courts—and upheld by the U.S. Supreme Court—as property "takings" (Bosselman and Callies, 1972). When land use regulations in the United States go beyond these functions and greatly reduce the monetary value of the property—the courts have generally ordered the regulating government to provide "just compensation" to the affected landowner.

Property values may be restricted in ways other than government land use regulation. The purchase of development rights (PDR), coupled with conservation easements, can keep land undeveloped for either a limited or a defined period of time. Several types of easements exist, and they all reduce a parcel's development potential (Table 7-1). For example, an easement may ensure access to a property that is accessible only by crossing another property. Easements allowing emergency vehicle access or utility maintenance vehicle access are also quite common.

Conservation easements, typically held by non-profit organizations, are often created to preserve open space. Maintaining ecosystem integrity and connectivity are important precepts of sustainable development, and the conservation easement is a useful tool in

TABLE 7-1 Common types and purposes of easements.

Type	Purpose
Access easements	Ensure physical access to or across a site from adjacent properties.
Utility easements	Provide physical access to install, replace, and maintain utility system infrastructure, such as power lines or underground piping.
Conservation easements	Restrict development potential and are often used to protect hiking trails and other recreational areas, and to maintain important ecosystem functions such as groundwater recharge.
Scenic easements	Protect vistas and viewsheds by preventing development that blocks or degrades those views.
Solar easements	Protect solar access to adjacent property

achieving these objectives. Scenic easements can also limit the scope and character of land development. The transfer of development rights (TDR) is a less common, but effective legal strategy for redirecting potential development from conservation areas to other more suitable locations.

7.5 PUBLIC INFRASTRUCTURE

The built environment is a complex array of private and public buildings, open spaces, and infrastructure. The public infrastructure includes streets, other transportation systems, and vast utility networks (for example, sanitary sewerage and potable water). The location and type of utility networks present or adjacent to the site are important information in the site planning process. The locations of existing transportation and utility systems are common design determinants that often influence key site-planning decisions. The location of site entrances and the placement of new buildings, for example, are decisions that may be driven directly by the location of the existing public infrastructure.

7.5.1 Circulation

Understanding existing circulation patterns is an important part of the site inventory process. Many mistakes have been made in both site planning and architectural design because established pedestrian and vehicle circulation patterns were either ignored or poorly understood. Site planners usually have leeway in determining how and where pedestrians enter a site, so existing circulation patterns must be taken into account. Failure to anticipate "desire lines" between existing and/or proposed entrances to the site, to buildings, or to other activity areas can create dangerous pedestrian–vehicle conflicts.

Mapping

The location of adjacent streets, driveways, drop-off zones, service areas, and parking lots is contextual information that often influences the spatial organization of the site plan. Existing average daily traffic volumes on adjacent streets and highways can be estimated and mapped. Different circulation systems (pedestrians, bicycles, vehicles) and volumes can be portrayed graphically by varying the color and width of the arrows (see Box 7–1, Figure 7-13). Existing conflicts between vehicles and pedestrians should be identified as well.

7.5.2 Utilities

Infrastructure is conventionally thought of as streets, bridges, and sanitary sewer systems. But the utilities serving a site often include other networks for the distribution of energy and potable water, telecommunications, and the removal of stormwater. New utility systems often account for a significant share of a site's development costs. In the site inventory, it is important to understand where the public utility systems are located (Figure 7-3). This information is needed to determine the locations where the new development will connect to these systems.

Mapping

Utility systems deliver energy, water, and information to the site and remove wastes and excess stormwater. A site utilities map commonly includes, therefore, these systems:

- Potable water

- Electricity

- Natural gas

- Telecommunications

- Stormwater sewerage

- Sanitary sewerage

An inventory of existing site utilities should include the locations of utility poles, overhead power lines, fire hydrants, and utility boxes, as well as the diameters of underground pipelines.

7.6 BUILDING AND NEIGHBORHOOD CHARACTER

Kevin Lynch (1960), in *The Image of the City*, proposed a typology to explain how people form cognitive maps, or mental images, of the built environment. The five functional elements, with examples of each, are as follows:

- Edges (for example, shorelines, roads, and hedgerows)

- Paths (for example, streets and walkways)

LEGEND
—ᴵᶠ→ EXISTING SEWER
—ˢᶠ→ EXISTING FORCE MAIN
○ EXISTING LIFT STATION
—■—■— SERVICE AREA BOUNDARY
--------- DRAINAGE BASIN BOUNDARY
—·—·→ PROPOSED FORCE MAIN
○ PROPOSED PUMP STATION
——→ PROPOSED SEWERS

CITY OF AUBURN
COMPREHENSIVE SEWER

FIGURE 7

Figure 7-3 Sanitary sewer service to the site of a land development project in Washington State. Source: R.W. Thorpe and Associates.

- Districts (for example, neighborhoods)

- Nodes (for example, entrances, plazas, and street and walkway intersections)

- Landmarks (for example, unique buildings, structures, and natural features)

This typology is particularly useful for assessing the character and function of the built environment.

The site's context must be understood if any new development is to make a positive contribution to the character of the area. This context includes the use, design, and placement of nearby buildings. Common residential building "types" include the following:

- Single-family and multifamily houses (for example, small footprints, pitched roofs, two stories)

- Multifamily residential towers (for example, 5 to 12 stories, subdivided living units, retail use of first floor)

- Mixed-use residential/commercial development (for example, ground floor retail or office uses, upper floor residential use, three to five stories, rectanglar and linear footprints)

In documenting a typology of building types within a commercial district, for example, the following building attributes may be analyzed (Pregliasco, 1988, p.15):

- Height

- Width

- Setback

- Proportion of openings

- Horizontal rhythms

- Roof form

- Materials

- Color

- Sidewalk coverings

- Signs

These building attributes are typically documented with photographs, annotated street elevations and sections, and maps.

Neighborhood character is also influenced by street and walkway arrangements, the mix of land uses, and the size, placement, and design of outdoor open spaces. Indigenous construction materials include locally quarried stone and collected boulders. Native and naturalized vegetation also contributes to a site's identity. Teed and others (2002), in an analysis of these attributes for neighborhoods in British Columbia, Canada, developed a typology consisting of six neighborhood patterns, ranging from rural to more urban. Existing neighborhood patterns—including local building materials and architectural styles—can be documented to guide context-sensitive site planning and architectural design. These "pattern books" can lead to new development or redevelopment that strengthens the local character and "sense of place" (Urban Design Associates, 2003).

Parks and public open space are integral community elements that should be considered in the inventory process. Especially if part of an integrated public open space system, these open spaces may provide not only visual amenities and outdoor recreational opportunities but also vital space for stormwater management. These open spaces may also perform essential ecological functions that could be enhanced or—at the very least—protected by careful site planning and design. Other community resources that contribute to a neighborhood's character include schools, libraries, and community centers. A site context map shows the locations of these important civic institutions.

Mapping

In addition to the mapping methods already discussed in this section (for example, Lynch's typology), figure-ground mapping is an effective technique for visually assessing the texture or "grain" of development near a site. This is a graphic method of portraying building patterns on or near a site (Figure 7-4). It involves mapping just two elements: building footprints and the spaces between the buildings. The pattern of solids and voids reveals the texture or sense of enclosure or openness of the built environment surrounding the site. This information can be useful not only in siting new buildings but also in determining the sizes and proportions of any new buildings' "footprints."

Figure 7-4 Figure-ground diagram showing building "footprints" superimposed on a vertical aerial photograph. This mapping technique facilitates a visual assessment of urban "texture" – an important contextual attribute.
Source: The HOK Planning Group.

7.7 HISTORIC RESOURCES

"Cultural resources are those tangible and intangible aspects of cultural systems, both past and present, that are valued by or representative of a given culture, or that contain information about a culture."

—National Park Service

Cultural resource assessments document the location, quality, and historic significance of buildings and other human-made elements, as well as prior land uses (Figure 7-5). Historic resources include bridges, buildings, walls, signs, and many other significant structures or elements built in previous eras. In the United States, the National Historic Preservation Act (NHPA) affords legal protection to buildings, bridges, and other structures registered on the list of nationally significant historic resources. Programs and policies aimed at protecting and restoring historic resources also exist at the state and local levels. The historic significance of a structure or neighborhood is based on several criteria, including age, quality, rarity, and representativeness (Ames and McClelland, 2002).

Cultural resources also include historic sites, such as forts, battlefields, parks, and archaeological sites. Archaeological finds, such as Native American artifacts, can have a significant impact on project planning and implementation. According to Talarico (1998, p. 250):

Rules governing finds vary according to the locality, the size of the site, and who is involved in the project. If the property is private, finds can be bulldozed, except where there's legislation that says otherwise. If there are ties to the federal government, even if the project is only partially funded by a federal agency, the site falls under the National Historic Preservation Act, administered by the Department of the Interior. The property must then undergo a phase-one archaeological analysis, during which test pits are dug. If anything of value is found, the act requires a more extensive phase-two dig. A phase-three dig is a full-blown excavation.

Mapping

Sanborn maps are detailed city maps that were originally created in the United States for the fire insurance industry. These maps are developed through field surveys, and they provide detailed information on building heights, "footprints," uses, construction materials, and other building attributes (Sanborn, 1999). Sanborn maps are commercially available as georeferenced vector or raster GIS data layers. More than 750,000 Sanborn maps have been donated to the United States Library of Congress (Sanborn, 1999).

In inventories of cultural resources, historic districts may be mapped to illustrate the site's cultural context (Figure 7-6). Historic districts may be mapped by local planning agencies as zoning "overlay districts," with special local land use controls. The architectural resources within historic districts also may be mapped (Figure 7-7).

Figure 7-5   Historic timeline showing major historic and cultural events occurring within the region of a greenway- planning project near St. Louis, Missouri. Source: The HOK Planning Group.

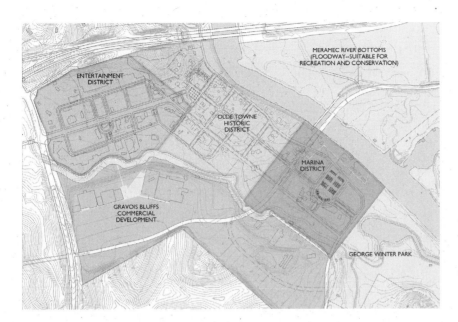

Figure 7-6   Inventories of cultural attributes include mapping of visually and functionally distinct urban districts. This map shows six districts, including one historic district in Fenton, Missouri. Source: The HOK Planning Group.

7.8   SENSORY PERCEPTION

In a classic essay on landscape perception, D. W. Meinig (1979) identifies ten possible ways in which knowledge, experiences, and values influence our perceptions of land and landscapes (Table 7-2). All of these perspectives are rational, but each one is a product of the unique "lens" with which each of us views the world.

Maslow's (1954) hierarchy of human needs suggests that basic needs must be satisfied before higher-level secondary and tertiary needs can be satisfied. Physical safety and security—along with food, clothing, and shelter—are the most basic needs in the hierarchy. Yet human perceptions of a site's safety and security vary among individuals of different age, gender, and other demographic attributes. Medical research is beginning to illuminate the powerful linkages between mind and physical well-being (National Center for Complementary and Alternative Medicine, 2005).

Our ability to see, smell, taste, touch, and hear give us access to extensive information about our surroundings. Human perception of land-based amenities—and disamenities—primarily involves three senses: hearing, sight, and smell. For most people, perceptions of a site are formed primarily through the sense of sight. A visual resource assessment is concerned with both visibility and visual quality. However, sound quality and air quality are also very relevant in land planning and design. The significance of each attribute depends on the site and its context, of course, but also on the program or intended uses of the site.

7.8.1   Visibility

A site's context plays an important role in land planning and design. Land use on adjacent sites can influence, in several different ways, the suitability of a site for a development or

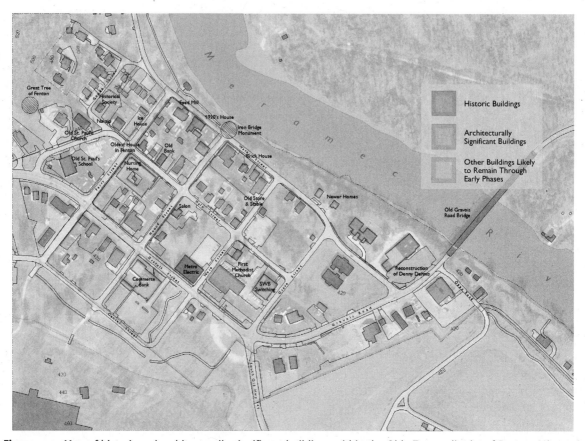

Figure 7-7 Map of historic and architecturally significant buildings within the Olde Towne district of Fenton, Missouri. Three classes of building significance are identified.
Source: The HOK Planning Group.

redevelopment program. A commercial project, for example, may benefit from good visibility to the site from adjacent streets, highways, and other off-site locations. Visibility is a form of advertising, and this site attribute is typically reflected in increased purchase prices or rental incomes.

The distance around a site that is relevant to how the site will be used in the future varies, of course, with what can be seen from the site. The identification of viewsheds, or areas visible from specific locations on the site, is amenable to automation within a GIS. Identifying viewsheds from topographic data alone becomes more complex, of course, when trees and tall shrubs are present to block views.

The most common seasonal influence on visibility to and from a site is vegetation. In temperate climates, viewsheds may vary seasonally, too, if the vegetation is deciduous. Deciduous trees and shrubs may form an effective screen during the time of the year in which the plants are in leaf, but during the remaining weeks and months, the leafless plants may provide very little screening.

TABLE 7-2 Ten perceptions of landscape meaning.

Landscape as	Associated Concepts
Nature	Fundamental Enduring
Habitat	Adaptation Resources
Artifact	Platform Utilitarian
System	Dynamic Equilibrium
Problem	Flaw Challenge
Wealth	Property Opportunity
Ideology	Values Ideas
History	Chronology Legacy
Place	Locality Experience
Aesthetic	Scenery Beauty

Source: Adapted from: D. W. Meinig, 1979.

Mapping

A visibility (or viewshed) map graphically shows the locations that can be seen from an individual viewing point. A "frequency seen" map characterizes the visibility of locations from two or more viewing points (Computer Terrain Mapping, 1997). Within a GIS, this map can be created by overlaying a series of one-point viewshed maps. A value of "1" is assigned to the visible areas on each layer, and areas that are not visible are assigned a value of "0." The viewshed maps are combined through a polygon overlay process, and the attribute values for all layers are summed. For example, when five viewshed maps are combined, the "frequency seen" or "visibility" values on the output layer could range from zero (locations that are not visible from any of the five viewing points) to five (locations that are visible from all five viewing points). Each visibility class could be depicted with a single color and/or texture.

The visibility of off-site features may be as important, on some projects, as visibility to on-site features. A site that is heavily forested yet relatively flat, for example, limits views on and off the site. In contrast, in landscapes with long, unobstructed views—as in mountainous terrain or on the open plains—the visible distance from the site can be substantial. At the site scale, an assessment of visibility may document the views from multiple vantage points (Figure 7-8).

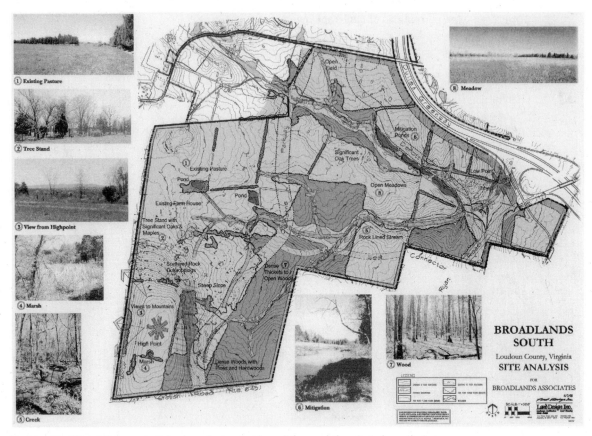

Figure 7-8 The visible context for a project extends well beyond the site's boundaries.
Source: Land Design.

7.8.2 Visual Quality

Visual quality plays an important role in land planning decisions. Two approaches, or paradigms, have been utilized in assessing landscape visual quality. The objectivist approach assumes visual quality (or lack thereof) is an inherent landscape attribute, whereas the subjectivist approach assumes that visual quality is merely in the eyes of the beholder (Lothian, 1999). Although it is true that conceptions of beauty are influenced by culture and experience, the only meaningful significance of this distinction is in the approach that is taken to assess visual quality.

The objectivist approach relies on experts in landscape aesthetics. Evaluations by experts take into account an area's scenic qualities, or visible attributes, which include form, proportion, line, color, and texture. The subjectivist approach shuns evaluations by trained experts in design or aesthetics. Instead, this approach relies on a representative, often randomly selected, group of individuals who provide their assessments of scenic quality.

Typically, these assessments or preferences are elicited for a carefully selected set of photographic scenes. A related approach is to provide cameras to the selected individuals and ask them to identify photograph scenes that they particularly like or dislike.

Jakle (1987, p.11) focuses on tourism and sightseeing in writing about landscape visual assessment, as follows:

> Tourists come as strangers with accompanying needs to orient to new places. What they see is novel and it attracts attention accordingly. As they seek interest and pleasure in their visual surroundings, they are sensitive to those aspects of landscape, to those places, which portend interest and pleasure.

Particularly in hilly and mountainous landscapes, where tourism is an important component of the local or regional economy, the skyline is a significant visual resource. Visual resources create, for tourists and for residents, memorable images of "place." At the University of Washington in Seattle, for example, the campus layout responds to distant views of Mount Rainier, Washington. Although this dormant volcano is many miles to the east, it is a prominent campus landmark. This visual linkage was strengthened by carefully preserving unobstructed sight lines to the mountain from major campus open spaces.

Prominent views to natural and cultural features are site amenities with social as well as economic value. The visual quality of the site itself, as well as visible off-site features, can be particularly important to the success of commercial, residential, and recreational projects. Residential real estate, for example, often places a premium on seclusion and screening from off-site locations. Proximity to a nearby highway, for example, is usually an undesirable feature that can eliminate sites from consideration for residential development. The visibility of unsightly on- and off-site features is also important. A landfill, overhead wires, and industrial sites are elements that, for many people, degrade a landscape's visual quality.

Views to historically significant buildings, prominent mountains, or other landmarks are important site attributes because they convey a clear sense of place (Figure 7-9). Vertical elements, such as buildings, trees, and landforms, have a substantial influence on visual quality. Restrictions on the heights of buildings in capitol cities are efforts to maintain the visual prominence of each city's capitol building—a landmark and symbol of the seat of government. In Washington D.C., for example, building height limits are more restrictive along the major streets created by the 1791 L'Enfant plan (Gutheim, 1977). Protecting scenic resources is a common public policy objective, from local to national levels of government. Moreover, whether aesthetically positive or negative, views and vistas are important considerations in context-sensitive site planning and design (Figures 7-10 and 7-11).

Mapping

Visual quality often is a function of an area's biophysical and cultural distinctiveness. Distinctive biophysical features include rock outcrops, water bodies, wooded areas, and isolated specimen trees. Distinctive cultural features include both historical and contemporary elements such as cemeteries, stone walls, pathways, as well as churches and

Figure 7-9 Inventory of important views from—and to— a prospective development site in Fenton, Missouri.
Source: The HOK Planning Group.

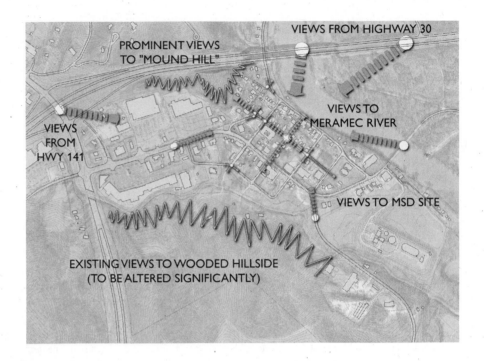

farmsteads (Figure 7-12). The abundance and arrangement of these built and natural features directly influences landscape scenic quality (Table 7-3).

A regional map of visual quality could be divided into a regular grid, and each grid cell rated for visual quality using one of four ordinal classes, as follows (Anderson, 1980):

- Very unique

- Unique

- Frequent

- Common

This approach also can be taken in documenting the visual quality of sites and other smaller areas. The mapping units depicted on a map of visual quality should conform to the dimensions of the spaces and features in the landscape. Therefore, the mapping units may not be uniform in either size or shape.

7.8.3   Noise and Odors

A site's perceptual quality is affected not only by what people can see but also by what they can hear and smell. Noise in the built environment is an attribute that may vary on a daily or seasonal basis. Noise—or lack of noise—has a significant impact on perceptual quality and

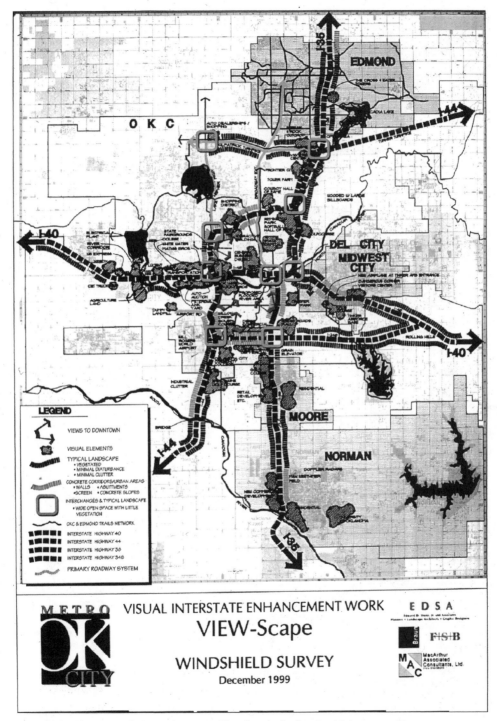

Figure 7-10 Windshield survey of views along 85 miles (130 km) of major highway corridors.
Source: Edward D. Stone, Jr., and Associates.

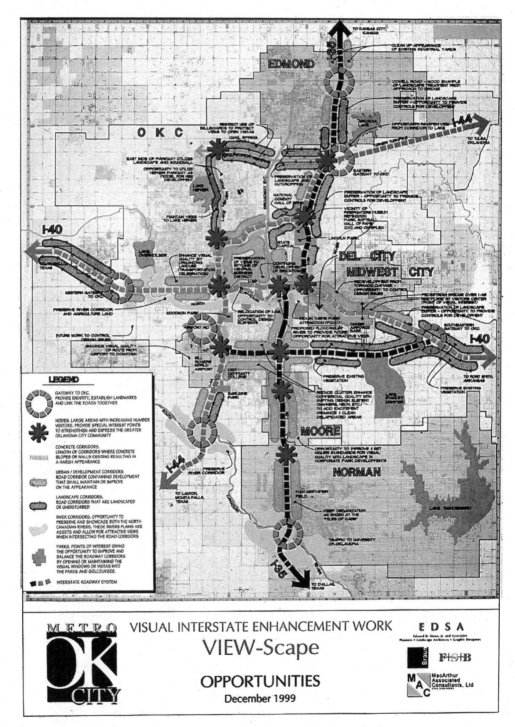

Figure 7-11 Opportunities for enhancing scenic quality within the areas visible from the major highway corridors. Source: Edward D. Stone, Jr., and Associates.

Figure 7-12 Pastoral, rural landscape with very high scenic value. Canton Appenzell, Switzerland.

recreational experiences in outdoor environments. In *The End of Nature,* McKibbon (1989) suggests that a wilderness experience includes freedom from the noise of chain saws.

Noise can be described in terms of intensity (perceived as loudness) and frequency (perceived as pitch). Both the intensity and the duration of noise exposure determine the potential for damage to the inner ear. Even sounds perceived as "comfortably" loud can be harmful (Rabinowitz, 2000, pp. 2749–2757). Sound intensity is measured as sound pressure level (SPL) on a logarithmic decibel (dB) scale. Permanent hearing loss can result from chronic noise exposures equal to an average of 85 dB(A) or higher for an eight-hour period (Morata et al., 1993, 245–254). However, four hours of noise exposure at 88 dB is

TABLE 7-3 Scenic quality rating criteria for natural and vernacular landscape assessments.

Criterion	Desirable Attributes
Landform	Steep, massive, sculptured, or extraordinary terrain
Vegetation	Variety of patterns, forms, and textures; sculptured forms (for example, gnarled trees)
Water	Clarity, dominating element
Color	Variety, contrast, and harmony
Scarcity	Distinctive or unusual within the region
Cultural modifications	Add favorably to visual variety and harmony

Note: Criteria are rated on a scale from 5 (highest) to 0 (lowest).
Source: U.S. Department of Interior, Bureau of Land Management Manual 8410 (Visual Resource Inventory).

considered to provide the same noise "dose" as eight hours at 85 dB (Clark and Bohne, 1999). Common noise sources and loudness levels, measured in decibels (dB), are as follows (Rabinowitz, 2000, pp. 2749–2757):

- ☐ Gunshot (140–170)
- ☐ Jet takeoff (140)
- ☐ Rock concert, chain saw (110–120)
- ☐ Diesel locomotive, stereo headphones (100)
- ☐ Motorcycle, lawn mower (90)
- ☐ Conversation (60)
- ☐ Whisper (30–40)

The Federal Occupational Safety and Health Administration (OSHA) has set noise standards for the workplace. When noise in work environments is louder than 90 decibels for more than eight hours, employers must ensure that workers wear earplugs or other hearing protection. Hearing protection is recommended for anyone exposed to 85 decibels or higher, especially if the exposure is for a prolonged time.

According to the U.S. Centers for Disease Control and Prevention, noise is an increasing public health concern (www.cdc.gov/nceh/hsb/noise/). Prolonged noise damages the inner ear's hair cells that carry sound to the brain. Not only can noise pollution cause hearing loss, but too much noise also can lead to other human health and development problems. For example, loud noise can delay reading skills and language acquisition skills in children (Hendrick, 1997, p.3G).

Odors also may pose a problem with sites near large industrial or animal confinement operations. The direction of the prevailing breezes is a particularly important attribute to consider when planning land development in the vicinity of these and other odor-producing activities.

7.9 CONCLUSION

Understanding a site's cultural context may require the collection and mapping of diverse data. Land use controls play an important role in limiting the range and intensities of permitted uses. These and other legal constraints typically have spatial dimensions that can be mapped. Historic resources may be present either on or adjacent to a site and may become significant design determinants. Visibility and visual quality also play an increasingly important role in influencing land use preferences and real estate value, and these, too, must be addressed in the site inventory. Finally, cultural context includes the physical infrastructure of streets, utilities, and buildings. Depending on the site planning program, any of these attributes can have a significant influence on how the land is ultimately designed and developed.

BOX 7-1   In Practice

Cultural Resource Assessment
Haifa, Israel

Site Planning
The HOK Planning Group
St. Louis, Missouri

Size
59 acres

Completed
2000

Project Goals
The Stella Maris Monastery on the western-most promontory of Mount Carmel overlooking the Mediterranean is the birthplace of the Carmelite Order. Built over the cave of the Old Testament Prophet Elijah, the Monastery and grounds command a spectacular panorama of Haifa Bay and the Mediterranean Sea below. HOK was commissioned to create a comprehensive master plan for the site.

   The program included a processional colonnade with adjacent prayer gardens, an amphitheater for 1000 persons, and inspirational artwork including a statue of the Prophet Elijah. Outside the religious zone, the proposed development includes multifamily residential, commercial space, a tourist-oriented commercial village, subterranean parking for cars and buses, and an upscale resort hotel.

Cultural and Historic Resources
The inventory of cultural and historic resources was focused by the need to ensure the sanctity of the monastery and religious zone while fitting compatible development on the remaining site. The inventory assessed land use, visibility, views, and pedestrian and vehicular circulation (Figure 7-12 and 7-13). The dramatic and historic setting also led the team to assess elevation and vegetation.

BOX 7-1   In Practice (continued)

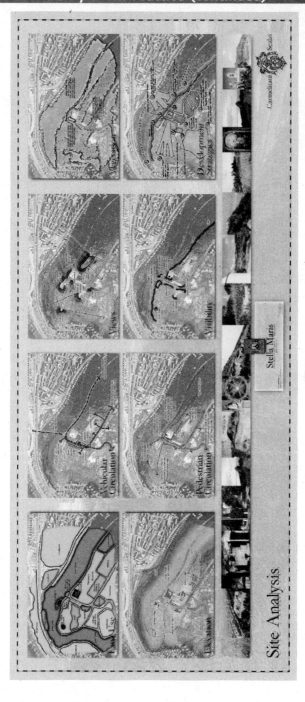

Figure 7-13 Composite set of site inventory maps. Individual maps depict views from the site and the site's visibility from surrounding areas in Haifa, Israel. Source: The HOK Planning Group.

BOX 7-1   In Practice (continued)

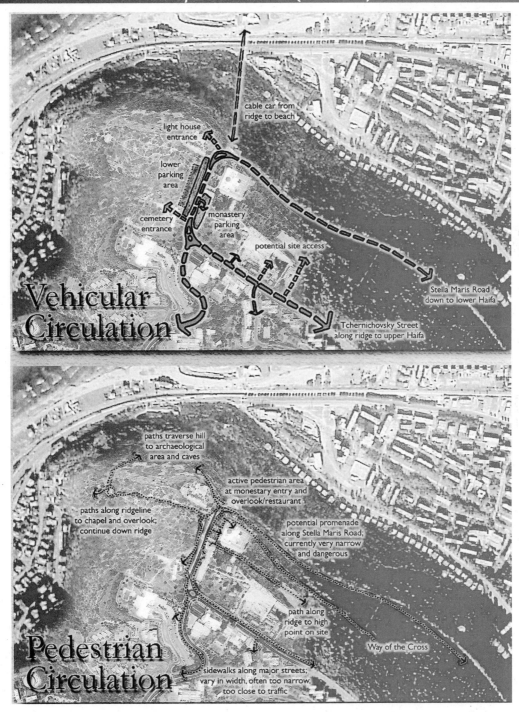

Vehicular Circulation

cable car from ridge to beach

light house entrance

lower parking area

cemetery entrance

monastery parking area

potential site access

Stella Maris Road down to lower Haifa

Tchernichovsky Street along ridge to upper Haifa

Pedestrian Circulation

paths traverse hill to archaeological area and caves

paths along ridgeline to chapel and overlook; continue down ridge

active pedestrian area at monastery entry and overlook/restaurant

potential promenade along Stella Maris Road; currently very narrow and dangerous

path along ridge to high point on site

Way of the Cross

sidewalks along major streets; vary in width, often too narrow, too close to traffic

BOX 7-1 In Practice (continued)

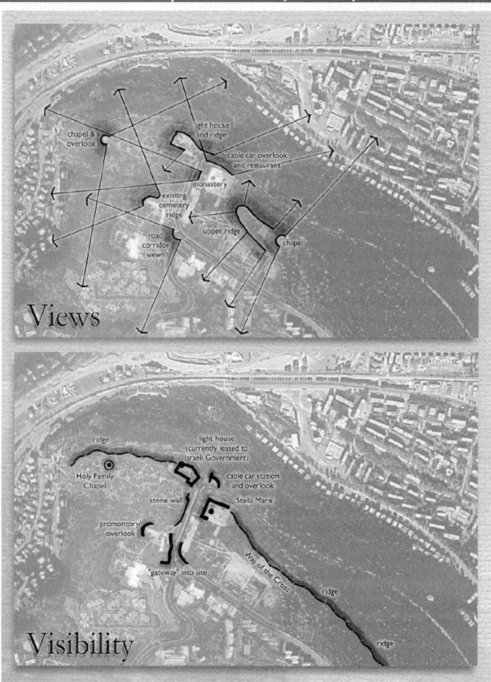

Site Analysis: Integration and Synthesis

Look and you will find it—what is unsought will go undetected.

—Sophocles

8.1   INTRODUCTION

Site analysis - which is much more than simply mapping the site's existing conditions - is essential to the design of sustainable built environments. The site inventory provides the physical, biological, and cultural data needed for this program-driven analysis (Figure 8-1). The site analysis is a *diagnostic* process that identifies the opportunities and constraints for a *specific* land use program (Figure 8-2).

Some parts of the site may be unsuitable for development because of inherent physiographic constraints in those locations (Table 8-1). These "endogenous" site constraints may include steep slopes, shallow bedrock, water, and wetlands. Other parts of the site may be suitable for development but relatively inaccessible. Lack of access to part of a site may be due to intervening constraints (Figure 8-3). The costs of extending roads and utilities to isolated site areas may be prohibitive. Consequently, pockets of undevelopable land can render the original program unfeasible. The discovery of site constraints, during the site analysis, is a common reason for revising a project's program.

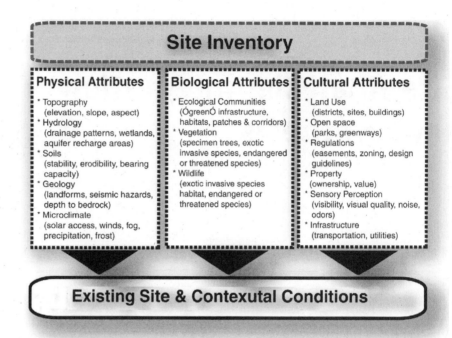

Figure 8-1 The site inventory produces mapped data on the existing conditions of the site and its context.

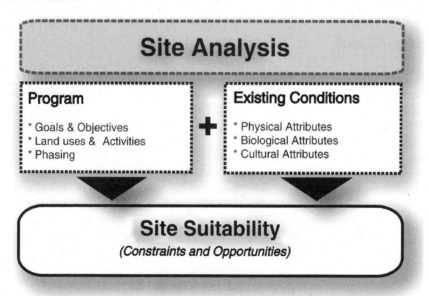

Figure 8-2 The site analysis assesses the site's opportunities and constraints—or design determinants—for a specific land use program.

TABLE 8-1 Selected development constraints. Any location on a site could fall into one or more of these constraint categories.

Constraint	Examples
Ecological infrastructure	Aquifer recharge areas, wetlands, surface water, critical wildlife habitat
Health or safety hazards	Floodplains, earthquake fault zones, areas susceptible to landslides
Physiographic barriers	Steep slopes, highly erodible soils, shallow bedrock
Natural resources	Prime farmland, sand and gravel deposits, specimen trees, scenic views
Historic resources	Historic buildings, archaeological sites
Legal restrictions	Zoning codes, subdivision ordinances, easements, deed restrictions
Nuisances	Noises, odors, unsightly views

8.2 SITE CARRYING CAPACITY

Sustainable development does not jeopardize the ability of future generations to meet their needs (World Commission on Environment and Development, 1987; Beatley and Manning, 1997). Therefore, sustainable development protects – and celebrates – each site's ecological integrity and cultural heritage.

Land development can create significant off-site impacts, or externalities, that impose economic and social costs on others. Yet skillful site planning can minimize these impacts and mitigate environmental degradation. Rather than using "brute force" engineering to overcome the intrinsic "difficulties" that a site poses for development, some sites—and portions of sites—should simply remain undeveloped. Refraining from developing in certain sensitive or unique areas can be justified from an environmental quality perspective and can be supported on economic grounds. Protecting significant natural and cultural resources, as part of the real estate development process, creates economic value (Bookout, 1994).

Residential subdivision design, for example, must involve much more than the efficient layout of streets and utilities. The most cost-efficient plan is often the rectangular grid layout that became popular in tract-home subdivisions in the 1940s and 1950s. Typically, however, the most profitable plan is one that takes advantage of the natural features on the site and provides other interesting design features or focal points (Peiser, 1992, p. 71).

Developing "with nature" is also fiscally prudent for the municipalities in which the development occurs. Development plans that respect inherent environmental constraints help to protect public health, safety, and welfare from natural hazards.

Figure 8-3 Constraints and opportunities may be on-site or off-site attributes that shape development suitability patterns and influence the spatial organization of program elements on the site.

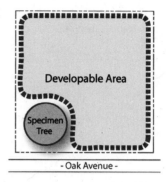

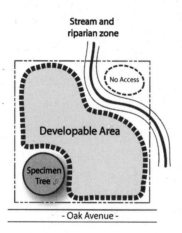

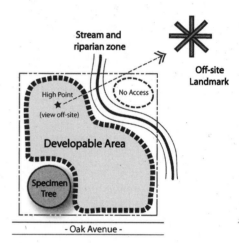

8.3   SUITABILITY ANALYSIS

8.3.1   Overview

In *Design with Nature,* McHarg (1969) advocates a land use planning process called "environmental determinism"—allowing the analysis of biophysical conditions to drive land use allocation decisions. McHarg's book brings map overlays and suitability analysis to the attention of many land planners and environmental scientists. Since McHarg's seminal contributions to the field, geographic information system (GIS) hardware and software has continually improved.

Suitability analysis, as Steiner defines (1991, p. 132), is "the process of determining the fitness, or the appropriateness, of a given tract of land for a specified use." Suitability analysis, therefore, is spatially explicit and program dependent. A location that is suitable for a particular land use is one that can accommodate the proposed development with the minimum amount of inputs or resources. For example, the U.S. Natural Resources

Conservation Service (NRCS) classifies the capability of soils for agriculture. Prime soils are those that require the fewest inputs for productive agriculture. Locations with prime soils require comparatively less irrigation, less fertilizers and pesticides, and less effort devoted to erosion control.

A suitability analysis involves the following three discrete steps:

1. Identify suitability criteria for each anticipated land use

2. Collect and map the relevant site attribute data

3. Identify and map the site locations with attribute values that meet the suitability criteria for the targeted land uses

On relatively large sites, especially where built elements will cover a minor fraction of the parcel's surface area, land use suitability analysis may be an appropriate first step in the site analysis. Typically, suitability is interpreted to mean the site's suitability for the construction of roads and buildings. In more rural areas, suitability may include the soil's capacity to accommodate on-site wastewater treatment systems or specific agricultural uses such as vineyards. Site inventory maps are required for this analysis.

An important step in evaluating a site's suitability for specific uses is the selection of attributes, sources of data, and suitability criteria. In selecting data themes and data sources, several factors should be considered, as follows (Anderson, 1980; Pease and Sussman, 1994, pp. 94–105):

- Data requirements (for example, for permitting applications to public agencies)

- Data relevance (for example, data are current and relate to the suitability criteria for proposed uses)

- Data reliability (for example, data are accurate in location and attribute classifications)

- Data availability (for example, data exist at the needed scale or can be affordably acquired)

Most suitability analyses involve the analysis of several site attributes. If conducted within a GIS, with site inventory maps in digital form, suitability maps can be generated for each proposed land use. Suitability maps can then be combined to create—on a single map—a synoptic analysis of multiple land use classes. In addition, statistics on the amount of site area in each suitability class can be derived from these maps.

8.3.2 Single Attribute Analysis

Data Partitioning
A GIS database consists not only of maps, but also of data tables that are linked to the points, lines, and polygons on the maps (Chrisman, 1997). Information about the location and

attributes of each map unit is stored as tabular data. The analysis of an individual attribute layer involves partitioning the spatial distribution of attribute values.

The analysis of a single attribute layer may have several objectives, but the primary objective usually is to find locations that meet one or more specified attribute conditions. These conditions create suitable—or unsuitable—places for one or more components of the proposed program. For example, this partitioning of attribute values can identity site areas that are either:

- greater than a specified minimum (for example, elevations at least one meter above sea level);

- less than a specified maximum (for example, slopes less than 20 percent); or

- within a specified range (for example, slopes with southwestern, southern, or southeastern aspects).

Spatial Buffering

Spatial buffering, or proximity analysis, is used to identify locations within a specified distance of one or more reference features. Chrisman (1997) distinguishes between buffers and setbacks (Figure 8-4), but the only significant difference between a buffer and a setback is the direction (outward or inward) in which the new area is created. The buffering distance and the area measured within each buffer zone can be easily adjusted. Moreover, buffering may be used to locate areas near:

Figure 8-4 Diagram of buffers and setbacks within a GIS. Source: Chrisman, copyright © 1997, p. 142, Figure 6-1. Reprinted by permission of John Wiley & Sons, Inc.

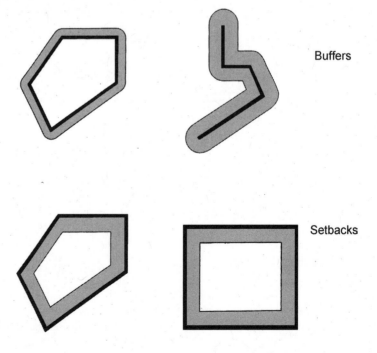

Buffers

Setbacks

- □ natural resources requiring protection from development (for example, wellheads, wetlands, habitats of legally protected species);

- □ cultural resources requiring protection from development (for example, historic buildings and battlefields);

- □ hazards posing significant risks to human life and property.

Possible analyses of buffer areas include the presence or absence of a specific attribute condition or value (such as vegetation type or slope gradient). In addition to simply indicating the presence or absence of some attribute value, these analyses reflect the interpretation and synthesis of project objectives. For example, buffering may be used to target areas on a site that most warrant protection or restoration, such as riparian corridors, wetlands, and other components of the landscape's "green" infrastructure. Buffering might identify, therefore, all areas within a specified distance of a stream. Adequate plant cover within riparian areas can significantly limit erosion, sedimentation, and chemical pollution of aquatic ecosystems by filtering stormwater surface runoff. Other benefits of riparian buffers include the conservation of terrestrial and aquatic habitat.

8.3.3 Multiple Attribute Analysis

Although complex spatial analyses are possible with a GIS, a small number of analytical functions are most useful for land planning purposes. A site suitability analysis typically involves overlaying two or more attribute layers (Figure 8-5). The intersection and union analyses are two of the most common, and useful, algebraic functions for analyzing multiple attribute layers. For a comprehensive review of these GIS operations, see Chrisman (1997).

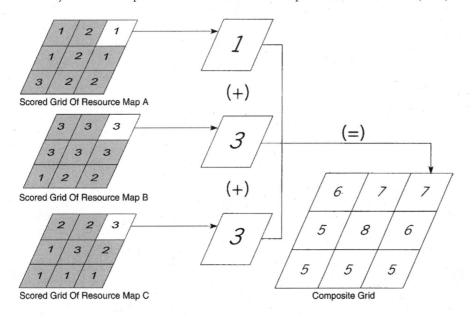

Figure 8-5 Overlay analysis using a linear combination approach. Source: Chrisman, copyright © 1997, p. 132, Figure 5-11. Reprinted by permission of John Wiley & Sons, Inc.

Union

The union of two sets of numbers yields a third set that contains each unique number in the two original sets, as follows:

$$\{1, 3\} \cup \{2, 3\} = \{1, 2, 3\}$$

In a GIS, the union function identifies locations where any of the specified attributes occur. For example, the analyst might want to identify all areas that pose severe constraints for excavation and subsequent construction of building foundations. Attribute values that could hinder excavation or construction include shallow depth to the water table and shallow depth to bedrock. In an overlay analysis using the union function, all site areas could be identified that meet either one or both of these conditions.

Intersection

The intersection of two sets of numbers yields a third set of numbers that are common to both original sets, as follows:

$$\{1, 3\} \cap \{2, 3\} = \{3\}$$

This algebraic function is the conceptual basis for another type of overlay analysis, identifying locations where two or more attribute conditions are spatially coincident (overlap). An intersection of multiple attribute layers might yield, for example, site locations with slopes of less than 8 percent and subsurface conditions suitable for the excavation of building foundations.

Other Functions and Cautions

Although computers are powerful tools for spatial analysis, there is always a risk of drawing invalid conclusions from inappropriate uses of the data. A GIS is capable of easily comparing "apples and oranges"—even when these comparisons could lead to erroneous conclusions (Hopkins, 1977; Chrisman, 1997). Weighting schemes, for example, are frequently used to assign priority values to key site attributes. The challenge in using weighting schemes is to identify weights that can be justified empirically. This is an area in which applied research is greatly needed.

The comparison of completely unrelated physical, biological, and cultural attributes is another potential concern. Although it is mathematically possible to weigh each different attribute and arrive at an algebraic sum, the significance of the values may be highly questionable. For example, a site analyst may consider visual quality, slope gradients, and soil erodibility to be the most important variables in assessing development suitability of a particular site. But how much weight should be placed on each of these variables? One could assign, for example, a 15 percent weight to visual quality, 25 percent weight to soil erodibility, and 60 percent weight to slopes. These are far from trivial decisions and the choices made can dramatically affect the conclusions of the analysis.

8.3.4 Data Accuracy

Data accuracy is another issue that warrants attention as spatial information technologies become more common. How accurate do data layers need to be? The answer to this question depends on the purpose for which the data will be used. A parcel boundary map, which is the basis for property transactions, must be highly accurate (for example, within a few centimeters). The spatial accuracy of other site attribute data, such as soil or vegetation type, can be less accurate, perhaps within a few meters.

Resource inventory maps created by state and federal governments, for example, are typically not intended to be the sole source of information for site-level decision making. Therefore, the boundaries of mapped attributes, such as landslide hazards or flood hazards, are inexact and may be inaccurate by several meters. The Environmentally Critical Areas Policies and Regulations adopted in Seattle, Washington (United States), recognizes these data limitations. The city's development controls are linked to site attributes (Table 8-2) rather than to constraint maps, as indicated in the following:

> When specific actions are proposed in or adjacent to mapped critical areas, more detailed review may be required. Projects located within a mapped area could be exempted from the regulations, if the applicant can demonstrate that the site does not, in fact, meet the definition of the critical area. Conversely, developments outside of the mapped area could be covered by the regulations, if it is shown that the site does, in fact, meet the definition. (Marks, 1997, p. 231)

8.3.5 Planning Applications

The U.S. Department of Agriculture's land evaluation and site assessment (LESA) system helps local and state governments protect prime, unique, or locally important farmland from development (Steiner et al., 1994). The LESA system has been used in determining the boundaries of agricultural zoning districts, identifying farms that are eligible for purchase of development rights (PDR) or transfer of development rights (TDR), and other land use policy objectives (Malloy and Pressley, 1994, pp. 262–273).

One criticism of the LESA system, as it was being used in the early 1990s, is that it mixed two disparate policy concerns in one aggregate index (Pease and Sussman, 1994, pp. 94–105). The LESA model grouped together agricultural productivity and potential for development. Given the objectives of the analysis, these two factors should have been evaluated separately. Another continuing challenge is data redundancy. The results of the analysis will be skewed if some constraints disproportionately influence the results because they are represented by multiple data themes (Pease and Sussman, 1994, pp. 94–105).

Suitability criteria for a given land use may vary substantially with differences in local and regional conditions. For example, maximum feasible slope gradients for housing development will vary with local factors such as soil and geologic conditions and climate. Locations with subfreezing winter temperatures are much more limiting because of the dangers that icy and slippery conditions create for pedestrians and vehicles. The steep street

TABLE 8-2   Criteria for defining and mapping environmentally critical areas in Seattle, Washington.

Critical Area	Attributes
Landslide hazards	Known landslide areas Slopes greater than 15 percent with specified geologic conditions Slopes greater than 40 percent Previously altered slopes greater than 40 percent
Liquefaction hazards	Identified by the U.S. Geologic Survey
Flood hazards	Areas on FEMA flood insurance maps
Abandoned solid waste landfills	Sites listed by the State Health Department Areas within 1000 feet of methane-producing landfills Sites identified by public or historical research
Toxic disposal sites	Sites listed by the State Health Department Sites discovered by historical research, site sampling, or during project review
Steep slopes	Areas over 40 percent slope
Riparian corridors	Class A Riparian corridors of year-round or salmonid water bodies Class B Intermittent streams without salmonids Buffers 100 feet from water body or 100 year floodplain (whichever is greater)
Wetlands	U.S. Fish and Wildlife Service inventory Areas that support a prevalence of vegetation typically adapted for saturated soil
Fish and wildlife habitat	Priority species habitat (identified by the State Department of Wildlife) All water bodies providing migration corridors and habitat for fish, especially salmonids

Source: Adapted from Marks, 1997, Table 18.1

gradients in San Francisco, California, for example, would be impractical in a city with snowstorms and freezing winter temperatures. San Francisco's street system—primarily a grid configuration imposed on a hilly landscape—has many street gradients between 20 and 30 percent. A common development code maximum for street gradients, in other cities, is typically 12 percent.

A suitability analysis can identify optimal locations for specific site uses or activities (Figure 8-6). For example, most land development projects require one or more vehicle entrances to the site. Site factors that might influence the selection of an entrance location include the vertical and horizontal alignment of adjacent roads, existing site amenities such

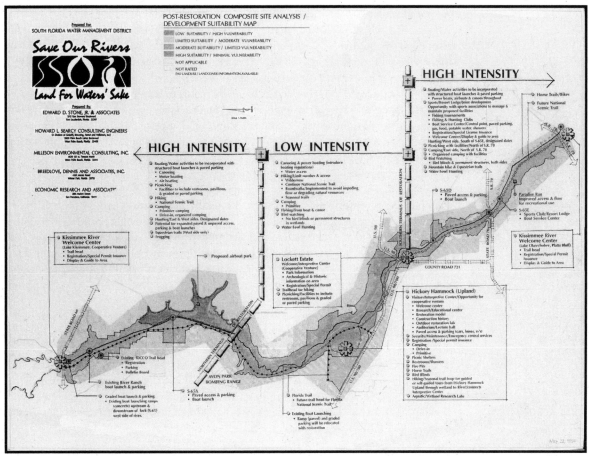

POST-RESTORATION COMPOSITE SITE ANALYSIS / DEVELOPMENT SUITABILITY MAP

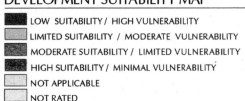

LOW SUITABILITY / HIGH VULNERABILITY

LIMITED SUITABILITY / MODERATE VULNERABILITY

MODERATE SUITABILITY / LIMITED VULNERABILITY

HIGH SUITABILITY / MINIMAL VULNERABILITY

NOT APPLICABLE

NOT RATED
(NO LANDUSE / LANDCOVER INFORMATION AVAILABLE)

Figure 8-6   Composite site analysis/development suitability map for the restoration of one stretch of the channelized Kissimmee River in central Florida. The project area, analyzed with a GIS, is divided by intensity of future uses.
Source: Edward D. Stone, Jr., and Associates.

as significant trees or landforms, and views from the site to the surrounding landscape. The suitability of potential locations for the new entrance could be analyzed by assessing elevation, adjacent land use, and a variety of other attributes. Possible locations for the entrance could be ranked according to the suitability of each alternative location. A map could portray this analysis with four suitability classes (ordinal scale): no constraints, minor constraints, moderate constraints, and severe constraints.

Site suitability is a function of the intended site uses. Consider, for example, a partially wooded and hilly site along a small stream. Several site attributes could be mapped, but not all of these attributes may be relevant to the program under consideration. A map showing the site's range of slope percentages (for example, 0–5 percent or 5–10 percent) is potentially useful because some land uses are better suited for gentle slopes, and other uses are better suited for steeper slopes. In gently rolling to nearly level terrain, topographic slope and aspect may have an insignificant effect on land planning and site design decisions. In steeper terrain, however, elevation, slope, and aspect can be highly important attributes, influencing the site's hydrology, visual quality, and plant and animal distributions (Figure 8-7, 8-8, and 8-9).

The site attributes relevant to a proposed nature conservancy may differ significantly from the site attributes relevant to a proposed multifamily housing development; for example, the inventory and analysis for the nature conservancy project would place a high priority on identifying the site's plant communities and wildlife habitats—from dry, upland, forested slopes to lowland marshes and bogs. In contrast, the inventory and analysis for the housing project would place a high priority on identifying areas without significant development constraints, such as steep slopes, shallow bedrock, or shallow water table.

8.3.6   Suitability and Development Regulation

The State Growth Management Act, passed in Washington State in 1990, requires local municipalities to adopt critical areas ordinances that protect wetlands, aquifer recharge areas (for potable water sources), fish and wildlife habitat conservation areas, frequently flooded areas, and geologically hazardous areas (Marks, 1997, pp. 227–240). The Environmentally Critical Areas Policies for Seattle states:

> The Critical Areas Ordinance should allow land to be developed in accordance with the constraints and opportunities provided by the land itself. All land is not the same. If a person purchases a parcel that is 80 percent wetland, it is significantly different than other types of property. The same is true with areas subject to either landslides or floods. If the owner purchased property that contained a wetland, a landslide area, or a flood plain. The Critical Areas Ordinance should recognize that the reasonable development potential of such properties is less than the reasonable potential of unconstrained sites. The ordinance should permit development that makes use of a site's natural opportunities and that recognizes its natural constraints (Marks, 1997, pp. 230–231).

Taking a similar approach, a model ordinance for traditional neighborhood development (TND) includes explicit criteria for determining a site's potential building capacity for a new housing development (Arendt, 1999). Several constraint categories, each with a different ratio, are used to determine the number of dwelling units permitted on the developable areas of the site (Table 8-3). To determine a site's "total adjusted tract

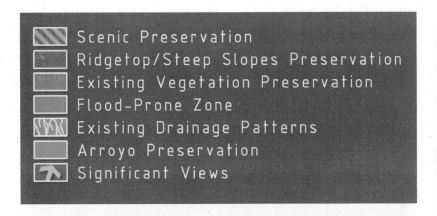

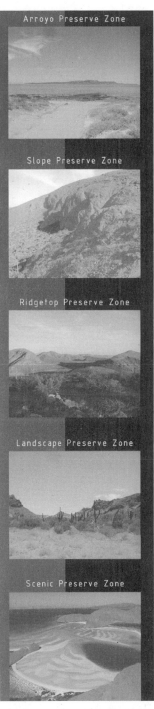

Figure 8-7 Site analysis identifying major land use determinants and proposed nature preservation zones in Bahia Balandra, Mexico. Source: The HOK Planning Group.

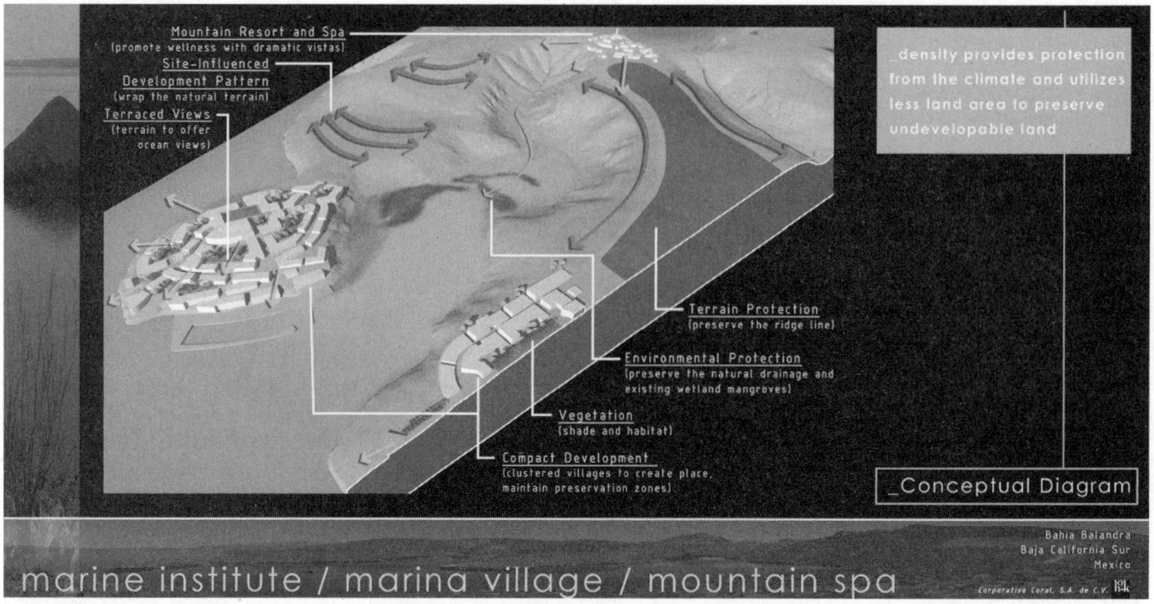

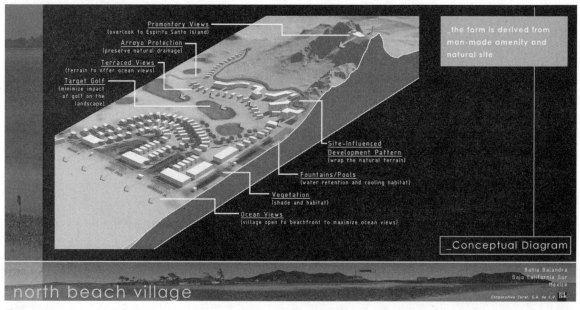

Figure 8-8 Three-dimensional concept diagram and analysis showing how the programmed uses will be adapted to the unique conditions of the site and its context. Source: The HOK Planning Group.

Figure 8-9 Concept diagram and analysis adapts the programmed uses to the site and context. Source: The HOK Planning Group.

TABLE 8-3   Constraints and ratios for calculating allowable development density that is transferred to the developable portions of the site.

Ratio	Site Constraint
0.00	Street rights-of-way Floodways within 100-year floodplain
0.05	Wetlands and "very poorly drained" soils Bedrock at the surface Rock outcrops and boulder fields Utility easements for high-tension electrical transmission lines (greater than 69 kilovolts)
0.25	Slopes greater than 25 percent gradient
0.33	"Poorly drained" soils (in unsewered areas) Bedrock within 42 inches of the surface (in unsewered areas)
0.50	100-year floodplains (excluding floodways or wetlands within floodplains) Bedrock within 36 inches of the surface (in unsewered areas)
0.75	"Poorly drained" soils (in sewered areas) Bedrock within 42 inches of the surface (in sewered areas) Slopes between 15 percent and 25 percent gradients
1.00	Unconstrained land

Source: Adapted from Arendt, 1999, p. 100, Table III.B.2.1.

acreage," the area of land in each of the constraint categories is multiplied by the development ratio and these values are summed (Arendt, 1999). This number (total adjusted tract acreage) is then multiplied by the dwelling density that is allowed in the zoning district. This results in the total number of dwellings (absent density bonuses) that can be built on the site.

Another similar, but broader, approach to guiding new development is provided by Nelesson (1994). This method includes an extensive array of physical, biological, and cultural attributes that constitute development constraints. Constraints are categorized into three levels: highest, severe, and moderate. These categories of constraints, with associated ratings, are used to determine the permitted number of dwelling units on the portions of the site without constraints. Nelesson (1994, pp. 116–117) recommends consideration of the following constraints:

- Open water

- Aquifer recharge areas

- High levels of toxic waste

- Low levels of toxic contamination (with cleanup or treatment potential)

- Historic or archaeological sites
- Class I and II agricultural soils (in an active farming community)
- Mature vegetation
- Major viewsheds
- Ridge tops

8.4   INTEGRATION AND SYNTHESIS

8.4.1   Site Constraints

Difficult Sites

A landscape's "green" or ecological infrastructure includes open water, wetlands, aquifer recharge areas, and unique landforms. Philip Lewis, Jr., pioneered the concept of environmental corridors in Wisconsin. These "e-ways"—representing environment and education—coincided with the location of physiographic constraints: water, wetlands, and steep topography (Lewis, 1996). Earlier, in Illinois, Lewis found that most of the state's significant ecological and cultural resources occurred at these locations.

Physiographic constraints are particularly important considerations in site selection. Depending on the desired uses of the site, these constraints can affect the project's social and environmental impacts; its functional or land use feasibility; in addition to the costs for construction, maintenance, and operation.

Building in difficult locations requires comparatively more time and money before, during, and after construction. Steep slopes, for example, are a significant constraint for many developed uses (Figure 8-10). Building foundations on steep slopes must be more complex—perhaps stepping down a hillside—and are, therefore, more costly to construct. In locations where site drainage is poor, or where subsurface materials are unstable, additional design and construction effort is needed to ensure the building's structural integrity. The construction process is also more complicated if the site is more vulnerable to development impacts such as soil erosion, groundwater contamination, and the degradation of critical wildlife habitat.

Acquiring development permits for difficult sites is complicated by the potential environmental impacts of the construction process as well as the post-construction uses of the site. Consequently, the development of sites with significant physiographic constraints may be economically—and politically—unfeasible.

In urban environments, microclimate can vary dramatically over short distances. Buildings can create outdoor areas that are relatively sheltered from the wind. In cooler climates, these pockets of calm air—especially if they have access to direct sunlight—can have much milder microclimates than other nearby windy or shaded sites. Exploiting these milder microclimates or consciously creating them provides valuable opportunities for meaningful outdoor open spaces.

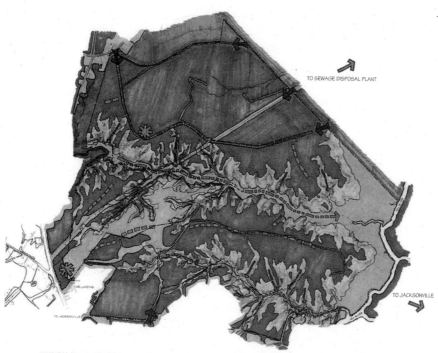

TO SEWAGE DISPOSAL PLANT

TO JACKSONVILLE

ONSLOW COUNTY INDUSTRIAL PARK
ONSLOW COUNTY, NORTH CAROLINA

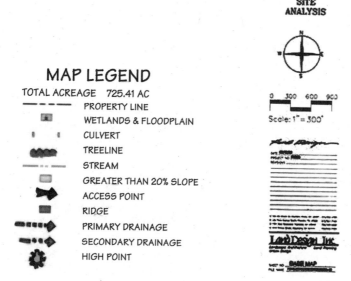

Figure 8-10 Site analysis showing development constraints: drainage patterns, ridges, and areas with slope gradients greater than 20 percent. This analysis also identifies potential site access points to a future industrial park in Onslow County, North Carolina. Source: Land Design.

SITE
ANALYSIS

0   300   600   900

Scale: 1" = 300'

MAP LEGEND

TOTAL ACREAGE   725.41 AC

PROPERTY LINE
WETLANDS & FLOODPLAIN
CULVERT
TREELINE
STREAM
GREATER THAN 20% SLOPE
ACCESS POINT
RIDGE
PRIMARY DRAINAGE
SECONDARY DRAINAGE
HIGH POINT

Yet, relatively harsh and uncomfortable microclimates also exist in urban areas. Tall buildings and groups of buildings may deflect or channel winds to create turbulent areas, or virtual "wind tunnels." A lack of solar radiation can also make outdoor spaces substantially colder than nearby areas with full exposure to the sun. Existing—or proposed—trees, buildings, and other structures on or near the site will cast shadows. Understanding these shadow patterns as they vary daily and seasonally is crucial to the site-planning process. An urban site analysis, especially, should utilize sun and shade diagrams created during the site inventory.

Natural Hazards

Ignoring or discounting potential hazards can lead to expensive—even deadly—disasters. Natural hazards that may impact a site are often weather related. During periods of good weather, the dangers may be absent, but the danger is greatest when relatively infrequent, but severe, weather events occur. Earthquakes, hurricanes, and other natural hazards occur at infrequent intervals. The recurring nature of these events suggests, however, that it's not a question of if, but when, a specific event will occur.

There is little that planners or builders can do to mitigate the effects of tornadoes on conventional wood-frame construction buildings. Hurricanes, in contrast, are weather events that raise significant land use planning implications. Hurricanes always form over water, so the risk they pose is greatest in coastal communities. Because hurricanes are long-lasting storms, their persistent rains saturate soils and exacerbate the threats of local flooding. Advances in building construction methods have reduced the risk of structural failures from storm wind loads (Simiu and Miyata, 2006). But a hurricane's main threat to life and property is the accompanying storm surge (Heinz Center, 2000).

Storm surges associated with hurricanes may create walls of water that are at least several meters above normal high-tide elevations. Development in low-lying areas is especially vulnerable. Moreover, mean sea level could rise up to one meter over the next century as the Earth's climate continues to warm (Mileti, 1999). That seemingly small increase could have devastating social and economic implications for many coastal areas. The least costly public policy option for managing this risk is to discourage development (and redevelopment) in these high-risk areas (Heinz Center, 2002).

Snow, ice, and rain storms create additional hazards. The 1993 floods of the upper Mississippi River demonstrated the destruction that can result when humans underestimate the forces of nature. Levees and dams—meant to channel and confine the river—were unable to contain the river during this flood season. The capacity of the upland areas to infiltrate stormwater runoff was reduced by the presence of buildings, roads, and other impervious surfaces. Flooding is exacerbated in landscapes where buildings, paving, and other impervious land cover substantially reduce the normal capacity of the land to retain and infiltrate stormwater. Earthquakes and volcanoes are also dangerous geological hazards. The shaking forces on buildings, bridges, utility lines, and other structures demand extraordinary design and construction to mitigate the risk (Dowrick, 1991; Erdey, 2007). If the risk can be avoided or reduced significantly by not building in the most active areas (fault zones), then this is clearly the prudent course of action.

Legal and Cultural Constraints

Urban and other built-up areas are complex environments. Site analyses, in this context, must examine much more than the site's physiographic conditions (Figure 8-11). A broad array of contextual information is needed to ensure that new buildings and other site elements will be visually and functionally compatible with the surrounding cultural context. Urban structure, for example, is an important contextual element that may not be obvious from the ground. The search for order and pattern should be part of the inventory and analysis process. Within an urban context, patterns of mass and space, and the relationships between these basic urban building blocks, can be assessed, in part, with figure-ground diagrams.

The assessment of context involves identifying neighborhood and community spaces and determining what activities and symbolic values are associated with those spaces. The spatial and temporal qualities of "place" are particularly relevant to urban in-fill projects. Jakle (1987, pp. 4–5) comments on the time and space dimensions of place:

Certainly, places as behavioral settings have spatial context. They also, however, have temporal dimensions because they open and close at set points in time and, thus, function for set durations of time, often with cyclical regularity. They are occupied by people (usually a limited range of types), by activities (usually a limited set of general behaviors), and by a limited array of furnishings supportive of those behaviors.

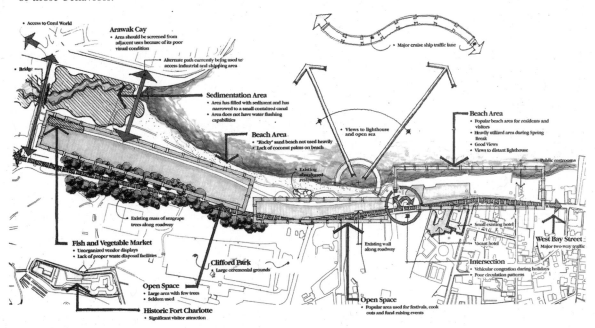

Figure 8-11   Site analysis showing prominent views, pedestrian–vehicle conflicts, cultural amenities, and a variety of other site and contextual information. Source: Edward D. Stone, Jr., and Associates.

Depending on the project's program, other analyses within an urban environment may be warranted. An analysis of pedestrian circulation within, and surrounding, the site would seek to identify potential entrance locations. This analysis should also identify problems, such as the following:

- Lack of walkway connectivity (unfulfilled desire lines)
- Inadequate capacity (congestion)
- Conflicts among vehicles, bicycles, and pedestrians (safety hazards)
- Lack of seating and other site furniture (amenities)

Similarly, an analysis of the site's architectural context would certainly seek to identify the positive attributes of the area's better designed buildings. Yet this analysis must also identify the existing problems or weaknesses of the area's architecture. These problems, which could be addressed in a comprehensive renovation and adaptive reuse program, include the following:

- Large, unarticulated building facades
- Facades covered with visually monotonous materials (for example, concrete and concrete block)
- Unbroken rooflines (the entire length of the building)
- Insufficient maintenance

Additionally, the analysis of urban streetscapes might reveal a variety of other potentially correctable problems. These include the following:

- Lack of spatial enclosure
- Poor-quality materials (for example, paving and seating)
- Lack of maintenance (for example, curbs, walkways, plantings)
- No unifying design theme (for example, materials, forms, proportions)
- Insufficient or excessive lighting
- Insufficient seating and other site furniture (for example, signs and trash containers)

8.4.2 Site Opportunities

A site analysis focuses on more than just site constraints, although this alone is enough to justify this activity. Significant site amenities have social, economic, ecological, and aesthetic value. These might include specimen trees or scenic views to natural features such as water or landforms, landmark buildings, or other significant cultural features (Figures 8-12 and 8-13). These physical assets, if integrated within a development plan,

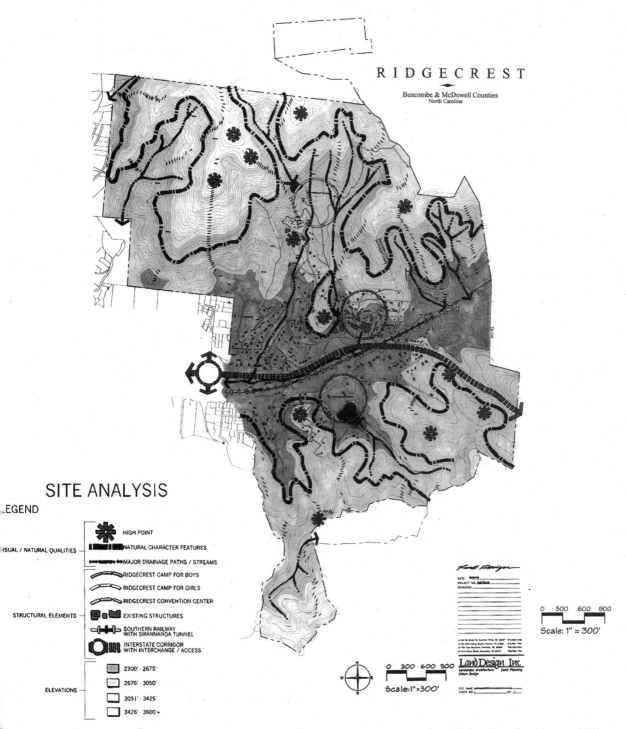

RIDGECREST

Buncombe & McDowell Counties
North Carolina

SITE ANALYSIS

LEGEND

VISUAL / NATURAL QUALITIES
- HIGH POINT
- NATURAL CHARACTER FEATURES
- MAJOR DRAINAGE PATHS / STREAMS

STRUCTURAL ELEMENTS
- RIDGECREST CAMP FOR BOYS
- RIDGECREST CAMP FOR GIRLS
- RIDGECREST CONVENTION CENTER
- EXISTING STRUCTURES
- SOUTHERN RAILWAY WITH SWANNANOA TUNNEL
- INTERSTATE CORRIDOR WITH INTERCHANGE / ACCESS

ELEVATIONS
- 2300' - 2675'
- 2676' - 3050'
- 3051' - 3425'
- 3426' - 3600'+

Scale: 1" = 300'

Figure 8-12   Site analysis showing major transportation corridors, drainage patterns, and site high points. The ridges and hilltops, which are clearly identified on the analysis, contribute to the site's visual quality. Source: Land Design.

Figure 8-13 Site analysis showing prominent views to a natural amenity (water). Analysis also identifies site high points and potential harbor locations. Source: Land Design

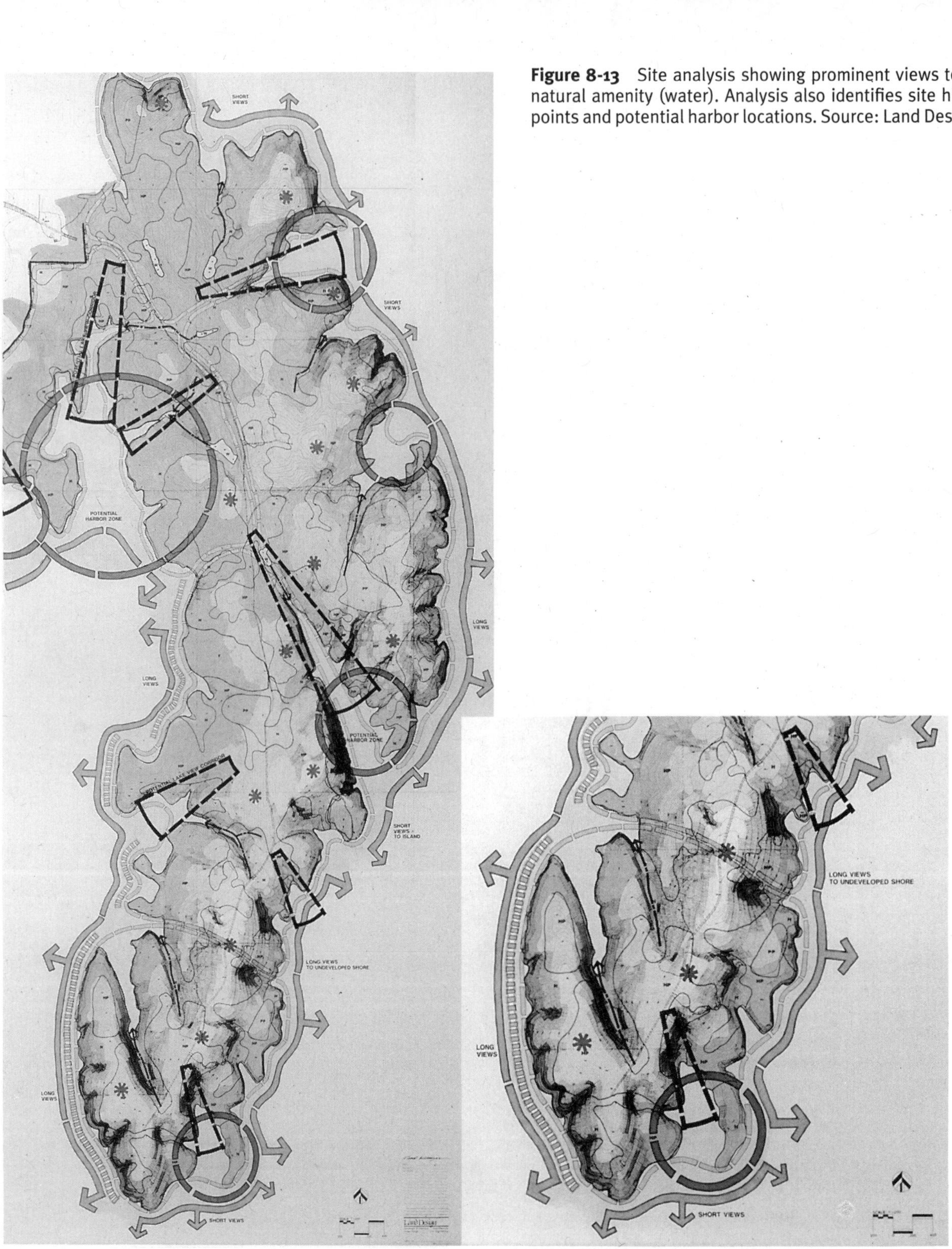

190

TABLE 8-4 Selected amenities and resources that may exist on or near a site, and warrant documentation in the site analysis.

Category	Examples
Visual amenity	Coastline
	Ridgeline
	Forest
	Golf course
Natural resource	Prime farmland
	Sand and gravel deposits
	Wetlands
	Aquifers
Cultural resource	Park
	Museum
	Historic district
	Archaeological site

can preserve a site's sense of place and enhance quality of life for future site users. Site amenities also include unique rock outcrops and historic or culturally significant buildings and structures (Table 8-4). Protecting or enhancing cultural amenities can add value to a completed project and make it more desirable to site users.

Site opportunities include locations on the site that are potentially useable for one or more project objectives—whether they entail real estate development (for example, construction of buildings, roads, and other facilities); environmental conservation or restoration to provide an on-site natural amenity; or a combination of these purposes. Together, the site's constraints and opportunities delimit one or more spatially explicit "envelopes" on the site that can suitably accommodate all or part of the project program (Figure 8-14). Like solving a jigsaw puzzle, design solutions that "fit the site" are often elegant compositions that capitalize on the site's natural and cultural attributes, creating a unique sense of place (Figure 8-15).

Sense of Place

The transformation of landscapes—most significantly since the end of World War II—has resulted from the interplay of many social, economic, and technological factors. Land use changes have been influenced by the international exchange of information and materials, and the implementation of public policies governing a range of activities, from transportation and economic development to school siting (Ben-Joseph and Szold, 2005). Design styles as well as construction methods and materials have become more standardized.

A community's character or sense of place results, in part, from the size, massing, and placement of buildings. Older, architecturally significant buildings are very important cultural components. Yet sense of place is also fundamentally influenced by the native landforms and vegetation, and other tangible and intangible elements within the built environment. New development that does not respond to local site conditions—including the surrounding context—contributes to placelessness.

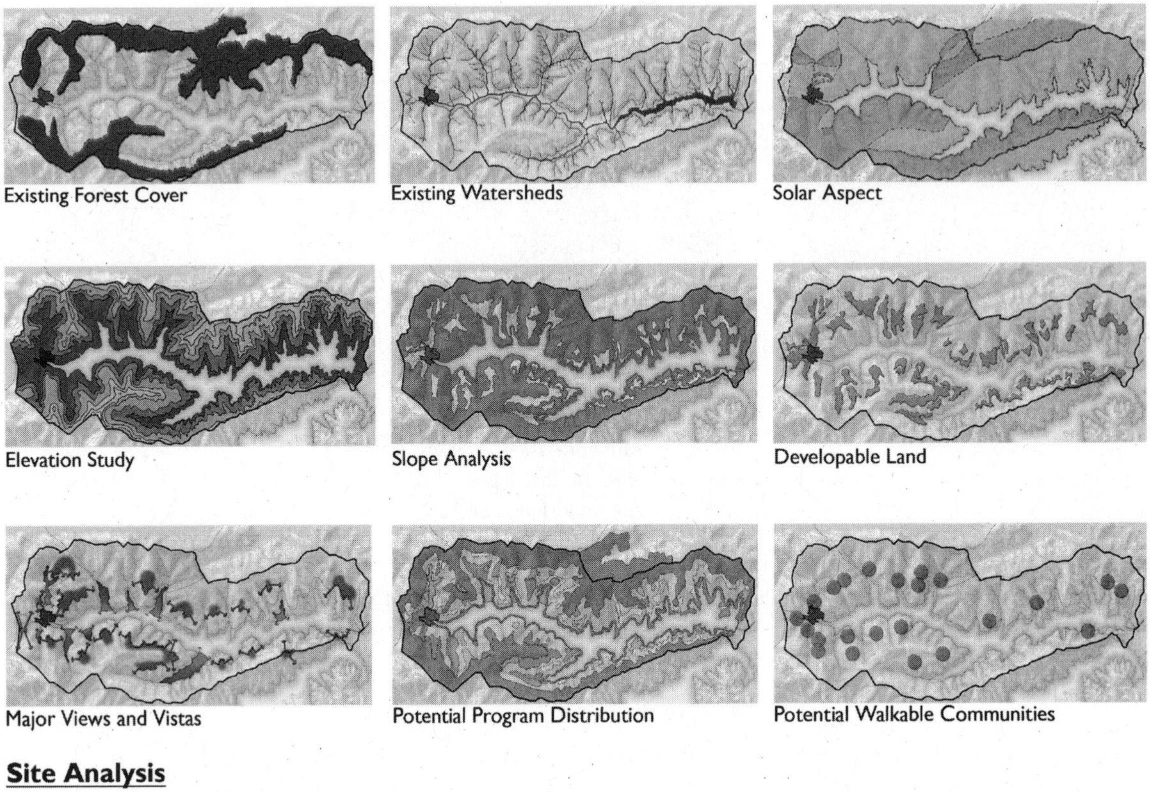

Existing Forest Cover

Existing Watersheds

Solar Aspect

Elevation Study

Slope Analysis

Developable Land

Major Views and Vistas

Potential Program Distribution

Potential Walkable Communities

Site Analysis

Figure 8-14 Composite set of site inventory and analysis maps in Lavasa, India. Source: The HOK Planning Group.

The biophysical and cultural context of a site encompasses local, community, and regional factors. Michael Hough (1990, p. 180) comments on the biophysical and cultural complexity of regional context:

Regional identity is connected with the peculiar characteristics of a location. . . . It is what a place has when it somehow belongs to its location and nowhere else. It has to do, therefore, with two fundamental criteria: first, with the natural processes of the region or locality—what nature has put there; second, with social processes—what people have put there.

Hough (1990, p. 186) also states:

The protection of natural and cultural history—the reuse and integration of the old into the new without fanfare, while avoiding the temptation to turn everything into a museum because it is old—lies at the heart of maintaining a continuing link with the past and with a place's identity.

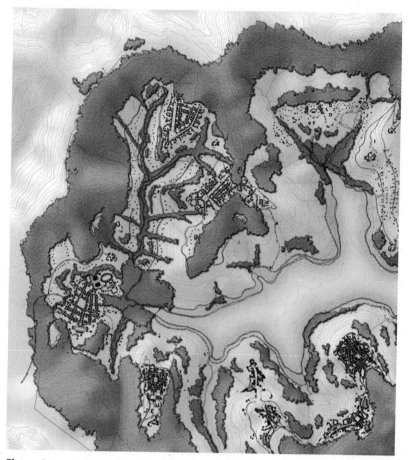

Figure 8-15 Master plan protects existing forests and drainageways, fits new development into the remaining "envelopes," and restores riparian vegetation. Source: The HOK Planning Group.

Contemporary references to earlier design styles, construction methods, and construction materials take into account—and create linkages to—the site's cultural history and intrinsic environmental character. A contextual approach to land development is a design ethic that seeks to create meaningful places that are also "good neighbors" (Box 8-1).

Yet placelessness occurs when buildings are constructed and sites are developed in ways that are not adapted to the site's historical and environmental context. Placelessness also results from a lack of attention to "space making." Too often, little or no attention is given to the creation of outdoor open spaces, their spatial organization and connectivity, or to their furnishing and refinement.

Cultural Significance

Our sense of hearing, sight, and smell help us form impressions about the quality of the environment. Our perceptions of a site could be determined, for example, by views of utility lines, parking lots, and by noise from commercial operations or from traffic on nearby highways (Figure 8-16). Environmental preferences drive our behavior concerning where we live, shop, work, and play. Amenities, as well as nuisances, play an important role in determining the desirability of a particular location. Off-site factors, including legal conditions, also may be significant (Figures 8-17). Analyses of the built environment examine how—and why—people use, or avoid, outdoor spaces. Post-occupancy evaluation of outdoor spaces is particularly useful for urban sites (Cooper-Marcus and Francis, 1999).

Natural as well as built features give neighborhoods unique identities. Morrish and Brown (1994), in *Planning to Stay*, suggest that neighborhood character is a product of the quality, accessibility, and convenience of the place. Specifically, character is derived from the following attributes:

- Location (on site and in the neighborhood)

- Scale (spatial—size and temporal—volume or rates, such as traffic)

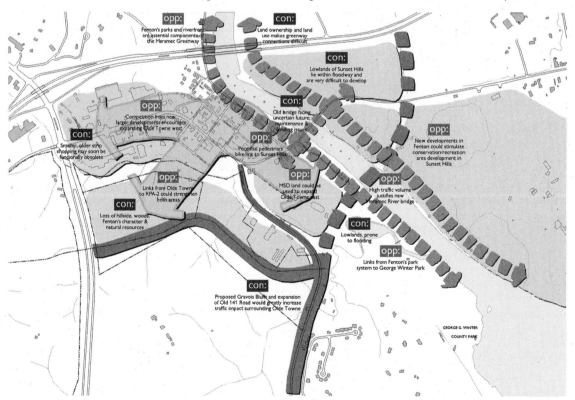

Figure 8-16 Opportunities and constraints diagram for the expansion of a historic village in Missouri. Source: The HOK Planning Group.

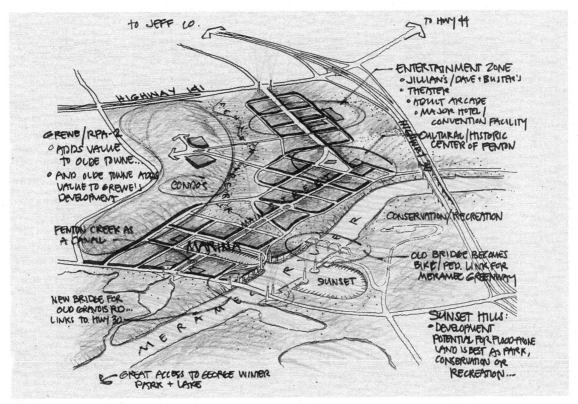

Figure 8-17   Aerial perspective urban analysis identifying important contextual factors. Source: The HOK Planning Group.

□ Mix (uses and their connections)

□ Time (sites change diurnally, seasonally, and over generations)

□ Movement (transportation—quality, convenience, speed)

Contextual or neighborhood character analyses may involve, therefore, assessments of the following neighborhood resources (Morrish and Brown, 1994):

□ Homes and gardens (for example, private)

□ Community streets

□ Neighborhood niches (for example, retail and services)

□ Anchoring institutions (for example, cultural, social, civic, employment/economic places)

□ Public gardens (for example, parks and greenways)

An important objective of the site analysis is to discover the special, interesting, and valuable features of the site and its context. These assets range from unique natural areas to culturally significant local places that—to someone unfamiliar with the neighborhood or community—may be overlooked.

8.5 CONCLUSION

Sustainable development requires the protection of ecological integrity and the conservation of natural resources, as well as cultural heritage. Yet land development can result, both during and after construction, in significant impacts that degrade the environment and impose a variety of economic and social costs on others. With careful site and contextual analysis, development can be designed to minimize these impacts and mitigate damage to the environment and society. Rather than attempting to overcome the intrinsic "difficulties" that a site may pose for development, some locations should simply remain undeveloped.

Each site presents a unique combination of physical, biological, and cultural conditions that preclude a "one-size-fits-all" approach to its planning and design. Development suitability is a function of the site's opportunities and constraints for a specific program. Opportunities are favorable, suitable, or advantageous locations on the site. These areas have attributes that are either essential for a programmed use or facilitate access to the area where the use will occur. Constraints are locations that are unsuitable or restricted for a particular use. Constraints exclude or prevent that use from occurring, or they increase the difficulty or cost of putting the use at that particular location.

BOX 8.1   In Practice

COMMUNITY PLANNING AND FARMLAND PRESERVATION

SOUTH LIVERMORE VALLEY, CALIFORNIA

Land Planner
Wallace, Roberts & Todd, LLC
San Francisco

Background
South Livermore Valley is in California's rolling hills of Alameda County (Figure 8-18). This has been a grape-growing and wine-producing area since the 1880s. As in other communities across North America, however, rural residential development began to significantly change this landscape. Standard zoning codes and subdivision ordinances were unable to protect the valley's rural character and viticulture industry. A participatory planning process, supported by a thorough analysis of the valley's biophysical and cultural conditions, informed a new approach for guiding growth and development within the valley.

Planning Process
An advisory committee was formed, consisting of concerned citizens and representatives from local municipalities. The four-year, consensus-building planning process, which began in 1987, ultimately resulted in the South Livermore Valley Specific Plan (City of Livermore, 1999). This plan sets the framework for development in a

Figure 8-18 The visual character of this California landscape is largely defined by hills and vineyards. Source: Wallace Roberts & Todd, LLC.

BOX 8.1   In Practice (continued)

14,000-acre (5600-hectare) area. The two major goals of the plan are to reinforce and rejuvenate the valley's wine-producing industry (Figure 8-19) and to preserve the area's rural character (Figure 8-20).

Design guidelines derived from careful study of historic regional precedents have resulted in development patterns and building forms that differ markedly from the typical suburban tract development in the area. The new development reinforces and enhances the valley's rural and historic character, while forging a distinctive new identity for the area's future (Figure 8-21).

Plan and Policy Implementation

Three strategies for accomplishing the community's goals were adopted:

1. *Specific Plan.* This land use plan targets new growth within seven distinct and noncontiguous subareas along six miles of Livermore's southern border (Figure 8-22 and 8-23). The total area allocated for new development is about 1500 acres (600 hectares), or about 1/10 of the entire planning area. Constraints maps and site analyses helped the planning team determine the preferred character and location of all new development (Figure 8-24 and 8-25).

   A "specific plan" is a mechanism made available to local governments by the State of California. It is essentially a planning and regulatory tool intended to implement a city or county general plan through policies, programs, and regulations. In the case of Livermore, it provides a fine-grain resolution to questions about how, where, and what development can take place—including detailed design guidelines to ensure consistency with the community's character—as well as establishes the means by which agricultural and natural resources are conserved. (Hammond and Roberts, 1999, p. 16)

BOX 8.1   In Practice (continued)

Figure 8-19   Development under the plan generates permanent protection of agricultural land and planting of new vineyards and orchard crops. Source: Wallace Roberts & Todd, LLC.

Figure 8-20   Conservation easements now protect 425 acres of open space. The Transfer of Development Rights program was implemented to permanently protect this scenic and environmentally diverse area as regional parkland. Source: Wallace Roberts & Todd, LLC.

BOX 8.1   In Practice (continued)

Figure 8-21 Protected open space provides a unique visual amenity at the community entrances. Source: Wallace Roberts & Todd, LLC.

BOX 8.1 In Practice (continued)

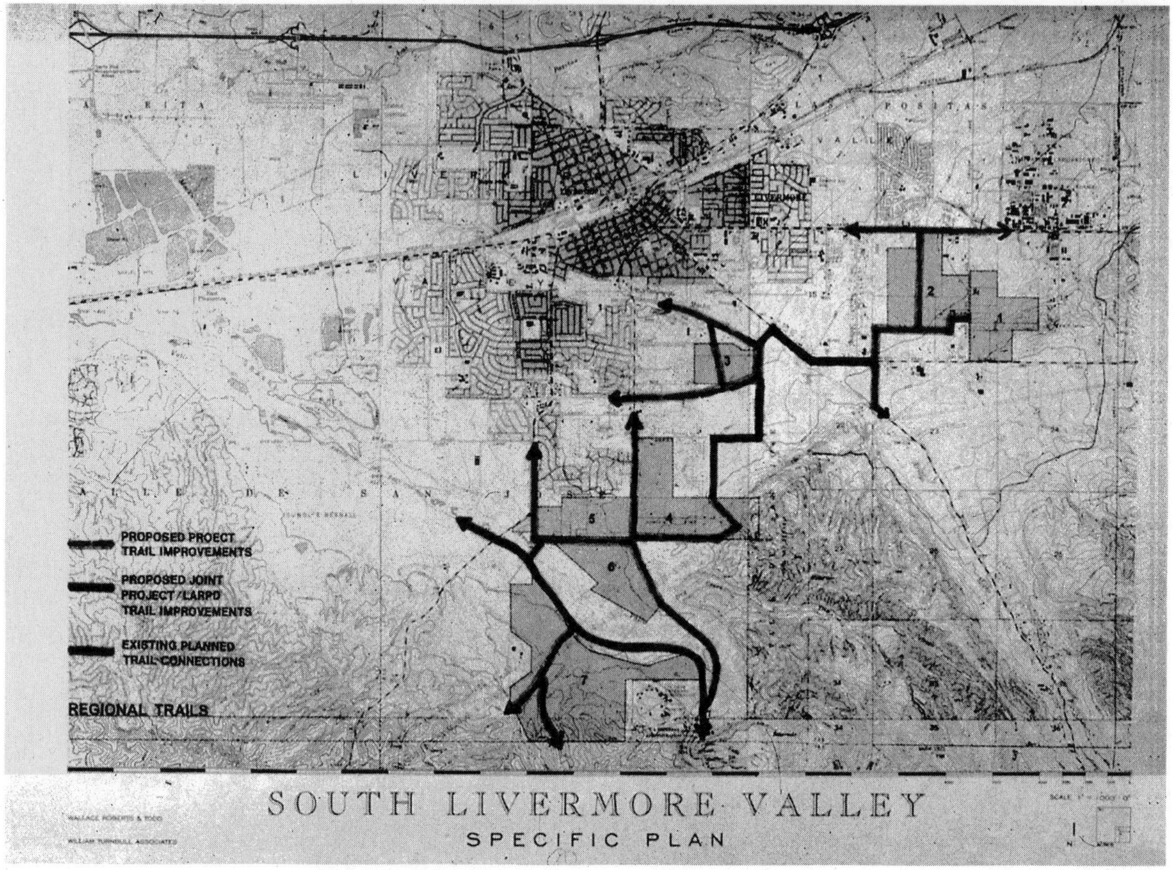

Figure 8-22 Community trails plan showing the seven development subareas. Source: Wallace Roberts & Todd, LLC.

BOX 8.1   In Practice (continued)

Figure 8-23   The plan contributed 6.5 miles of new multiuse trails that extend the length of the valley, connecting the new neighborhoods and creating an important recreational resource for the broader community. Source: Wallace Roberts & Todd, LLC.

BOX 8.1   In Practice (continued)

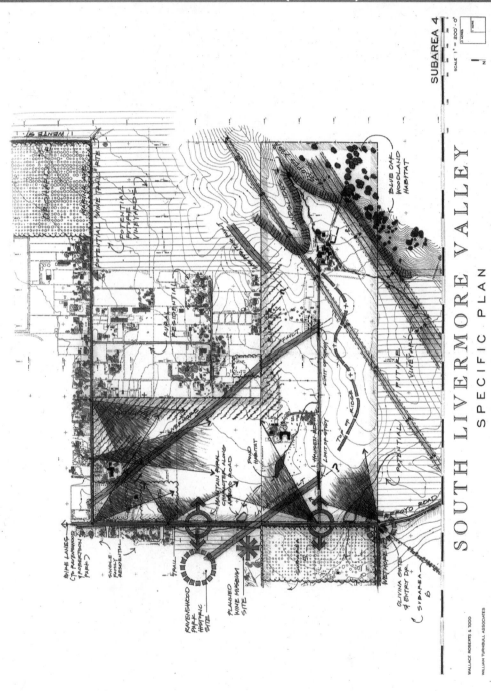

Figure 8-24 Site analysis for one of the seven development subareas. Source: Wallace Roberts & Todd, LLC.

BOX 8.1   In Practice (continued)

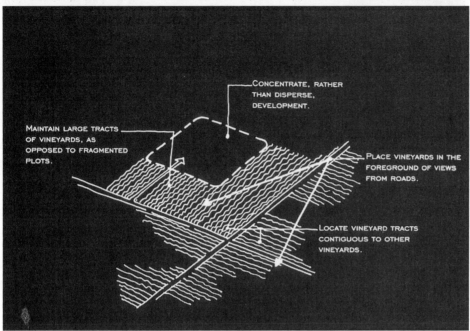

Figure 8-25 Site development design guidelines for a future commercial site. Source: Wallace Roberts & Todd, LLC.

BOX 8.1   In Practice (continued)

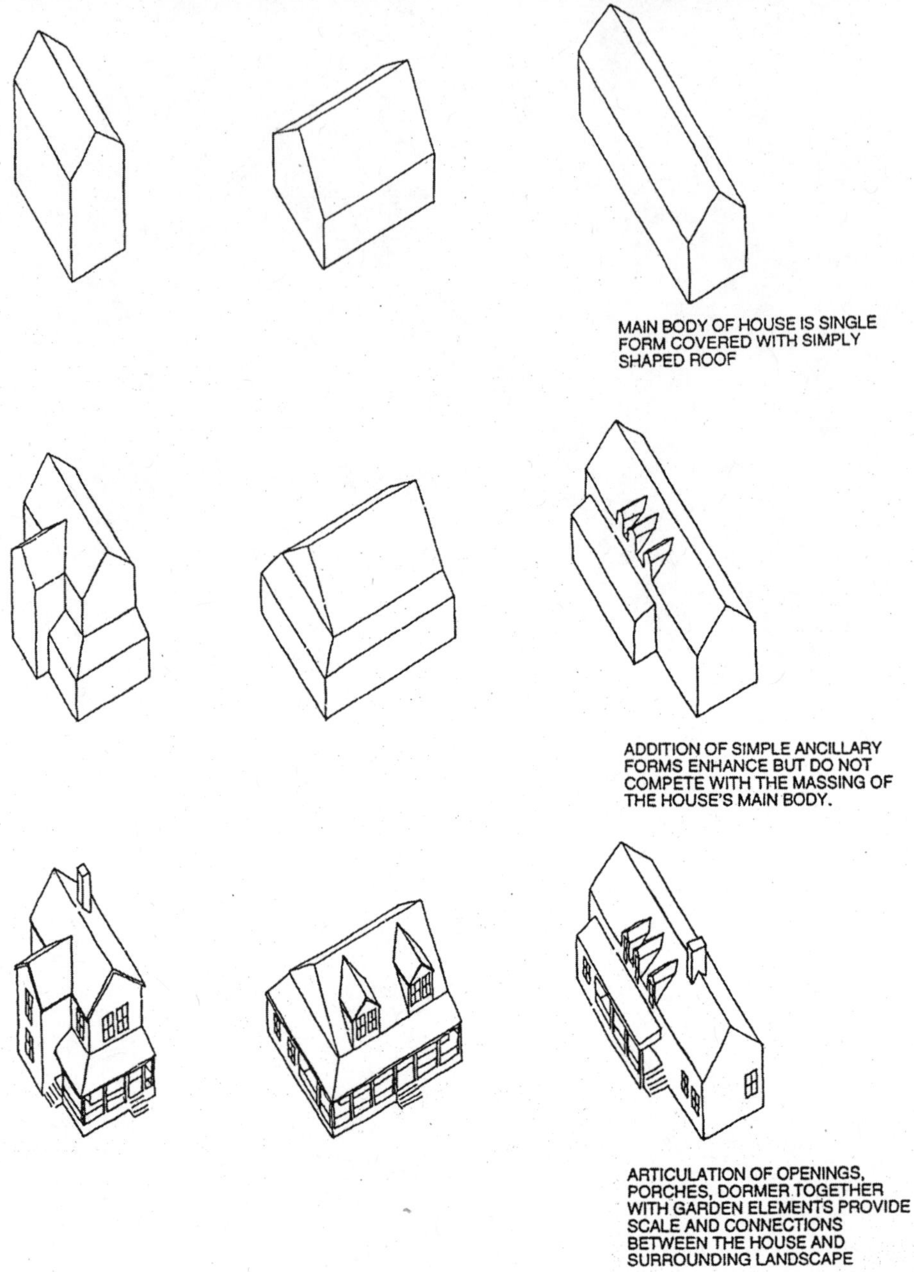

MAIN BODY OF HOUSE IS SINGLE
FORM COVERED WITH SIMPLY
SHAPED ROOF

ADDITION OF SIMPLE ANCILLARY
FORMS ENHANCE BUT DO NOT
COMPETE WITH THE MASSING OF
THE HOUSE'S MAIN BODY.

ARTICULATION OF OPENINGS,
PORCHES, DORMER TOGETHER
WITH GARDEN ELEMENTS PROVIDE
SCALE AND CONNECTIONS
BETWEEN THE HOUSE AND
SURROUNDING LANDSCAPE

Figure 8-26   Design guidelines and illustrations showing examples of desired building massing and façade articulation. Source: Wallace Roberts & Todd, LLC, with Turnbull Griffin Haesloop Architects.

BOX 8.1   In Practice (continued)

Figure 8-27 Completed homes designed to conform with the plan's guidelines for architectural massing and facade articulation. Source: Wallace Roberts & Todd, LLC, with Turnbull Griffin Haesloop Architects.

BOX 8.1 In Practice (continued)

2. *Incentives.* The plan creates a density bonus to encourage compact development, while protecting and enhancing the valley's agricultural activities. One new residential unit is allowed for each 100 acres (40 hectares), but four additional residential units are allowed if 90 percent of the 100 acres is legally protected in perpetuity (with agricultural easements), and these 90 acres (36 hectares) are planted with orchards or vineyards. Unlike many other agricultural uses, orchards and vineyards are economically viable in smaller areas.

3. *Implementation.* A nonprofit land trust, funded through development fees ($10,000 per unit), manages the agricultural easements required by the plan. The land trust also buys additional easements to help achieve the plan's agricultural preservation goals.

Design Features

The plan limits the visual impact of new development on the valley's rural, agricultural character. The plan also maximizes open space amenities, including an extensive hiking trail network, which has benefited tourists as well as residents. Standards and guidelines require that development patterns, details, and materials enhance the valley's historic wine country character (Figure 8-26). This is accomplished through the development of narrow, tree-lined streets with drainage swales (rather than curbs and gutters), short blocks, and traditional architectural styles (Figure 8-27).

Successful Implementation

Productive agricultural open space has become the defining characteristic for the new neighborhood's in South Livermore Valley. The community's development mitigation program not only requires conservation easements to protect agricultural land but also requires planting of the agricultural acreage and bonding for eight years to ensure that crops are established and maintained.

The South Livermore Valley Specific Plan received the 2006 National Outstanding Award for Implementation from the American Planning Association (APA).

part IV

Design and Implementation

This final section of the book has three chapters that focus on the form-giving phases of the site planning process. Chapter 9, Conceptual Design, concerns the spatial organization of basic project components, which are open space, circulation systems, and building "pods" or "envelopes." Chapter 10, Design Development, addresses the articulation—or more detailed design—of these project components. Chapter 11, Project Implementation, concludes the book with an overview of the construction documentation process and the roles that communities play in reviewing site development proposals.

c h a p t e r 9

Conceptual Design

"Make no little plans; they have no magic to stir men's blood and probably themselves will not be realized. Make big plans; aim high in hope and work, remembering that a noble, logical diagram once recorded will never die, but long after we are gone will be a living thing, asserting itself with ever-growing consistency."

— Daniel H. Burnham (1893)

9.1 INTRODUCTION

Designing better communities requires *vision*—for what the future could be. "Smart growth," "new urbanism," and "sustainable design" are three related planning paradigms for building better communities. These paradigms pay close attention to the physical configuration of the built environment. Moreover, they strive to improve upon the development patterns established during the last half of the twentieth century. The suburban sprawl of recent decades has not only degraded environmental quality in the United States, but it also has produced pedestrian-unfriendly communities that contribute to obesity and diminished public health (Frumkin, Frank, and Jackson, 2004). Communities aspiring to become more sustainable—and livable—are taking steps to attain the following attributes:

- Open space systems that protect site natural resources and provide recreational opportunities.

- Site and architectural designs that enrich public open spaces, especially streetscapes, and create neighborhoods with a clear sense of identity.

- Mixed and integrated uses (i.e., housing, shops, workplaces, schools, parks, and civic facilities) with a diversity of housing types and prices.

- A center that combines commercial, civic, and cultural uses, including other compact development to minimize infrastructure costs and limit environmental impacts.

- Multimodal transportation systems (i.e., pedestrian, bicycle, transit, automobiles).

Sources: Daniels, 1999, Western Australian Planning Commission, 2000, Barnett, 2003.

Public policy decisions to protect open space and develop multimodal transportation systems involve coordination on a community-wide, and even regional, scale. Yet, these efforts must be coupled with sustainable development at the site, or parcel, level. Site scale development—usually on privately owned property—is the primary way in which communities change, for better or worse.

9.2 CONTEXT-SENSITIVE DESIGN

Sustainable, context-responsive site planning has three fundamental precepts:

- Design with nature

- Design with culture

- Design places for people

These general precepts give rise to a more explicit set of principles for physical planning at the site scale. Many of these "best practices" are explained in this chapter, and in Chapters 10 and 11.

Responsiveness to site and contextual conditions demands consideration of a diverse set of physical attributes and regulatory constraints. These location-specific conditions include the following:

- Sun and wind exposure

- Lot size and shape

- Location in relation to transportation systems (for example, corner of prominent intersection)

- Significant vegetation, topography, and other natural features

- Prominent vistas and views of natural or cultural landmarks

- Building scale and character

Conceptual design in site planning follows—and flows directly from—the site inventory and analysis. Analysis of the site and its context typically reveal biophysical and cultural features that limit the number of feasible design configurations. Sites that have few, if any, significant biophysical or cultural features are often the most challenging to design. The absence of significant site features or constraints allows for a much wider range of feasible options for organizing activities and structures on the site. The lack of site character also makes it more challenging to create a unique sense of place.

Conversely, sites with significant natural or cultural features have the greatest potential to inspire context-sensitive plans that "fit" the site. A site with a large, picturesque specimen tree, for example, limits options for site use to locations that will not result in damage to the tree (see Figure 8-3). Another example is a stream on the site that restricts building options to higher elevations that are not prone to flooding and, if developed, not likely to degrade the stream's aquatic and riparian habitats. In both of these scenarios, "designing with nature" results in context-sensitive site plans that incorporate—rather than destroy—significant natural amenities.

9.3   DESIGN DETERMINANTS

Significant site and contextual conditions are design determinants that shape, or inform, the development of sustainable site plans. Design determinants include on-site (intrinsic) and off-site (extrinsic) factors. A thorough site and contextual analysis will identify important design or form determinants for any given project. Design determinants provide the basis, or rationale, for organizing and articulating the program on the site.

9.3.1   Program and Preferences

Obviously, the project's objectives—or program—plays an obvious role in determining how a site is designed. Typically, the client's preferences determine the type and extent of planned activities on the site (see Chapter 4). These activities range from private-sector real estate development to public-sector nature conservation and restoration. Depending on the type of project, the client may even have preferences regarding design style, theme, or character. In some projects, the future users of the site may play a significant role in influencing the design of the site. This is particularly common with public sector projects, such as parks, libraries, and schools.

9.3.2   On-Site Form Determinants

Design determinants include intrinsic site features that are retained, undisturbed, in the site plan. A steep, wooded slope or other natural or cultural feature lends character to the site and contributes to the site's unique sense of place. These elements can be viewed as development constraints that, if disturbed, would have negative environmental or community impacts. Yet these site features also create opportunities to incorporate natural or cultural amenities into the site plan. These amenities can add significant value to real estate (Bookout, 1994).

Important on-site form determinants include the following:

□ Physical conditions (for example, natural features such as drainageways, significant habitats, and steep slopes; cultural features; microclimatic factors, such as wind and solar access; site size and shape)

□ Regulations and standards (for example, zoning codes, building codes, land development codes, and design guidelines)

The site's boundary—or interface with off-site properties or public infrastructure—is a particularly important site planning consideration. The periphery or edge of the site is particularly meaningful when the site is small or linear in shape. The movement of water and wildlife typically transcend the site boundaries of most land development projects. Ecological linkages between the site and the surrounding landscape can be maintained—and strengthened—through undeveloped open spaces or conservation areas. These open spaces not only have significant ecological value but also can provide recreational and educational opportunities, in addition to visual amenity value.

9.3.3 Off-Site Form Determinants

Off-site features often influence the location and organization of program elements on the site. The number and location of entrances to the site, for example, are determined, in part, by the physical conditions just beyond the site's boundaries. Adjacent streets or transit stops suggest preferred locations for providing access to the site. Land development regulations also routinely affect the design of site entrances. Local development regulations commonly limit the number of entrances, or "curb cuts," to a site and impose a minimum distance requirement between site entrances and nearby street intersections.

Potential conflicts might exist between on-site and off-site uses or features, and these must be reconciled at the conceptual design phase. Off-site conditions can include nuisances, such as a busy highway, that impact the site with noise, odors, and undesirable views. When conflicts do exist, the arrangement of program activities or uses must try to mitigate those conflicts. Uses that are less sensitive to negative impacts can be sited closer than other, more sensitive, uses. Screening also may be needed, and this function can be shown diagrammatically on the concept plan. The selection of screening materials—which may include walls, fences, berms, and/or vegetation—occurs later, however, in the design development process.

Other design determinants include off-site features such as a prominent, iconic building. A state or provincial capitol building, a church or cathedral, or even a well-designed school or library could be a local landmark that influences the design of nearby buildings and sites. Other off-site form determinants include the following:

□ Neighborhood, community, and regional character. (For example, building styles or materials that may be "echoed" in new buildings or site designs.)

□ Nearby buildings and infrastructure. (For example, sites at the intersection of two major streets or on a visible hilltop demand special design treatment; an off-site landmark may influence the placement of circulation pathways—on-axis with the landmark; or the siting of a building to give it a prominent view of the landmark.)

The Capitol District in Washington D.C., for example, is replete with historic buildings and national monuments that are strategically located in a highly organized geometric configuration (Newton, 1971). L'Enfant's eighteenth-century plan for the nation's capital established axial relationships between prominent landmarks, creating interlocking shafts of space that to this day form a visibly cohesive and unique urban milieu. The "shaft of space," visually linking prominent elements within the built environment, is a classic ordering or organizational device in urban design (Bacon, 1974, p.70–71). In *Design of Cities*, Edmund Bacon does a masterful job of explaining the historic use of this technique in context-sensitive urban design.

9.3.4 Design Theory

Design theory is a set of guiding principles and strategies for making design decisions. In site planning, design theory encompasses the decision making process (for example, conduct the site analysis before embarking on conceptual design). Design theory also encompasses assorted "rules of thumb" for organizing program components on any given site, and for articulating those components through more detailed design. These design principles are based on a continually evolving body of knowledge informed by history, the arts, and the sciences. The successful application of design theory, in site planning, requires creativity—which, fortunately, can be nurtured through education and experience.

9.4 CREATIVITY AND CONCEPTUAL DESIGN

Problem solving is an important part of the site planning process. Site selection, for example, is largely an optimization problem aimed at finding an available site that can best satisfy the project objectives. Once a site is selected, identifying its constraints and opportunities is an effort to understand the "puzzle" that the site poses for the program under consideration. Solutions to this puzzle are sought during the conceptual design phase and, in more detail, through subsequent design development and construction documentation. Donald Schoen, in *Educating the Reflective Practitioner*, writes (1987, p.42):

Designers juggle variables, reconcile conflicting values, and maneuver around constraints—a process in which, although some design products may be superior to others, there are no unique, right answers.

An acceptable site plan is not only one that best meets the project objectives—as defined by the client, of course, but also by the community in which the site is located. Community goals—expressed in various ways including comprehensive plans, zoning codes, and development review standards—generally seek to promote public health, safety, and welfare.

Creative problem solving, as summarized by Kvashney (1982, p. 107), involves the pursuit of five things: facts, problems, ideas, solutions, and acceptance (of the solutions). Each of these is evident in the site planning and design process. The programming and site inventory phases, for example, involve fact finding. The site analysis utilizes these facts to assess the site's suitability for a specific program or set of objectives. This assessment identifies "problems" (constraints) and "ideas" (opportunities). Conceptual design and subsequent design development generate "solutions" that seek to avoid or, in some cases, overcome the site's constraints and capitalize on the site's opportunities. These solutions are communicated, evaluated, and—if approved by the client and other key stakeholders—implemented.

Site planning, therefore, involves judgments of relevance (for example, what site attribute data to collect) and of spatial relationships (for example, how would a site attribute affect a potential program activity). Site planning also involves acts of creating, including arranging and articulating project components (for example, different land uses), and assessing the implications of those decisions (for example, determining how a particular arrangement will affect society, economy, or the environment in the future).

Site planning excellence can make significant contributions to the development of sustainable built environments. However, there are significant consequences for poor site planning. These impacts range from exposing people to life and property risks to making people endure inconvenience and visually unattractive surroundings. Protecting public health, safety, and welfare is the primary reason for licensing professional landscape architects, architects, and engineers.

Good design, according to Richard Seymour (Lawson, 2004), results from "the unexpectedly relevant solution, not wackiness parading as originality." In *How Designers Think*, Brian Lawson (2006, p.153) elaborates on the important distinction in design between "originality" and "creativity," as follows:

> In the competitive and sometimes rather commercial world of design, the novel and startlingly different can sometimes stand out and be acclaimed purely for that reason. But being creative in design is not purely or even necessarily a matter of being original.

Robert Venturi, the noted architect, echoes this sentiment by commenting that, for a designer, "it is better to be good than to be original" (Lawson, 2004).

Creative designers find appropriate—and sometimes elegant—solutions to design challenges. Donald Schoen, writes (1987, p.41):

> Designing in its broader sense involves complexity and synthesis. In contrast to analysts or critics, designers put things together and bring new things into being, dealing in the process with many variables and constraints, some initially known and some discovered through designing.

The ability to create appropriate design solutions can be nurtured through education and training. One of the best ways to becoming more creative and increase one's capacity to design well is to build one's "design vocabulary."

A comprehensive knowledge of good design—its principles and varied forms of expression—can be acquired by analyzing relevant precedents. Design precedents may be real or imagined places, including natural and built environments. Precedent studies, ranging from formal post-occupancy evaluations to brief, informal meanderings through a foreign city, examine the ways that designers create places for specific purposes and in response to site and contextual conditions. Examples of great design—as well as design failures—yield valuable lessons that strengthen the designer's "tool kit" and capacity to arrive at creative and appropriate design solutions. Kneller (1965) writes:

> One of the paradoxes of creativity is that . . . we must familiarize ourselves with the ideas of others. These ideas can then form a springboard from which the creator's ideas can be launched.

Many good designers, even seasoned practitioners, are "students of design." They are inquisitive observers of the built environment, continually assessing what works and what does not work—and mentally filing that information away for future reference. Hertzberger (1991) comments on this phenomenon:

> Everything that is absorbed and registered in your mind adds to the collection of ideas stored in the memory: a sort of library that you can consult whenever a problem arises. So—essentially—the more you have seen, experienced, and absorbed, the more points of reference you will have to help you decide which direction to take: your frame of reference expands.

9.5   THE CONCEPTUAL DESIGN PROCESS

The conceptual design process is the time to explore, evaluate, and compare. Adaptation and revision, therefore, are an inherent part of fitting the program to the site. Exploring alternative concepts—or spatial configurations—does not require a substantial time investment. Yet, this can pay substantial dividends by improving the quality of the final site plan, which—ultimately—impacts the character, livability, and sustainability of the built environment.

To skip the conceptual design phase is to omit a crucial step in the site planning process. There are two important reasons to design conceptually before advancing to more detailed site design. First, conceptual design can be done more quickly than detailed design. Second, conceptual design is effective, even at small scales of representation (i.e., plans or maps). The proverbial "back of the envelope" diagram is feasible at the conceptual level because conceptual design is concerned with the "big picture." In site planning, this means organizing or spatially arranging, on the site, the project's major components. Once the program and the site's context are well understood, multiple concept plans can be—and should be—developed *before* proceeding to more detailed design.

Figure 9-1 Conceptual design considers program, community goals, and site and contextual conditions.

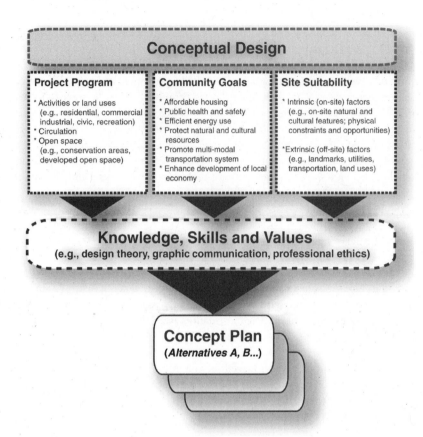

The conceptual design phase can be an exhilarating time in the site planning process. It is at this stage when the designer seeks an organizing structure for the program that respects the site's natural and cultural features and provides the spatial framework for subsequent site and architectural design (Figure 9-1).

Site design typically occurs in incremental steps, beginning with the general organizational decisions concerning what goes where on the site (i.e., conceptual design). The resulting organizing framework or pattern brings order in a coherent, functional way. Clearly organizing the built environment promotes orientation, or way finding, and helps to provide a strong sense of place. In addition to accommodating the project's program (i.e., uses and densities), the plan must also conform to the community's goals and development standards. The design process then proceeds to the more specific or detailed articulation decisions. This may not be the only way to approach the design, but it is an efficient, effective, and repeatable approach.

Conceptual design activities vary, somewhat, depending on the site and program. The process shown below is a synthesis of approaches, including the process advocated by Ian McHarg (1969) in his classic work, *Design with Nature*. This land planning approach is particularly appropriate for relatively large sites with significant natural or cultural resources.

Step 1: Delineate primary and secondary conservation areas.

Development projects on large sites are more likely to devote a substantial proportion of the site to open space. This is especially true if the site includes significant environmental features such as wooded areas, steep slopes, or a stream or wetland. Randall Arendt (1999, p. 75–77), in *Growing Greener: Putting Conservation into Local Plans and Ordinances*, suggests three basic objectives in designating these open spaces:

☐ Conservation areas should include the property's most sensitive resource areas

☐ Fragmentation of conservation areas into smaller, non-contiguous parcels should be minimized

☐ Conservation areas on a property should be linked, ideally, to community and regional open space systems

Conversely, site planning projects on smaller, urban sites may have little or no conservation open space. Redevelopment projects, especially, tend to be more site-intensive. Nevertheless, these sites still may be designed to include open space for outdoor recreation, stormwater management, or other important site functions.

Step 2: In the remaining site areas, delineate the locations that are suitable for development. These areas are where the project's program elements (i.e., buildings and associated infrastructure, as well as additional developed open space) will be located.

Step 3: Within the areas suitable for development, delineate the development "pods," considering their accessibility.

Attention must be paid to the sizes and shapes of the developable "pods" or envelopes. The activities or uses that will be accommodated within the buildings will dictate, to some extent, the minimum and maximum dimensions of these pods. Each pod should accommodate not only the anticipated building footprint but also the spaces required for pedestrian access and amenities, vehicle parking and building services, and associated "hard" and "soft" landscaped areas.

Step 4: Locate the primary and secondary circulation systems, considering the sizes and shapes of the remaining developable areas.

Circulation systems, as well as open space systems, are key site elements that can help organize the other program elements.

The concept plan explains the intended functional relationships among the site and project components. The plan may be supplemented with a concept statement that is a brief, written articulation of the design intent of the proposed concept plan. Character sketches, or image boards with photographs, may also convey the design concept—before proceeding with detailed site design.

9.6 ANATOMY OF A CONCEPT PLAN

Concept plans depict the spatial framework for subsequent detailed design. Conceptual site plans typically show three major site components: open spaces (both conservation areas and developed open spaces), circulation systems, and building pods or "envelopes." The scale of the concept plan determines the amount of detail that can be shown effectively. The plan's scale is usually a function of the size of the area being considered.

A conceptual land use plan for a 2,000-acre (809-hectare) site, for example, might show only general land use categories, such as residential, commercial, and recreational uses. Or, within the residential category, the plan might identify areas where certain housing densities will be located. These densities are typically expressed as dwelling units per area (acres or hectares). The concept plan for a project of this size might be drawn at a scale of 1:4800 (1 inch = 400 feet) or smaller.

In contrast, a concept plan for a 10-acre (4-hectare) site might provide much more detailed information about the proposed development. It could, for example, show the preferred locations for buildings and building entrances. This concept plan might be drawn at a scale of 1:480 (1 inch = 40 feet).

9.6.1 Open Space

Nature's Infrastructure

Open spaces help ecosystems maintain their structure and function. Natural landscape corridors, for example, accommodate several important ecological functions (Dramstad et al., 1996, p. 35–40), as follows:

- Habitat (for upland species and refuge for floodplain species displaced by flooding or lateral channel migration)

- Conduit (for individual upland animals)

- Filter (remove dissolved-substance inputs from overland stormwater runoff)

- Source (food and cover)

- Sink (during flooding, absorb floodwaters and trap sediment)

Protecting natural drainage corridors and other key areas can minimize a development's hydrologic and ecological impacts (Forman, 1995; Dramstad et al., 1996). A site's hydrologic infrastructure includes streams and their buffers, floodplains, wetlands, steep slopes, high-permeability soils, and woodlands (Prince George's County, 2000). To prevent the degradation of this important "green" infrastructure, buildings and circulation systems should not be sited in these areas. Undeveloped open spaces can also buffer developed areas from natural hazards, such as floods and landslides. These buffer zones are especially important in coastal areas where flooding from storm surges threaten both life and property (Figure 9-2).

Open space in the built environment serves many important functions (Table 9-1). Both natural and developed open spaces add aesthetic amenity, provide opportunities for outdoor recreation, and stimulate local economic development (Box 9-1). Trees, water, and other natural features are important to a community's identity and quality of life.

Figure 9-2 Coastal dune vegetation controls erosion and stabilizes protective dunes in Florida (United States).

Natural areas—both large tracts and linking corridors—can be integral elements of a community's open space infrastructure (Figure 9-3). A comprehensive, community open space system should protect the most valuable— and vulnerable—landscape components (Ahern, 1991; Stenberg et al., 1997). These typically include the following:

TABLE 9-1 Examples of beneficial functions of conservation open space.

Components	Functions or Benefits
Water	Outdoor recreation Visual amenity Aquatic and riparian habitat
Wetland	Groundwater recharge Flooding mitigation Plant and wildlife habitat
Forest	Microclimate amelioration Wildlife habitat Visual amenity
Steep slopes	Aquifer recharge Plant and wildlife habitat Visual amenity

Figure 9-3 Seasonal flooding along the Mississippi River in Minnesota (United States).

- □ Surface waters

- □ Wetlands

- □ Steep slopes

- □ Highly erodible or unstable soils

- □ Forested or wooded areas

- □ Floodplains and coastal zones subject to storm surge

Not every important natural area can be in public ownership. This is economically infeasible at the community or regional scales. Nevertheless, sustainable approaches to development on private property can protect and enhance these valuable natural resources.

Open space networks can provide the spatial structure around which buildings and circulation systems are organized. Development that integrates open space is a feature common to many master planned residential communities. Conservation subdivisions, for example, typically reserve at least half of the site in undeveloped open space. Arendt (1999, p.12) recommends that 60 to 70 percent of conservation subdivisions remain as open space in unsewered rural areas where significant portions of the site must be dedicated to "leach fields" for the absorption of wastewater effluent. In areas with sanitary sewer service, dedicated open space may be reduced to 40 to 50 percent of the site.

Managing stormwater on-site helps reduce construction costs associated with conventional stormwater drainage infrastructure. Bioinfiltration areas within the site's open space promote stormwater infiltration and groundwater recharge. Prairie Crossing, outside of Chicago, Illinois, is an award-winning residential community whose spatial organization revolves around open space—and the stormwater management that occurs within that open space (www.prairiecrossing.com). Another project designed around water is the Indian Trace project, in Florida, designed by Environmental Planning and Design (EPD) (Box 9-2).

Developed Open Space

Developed open spaces may be paved or unpaved "green" areas that are designed for pedestrians, and typically used for commercial, civic, or recreational purposes (Figure 9-4). At the conceptual design phase, detailed open space design is premature. However, the tentative locations of formal and informal open spaces can be established at this stage of the design process. Well-designed open space often has a strong sense of enclosure, which is commonly the result of carefully placed buildings, walls, or other vertical elements (Figure 9-5).

Open space is the central feature of contemporary "links-style" golf course communities. The most visually appealing golf courses, which also "fit" well into the landscape, utilize natural drainage patterns as golf course hazards. Where the natural drainage patterns and vegetative cover have been disturbed, restoration may not only reestablish hydrologic function but also enhance the area's visual quality. This environmentally responsive approach to golf course architecture also reduces the course's construction and long-term maintenance costs, and protects existing plant and animal habitats. This context-sensitive design approach also creates memorable playing experiences for golfers.

Figure 9-4 Major linear urban space with strong spatial enclosure from bordering trees in Paris, France.

Figure 9-5 Large urban plaza serving as the city's central civic space in Toulouse, France.

9.6.2 Circulation Systems

Circulation systems are the infrastructure that provides access to and from the site, as well as mobility on the site. Integrated transportation solutions create more options for mobility by vehicles, pedestrians, bicyclists, and users of public transit. According to the U.S. Federal Highway Administration (FHWA), context-sensitive transportation planning, seeks to develop a transportation network "... that complements its physical setting and preserves scenic, aesthetic, and historic and environmental resources while maintaining safety and mobility."- Providing viable transportation alternatives within pedestrian-friendly, mixed-use neighborhoods, for example, can help reduce traffic congestion within the broader community, as well as air pollution associated vehicle miles traveled (VMT).

Organizing a site's circulation systems requires an understanding of the site's context—specifically, the existing circulation systems serving the site. The entry and arrival sequences to destinations on the site must begin at one or more points of access to the site's periphery. Entrances to the site, or to buildings and major pedestrian walkway intersections, are places where plazas or seating areas may be developed. These nodes warrant special design treatment, including special paving, lighting, planting, and furniture.

Other design objectives related to circulation include establishing gateways and creating a strong sense of arrival. The entrance driveway to a new building might be located, for example, "on-axis" with the proposed building or some other significant on-site or off-site feature. The "visual anchor" for the axis, an imaginary line, could be a large specimen tree, a hill, prominent landform, or some other visually interesting feature.

Circulation systems, especially for pedestrian use, are often organized in one or more geometric patterns or configurations, as follows:

□ Linear pattern. [Walkway systems are commonly used for recreational corridors; may parallel natural features such as streams, rivers, or oceanfront (Figure 9-6); can be curvilinear, zigzag, or straight linear patterns.]

□ Grid pattern. (Walkways parallel street network in urban areas; advantages include ease of orientation and flexibility in route selection.)

□ Loop pattern. (Walkway may connect and organize a series of open spaces, a cluster of buildings, or other activity nodes.)

□ Radial pattern (Walkways converge to form intersections that can be designed as plazas, squares, or other important pedestrian nodes.)

□ Spiral pattern (Walkway is appropriate for ceremonial processions that descend or ascend toward a special destination; common in sculpture gardens, memorials, and other contemplative outdoor spaces.)

Utility systems are also important components of a site's infrastructure. These systems physically connect individual buildings with off-site utility systems and facilities. Typically, major utility lines are located within streets' rights-of-ways or within other circulation

system corridors. Many of these systems require extensive underground networks of pipes and associated structures.

After implementation, most site development projects require continuing inputs of resources, such as potable water and electricity. These inputs may be delivered to the site through the utility infrastructure. Other utility linkages may include gas, electric, telephone, and television cable. Development projects also generate continuing outputs, such as sanitary waste which is either treated on-site or collected at an off-site treatment facility. The site's utility systems are not commonly shown on the concept plan, unless the site is particularly small and the concept plan is relatively large in scale.

9.6.3   Building Envelopes or Pods

The site analysis may identify locations that are suitable for development or, more specifically, building construction. These locations may be one or more distinct zones, "pods," or "envelopes." A development pod for a single building may be large enough to accommodate the building along with sufficient space for parking, service areas, and landscaped pedestrian areas associated with the building.

Open space networks are the "green infrastructure" that protects the structure and function of the natural environment. These open spaces may also serve as amenities for buildings that are clustered on the remaining parts of the site. Clustering reduces a development's impervious cover and lowers construction costs for streets, utilities, and other infrastructure. Clustering can also minimize site disturbance and, if the buildings is carefully sited, preserve natural drainage networks and other natural or cultural features.

Figure 9-7 Building "steps back" from the street, reducing its scale at the street level, while improving solar access and creating useable outdoor terrace space for each residential unit in Zurich, Switzerland.

The construction and operation of buildings consumes substantial amounts of energy, water, and materials. Building siting can have a significant effect on the building's design and operation. Energy use for cooling, heating, and lighting, for example, is not only influenced by the building's design, of course, but also by its location and orientation on the site (Figure 9-7). Seasonal wind direction and velocity and solar exposure are climatic factors that should be considered when siting building pods. In the northern hemisphere, south-facing slopes, for example, may be ideal locations for solar buildings.

Many notable examples of architectural design receive recognition because the buildings are superbly designed in response to the conditions of their sites. Exceptional works of architecture achieve compatibility with the site and context in simple, yet often, elegant ways. Frank Lloyd Wright's Falling Water is a building that fits its site well, and the building's form actually mimics the cascading form of the site's streambed (see www .paconserve.org/index-fw1.asp). Another example of site-driven architecture is the collaboration of Robert Venturi and Lawrence Halprin on the Sea Ranch project in California (see www.greatbuildings.com/buildings/Sea_Ranch_Condominium.html). The windblown conditions of the northern California coastal landscape were major design determinants. The project's outdoor spaces, as well as the arrangement of buildings, vegetation, and berms, were all influenced by concern for the local microclimate.

9.7 CONCEPT PLAN GRAPHICS

The concept plan is a relatively simple diagram that shows how a project's major program elements relate to each other functionally and, potentially, visually. Concept plans often provide contextual information about the site's biophysical and cultural features—or design determinants—that will be integrated into the development or redevelopment project (Figure 9-8).

Concept plans are spatially explicit, which simply means that the project's components are shown approximately where they are to be located on the site. Information regarding the dimensions of streets, buildings, or other site elements—as well as the types of materials needed to build these structures—is not typically conveyed on the concept plan. These more detailed design decisions occur during the subsequent design development and construction documentation phases.

A basic principle of effective diagramming is to exclude noncritical or extraneous information (Monmonier, 1996). A city subway map, for example, is useful because of what

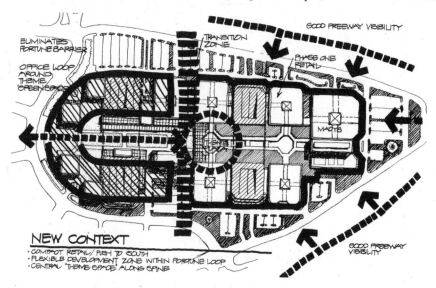

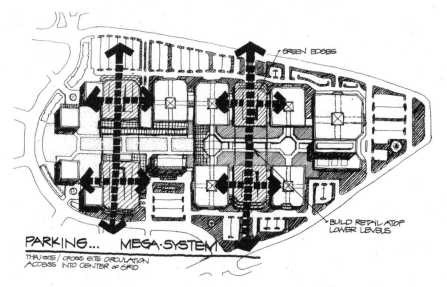

Figure 9-8 Concept diagrams showing proposed uses and important spatial relationships. The central axis for this development project is a bold and effective organizing element. Source: The HOK Planning Group.

Figure 9-8   (continued)

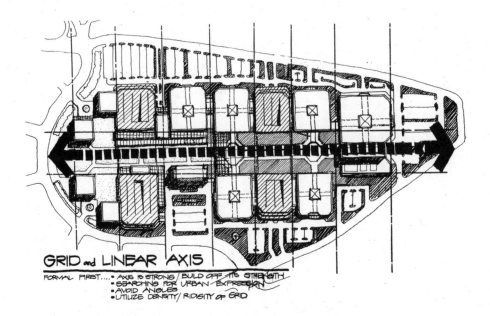

GRID and LINEAR AXIS

FORMAL FIRST.... • AXIS IS STRONG / BUILD OFF ITS STRENGTH
• SEARCHING FOR URBAN EXPRESSION
• AVOID ANGLES
• UTILIZE DENSITY / RIDIGITY of GRID

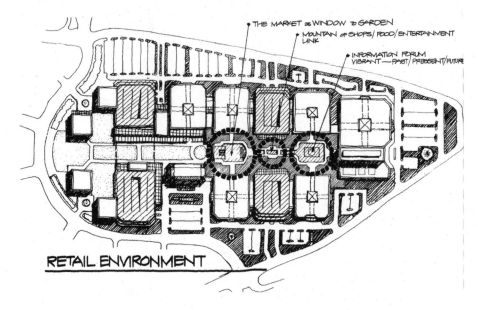

• THE MARKET as WINDOW to GARDEN

MOUNTAIN of SHOPS / FOOD / ENTERTAINMENT LINK

• INFORMATION FORUM
VIBRANT — PAST / PRESENT / FUTURE

RETAIL ENVIRONMENT

TABLE 9-2 Examples of proposed and existing elements that may be conveyed graphically on a conceptual site plan.

Categories	Specific Components
Open space	Active recreation areas
	Passive recreation areas
	Conservation areas
Vehicle circulation	Streets and site entrances
	Passenger drop-off zones
	Parking areas
	Loading docks and service areas
Pedestrian circulation	Walkways
	Site and building entrances
	Plazas, patios, and other nodes
	Street crosswalks
Other circulation	Bikeways
	Public transit stations or stops
Buildings	Various uses
Utilities	Easements for pipes or lines
	Sanitary lift stations
Views	Prominent views from the site
	Prominent views to the site

the map leaves out, as well as what the map includes. The locations of buildings, highways, or a myriad of other geographic information are not included on a subway map for a simple reason—it would diminish the map's clarity and, therefore, effectiveness as a guide to subways riders.

Concept plans convey information graphically with text and, typically, three basic geometric objects: polygons, lines, and points (Table 9-2). Notes, or annotations, are also useful in conveying information about the intended functional and visual relationships among the proposed site uses. Effective graphic communication enables the efficient review of concept plans by colleagues as well as by public planning staff, elected officials, and other stakeholders.

9.7.1 Zones

On a concept plan, major uses of the site are typically portrayed diagrammatically as zones or "bubbles." As the concept plan is refined, these activity or land use zones may be further subdivided to show building locations and minor circulation patterns. As the planning process moves further into the design development phase, these zones or development "pods" are then subdivided into smaller areas and eventually each area is designed in detail

Figure 9-9 Refining a concept plan involves subdividing initial "bubbles" or zones into smaller, more detailed components.

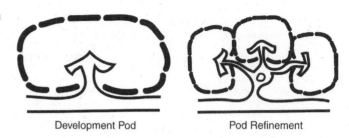

Development Pod   Pod Refinement

(Figure 9-9). In addition to showing the locations of proposed development zones, concept plans show the open spaces that will not be developed.

9.7.2   Paths and Edges

Proposed activities on a site may relate to each other both functionally and visually. Desired views between locations on the site, or between locations on and off the site, for example, can be depicted graphically with arrows and/or annotated labels. Conversely, screening of undesirable views may be warranted, and this also can be portrayed graphically. Linear elements on a concept plan may represent the following:

- Axial relationships
- Circulation systems (for example, pedestrian, bicycle, and vehicles)
- Stormwater drainage patterns
- Utility lines (above ground and subsurface)
- Views (favorable and unfavorable)
- Edges (for example, abrupt changes in topography)

Color, texture, and line weight help to distinguish these disparate types of site information.

9.7.3   Nodes and Landmarks

The concept plan also may identify nodes and landmarks. These may be locations of either proposed buildings or other site features, or significant existing buildings that will remain on or off site. Nodes may be highlighted graphically and typically include the following:

- Entrances to the site or buildings
- Intersections of pedestrian and vehicle circulation systems
- Scenic high points or scenic overlooks

Landmarks include the following:

- □ Specimen trees

- □ Bridges

- □ Unique buildings

- □ Hilltops or other topographic features

Sections and Other Graphics

On some projects, especially urban projects, the vertical organization of a project's uses is expressed at the conceptual design phase. Conceptual sections or aerial perspectives may be used to explain the type and arrangement of uses within buildings and in nearby areas outside of the building (see Figure 9-15 later in this chapter). Concept plans also may be supplemented with image boards—an organized set of photographs or sketches that convey the desired "character" of the proposed development or redevelopment. Typically, these are photographs of comparable projects or precedents. A project's "character" results, in part, from building massing, scale, and placement. It also stems from the choices of forms and materials and how they are combined (i.e., design style).

9.8   CONCEPT EVALUATION AND REFINEMENT

As communities and regions increase in population, undeveloped sites become increasingly important ecologically and hydrologically. Concern for environmental quality and community sustainability is leading to greater scrutiny, by local governments and citizens, of the potential development impacts.

The design review process at local levels of government examines the potential negative impacts of proposed development projects on public health, safety, and welfare. Some of the questions posed by planning department staff who review site plans include the following (Wyckoff, 2003, pp. 61–64):

- □ Is the proposed use of the site consistent with the existing zoning classification of the parcel?

- □ Have any risks of natural hazards from flooding, erosion, slumping of steep slopes or sandy soils, subsidence or other natural event been adequately considered?

- □ Are the proposed locations of structures and uses relative to wetlands, groundwater recharge areas, and floodplains adequate?

- □ Would any endangered plant or animal habitat be affected?

- □ Have any significant views and/or unique natural features been adequately considered?

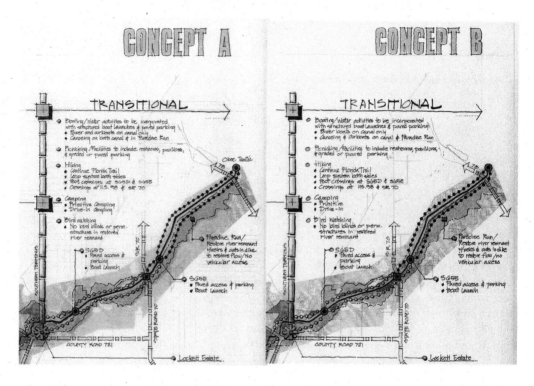

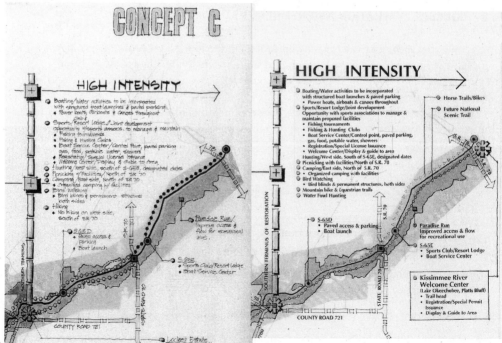

Figure 9-10 Kissimmee River restoration concept plan alternatives and the final plan for a segment of the river corridor. Source: Edward D. Stone, Jr., and Associates.

☐ Does the proposed plan minimize negative impacts (especially noise, dust, odor, light, vibrations) on adjoining land uses?

These are among the many questions that site planners should ask themselves during the conceptual design phase—prior to external regulatory reviews. The strengths and weaknesses of alternative concepts should be systematically evaluated using these or other similar questions. Descriptive statistics that compare existing site conditions with the proposed site conditions can be helpful in evaluating the merits of a conceptual site plan. The systematic comparison of alternative concepts can also expedite the process of developing a final site plan that combines the best features of each concept alternative (Figure 9-10).

9.9 CONCLUSION

Conceptual design is an iterative process involving the spatial organization of the project's basic components. More detailed design comes afterward. Many possible alternatives exist for arranging programmed activities or uses on a site. The complexity of this task can be reduced by careful analysis of existing site and contextual conditions. Design determinants—revealed through the site analysis—often suggest the spatial framework for fitting the program to the site. A systematic and analytical approach to conceptual design is capable of producing defensible site planning decisions and, ultimately, higher-quality built environments.

BOX 9.1   In Practice—Greenway Planning

CHOUTEAU GREENWAY, ST., LOUIS, MISSOURI

Owner/Developer
City of St. Louis, Missouri

Consultants
The HOK Planning Group, St. Louis, Missouri
McCormack Baron Associates, Inc., St. Louis, Missouri

Overview
The City of St. Louis commissioned a conceptual master plan for Chouteau Lake and Greenway. The program included a 5-mile greenway and a 15-acre lake. Phase III Concept Planning was completed in the spring of 2006.

Site and Contextual Analysis
The region's settlement history and current environmental and cultural context were significant influencing factors on this Greenway-planning project (Figure 9-11). The Chouteau Greenway is a major component of the region's emerging network of greenways, parks, and recreational trails (Figure 9-12). Other linear parks and open space corridors will eventually link a major park on the city's west side with the Mississippi River and the Gateway Arch on the east. Ecology, sustainability, recreation, and natural and cultural resource interpretations are key program elements (Figure 9-13). An important additional justification for this public investment is that the greenway is expected to be a catalyst for adjacent redevelopment and neighborhood revitalization (Figure 9-14).

BOX 9.1 In Practice (continued)

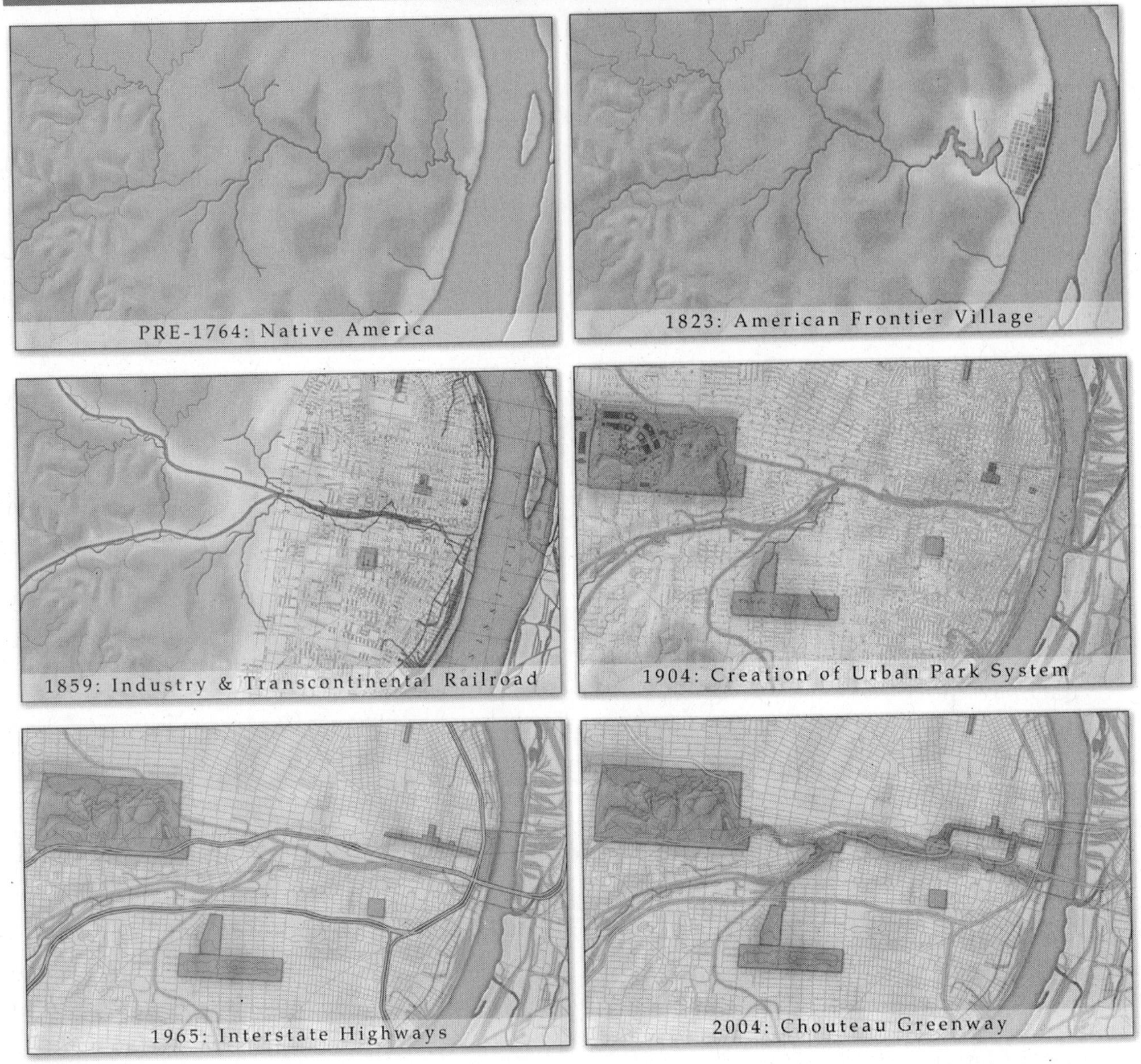

PRE-1764: Native America

1823: American Frontier Village

1859: Industry & Transcontinental Railroad

1904: Creation of Urban Park System

1965: Interstate Highways

2004: Chouteau Greenway

Figure 9-11
Evolution of land use patterns in the St. Louis region is portrayed graphically over a several hundred-year period. Source: The HOK Planning Group.

BOX 9.1   In Practice (continued)

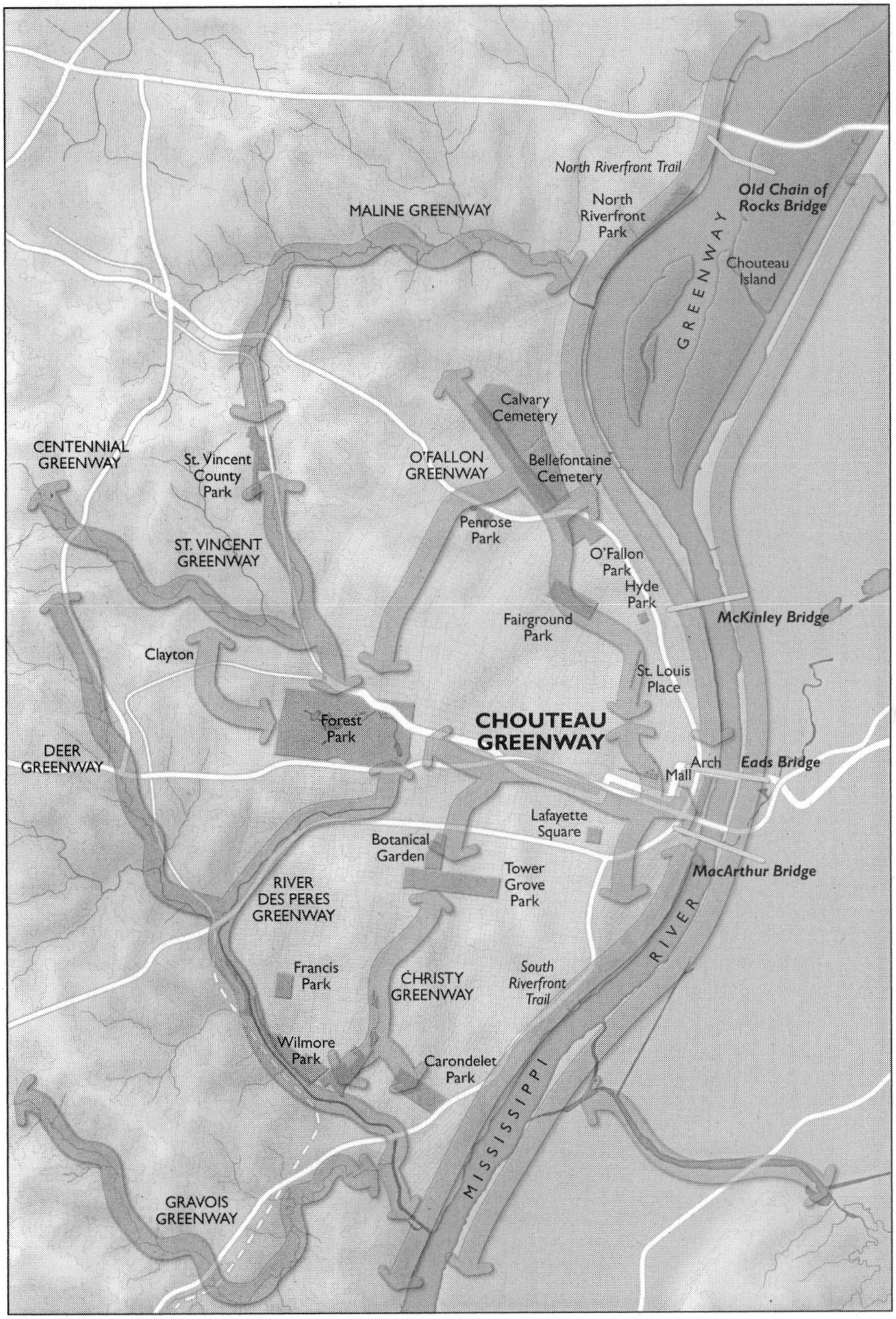

Figure 9-12 Regional network of greenways, parks, and recreational trails. Source: The HOK Planning Group.

BOX 9.1   In Practice (continued)

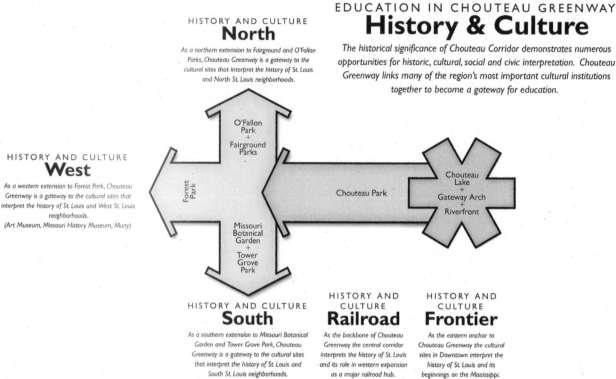

HISTORY AND CULTURE
North

As a northern extension to Fairground and O'Fallon Parks, Chouteau Greenway is a gateway to the cultural sites that interpret the history of St. Louis and North St. Louis neighborhoods.

EDUCATION IN CHOUTEAU GREENWAY
History & Culture

The historical significance of Chouteau Corridor demonstrates numerous opportunities for historic, cultural, social and civic interpretation. Chouteau Greenway links many of the region's most important cultural institutions together to become a gateway for education.

HISTORY AND CULTURE
West

As a western extension to Forest Park, Chouteau Greenway is a gateway to the cultural sites that interpret the history of St. Louis and West St. Louis neighborhoods.
(Art Museum, Missouri History Museum, Muny)

O'Fallon Park + Fairground Parks

Forest Park

Chouteau Park

Chouteau Lake + Gateway Arch + Riverfront

Missouri Botanical Garden + Tower Grove Park

HISTORY AND CULTURE
South

As a southern extension to Missouri Botanical Garden and Tower Grove Park, Chouteau Greenway is a gateway to the cultural sites that interpret the history of St. Louis and South St. Louis neighborhoods.

HISTORY AND CULTURE
Railroad

As the backbone of Chouteau Greenway the central corridor interprets the history of St. Louis and its role in western expansion as a major railroad hub.

HISTORY AND CULTURE
Frontier

As the eastern anchor to Chouteau Greenway the cultural sites in Downtown interpret the history of St. Louis and its beginnings on the Mississippi.

Figure 9-13   Diagram showing important program goals and elements. Source: The HOK Planning Group.

Design Concept

The design concept for this urban corridor includes a five-mile greenway through the heart of the city and a 15-acre lake and adjacent public open space lake just south of Downtown St. Louis (Figure 9-15). In conjunction with the St. Louis Metropolitan Sewer District, streetscape design guidelines were established to incorporate innovative stormwater drainage strategies, new pedestrian and bicycle facilities, and interpretive features relating to the theme of personal and environmental health (Figure 9-16). These features demonstrate a commitment to sustainable design practices that will gradually be implemented throughout the greenway corridor's public realm and private development (Figure 9-17).

This planning work won an Honor Award, in 2000, from the American Institute of Architects, St. Louis Chapter.

BOX 9.1   In Practice (continued)

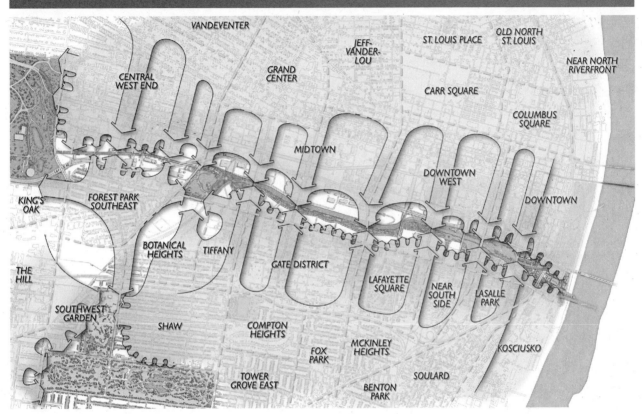

Figure 9-14 Diagram portraying the Greenway's expected social and economic impacts on adjacent neighborhoods. Source: The HOK Planning Group.

BOX 9.1 In Practice (continued)

Figure 9-15 Aerial perspective rendering of the completed urban greenway. Source: The HOK Planning Group.

BOX 9.1   In Practice (continued)

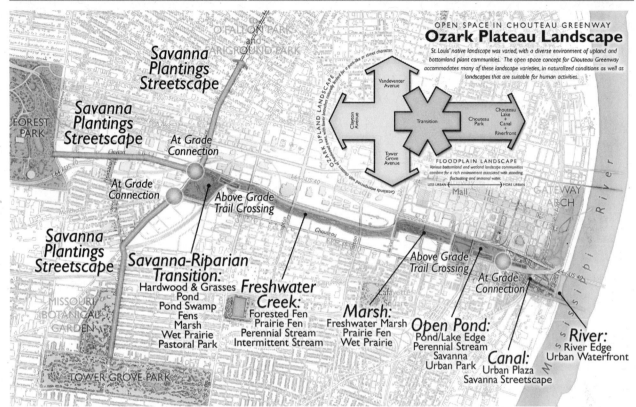

Figure 9-16   Greenway concept plan reinforcing the sustainability theme. Source: The HOK Planning Group.

BOX 9.1   In Practice (continued)

Clayton Avenue Demonstration Trail:
Stormwater Retention Concept

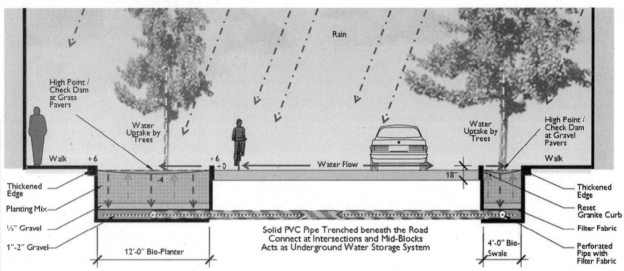

Figure 9-17   Street section demonstrating a sustainable approach to urban infrastructure. Source: The HOK Planning Group.

BOX 9.2   In Practice—Community Planning

INDIAN TRACE BROWARD
COUNTY, FLORIDA

Owner/Developer
Arvida Corporation, Miami, Florida

Traffic Engineer/Economist
Wilbur Smith and Associates, Miami, Florida

Engineer
Gee and Jenson, West Palm Beach, Florida

Land Planner
Environmental Planning & Design (EPD), Miami Lakes, Florida

Overview
This new town project was planned for 10,000 acres (4000 hectares) along the western edge of a large, urbanized, and rapidly growing metropolitan area along the southeastern coast of Florida. Indian Trace is a planned unit development (PUD) designed to ultimately accommodate about 100,000 residents. A two-year research, analysis, and planning effort culminated in the conceptual master plan summarized here. The process involved many local, state, and federal

BOX 9.2   In Practice (continued)

agencies; citizen groups; and a wide array of leading planners, engineers, economists, and ecologists. The projected build-out period for this new town is forty years.

Site Analysis

The 16 square-mile (41 square-kilometer) site is bounded by four major existing or proposed highways. To the north and west of these highways are protected Everglades Conservation Areas. Long-range projections of population and land use were provided by the Broward County Area Planning Board and the County Planning and Zoning Department. The site, the local environs, and the larger region were all examined during the site inventory and analysis.

The analysis of a site topographic survey and aerial photographs was supplemented by field investigations of soil, water, vegetation, and wildlife. More than 30 "eco-determinant" maps were created to define the site's ecological context and long-range constraints and possibilities. These maps addressed climate (Figure 9-18), hydrology (Figure 9-19), and a wide variety of other biophysical attributes. Vegetation on this site includes an abundance of invasive exotic species (i.e., Melaleuca, Brazilian Pepper, Australian Pine). No endangered animal species were found. Relatively shallow groundwater, low-site elevations in relation to mean sea level (MSL), and abundant seasonal rainfall were important land use constraints.

Significant cultural factors that influenced the conceptual land use plan included the locations of various public facilities and infrastructures. Regional transportation systems, schools, public safety and medical facilities, and overall land use patterns were considered, along with many other cultural attributes. For each of these elements, existing conditions, as well as community and regional plans for the future, were assessed.

Design Features

1. *Open Space*. An extensive open space system defines neighborhoods and provides recreational and visual amenities (Figure 9-20). In addition to the lakes, waterways, and wetlands ("blueways"), the plan also creates a diverse array of upland green space. Together, the water areas and the green spaces create a clearly defined framework for future development.
2. *Water*. The water resources management plan is designed to prevent flooding, protect water quality, replenish underground reserves, and develop surface water storage areas as community amenities (Figure 9-21). Approximately 3000 acres (1200 hectares) are allocated to lakes, waterways, and other water storage areas. Stormwater runoff will be filtered by grassed swales and buffer strips adjacent to lakes and waterways. The normal water elevation in the lakes will be 4.0 feet above mean sea level. During rainy periods, discharge to the South New River Canal will occur, at a limited rate, when the system reaches 5.0 feet above MSL.
3. *Neighborhoods*. Residential population on the site will be distributed as a gradient from low density in the southwest to medium densities in the northeast. Neighborhoods will vary in shapes and sizes to accommodate a variety of housing types, ranging from semirural "villages" to apartment complexes with urban densities (Figure 9-22). Average housing density will be 4.08 dwelling units-per-gross acre (0.4 hectare). Neighborhood gathering places, focal points, and recreation activities are designed to be within easy walking or biking distances of residents. Commercial and civic uses are planned for neighborhood centers. In addition, all of the schools, major cultural facilities, and commercial districts are strategically located in proximity to at least two neighborhoods.
4. *Circulation*. The plan's multimodal transportation network includes a regional public transit node and a hierarchy of freeways, arterial parkways, collector roads, and local streets (Figure 9-23). The plan also includes separate bus lanes, mini-transit routes, and an extensive walking and biking trail system. Two-lane roads designed for low speeds and limited traffic volumes will be common in many neighborhoods. Limited building frontage will be allowed along major parkways and collector roads. The right-of-way for parkways will accommodate walkways and bicycle paths. Utility

BOX 9.2　In Practice (continued)

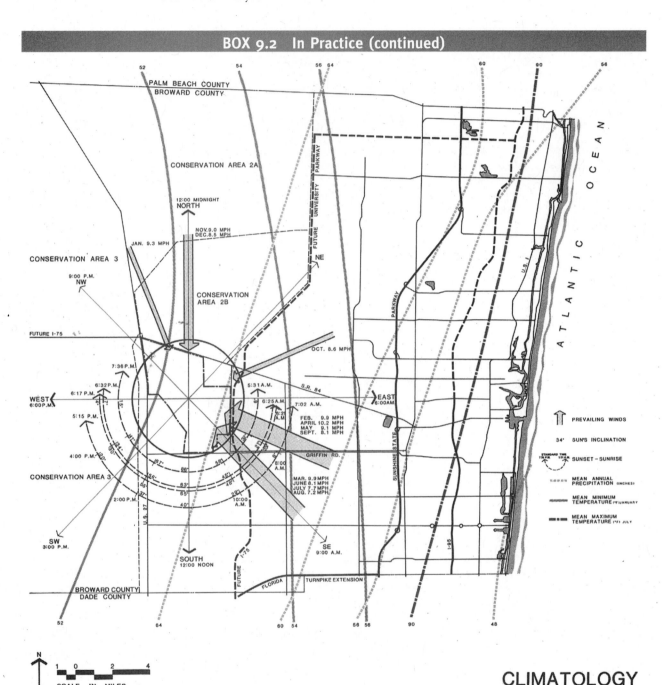

Figure 9-18　Map of climatic factors influencing the site. This map shows the direction of winter winds, average seasonal precipitation, seasonal times of sunrise and sunset, and average seasonal temperatures. Source: Environmental Planning & Design.

BOX 9.2   In Practice (continued)

lines for water distribution and wastewater collection will parallel the site's network of major roads and streets (Figure 9-24).

5. *Recreation*. Upon completion, the new town will contain more than 20 acres (8 hectares) of recreational land for each 1000 residents. These recreational areas include several school/neighborhood parks, five larger urban parks, one regional park, and two golf courses (Figure 9-25).

6. *Community Center*. A planned community center will accommodate civic, cultural, and commercial uses, along with a regional transit terminal. Industrial uses planned for areas outside of the community center include a regional goods distribution center and assorted research-oriented light industry.

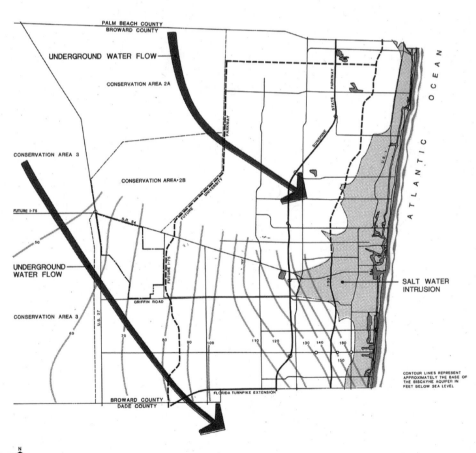

Figure 9-19 Map of groundwater showing locations of salt water intrusion, aquifer depths, and direction of groundwater flow. Source: Environmental Planning & Design.

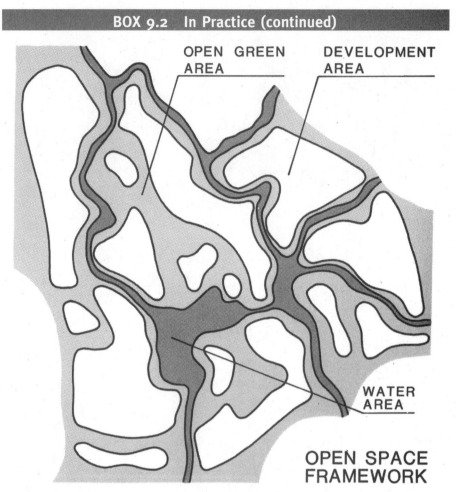

Figure 9-20 Conceptual diagram of the proposed open space system, providing the spatial framework for future development. Source: Environmental Planning & Design.

BOX 9.2 In Practice (continued)

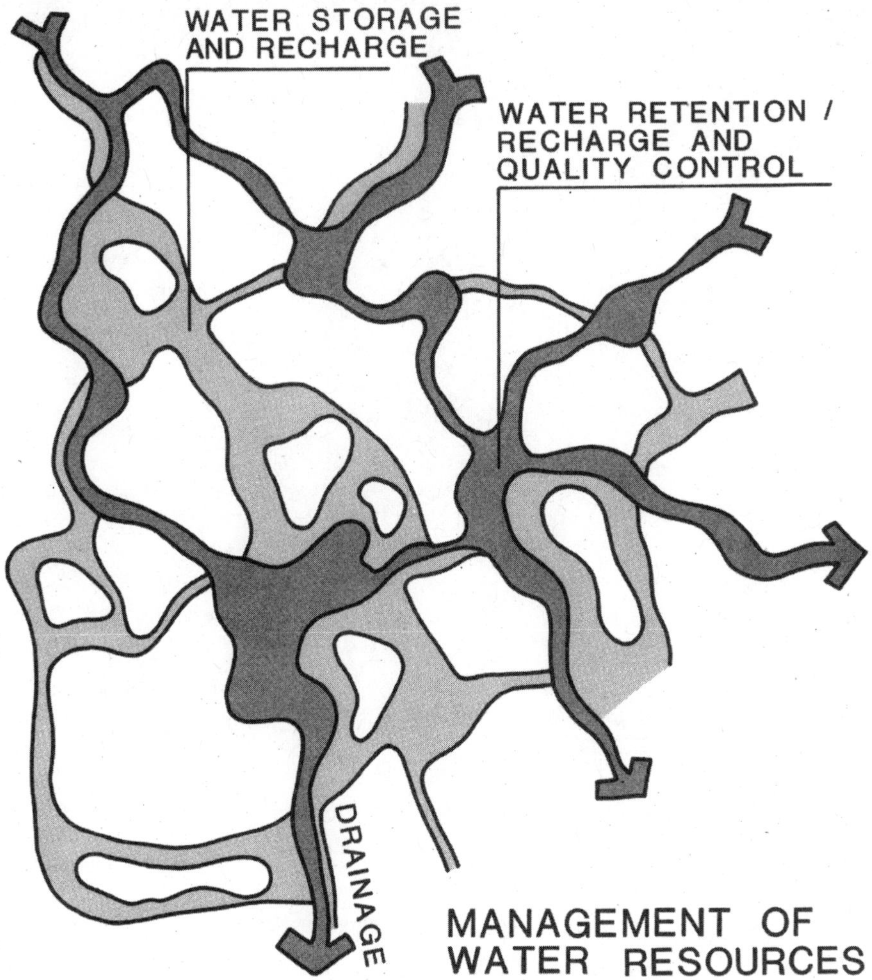

Figure 9-21 Conceptual diagram of the water resources management plan. Source: Environmental Planning & Design.

BOX 9.2   In Practice (continued)

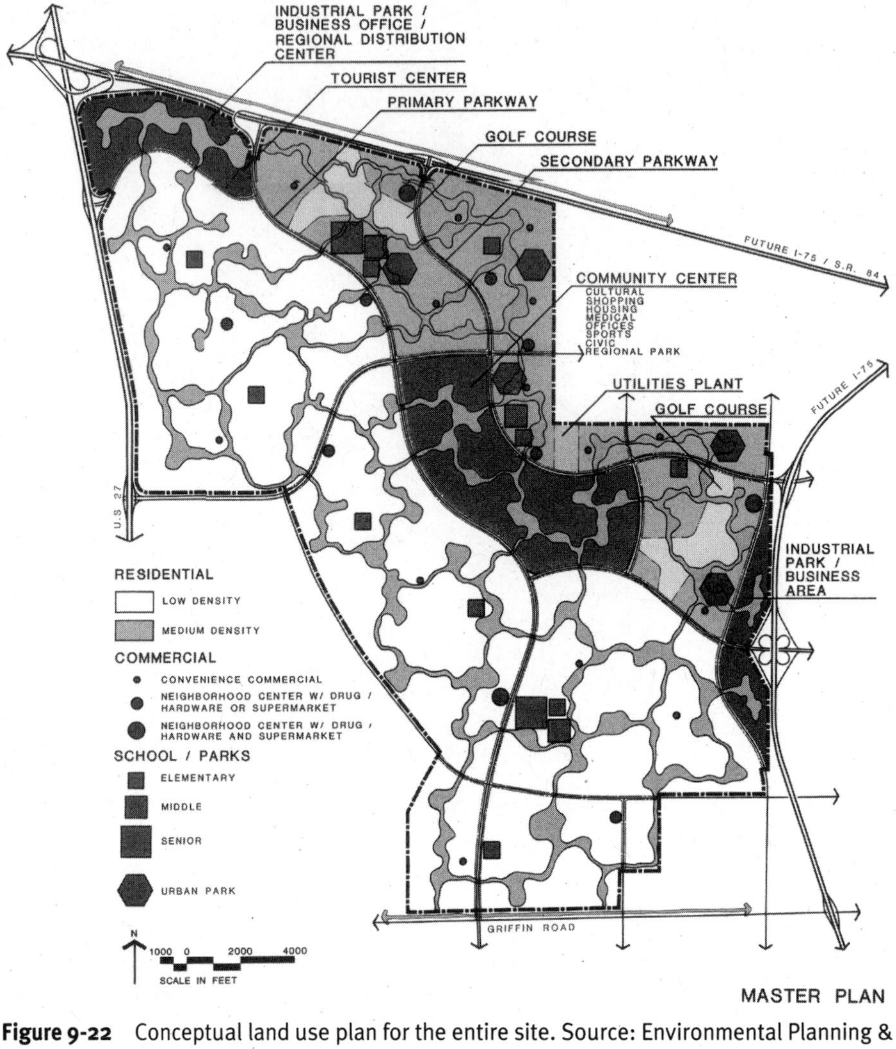

Figure 9-22   Conceptual land use plan for the entire site. Source: Environmental Planning & Design.

BOX 9.2   In Practice (continued)

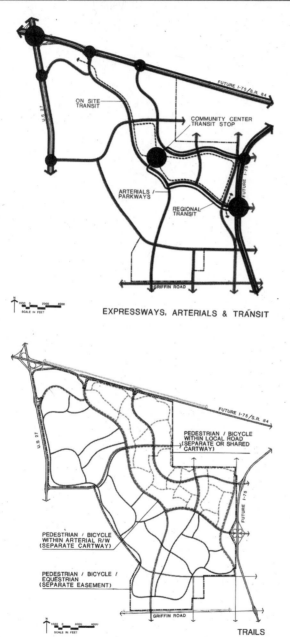

Figure 9-23   Conceptual diagrams of the proposed circulation system. A hierarchy of components includes arterial highways, public transit stops, local streets, walkways, and bike paths. Source: Environmental Planning & Design.

BOX 9.2   In Practice (continued)

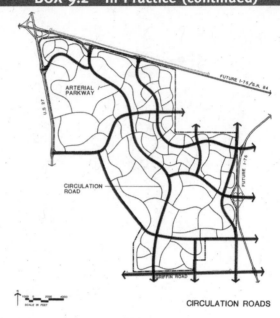

Figure 9-23 (Continued)

BOX 9.2   In Practice (continued)

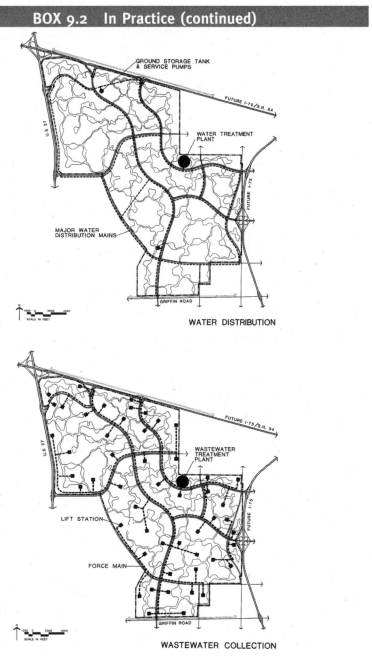

Figure 9-24   Conceptual diagrams of proposed water distribution and wastewater collection systems. Source: Environmental Planning & Design.

BOX 9.2   In Practice (continued)

Figure 9-25 Conceptual diagrams of the proposed recreation, parks, and open space systems. The hierarchy of open spaces spans a range of spatial scales: regional/urban, community, and neighborhood. Source: Environmental Planning & Design.

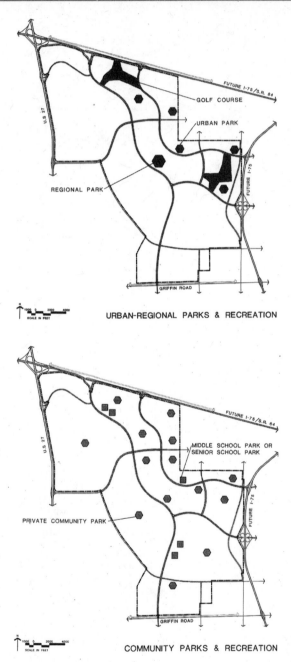

BOX 9.2   In Practice (continued)

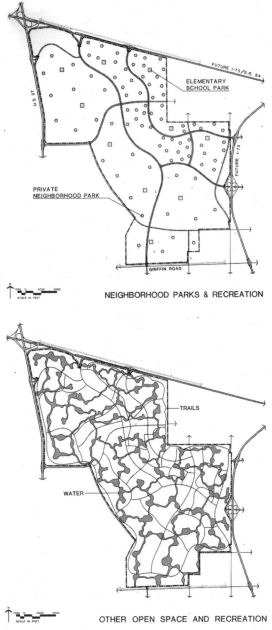

NEIGHBORHOOD PARKS & RECREATION

OTHER OPEN SPACE AND RECREATION

Figure 9-25   (continued)

Design Development

In the end, our society will be defined not only by what we create, but by what we refuse to destroy.

—John Sawhill, former president, The Nature Conservancy

10.1 INTRODUCTION

Good site planning brings order and harmony to the built environment. The concept plan spatially organizes the buildings, circulation systems, and open spaces on the site. Design development is the refinement or "articulation" of the concept plan. Both broad—and fine-scale design decisions determine how well the site accommodates its intended uses. These decisions also determine the project's positive and/or negative impacts on the environment and the surrounding community. This chapter examines the detailed site design decisions that influence the sustainability and "livability" of the built environment.

10.2 SUSTAINABILITY AND LIVABILITY

Smart growth "principles" are relatively broad policy goals that help guide both capital investment in public infrastructure and the regulation of land development over a hierarchy of scales, from the regional to the local. Creating sustainable and livable communities requires implementation, however, at the site scale.

The Extended Metabolism Model (Newman and Kenworthy, 1999), underlying the State Sustainability Strategy for Western Australia, suggests that sustainability and livability are not only complementary goals but also are essential for the development of quality built environments (Western Australian Planning Commission, 2000):

> ...for a settlement to be sustainable, resource consumption (such as land, energy, water, and materials) and waste (solid, liquid, and gaseous) must be reduced, while simultaneously improving livability (in areas such as income, housing, health, education, and community).

Ensuring that future generations have the resources they need to pursue their goals is a core precept of sustainable development. Sustainable communities strive not only to live lightly on the land but also to be livable as well. Achieving smart growth principles at the neighborhood and community levels is unattainable without appropriate design and implementation decisions at the site scale. Sustainable site planning—as discussed in Chapter 1—entails five actions. These are as follows:

- □ *Protect* the environment from unnecessary impacts (for example, soil, air, water)

- □ *Restore* environmentally degraded areas (for example, habitats, soil, air, water)

- □ *Recycle* already developed sites (for example, shopping centers and brownfields)

- □ *Create* compact, distinctive, walkable places (for example, smart growth)

- □ *Conserve* resources (for example, use of energy, water, building materials)

Livable communities are safe, visually attractive, and pedestrian-friendly. How does a site planner help meet these broad policy goals when making design decisions to modify an individual parcel of land? In other words, how are the smart growth and sustainability goals translated into design theory—and design guidelines?

10.3   DESIGN THEORY

Design theory is a body of ideas, principles, and techniques for designing buildings, plazas, and other elements of the built environment. These normative "rules" are culturally influenced and because they embody the "best practices" within a design field, they may change over time with the acquisition of additional experience or knowledge, or the evolution of economic, legal, or social conditions. Examples of good site planning and design are as instructive as examples of poor site planning and design.

In the United States, many older neighborhoods built before the deleterious effects of extensive highway building and single-use zoning, for example, are attractive and visually cohesive. This visual quality is achieved through the consistent repetition of scale, proportion, and other attributes. These neighborhoods have a unity and human scale that have made them models or "patterns" for contemporary urban design (Urban Design Associates, 2003).

A Pattern Language, by Christopher Alexander and other collaborators (1977), is an encyclopedic collection of solutions to diverse design problems common in urban and architectural design. Historic as well as contemporary precedents are essential for robust and relevant design theory. Brian Lawson (2004, p.96) writes:

> Precedents are often either whole or partial pieces of designs that the designer is aware of. They may be previously employed solutions by the same designer, by famous designers, buildings, landscapes, or towns seen on study visits or even on holiday....Before the introduction of photography and modern methods of reproduction, travel was essential in the education of a young designer who would be expected to take the grand tour to build up this knowledge.

Design theory, as it concerns site planning and design, addresses not only the functions of the site but also its form or appearance. Throughout the built environment, appearances influence the economic success of products ranging from automobiles to toasters and televisions. Appearances also influence the economic success of places—from individual houses or housing projects to entire neighborhoods, communities, and even regions. Underlying these economic effects, of course, is the issue of preference (National Park Service, 1995). All of us have preferences that influence, in one way or another, our behavior—including where we live, the places we visit, and the things we own or rent. For practical reasons, including location and income, few people—if any—are able to fulfill each and every one of their preferences.

10.3.1 Why Do Appearances Matter?

Design theory is concerned with form—and indirectly appearance—because the form of the built environment directly affects its function. The spatial organization and articulation of the built environment—its buildings, open spaces, and transportation systems—are fundamental determinants of community sustainability and quality of life. Urban form also concerns the physiognomy, or visible outer surface, of the built environment. "Beauty is in the eye of the beholder" is a well-known aphorism often used to argue against "appearance regulations" concerned with community aesthetics. This assertion may, in fact, be valid if the appearance issue under consideration is relatively minor (for example, the color of a house).

Yet not all "beholders" of beauty have equivalent—let alone adequate—knowledge and skills of appreciation as they pertain to the design of the built environment. Acquiring expertise in urban design is far from a trivial issue. Nevertheless, an appreciation for well-designed built environments is not the exclusive domain of professional planners, architects, and landscape architects. The design of the physical environment affects quality of life and, consequently, location preferences for housing choices and other location decisions that people make in their daily lives. Richard Florida (2002), in *The Rise of the Creative Class*, writes that better educated, higher income professionals essentially "vote with their feet" and seek regions and cities with a high quality of life, which is often the result of plentiful public open space, environmental quality, and visually attractive built environments.

Increasingly, communities—small and large—are recognizing the value of excellence in urban design. The City of Aberdeen, South Dakota (USA), for example, includes an entire chapter, titled "Community Appearance," in its Comprehensive Plan. The following statement sums up the rationale for the city's legitimate concern for community aesthetics (City of Aberdeen, 2004, p.8–1):

> Simply put, beauty adds value to the community. The appearance of a community is one of the foremost influences of value and, hence, one of its most regarded assets. Residents take pride in their community and its attractive and interesting places. Businesses also like to locate in attractive environments, which improve their ability to recruit employees, host clients and investors, and continue to invest in their facilities.

Clearly, the organization and articulation of the built environment influences human experiences and preferences. The scale and character of a community, for example, determines how easy or difficult, and how pleasant or unpleasant, it is to live within the community. Every community, therefore, should closely examine the quality of their built environment and ask a variety of questions. Do most school children walk to school, or does vehicle traffic make it too dangerous? Do tourists visit? Do prospective employees, with skilled workforce needs, move here? If not, why not?

10.3.2   Spatial Organization of the Three-Dimensional Built Environment

Open space is a vital component of any community, and its location and design play a very important role in how the community is experienced. Space—whether inside buildings or outdoors—is defined by a ground plane, and to varying extents, a vertical plane and overhead plane. Many of the best-designed outdoor spaces are well defined. Buildings, landforms, trees, and other physical elements enclose space and create outdoor "rooms" and "corridors." Many of the functions performed by the ground, vertical, and overhead planes are summarized in Table 10-1.

Any built environment can be viewed as a three-dimensional "design" that, at it's most basic, sculptural level is composed of masses and voids. These three-dimensional compositions are derived from elements in the ground or "floor" plane and, in many instances, also in the vertical or "wall" plane and the overhead or "ceiling" plane. Visible masses are the building blocks that shape the character and visual quality of the built environment. These elements may be spatially arranged to enclose or define connected sequences of outdoor spaces or "rooms."

Many different design fields—automobile design and furniture design, for example—are concerned with the appearance of their products. Good design, from an aesthetic or visual perspective, creates an integrated and harmonious ensemble of forms, colors, and other visible qualities that, together, comprise a coherent and unified whole. More than 80 years ago, in *The Principles of Architectural Composition* (1924), Howard Robertson skillfully explained the importance of design theory to architectural design. Similarly, important

TABLE 10-1 Selected design functions of the three spatial planes within outdoor built environments.

Plane	Design Function
Ground	Separation
	Orientation
	Enclosure
	Linkage
Vertical	Screening
	Enclosure
	Background
	Direction
	Transition
	Framing
	Buffering
Overhead	Screening
	Enclosure
	Shading
	Weather protection

seminal books have been written on site planning and design, including *Site Planning*, by Kevin Lynch (1962), and *Landscape Architecture: The Shaping of Man's Natural Environment*, by John Ormsbee Simonds (1961). Design theory applied to the built environment continues to evolve, in part, from precedent studies of historic and contemporary built environments and from research in urban design, landscape ecology, and related fields.

10.3.3 Principles of Composition

Perceptions of the built environment's visual quality are, in part, a function of the organization of visible attributes or qualities—such as color, shape, size, and texture. Although many terms have been used in discussing the aesthetics of the built environment, for the sake of simplicity, these terms can be reduced to three major principles of composition. Unity, balance, and emphasis are three fundamental principles that, when skillfully applied in the design of the built environment, not only create places with high visual quality, but also contribute to those areas' identity or sense of place.

Unity
Unity is the most comprehensive of the three principles. Visual unity is achieved through the following:

- *Repetition* of similar qualities (for example, color, form, texture) and similar elements (for example, buildings)

- *Simplicity,* limiting the number or "palette" of different qualities and elements

Figure 10-1 Unity in nature. The rocky coastline near Monterey, California, exhibits a simple palette of repeated forms, colors, and textures.

□ *Rhythm* (placing elements in an ordered arrangement)

□ *Proportion* (relating sizes of elements to each other)

In nature, landscapes undisturbed by development or other significant human activities epitomize the principle of unity (Figure 10-1). Vernacular landscapes throughout the world also exhibit this appealing characteristic—visual unity with subtle, yet, extensive variation (Figure 10-2). Unity does not require rigid uniformity or repetition of identical objects. In fact, some variation of attributes—or how those attributes are combined—can lead to very high visual quality (Figure 10-3 and 10-4).

Unity in the built environment implies both internal coherence and compatibility with the surroundings. This visual coherence may occur over a range of spatial scale, from landscapes and communities down to neighborhoods, blocks, and individual sites (Figure 10-5). An urban infill project, for example, may be surrounded by a rich context of buildings, pavement, street furniture, and vegetation. Each of these elements has visible attributes that contribute to the identity of the place.

A visually unified composition typically derives its coherency from the application of a proportioning system. A proportion is the relationship between one part and another, or between one part and the whole. Proportioning systems are expressed as a set of ratio equalities, as follows:

Figure 10-2 Unity in a vernacular landscape that shows similar forms, sizes, and colors of housing on the island of Capri.

Figure 10-3 Unity at the district or neighborhood level in Florence, Italy.

Figure 10-4 Unity at the street block scale: historic townhouses in Baltimore, Maryland. Note: repetition of vertical lines and rectilinear forms and openings (windows and doors) with nearly equal sizes and proportions.

Figure 10-5 Unity at the site and building scale. Historic cathedral and leaning tower of Pisa exhibit the rhythmic repetition of form, color, size, and line.

$$a/b = c/d = e/f$$

where, for example,

a = building height, b = building width

c = window height, d = window width

e = brick height, f = brick width

Designs may be internally consistent, yet, in jarring visual conflict with their surroundings. "Heroic" works of architecture certainly have their place, particularly when form follows function—and the function is devoted to community or civic purposes (for example, a museum or performing arts center). "Contextual" buildings, however, are particularly important in neighborhoods and communities. Together, the best examples of contextual architecture contribute to human-scaled, and visually unified, places.

Existing built environments—if well designed—provide contextual "rules" or standards for designing new buildings and sites in the vicinity. These contextual issues concern material choices as well as the sizes and proportions of buildings and other site elements. The bay widths of a prominent historic building, for example, could be replicated in the design of a contemporary building on the same street and block. Similarly, on the ground plane, paving patterns adjacent to the new building could "echo" the bay widths expressed in the building's massing and façade articulation. This would be an example of architectural design that respects its context.

Aesthetics—and proportion, specifically—have been important in urban design through the ages. Plato developed a theory on the aesthetics of proportion in the fourth century A.D. Andrea Palladio published *The Four Books on Architecture* in 1570 in which he examined the importance of proportion in architecture. For thousands of years, the proportions of the human body have inspired architects to design buildings that carefully control proportion in both massing and façade articulation. Marcus Vitruvius Pollio, a Roman architect (30 B.C.–46 A.D.), wrote:

> Hence, no building can be said to be well designed, which wants symmetry and proportion...they are as necessary to the beauty of a building as to that of a well-formed human figure...
>
> — Vitruvius, Book III, Chapter 1

Leonardo Fibbonacci was, perhaps, the greatest European mathematician of the Middle Ages. Born in Pisa, Italy, in about 1175 A.D., he is known for the discovery of a remarkable series of numbers that begins as follows:

$$1, 1, 2, 3, 5, 8, 13, 21, 34, 55 \ldots \ldots$$

The Fibonacci sequence is created by adding the previous two numbers in the series together to form the next number in the sequence, and so on. The ratios derived from the Fibbonacci series—especially 1:1, 1:2, 2:3, 3:5, and 5:8—are at the heart of great architecture and urban design worldwide. If any two successive numbers in the Fibbonacci sequence are divided (for example, 5/8), the result or quotient approximates the Golden

Ratio (.618). The golden ratio, or golden section, is the proportioning system that underlies the design of ancient Greek and Roman temples, such as the Parthenon in Athens, Greece (Herz-Fischler, 1998).

The importance of proportion in the built environment is a crucial and enduring concept. Yet with the continuing commercialization of the design-build industries—at least in North America—the quality of design in the built environment has arguably declined since the mid-twentieth century. In the very timely book, *What Not to Build: Do's and Don'ts of Exterior Home Design*, Edelman, Gaman, and Reid (2006) show just how bad single-family housing design can get—and how the houses could be made better if the builder had understood, then applied, basic design principles concerning, for example, massing, scale, and proportion.

Balance

Balance refers to the visual "weight" associated with color, form, texture, and other visible qualities of the built environment. Balance is a relative term, with the "weight" of an element or composition being important in relation to a reference point or line (or axis). In the built environment, balance is often achieved in relation to an imaginary line or axis imposed on the ground plane, typically, and also on the wall plane. Point and radial symmetry are powerful techniques for organizing buildings and open spaces, especially in denser urban environments (Figure 10-6). A balanced composition successfully manages:

Figure 10-6 Piazza San Pietro in Rome, Italy. In addition to unity, the building and plaza composition demonstrates both radial and bilateral symmetry.

- □ *Weight* of visible attributes [for example, a symmetric or asymmetric combination of elements in relation to a line or point; symmetry may be bilateral (axial) or radial (point)]

- □ *Scale* (for example, the size of certain elements correspond to the average size of the human body)

Emphasis

Emphasis, the third major aesthetic principle of composition, is established when a building or other design element is distinct, in some way, from other nearby elements. This is often accomplished, as follows:

- □ *Contrast* adds interest or creates focal points (for example, unique, eye-catching focal points created by contrasts in color, form, size, number, line, texture, or placement in relation to its surroundings)

- □ *Hierarchy* (establishes visually dominant and subordinate elements)

An "iconic" building, bridge, or other element in the built environment is notable because it is unusual in some way. The special nature of an iconic structure may result from internal contrasts, such as a building with a tower or other dominant feature (Figure 10-7), or the iconic status may result from external contrasts with the surroundings. A prominent location also may contribute to a structure's iconic status, but this is not a requisite characteristic (Figure 10-8). Conversely, a prominent location could be the sole reason for a structure's iconic status.

10.3.4   Creating Order

Geometry is important in the organization and articulation of the built environment. Geometric frameworks provide consistency in organizing and arranging disparate materials and components. Drawing from a synthesis by Motloch (2001, p. 147–150), three primary geometric themes are summarized below.

Rectilinear Theme

In a rectilinear framework, elements are organized as follows:

- □ Straight lines (line)

- □ Right angles (line and texture)

- □ Squares and rectangles (form, color, texture)

Rectilinear configurations are easiest to implement because of the nature of most building materials and construction methods. Although exceptions certainly exist, a rectilinear approach is typically used in designing the façades of most buildings. The shapes of doors, windows, and the building itself, for example, are usually squares or rectangles

Figure 10-7   Contrast between vertical tower and shorter surrounding buildings in the village center in Reston, Virginia.

Figure 10-8 The iconic Golden Gate Bridge, linking San Francisco with Marin County, California. The bridge "stands out" from its surroundings because it contrasts in form, color, function, size, and placement. Source: Bridget Lang.

(Figure 10-9). Attention to proportion, of course, provides a time-tested rationale for choosing the dimensions of the framework.

Angular Theme

In an angular framework, the parts or key elements are organized as follows:

- Points

- Radiating lines and acute or obtuse angles

- Triangles and hexagons

Angular themes are less common in the built environment than rectilinear themes. Angular elements may provide contrast in an otherwise rectilinear composition (Figure 10-10). A clock tower, for example, is essentially a rectilinear form—except for the tower's top or peak, which is triangular in shape.

Curvilinear Theme

In a curvilinear framework, the key parts or elements are organized by the following:

- Generative points

Figure 10-9 Rectilinear framework organizes the massing and articulation of the mixed-use Mizner Court building in Boca Raton, Florida.

Figure 10-10 Hexagonal forms expressed in the ground plane in the waterfront plaza in Zurich, Switzerland.

□ Arcs and tangents

□ Circles and semi-circles

Curvilinear themes in the wall plane are often expressed or "echoed" in the ground plane (Figure 10-11).

Combined Themes

The rectilinear, angular, and curvilinear frameworks are frequently combined to create hybrid themes where two or more geometric patterns are juxtaposed (Figure 10-12).

Figure 10-11 Curvilinear form of the wall plane is "echoed" below in the ground plane (stairs and planter edge) in San Francisco, California.

10.4 OPEN SPACE

Protecting sensitive natural areas is a fundamental goal of good site planning. These open spaces provide a wide range of environmental, economic, and social goods and services and are essential components of sustainable and livable communities. Open spaces in the built environment span a diverse range of modification, from the relatively undisturbed natural or conservation open spaces to the developed open spaces, including entirely paved, architectonic urban plazas. Examples of each open space type, with various characteristics and functions, are as follows:

Figure 10-12 View from the Hancock Tower in Boston, Massachusetts, showing combined geometric frameworks juxtaposed in the built environment.

Conservation open space

- ☐ Woodland

- ☐ Grassland

- ☐ Water

Developed "hard" open space

- ☐ Plaza

- ☐ Promenade

- ☐ Courtyard

Developed "soft" open space

- ☐ Lawn

- ☐ Garden

- ☐ Park

Clustering buildings and infrastructure leaves the remaining site areas for other uses such as permanent open space. With skillful site planning—based on a thorough site analysis—clustering can protect environmentally sensitive areas and also provide an attractive setting for housing or other site uses. Not all local development regulations allow clustering, however, and this is an area in need of public policy reform.

10.4.1 Conservation Open Space

Conservation open space provides a range of benefits that society values, including the protection of natural resources, opportunities for outdoor recreation, and aesthetic amenity (Kline and Wichelns, 1998). Kline (2006, p.645) writes:

> . . .key socioeconomic trends—most notably, population growth, rising incomes, development, and increasing open space scarcity—motivate interest and support for preserving open space, when open space lands remain unprotected.

Communities in the United States protect open space and critical environmental areas—or green infrastructure—in different ways (Figure 10-13). Purchasing the lands is an effective, yet relatively expensive, approach. Nevertheless, between 1999 and 2005 U.S. voters approved 827 public referenda to finance open space preservation programs: 25 at the state level, 148 at the county level, 631 at the municipality level, and 23 by other jurisdictions (Trust for Public Land, 2005). Financing methods varied widely, including raising sales and property taxes, borrowing the money by issuing bonds, and raising state income taxes (Kline, 2006). Other techniques for protecting open space include regulatory approaches that restrict development rights on lands with significant environmental resources.

Figure 10-13 Conservation open space in San Francisco, California. Source: Bridget Lang.

10.4.2 Developed Open Space

Communities can limit urban sprawl and reduce the loss of open space by encouraging the redevelopment of previously developed sites. This alone, however, does not ensure that the development will be compact, pedestrian-friendly, or consistent with any other sustainability or livability goals. Without appropriate site and building design, these goals cannot be met.

Meaningful outdoor spaces are an essential component of a well-designed community. Developed open space includes both "soft" and "hard" spaces. These outdoor "rooms" and "corridors"—when human-scaled, appropriately furnished, and functionally linked—are vital to community livability (Figure 10-14 and 10-15). Public parks, waterfronts, and other open spaces are often the sites of farmers markets, art exhibitions, musical performances, and other events that not only attract tourism, but also enhance a community's quality of life and economic competitiveness (Diamond and Noonan, 1996).

Well-designed open spaces can strengthen a community's identity or "sense of place," add value to real estate within the community (Bookout, 1994), and provide a safe environment that is conducive to active living (Frumkin, Frank, and Jackson, 2004). "Lost" spaces—typically poorly defined and often neglected—are missed opportunities to improve the visual quality, human scale, and walkability of the built environment (Trancik, 1986). The most

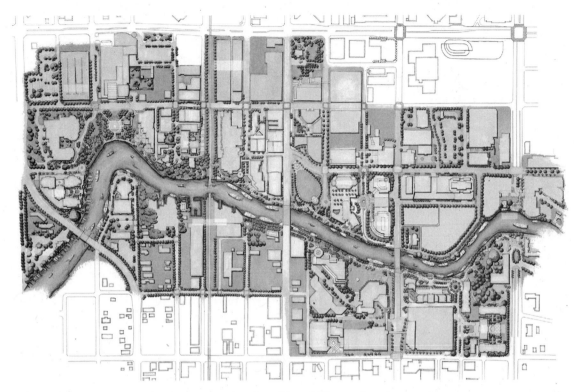

Figure 10-14   Master plan showing a recreational corridor within an urban context. Fort Lauderdale, Florida. Source: Edward D. Stone, Jr., and Associates.

popular outdoor spaces tend to be human-scaled with a moderate to strong sense of enclosure. These outdoor rooms are often designed exclusively for pedestrians.

Open spaces are created by the strategic arrangement of site elements. The primary method of enclosing outdoor space is by organizing the built environment's solids or mass—primarily buildings. Sense of enclosure is influenced by the height of the defining wall planes and the dimensions of the open space. An outdoor space's "sense of enclosure" is strong at a height/width ratio of 1:2 or 1:3 (Figure 10-16). Depending on the context and function of the open space, the ideal height/width ratio may range from 4:1 to 1:4.

Buildings have a significant effect on microclimate, which is an important consideration in the design of outdoor urban spaces (Whyte, 1980). In warmer climates, shade is valued for its cooling effects. Plants serve many different, yet vital, functions in the built environment, including providing shade (Table 10-2). In cooler climates, sunlight in public spaces is not only valued but also mandated by ordinance in some cities (San Francisco Recreation and Park Department, 2006).

Developed open space varies by the intended uses of the space. Semi-public open spaces, for example, tend to be closely associated with buildings that are open to the public.

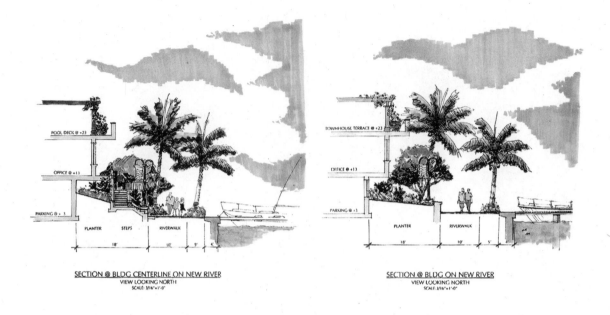

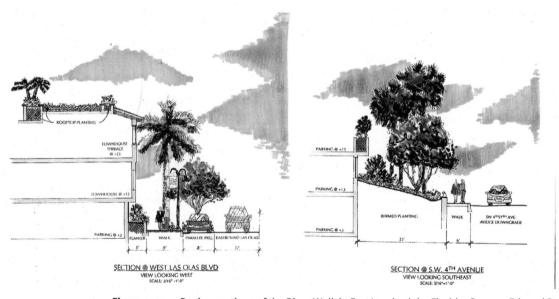

Figure 10-15   Design sections of the River Walk in Fort Lauderdale, Florida. Source: Edward D. Stone, Jr., and Associates.

Figure 10-16 Building height, in relation to the width of the streetscape, determines an open space sense of enclosure. Zurich, Switzerland.

Entrance forecourts and terraces for restaurants and other commercial uses are common examples of semi-public space. Private, outdoor open space is generally associated with housing—balconies, patios, decks, and other similar outdoor spaces for the exclusive use of residents and their guests. A variety of meaningful public, semi-public, and private outdoor spaces is essential for public health and community well-being.

10.5 CIRCULATION SYSTEMS

Physical planning at the site scale is where many of the broad neighborhood and community goals are realized. Livability connotes a walkable, safe, and healthy environment served by a multimodal and highly interconnected transportation system. Livable communities provide the following:

□ Transportation choices (for example, walking, bicycling, and transit)

□ Interconnected transportation modes

□ Networks of streets with high levels of connectivity and short blocks

□ Concentrated activity centers around transit service

□ Sidewalks in all new developments

Source: International City/County Management Association (2002). *Getting to Smart Growth: 100 Policies for Implementation*, www.smartgrowth.org.

TABLE 10-2   Selected uses of plants in the built environment.

Objective	Specific Use
Architectural	Defining (enclosing) space
	Creating linkages between buildings or spaces
	Controlling or directing circulation
	Marking the location of an entrance (for example, way finding and orientation)
	Separating incompatible activities
	Screening undesirable views
	Framing desirable views or focal points
	Softening building corners and walls
	Providing scale (human)
Engineering	Controlling erosion
	Shoreline stabilization
	Slowing and filtering stormwater runoff
	Intercepting and facilitating stormwater infiltration
	Reducing wind velocity
	Buffering noise
	Shading solar radiation
Ecological	Creating wildlife habitat (for example, food, cover, and shelter)
	Providing corridors for wildlife movement
	Improving air and water quality
	Ameliorating microclimate (for example, shading, wind buffering)
	Reducing urban "heat-island" effect

Source: Booth, 1983; Brooks, 1994.

10.5.1   Pedestrian Circulation

The built environment can either impede or contribute to active living—which is essential for public health (Jackson and Kochtitsky, 2001). However, over the last thirty years, population growth coupled with urban sprawl have made communities unsafe for pedestrians—particularly school-age children and the elderly. In 1969, nearly half of all school-aged children in the United States walked to school; by 1995 that ratio had dropped to just ten percent (Quraishi et al., 2005, p.2). Metropolitan areas with higher population densities tend to be safer for pedestrians than more sprawling and sparsely populated metropolitan areas (Quraishi et al., 2005).

Conflicts between pedestrians and vehicles frequently result, unfortunately, in pedestrian injuries and deaths. In fact, a leading cause of injury-related death among children is pedestrian-related collisions (Centers for Disease Control and Prevention, 2002). For this reason, and many others, designing the built environment demands close attention to the needs of people—not just in vehicles, but people as pedestrians. Far too many communities in the United States have failed—through lack of knowledge or neglect—to ensure that the needs of pedestrians are adequately met.

Research suggests that, on average, people are willing to walk a maximum of one-half mile (.804 km) for "premium transit and rail service" and one-quarter mile (.402 km) for other bus service (Kulash, 2001). In safe and easily walkable neighborhoods, basic services are located near homes, jobs, and transit—and vehicle traffic is "calmed" by the design of the transportation infrastructure (see www.Context SensitiveSolutions.org).

Pedestrian circulation systems at the site scale perform three important functions that make the sites safer and more comfortable for pedestrians. They provide: (1) access to the site, (2) mobility within the site, and (3) outdoor spaces for socializing and individual activities such as reading or eating. William Whyte (1980), in *The Social Life of Small Urban Spaces*, examines the key characteristics of successful outdoor urban spaces in New York City. These attributes, which foster social life in outdoor spaces, include: (1) seating; (2) food and/or entertainment; (3) locations with both sunshine and shade; and (4) nearby sources of people (for example, office buildings). Whyte's research demonstrates that pedestrian circulation systems not only facilitate pedestrian movement but also provide meaningful places for outdoor living.

Well designed pedestrian circulation systems provide a clear sense of entry and arrival to the site (Figure 10-17). They also provide places for lingering, such as the following (Hall, 1966):

□ Nodes, providing opportunities for social interaction

□ Oases, providing opportunities for quiet respite

□ Niches, providing opportunities for prospect with refuge

Whether at the community, neighborhood, or site scales, a convenient, safe, and fully functional pedestrian circulation system must meet the following design criteria: (1) separation, (2) connectivity, (3) capacity, (4) accessibility, and (5) amenities. Each of these design principles is summarized below.

Separation

□ *Separate* pedestrians from vehicles and, where systems intersect, identify the walkway with paving changes, markings, or refuge islands to reduce pedestrian crosswalk distances (Figure 10-18).

□ *Minimize* pedestrian conflicts with vehicles, transit, and bicycles.

□ *Minimize* pedestrian risks to natural hazards (for example, steep cliffs) or other dangers.

□ *Provide* vehicle-free zones for pedestrians, especially in commercial centers, multi-family housing developments, schools and campuses, and other areas with large numbers of pedestrians.

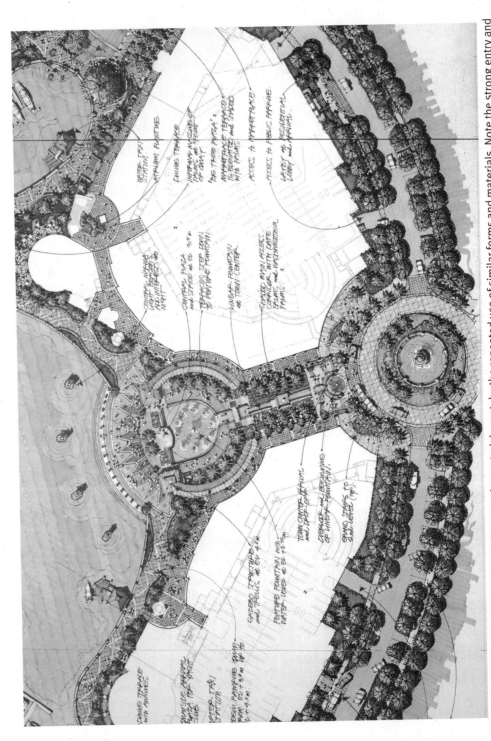

Figure 10-17   A unified outdoor environment is created, in part, by the repeated use of similar forms and materials. Note the strong entry and arrival sequence and the bilateral symmetry along the project's central axis. Source: Edward D. Stone, Jr., and Associates.

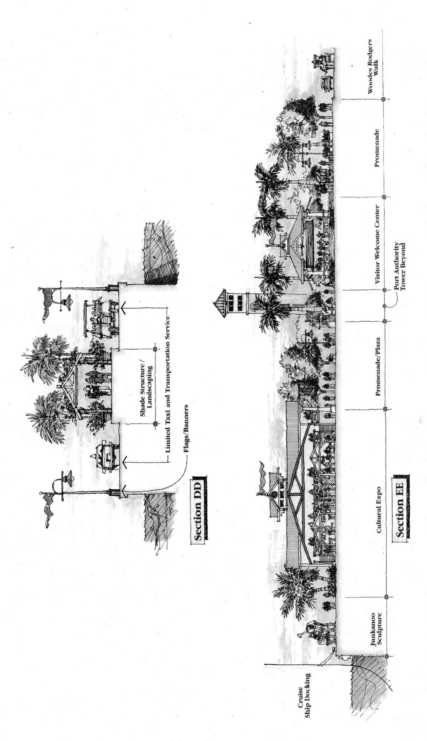

Figure 10-18 Section DD of a proposed pier communicates an important design principle: separate incompatible vehicle and pedestrian circulation systems. Source: Edward D. Stone, Jr., and Associates.

Connectivity

☐ *Satisfy* pedestrian "desire lines" with convenient linkages between common destinations (for example, building entrances, transit stops, parking lots, plazas).

☐ *Minimize* the number and distance of walkway interruptions (for example, across large parking lots).

Capacity

☐ *Provide* a hierarchy of pathways, each with sufficient width to accommodate expected pedestrian traffic.

Accessibility

☐ *Provide* disabled users direct access from parking spaces to pedestrian walkways and from walkways to building entrances (Figure 10-19).

☐ *Ensure* that all walkway gradients are safe to navigate even in inclement weather (Figure 10-20).

The Americans with Disabilities Act (ADA) is a federal civil rights law (1992) that prohibits the exclusion of people with disabilities from everyday activities (for example, shopping, attending movies, eating in restaurants). ADA requirements affect private businesses of all sizes and non-profit organizations. Tax credits and deductions offset many costs of providing access to people with disabilities. ADA has less-stringent requirements for existing facilities built before 1993.

Figure 10-19 Direct access provided from a disabled parking space to an adjacent walkway.

Figure 10-20 Pedestrian access on sloping terrain can be an elegant, sculptural element (San Francisco, California).

Amenities

- *Special paving* (to define entrances to buildings and sites, and at major pedestrian intersections)

- *Lighting* (human scale fixtures and adequate lighting)

- *Furniture* (seating in sun and shade), *kiosks and signs, trash receptacles, drinking fountains*

- *Seating areas* (nooks, niches, and scenic overlooks)

- *Vegetation* (trees, shrubs, annuals, and perennials)

- *Public art* (Figure 10-21)

- *Decorative fountains*

Pedestrian amenities are essential elements of livable communities, providing outdoor comfort and contributing to a community's sense of place (Figure 10-22). For example, high-quality pedestrian spaces incorporate "special" paving—such as brick or granite or concrete pavers—to define and visually enrich the space by adding color and texture to the ground plane (Figure 10-23).

10.5.2   Bicycle Circulation

Bicycle circulation can safely occur in the traffic lanes of low-speed, low traffic streets or drives. Streets with higher traffic volumes and speeds require dedicated bicycle lanes to

Figure 10-21 Sculpture by Henry Moore, an example of public art within the built environment (Zurich, Switzerland).

safely accommodate bike traffic. More importantly, off-street bicycle paths or bicycle/pedestrian paths should be added where feasible (Figure 10-24). Community transportation is not confined to the public realm. Safe linkages from site circulation systems to community circulation systems are essential for more sustainable and livable built environments.

10.5.3   Vehicle Circulation

Transportation network patterns have a direct influence on land development patterns. Sustainable communities reduce the number and distance of vehicle trips by mixing land uses and ensuring that safe and comfortable alternatives exist for pedestrians, bicyclists, and transit riders. Shorter blocks, with lengths between 300 and 500 feet (91.4 and 152.4 meters), improve neighborhood walkability (Ewing, 1999, p.4). Interconnected street networks with high levels of connectivity also tend to reduce traffic congestion by distributing traffic across a greater number of streets, rather than concentrating traffic on a small number of arterial or collector streets.

Entry and arrival sequence

Entry and arrival sequences are as important to vehicle circulation systems as they are to pedestrian circulation systems. The entrance experience to a site can be enhanced—and even celebrated—by good design (Figure 10-25). Corner lots at street intersections are particularly important locations because of their high visibility. When not carefully sited, large parking lots negatively impact visual character and diminish the site entry and arrival experience.

Vehicle parking is provided by either surface lots or parking structures. Structures, although much more costly to build, have the advantage of accommodating more vehicles within a smaller site area or "footprint," therefore, making more of the site available for other uses. Parking can be provided in stand-alone structures, in underground structures beneath buildings, or on upper levels of buildings that have commercial uses on the lower levels. On sites with high land costs—particularly in locations that are served by transit—this mixed-use approach has the advantage of supporting higher density development.

Like any major component of the built environment, the design *and* placement of parking lots determine not only how well they perform their intended function but also their impacts on pedestrians and the environment. Parking lots often have unintended consequences. For example, poorly designed or improperly sited parking lots may impede pedestrian circulation, diminish visual quality, and weaken a community's sense of place.

Organize Vehicle Circulation and Parking

Vehicle circulation is best organized by non-paved surfaces that define the lot's parking bays and aisles. The primary organizing structures are landscaped peninsulas extending from the parking lot edges, and interior landscaped islands. Restricting vehicles to defined circulation and parking patterns has several benefits, including improving driver orientation or way finding. It also minimizes pedestrian/vehicle conflicts and minimizes the lot's impervious surface areas (Figure 10-26). In addition, sufficient lighting and landscaping enhance the quality of the pedestrian experience walking to and from parked vehicles.

Pedestrian—vehicle conflicts are common where the built environment has been designed exclusively for vehicles. When parking lots are not designed by qualified site-planning professionals, pedestrians are commonly relegated to use the vehicle circulation system because walkways were not provided. The quality of the built environment—certainly in the United States—could be substantially improved simply through better design of all parking lots.

Bay configurations may be single loaded (parking on one side of aisle) or double loaded (parking on both sides of the aisle). Parking spaces may be oriented perpendicular to the aisle or angled (usually 45 or 60 degrees) to the aisle. To prevent driver confusion, a perpendicular arrangement of parking spaces serves two-way aisle circulation. Angled spaces are better served by one-way circulation.

Integrate Green Space

Plantings within and adjacent to parking lots provide seasonal interest and foster sustainable approaches to stormwater management. By intercepting precipitation, filtering stormwater runoff, and facilitating groundwater infiltration, planted areas help to reduce development impacts on the local hydrologic system. Trees in and adjacent to parking lots shade pavement, which helps to reduce local heat island effects and reduce air pollution (Figure 10-27). Trees need healthy roots. Planting islands must be large enough to permit healthy root growth. The width of one parking space (about 9 feet or 2.74 meters) is a reasonable dimension for islands or peninsulas planted with shade trees. Even the proverbial "sea of asphalt"—seemingly ubiquitous in suburban shopping malls across the United States—can be retrofitted with tree islands (Figure 10-28).

On sloping sites, surface parking lots with islands running parallel to the contours can "take up the grade" of the slope and, by terracing the paved aisles and bays, significantly reduce the cross-slopes on the surfaces used by vehicles and pedestrians (Figure 10-29). This terracing approach is particularly beneficial in colder climates where freezing temperatures can make icy, sloped pavements very dangerous for pedestrians. If the lot is graded to encourage surface runoff into the islands, these green spaces can srve as bioinfiltration swales or rain gardens that retain stormwater and promote groundwater recharge (Figure 10-30).

Disconnect Impervious Surfaces

Impervious surfaces disrupt the landscape's natural hydrologic cycle by impeding stormwater infiltration, and by altering natural runoff patterns and volumes. The impacts of site development can be mitigated, somewhat, by integrating green spaces within parking lots

Figure 10-22 Fountain and landscaping amenities for pedestrians (Boca Raton, Florida).

Figure 10-23 Special paving accentuates a building's entrance along an urban streetscape (San Francisco, California).

to disconnect these impervious surfaces. Parking lot edges that are curbless or have openings in the curbs allow stormwater runoff to filter into turf or bioretention areas. Porous paving (Figure 10-31) is another fine-scale method for disconnecting impervious surfaces (Ferguson, 2005).

Service and Emergency Vehicles

Grocery stores, department stores, and other commercial buildings regularly receive product deliveries. A loading dock may be an essential program component on some site-planning projects (Figure 10-32). In addition to receiving deliveries, most buildings generate wastes or recyclable materials that are temporarily stored on site and picked up regularly by service providers. Dumpsters for trash and recycling containers may be part of the program as well. Emergency vehicles also require access to sites for fire protection and medical emergencies. These large trucks require much more space for turning than automobiles. These turning radii, which vary by truck length, wheel-base, and number of axles can be significant determinants in designing service areas and providing emergency access to buildings.

10.6 BUILDINGS

The design development process involves decisions about the articulation of elements generally defined on the conceptual site plan. If a development "pod" on a concept plan is

Figure 10-24 Lakefront bicycle path in Geneva, Switzerland.

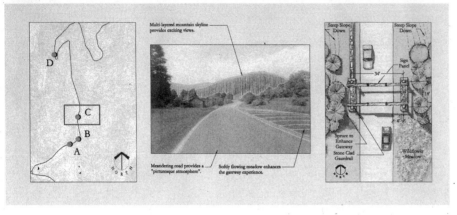

Key Map   Visual Analysis   Plan View

Proposed Gateway in Location C

Figure 10-25 Proposal for a park entrance and sign. Visual quality of the surroundings is a major design determinant. Source: Land Design.

designated as single-family housing, for example, the next step might be to add walkways in addition to the individual building lots or parcels. If the pod will be a multifamily housing cluster, design development would focus on determining the size, shape, and location of the "footprint" for the building or the building's ensemble.

In the design of urban infill projects, new buildings are expected to be "good neighbors" and "fit in" contextually—at least when the nearby buildings are well designed. This "fitting in" is often achieved by "echoing" the massing, scale, proportion, or other design attributes of nearby buildings. Visually cohesive downtown commercial districts have buildings that tend to complement one another in form and function (National Mainstreet Center, 1995).

Besides the important issue of building design, the placement or siting of a building has a substantial influence on the character and

Figure 10-26 Walkway within a parking lot separates pedestrians from vehicle traffic.

scale of the built environment. Factors that should be considered in siting a building include the terrain, the climate, and proximity to nearby streets and buildings. Scale is especially important in the design of streetscapes and other open spaces in which people walk, sit, and pursue other activities. Scale is determined, in part, by the placement of buildings and, therefore, the distances between them.

10.6.1   Precedent and Architectural Design

The articulation of a building's exterior involves choices regarding materials, colors, and forms, as well as several other attributes. Buildings achieve contextual compatibility by "echoing" the attributes of well-designed precedents within the site's neighborhood, community, or region. Distinctive bungalows, a housing style popularized in the later 19th and early 20th centuries, are particularly fitting in new urbanist communities, where great attention is given to the quality of the architectural design (Figure 10-33).

When a distinct building style is repeated over time in sufficient density, the precedent or style may be identified with a particular city or region. Frank Lloyd Wright's architectural legacy from the early twentieth century, for example, has spawned a strong—and growing influence on contemporary architectural design in the Midwest (United States). His horizontal, landscape-hugging buildings in

Figure 10-28   A new tree island created within an existing shopping center parking lot.

Chicago, Milwaukee, and Madison, for example, are iconic structures that virtually define the prairie style.

Architectural styles associated with specific cities or geographic regions are not uncommon. San Francisco, for example, is world-renowned for it's Victorian architecture. The vertical massing, pastel colors, and highly articulated facades of row houses and mansions define the older streetscapes and neighborhoods of this hilly, picturesque "City by the Bay." Similarly, Miami, Florida, is closely identified with palm trees and the rounded forms and pastel colors of art deco architecture.

10.6.2   Building Uses

Sustainable and livable neighborhoods bring residential, commercial, and civic uses, and outdoor recreation, together in close proximity. Residential and commercial uses, for example, may be in separate buildings located close together—or within individual buildings—typically, with professional offices, restaurants, and retail uses on the first one or two stories, and residential uses on the stories above. This enables residents to live within walking distance of where they shop and, potentially, where they work. When these different uses are close to each other, spatially, and are served by well-designed pedestrian circulation systems, residents and employees are able to drive less and walk more for at least some of their daily trips.

Mixed-use redevelopment is very gradually changing the face of suburban America, as well as many downtowns. The development of new neighborhood centers—especially when located near public transit—is a positive step toward more sustainable and livable communities. Yet higher-density infill development places a premium on outdoor open spaces that are well-designed and safely connected by adequate walkways. As Jan Gehl (2003) aptly states: "Life takes place on foot."

Other convenient modes of transportation are important, as well. Although commuter rail, light rail, and streetcars require substantial public investment, these slowly reemerging forms of transit increase the viability of higher density redevelopment. Transit routes that serve compact, higher-density neighborhoods, with more people, are simply more cost effective. In less dense neighborhoods, convenient transportation alternatives also include energy-efficient bus service.

10.6.3   Building Design

Massing

A building's scale is a function of both massing and articulation. Buildings that are in scale with the human body tend to be well articulated at the ground level

Figure 10-29 Parking lot on a sloping site. The planted island reduces the cross-slope or gradient of the adjacent parking bays.

Figure 10-30 Bioretention swale collects and filters stormwater runoff from parking surfaces and facilitates groundwater recharge.

Figure 10-31 Porous paving (concrete grid) in a commercial parking lot.

and at least the first one or two stories above that (Figure 10-34a and b). This is the zone that has the greatest visual impact on pedestrians entering or walking past the building. Human-scaled streetscapes, typically, are enclosed by buildings that are two to four stories in height. If the buildings are taller, the higher stories are recessed, or "stepped back," from the streets' edges. This context-sensitive massing is far superior—from a pedestrian's perspective—than the alternative: cavernous streetscapes crowded by tall buildings that dwarf the pedestrians below.

Besides the unavoidable visual impacts, tall, closely spaced buildings also have significant effects on streetscape microclimate. They often cast the streetscapes into near-perpetual shade. In blustery weather conditions, the buildings create downdrafts and funnel the wind—creating very pedestrian unfriendly wind tunnels. In contrast, a building that has a height of two to four stories at the street edge adds a sense of urbanity and enclosure, without creating visually overwhelming edifices.

The Affordable Housing Design Advisor (www.designadvisor.org), a U.S. Department of Housing and Urban Development website, recommends "visual and architectural complexity" in affordable housing—not as a frivolous gesture but as an integral part of the project's design. For example, recommendations include the following:

Consider breaking a large building into smaller units or clusters. Consider variations in height, color, setback, materials, texture, trim, and roof shape. Consider variations in the shape and placement of windows, balconies, and other façade elements. Consider using landscape elements to add variety and differentiate units from each other.

Articulation

Regardless of a building's height along the street edge, the design of the building's first story, especially, is critically important to a livable streetscape. *Transparency* is particularly important in the design of buildings in downtown commercial districts, neighborhood centers, and other similar streetscapes intended for pedestrians. A building with extensive windows on the first floor is not only visually interesting but also allows a visual relationship between the building's interior and exterior. This contributes to a more inviting presence and a sense of belonging to the community. Conversely, when a building's ground floor at the streetscape is a blank wall, or one with few openings of any consequence, the visual effect may be perceived as hostile, or antisocial.

Façade openings—windows and doors—create more inviting streetscapes. Building entrances, when placed along major pedestrian walkways, are more convenient for the

Figure 10-32 Recessed loading dock for a suburban office building.

Figure 10-33 A single-family house, designed in the bungalow style and built in the 1990s, within a neotraditional neighborhood in Middleton Hills, Wisconsin. Source: Bridget Lang.

Figure 10-34a Human-scaled and environmentally responsive site planning in Ciudad Mitras, Mexico. Source: The HOK Planning Group.

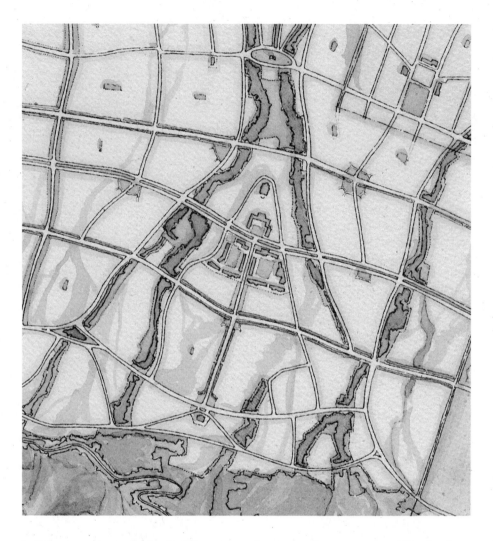

buildings' occupants. A visually interesting pedestrian environment may add pedestrian-friendly features such as awnings, articulated façades, and streetfront display windows. Choices of construction materials are driven by several factors, including material durability, cost, and appearance. Which materials are used, and how they are combined, determines—to a large extent—if the project is attractive and if it fits in with its surroundings. Neighborhood design guidelines for the Seattle, Washington aptly state (City of Seattle Department of Planning and Development, 2005, p.12):

> A contextual design approach is not intended to dictate a historicist approach, but rather one that is sensitive to surrounding noteworthy buildings and style elements.

Figure 10-34b Urban open space defined by human-scaled architecture in Ciudad Mitras, Mexico. Source: The HOK Planning Group.

Not all new buildings must conform, visually, to their surroundings. When the new building will serve a prominent civic function—such as a library, school, or hospital—departure from the norm may be in order and, indeed, desirable. Because of their special uses or purposes, these are often the important iconic buildings within the community—deserving a more prominent visual presence.

10.6.4 Building Siting

Good site planning is concerned with the siting or placement of buildings in response to specific site and contextual conditions. Earlier chapters addressed a variety of biophysical, cultural, and legal factors, or design determinants, that influence how and where buildings are placed on a site. These influences are not universally constant, but vary across the urban to rural continuum. What may be appropriate in either a rural or suburban environment, for example, may be completely inappropriate in an urban setting. Context, therefore, is especially important for decisions concerning a building's siting. Site conditions play a very significant role in building design and placement (Table 10-3).

Building footprints, as well as their placement, should be adapted to fit the site. Hilly sites may lead to the design of a building in which both the foundation and the floors of the building "step down" the hillside. Both functional and visual indoor–outdoor relationships may also influence the design of the building and site (Figure 10-35).

TABLE 10-3 Examples of site conditions that influence building design, particularly in rural and suburban settings.

Topography (Slope, Aspect, and Elevation)
Structural wind loading
Architectural elevations

Soil Types, Textures, and Load-Bearing Capacity
Foundation location and engineering

Vegetative Cover and Existing Native Plant Populations
Solar load access and avoidance
Construction boundaries and site drainage
Maintenance strategies

Wildlife Migration and Nesting Patterns
Footprint location and site clearing

Geologic and Seismic Conditions
Foundation type and location
Structural specifications

Parcel Shape and Adjacent Land Uses and Buildings
Capacity to accommodate a proposed building size
Building access points

Utility Easements or Corridors, Lines, and Sizes
Footprint location
Location of building tie-in to utilities

Micro-Climate Factors (For Example, Solar and Wind Loads)
Layout for solar orientation
Location of entrances, windows, and loading docks
Location of air inlets and exhaust

Circulation Networks For Pedestrians, Bicycles, Vehicles, and Transit
Walking distance and orientation to other pedestrian destinations
Fire protection

Source: Los Alamos National Laboratory Sustainable Design Guide (Ch.3 Building Siting, p.37).

According to the U.S. Green Building Council (USGBC), green design and construction practices significantly reduce or eliminate negative impacts of buildings on occupants—and on the environment. Green buildings are healthier buildings, providing more natural daylight and fresh air. The LEED (Leadership in Energy and Environmental Design) Green Building Rating System for new construction focuses on five areas: sustainable site planning, safeguarding water and water efficiency, energy efficiency and renewable energy, conservation of materials and resources, and indoor environmental quality (see www.usgbc.org).

Principles for siting buildings, particularly in rural and suburban settings, include the following (U.S. National Park Service, 1993):

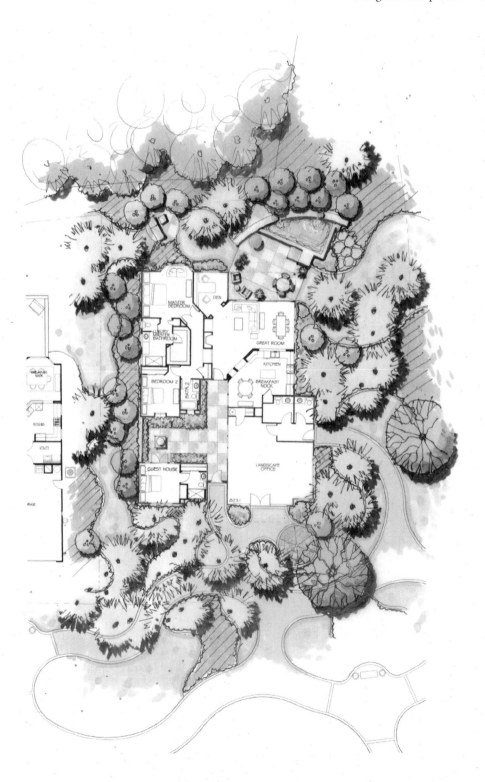

Figure 10-35 A site plan that shows landscape/building relationships for a new single-family residence. Trees and shrubs define outdoor spaces, provide shade, screen views, and perform a variety of other design functions. Source: Edward D. Stone, Jr., and Associates.

◻ Reuse previously disturbed sites to conserve open space, and minimize site-clearing, excavation, and disturbance of natural habitats, to reduce costs and minimize soil compaction.

◻ Preserve existing vegetation, which can reduce landscape maintenance costs, add character to the site, and provide energy-conserving shade and wind protection; select plants that are appropriate for the soil type and microclimate and restore natural habitats.

◻ Take advantage of natural site features, such as topography, sunlight, shade, and prevailing breezes, to promote energy conservation and natural ventilation.

◻ Maximize benefits for building and site occupants (for example, thermal comfort, access to fresh air, acoustic privacy, aesthetic views, functional outdoor space).

◻ Orient the building with the long side on the east-west axis to allow for the greatest winter solar gains and to minimize cooling loads from excessive solar heat gain.

◻ Minimize stormwater runoff and mitigate erosion to reduce topsoil loss and protect surface water quality; minimize groundwater and surface water pollution by eliminating supplemental irrigation and fertilizing.

◻ In colder climates, locate driveways, parking, entrances, and loading docks on the south side of buildings to minimize snow and ice build-up; minimize ground-level wind loads with vegetation, walls, fences, berming, or earth sheltering to act as windbreaks and to minimize snow build-up.

Building siting must also respond to regulatory requirements for development. Required building setbacks or build-to lines, for example, influence building placement. Floor area ratio (FAR) is another common zoning requirement that limits the size and site coverage of new buildings.

"Form-based" development codes are becoming increasingly common in the United States. These land use controls provide specific goals and standards for architectural design and site planning. Design guidelines typically seek to ensure that new development is responsive to site and context and also enhances the character of the community and neighborhood. Neighborhood design guidelines prepared by the City of Seattle Department of Planning and Development, for example, address this broad range of design concerns (Box 10-1).

10.7 CONCLUSION

Site planning's design development process involves the refinement, or articulation, of the conceptual site plan. Design theory—applied to each unique program and site—provides many of the rules or "best practices" for guiding this process. Site planning can play a vital role in improving the sustainability and "livability" of the built environment.

Figure 10-36 Three-dimensional model of the site concept plan. *Source:* The HOK Planning Group.

The spatial organization of the site—horizontally and vertically—must be effectively communicated to the client, other project consultants, and other stakeholders—particularly for design review by the public sector. Site planners commonly convey their design ideas with plans, sections or elevations, perspective sketches, and/or models (Figure 10-36). A project's proposed character—or spatial articulation—must be clear (Figure 10-37 and 10-38). Project phasing is often very important, as well.

Character Studies

Figure 10-37 Design character studies for a subtropical waterfront resort. Source: Edward D. Stone, Jr., and Associates.

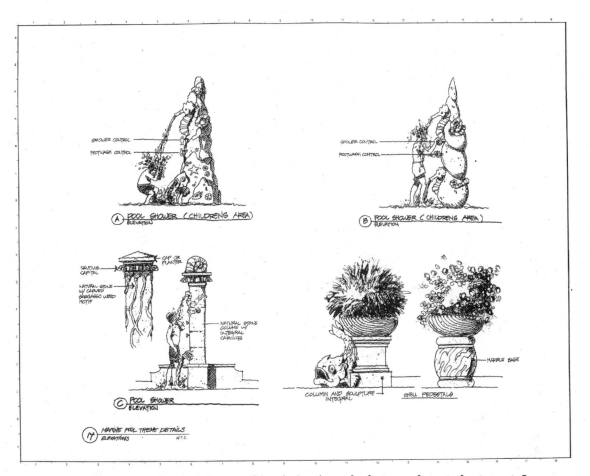

Figure 10-38 Character studies depicting a unifying design theme for features of a waterfront resort. Source: Edward D. Stone, Jr., and Associates.

BOX 10.1   Design Guidelines (Urban Context)

WALLINGFORD NEIGHBORHOOD DESIGN GUIDELINES

EFFECTIVE MAY 6, 2005

CITY OF SEATTLE, WASHINGTON

DEPARTMENT OF PLANNING AND DEVELOPMENT

The following design guidelines generally apply citywide. Additional guidelines, specific to the Wallingford Neighborhood, are omitted for the sake of brevity.

Site Planning
☐ Respond to site characteristics.

☐ Reinforce existing streetscape characteristics.

BOX 10.1   Design Guidelines (Urban Context)

☐ Make the site's entry clearly identifiable from the street.

☐ Encourage human activity on the street.

☐ Maximize opportunities for usable, attractive, well-integrated open space.

☐ Minimize the impact of automobile parking and driveways on the pedestrian environment and adjacent properties.

☐ Minimize parking on commercial street fronts by locating parking behind the building.

☐ Orient buildings on corner lots toward the corner and public street fronts, keeping parking and automobile access away from the corner.

Height, Bulk, and Scale

☐ Provide a sensitive transition to nearby, less-intensive zones.

☐ Cornice and rooflines should respect the heights of surrounding structures.

☐ Traditional architectural features such as pitched roofs and gables are encouraged on residential project sites adjacent to single-family and low-rise zones.

☐ Consider upper-level setbacks (5 feet) to limit the visibility of floors that are above 30 feet.

☐ Consider dividing buildings into small masses with variation of building setbacks and heights to preserve views, sun, and privacy of adjacent residential structures and sun exposure of public spaces, including streets and sidewalks.

Architectural Elements and Materials

☐ In existing neighborhoods with a well-defined and desirable character, new buildings should be compatible with the architectural character and siting pattern of neighboring buildings.

☐ Traditional early twentieth century commercial structures on the first story provide the streetscape with visual interest and human scale. These include the following:

- Solid kick panels below windows
- Large storefront windows
- Multipane or double hung windows with transoms or clerestories
- High level of fine-grained detailing and trim
- High-quality materials, such as brick and terra-cotta
- Canopies
- Variable parapets
- Cornices

☐ Distinguish the base, middle, and top of mixed-use buildings.

- Ground floors with transparent, open facades for commercial uses at street level (for example, windows cover 50-80 percent of the ground floor façade and begin approximately 24 to 30 inches above the sidewalk)

BOX 10.1   Design Guidelines (Urban Context)

- Middle floors are articulated to distinguish individual floors, etc.
- Tops of buildings may include gables with overhangs, parapets, and cornices; the roofline or top of the structure should be clearly distinguished from its façade walls.

☐ Building massing and detailing should create a well- proportioned and unified building form, with features expressing the functions within the building.

☐ Human-scaled architectural features, elements, and details should be incorporated in the design of new buildings.

Pedestrian Environment (Ground Plane, Ground/First Story)
☐ Pedestrian open spaces and building entrances, especially for residential uses, add activity on the street and allow for visual surveillance for personal safety.

☐ Continuous, well-lighted, overhead weather protection improves pedestrian comfort and promotes a sense of security.

☐ Avoid blank walls facing the street, especially near sidewalks.

☐ Minimize the visual and physical intrusion of parking lots on pedestrian areas.

☐ Personal safety and security: pedestrian-scale lighting (12–15 feet high pole fixtures or bollard fixtures).

Landscaping
☐ Planters at entryways are encouraged.

☐ Special paving, trellises, screen walls at the perimeter of parking lots, planters, site furniture, and plantings.

☐ Retain existing trees wherever possible.

Project Implementation

The most successful countries place high value on their buildings and on the spaces between their buildings.

—*Architecture + Design Scotland*

11.1 INTRODUCTION

Skillful site planning and architectural design can yield significant social, economic, and environmental benefits. A well-designed project, moreover—supported by a thorough analysis of the site and its surrounding context—is in many cases not any more expensive to build than a poorly designed project. Fortunately, savvy real estate developers have come to understand this. In a panel discussion convened by *Architectural Record* magazine, Dennis Carmichael, a landscape architect with EDAW, Inc., asserted (Dean, 1997, p. 49):

> . . . developers have learned that a good design equals return on investment. Rather than bulldozing a site into submission, they now try to celebrate its intrinsic qualities.

Unfortunately, in the United States, design excellence in the built environment remains an elusive goal. Examples of poor site planning and development abound—as many of the photographs in this chapter illustrate. It is incumbent, therefore, on the planning and design professions to learn from the mistakes of the past and take the steps necessary—within the public, non-profit, and private sectors—to incrementally improve the quality of the built environment. This includes developing, refining, and implementing the "best practices" in each allied field.

In the United States, for example, the Leadership in Energy and Environmental Design (LEED) Green Building Rating System[TM] provides explicit benchmarks for the design, construction, and operation of green buildings and related site development (see www.usgbc.org). LEED promotes a holistic approach to sustainability by focusing on building and site performance in five areas affecting human and environmental health, as follows:

- □ Sustainable site development

- □ Water savings

- □ Energy efficiency

- □ Materials selection

- □ Indoor environmental quality

Current LEED guidelines for measuring and documenting "green" development include the following areas:

- □ New commercial construction

- □ Major commercial renovation projects

- □ Existing building operations and maintenance

- □ Multiple buildings and on-campus building projects

- □ Neighborhood development

- □ Schools

- □ Homes

The U.S. Green Building Council (USGBC) is also developing LEED guidelines that will address new retail construction and healthcare facilities. The new LEED for Neighborhood Development (LEED-ND) rating system integrates the principles of smart growth, new urbanism, and green building. This standard for neighborhood design is the result of collaboration among three major non-profit organizations: the U.S. Green Building Council, the Congress for the New Urbanism, and the Natural Resources Defense Council.

11.2 QUALITY BY DESIGN

11.2.1 Reclaiming the Built Environment for Pedestrians

Good site planning can play a vital role in helping communities and neighborhoods reconnect with their pasts and maintain or strengthen their character and sense of place.

Figure 11-1 Although this building is fronting a public street, the poorly articulated façade and closeness to the street creates a very hostile pedestrian environment.

Along with historically authentic development, sustainable and livable development creates safe and pleasant outdoor environments for pedestrians (Figure 11-1). Pedestrian-friendly, mixed-use development includes housing, shops, restaurants, and other services, and neighborhoods with human-scaled buildings and streetscapes (Figures 11-2 and 11-3).

Context-sensitive transportation planning, for example, preserves scenic, aesthetic, and historic and environmental resources while creating multiple alternatives for safe and efficient transportation within a community. Transportation planning must be a collaborative effort that includes not only professional engineers, but also draws upon the skills of urban planners, landscape architects, and other professionals. Sustainable and livable communities place less emphasis on minimizing traffic delays and much more emphasis on traffic calming and increasing safe and convenient transportation alternatives.

These communities build pedestrian and bicycle circulation systems that are separate from the vehicle circulation system (Figure 11-4). When embedded within compact,

Figures 11-2 and 11-3 Residential "garagescapes" visibly convey the importance of the automobile in the United States. These also pose an uninviting barrier to visitors and neighbors.

Figures 11-2 and 11-3
continued

Figure 11-4 Though cul-de-sacs are residential streets that may have light vehicle traffic, should pedestrians be forced to "share" the street with vehicles?

Figure 11-5 A barrier wall, a lack of street trees, and insufficient separation from the street and parking lot create a hostile "no-man's zone" for pedestrians.

Figure 11-6 A poorly constructed stairway conveys the message that pedestrian safety and comfort are unimportant in this built environment.

mixed-use neighborhoods, well-designed pedestrian and bicycle networks can reduce daily vehicle trips and daily vehicle miles traveled, and reduce the polluting impacts of vehicles on the environment (Figure 11-5). Enabling safe and convenient walking and bicycling (Figure 11-6) has the added benefits of facilitating active living and enhancing a community's quality of life.

11.2.2   Restoration and Redevelopment

Agricultural development in the United States has involved woodland clearing, wetland drainage, and extensive topsoil erosion. Urban development has involved the industrialization of waterfronts and riparian areas and the fragmentation of wetlands and forests for highway construction. Along with forestry, mining, and other human activities, these land uses have left a legacy of environmental impacts that, today, present opportunities for redevelopment, remediation, and/or restoration.

Urban waterfronts, for example, which were often developed—particularly in the late nineteenth and early twentieth centuries—with railroad yards and heavy industry are potentially highly valuable community resources. When properly redeveloped—and ecologically restored—these locations become catalysts for economic activity and community pride.

Correcting mistakes and mitigating the impacts of previous site uses are an important part of sustainable site planning. Ecological restoration can have the greatest positive impacts on the environment if these efforts are judiciously targeted to ecologically critical areas. Riparian restoration, for example, is a good example of targeted remediation that produces important results, including:

☐ buffering aquatic habitats from contaminated stormwater runoff from upland, developed areas;

☐ creating ecotone habitat for native plant and animal species;

□ bioengineering solutions for shoreline stabilization to reduce erosion and sedimentation of water bodies;

□ adding aesthetic amenity through soil stabilizing plantings that are far superior, aesthetically, to "hardened" shoreline treatment (for example, stone rip-rap).

A thorough site analysis, of course, can provide the "road map" for targeting ecological restoration activities.

11.2.3   Stormwater Management

The proportion of a watershed covered by impervious surfaces is a key indicator of the potential hydrologic impact of urban development (Arnold and Gibbons, 1996). On developed sites, poorly managed stormwater runoff may increase the *quantity* of runoff and contribute to local flooding (Figure 11-7). Degraded runoff *quality* in developed and developing areas may contribute to four kinds of pollution, as follows:

□ Thermal pollution (runoff with elevated temperatures)

□ Sedimentation (sand, silt, clay)

□ Chemical pollution (hydrocarbons, heavy metals, fertilizers, pesticides)

□ Pathogens (bacteria and viruses)

The spatial structure of the built environment affects the movement of water, nutrients, and sediment within the landscape. Land development changes the distribution, or *quantity*, of water within a watershed. Groundwater depletion, for example, occurs when groundwater pumping is not balanced by groundwater recharge. The result of this imbalance is a gradual depletion or "mining" of groundwater resources.

Figure 11-7 Excessive impervious surfaces—in this case a 110-feet (33.53 meters) wide cul-de-sac—are expensive to build and maintain, negatively impact runoff quality and quantity, and are completely out of scale with their intended transportation function

Figure 11-8 Exceedingly wide streets and inconsequential street tree plantings clearly signal that this subdivision was designed (and approved) for the convenience of motorists—not pedestrians.

Methods of managing stormwater in the United States have changed dramatically over the past century, resulting in an overlapping series of management paradigms (Reese, 2004). This evolution has largely been in response to significant environmental impacts—often created by previous management practices that exacerbated land development's hydrologic and ecological impacts (Figures 11-8, 11-9, 11-10, and 11-11). Governments in the United States have taken a more aggressive role in regulating development impacts. An increasingly common requirement is that peak runoff rates, average runoff volumes, and average annual total suspended solid (TSS) loadings be maintained at levels that do not exceed predevelopment levels (U.S. Environmental Protection Agency, 1993).

Low-impact development minimizes hydrologic impacts by facilitating stormwater infiltration and groundwater recharge, removing waterborne pollutants and maintaining other important hydrologic functions. Objectives include the following (Prince George's County, 2000):

- Avoid development of the hydrological infrastructure (for example, streams and their buffers, floodplains, wetlands, steep slopes, high-permeability soils, and woodlands).

Figure 11-9 Narrow planting islands surrounded by pavement ensure the stunting (or imminent demise) of even the hardiest tree species.

Figures 11-10 and 11-11
A "brute-force approach" to
conveying stormwater runoff as
quickly as possible to the
nearest detention pond—or
worse—to a wetland or water
body.

- Protect existing native trees, shrubs, grasses, and forbs.

- Limit site clearing and soil disturbance to the areas required for building footprints, construction access, material storage, and safety setbacks.

- Control stormwater at the source (for example, minimize and mitigate land development impacts at, or near, the site disturbance).

- Disconnect impervious surfaces to increase infiltration and reduce runoff.

- Disperse drainage from roofs and other large impervious surfaces to lengthen flow paths and encourage slow, shallow runoff over vegetated, pervious surfaces.

▫ Use simple, small, nonstructural methods (for example, grassed swales and shallow basins with gentle side slopes, "rain" gardens.

▫ Plant with native or naturalized vegetation.

Sustainable site planning must also ensure that a project's implementation minimizes adverse impacts and includes appropriate restorative measures. For example, vegetated buffer zones can protect critical environmental areas from contaminated runoff and facilitate infiltration and groundwater recharge. Native and naturalized plant materials significantly reduce both planting costs and maintenance costs for irrigation, mowing or pruning, and pest control. In the Midwest (United States), for example, maintaining irrigated turfgrass costs as much as six times more than the cost of maintaining a native prairie or wetland community (Applied Ecological Services, 2000).

"Green roofs" and "rain gardens" can also reduce off-site runoff, while creating ecological and aesthetic amenities that reduce operation and maintenance costs for buildings and sites. Vegetated rooftops reduce energy requirements for heating and cooling buildings, reduce stormwater runoff and urban heat island effects, and create habitat for beneficial insects. Disbursing rooftop runoff over a pervious surface before it reaches an impervious surface can decrease the annual runoff volume from residential development sites by as much as 50 percent (Kwon, 2000). Of course, green roofs can also provide outdoor "refuge" space for humans.

11.2.4 Erosion Control

Erosion control is based on two main concepts (U.S. Environmental Protection Agency, 1993): disturb the smallest area of land possible for the shortest period of time and stabilize disturbed soils to prevent erosion from occurring (Figures 11-12, 11-13, and 11-14). During construction, effective stormwater management controls erosion, retains sediments on the site, and facilitates runoff retention and infiltration. Sediment discharges

Figures 11-12, 11-13, and 11-14
Unlike these construction sites, sustainable development minimizes site disturbances and employs protective measures to limit soil compaction, soil erosion, and the sedimentation of terrestrial and aquatic habitats.

Figures 11-13 and 11-14
continued

from construction sites can be many times greater than the discharges from undeveloped areas. Moreover, heavy metals, nutrients, and other pollutants can attach to sediments carried by the stormwater runoff. Nonpoint source pollution controls reduce the potential impacts of runoff both during and after construction.

By preventing the onset or start of soil movement, erosion can be minimized. Primary erosion control methods for construction sites include the following (U.S. Environmental Protection Agency, 1993):

□ Schedule clearing and grading to avoid periods of highest erosion potential (spring thaw) and favor periods of the year with lowest erosion potential (dry season).

□ Stage-land disturbance activities to expose only the area currently under construction. As soon as the grading and construction in an area are complete, stabilize the area with seeding, sodding, and, on steeper slopes, matting or mulching.

□ Restrict clearing to the areas essential for construction. Physically mark off the proposed land disturbance limits to ensure that only the required land area is cleared. Fencing should be used to protect tree root systems from cutting, filling, and compaction caused by heavy equipment.

□ Locate potential nonpoint pollution sources (for example, material stockpiles, borrow areas, construction access roads) away from steep slopes, highly erodible soils, and areas that drain directly into sensitive water bodies. Cover or stabilize topsoil stockpiles.

□ Divert runoff away from exposed areas or newly seeded slopes. Construct benches, terraces, or ditches at regular intervals to intercept runoff.

□ Minimize the length and steepness of slopes. Use retaining walls to decrease the steepness of a slope and reduce runoff velocity.

□ Stabilize drainage channels with erosion-resistant lining (for example, grass, sod, riprap).

□ Add check dams in swales or channels to reduce the runoff velocity.

11.2.5   Sediment Control

Effective erosion control reduces the size and cost of needed sediment control structures. Sediment controls capture sediment that is transported in stormwater runoff during the construction process. Detention (gravitational settling) and filtration are the main techniques for removing sediment from runoff. Construction site sediment controls include the following (U.S. Environmental Protection Agency, 1993):

□ Sediment basins

□ Sediment traps

□ Filter fabric fencing

□ Straw bale barriers

□ Drain inlet protection traps

□ Vegetated filter strips

In addition, construction entrances should be placed in locations where equipment will be less likely to track mud and other sediment off the site.

11.3   CONSTRUCTION DOCUMENTATION

Project implementation is a process of converting ideas into reality. Typically, this requires construction documents, which consist of construction drawings and written construction specifications. Construction documents become a legally binding contract to implement the project as designed. These documents are also the basis for construction cost estimates.

11.3.1 Construction Drawings

Construction drawings include plans, sections, elevations, and details. The construction plans are central elements of the construction documents (CD). Four plans, in particular, provide essential site engineering and construction information, as follows:

- *Layout plan (horizontal control).* Locates buildings, streets and parking areas, walkways, utility lines, and other site elements in relation to the site's boundaries.

- *Grading plan (vertical control).* Locates existing contours (dashed lines); proposed contours (solid lines); and proposed spot elevations at high points, low points; and pavement corners in relation to a local elevation benchmark. Drainage swales and storm drain systems are also included.

- *Utilities plan (subsurface and surface utilities).* Locates sanitary sewer systems, on-site wastewater disposal and treatment systems, drinking water distribution lines, electrical supply lines, lighting, and telecommunication cables. Typically specifies type (for example, sanitary sewer) and size or capacity (for example, pipe diameter).

- *Planting plan (trees, shrubs, vines, and groundcover).* Locates new plant materials, including the desired spacing between plants. Plant quantities, sizes, and root conditions are included in a table or schedule.

Other plans that may be included, as follows:

- *Demolition plan (site preparation).* For infill sites, especially, identifies the buildings, utility structures, and other site elements that will be either removed, adapted, or protected.

- *Irrigation plan.* Locates the site irrigation system. Sustainable site planning minimizes the need for supplementary irrigation by specifying native and natural plant materials.

- *Erosion and sediment control plan.* In some jurisdictions, an erosion and sediment control plan (ESC) must be submitted before development permits can be issued (U.S. Environmental Protection Agency, 1993). Typically, an erosion and sediment control plan includes the following information (U.S. Environmental Protection Agency, 1993):

  - Description of predominant soil types
  - Site grading details, including existing and proposed contours
  - Design details and locations for structural controls
  - Provisions to preserve topsoil and limit disturbance
  - Details of temporary and permanent stabilization measures
  - Description of the construction sequence

Construction details may be plans, sections, or elevations. As computer technology has become an integral tool in site planning and design, construction detailing has become more efficient (Cook, 1999). With the advent of computer-aided design (CAD) software, construction details are now saved as digital files and modified as needed for site- and project-specific requirements. For more extensive information on the construction documentation process, see *Site Engineering for Landscape Architects*, by Strom et al. (2004).

11.3.1 Construction Specifications

Construction specifications supplement the construction drawings. Typically, specifications include information that is conveniently assembled in report form, rather than directly on the construction drawings. The *general specifications* cover topics such as bidding requirements, required insurance and bonding, as well as incentives for completing construction before the final completion date.

Competitive bidding is practiced by public clients for all but small projects and by private clients for most large projects (Sauter, 2005). Contractors propose, or bid, to complete the project—at a specified cost—based on the information conveyed by the construction documents. Typically, the client opens the sealed bids or proposals at a designated time and place to allow the bidding contractors to attend and observe the process.

The *technical specifications* are written descriptions of the procedures and materials required in implementing either a development or restoration project. They include information about the quality of materials, construction methods and standards, and work safety requirements. Some of these requirements are based on industry or government standards, such as those of the American Society for Testing and Materials (ASTM).

The construction documents ensure that the project implementation costs are considered in the contract bidding process. If the project for the site includes one or more buildings, a full set of construction plans, details, and specifications also would be prepared for each building.

11.4 CONTRACT ADMINISTRATION

Contract administration and construction supervision are different processes. Construction supervision is the responsibility of the general contractor and the various subcontractors building the project. The contractors directly supervise the work, which may involve earthmoving, demolition of existing buildings; the construction of new buildings, roads, and other site structures; and landscaping. The designers, whether architects, landscape architects, or engineers, are typically agents of the client. These agents, or consultants, protect the owner's interests through contract administration. Contract administration ensures that the project's implementation reflects the intent of the approved plans and that the work—including landscaping, for example—is completed as specified in the construction documents. If the work is not completed as specified, the local governing agency can require that it be completed, before issuing the project's "Certificate of Occupancy."

11.5 PERMITTING AND APPROVALS

11.5.1 Development Controls

If site planning and architectural design skills were easy to acquire and then broadly applied in shaping the built environment, the need for land development controls would be far less critical. In the real world, however, there is ample evidence to suggest that poor design in the built environment is quite common. In spite of great wealth and robust design professions, the United States is home to some of the most pedestrian unfriendly—and ugly—development anywhere.

Government's primary purpose is to protect the public health, safety, and welfare. Municipalities may try to protect public health, safety, and welfare in the four following ways (Chapin and Kaiser, 1985):

- Public investment (for example, transportation and utility system infrastructure, parks, and open spaces)

- Regulations (for example, zoning and subdivision ordinances and building codes)

- Incentives and disincentives (for example, preferential taxation and zoning bonuses)

- Land use planning (for example, comprehensive plan and capital improvements plan)

Local governments in the United States are divided into three branches, each of which has specific functions, as follows:

- Legislative branch (writes and enacts laws)

- Executive branch (administers laws)

- Judicial branch (interprets laws)

The legislative branch at the local level consists of a city council that writes and enacts local laws (ordinances or codes). Although these elected officials are the final authorities for the regulation of land development within the city's jurisdiction, they typically are advised by a planning commission of local citizens appointed by the mayor, the head of the executive branch (Owen, 1994). Many cities have a planning department, also in the executive branch, with a staff that prepares and administers the planning ordinances and policies. Collectively, these plans and policies determine if, when, where, and how land development can occur.

Achieving sustainability as a society requires collective action at multiple scales, from the regional level to the community level and, ultimately, to the neighborhood and site levels. Public policy can play a critical role in facilitating sustainability by reducing barriers and creating incentives for sustainable decision making.

Zoning Codes

Comprehensive plans are community-level land use plans that provide a "vision" for orderly growth and development (see Chapter 7). These plans are implemented, in part, through zoning codes and other land use regulations. A typical zoning code divides a community into many relatively small planning districts. Although some development standards or requirements apply throughout a community, additional rules commonly apply to individual districts or zones within the municipality's jurisdiction. Zoning regulations address three sets of issues within each zone (Meck et al., 2006, p. 2–1, 2–2):

1. *Permitted use of land and buildings.* General use categories include residential, commercial, and industrial. A variance may be requested if, due to unusual circumstances, compliance with the zoning requirements would pose a hardship on the land owner. Nonconforming uses may be permitted with "conditional use permits." A zoning change may be granted if it would benefit the general welfare of the community and if the change would be consistent with the objectives of the comprehensive plan.

2. *Intensity of the use.* For residential uses, intensity is expressed as dwelling unit density—minimum lot sizes for single-family residential districts and number of dwelling units per acre/hectare for multifamily residential districts. For nonresidential districts, intensity may be expressed as floor area ratio (FAR) (how many square feet of building can be built on an area of land) or building height (number of stories allowed).

3. *Height, bulk, and other dimensional standards.* These standards define, in three-dimensions, the portion of the lot that can be occupied by buildings. They may limit the percentage of the site covered by a new building, the building's FAR, and the building's height and bulk. Other standards influence the location of buildings on the site by specifying minimum lot sizes and required building setbacks from property lines. Zoning standards may also govern, for example, the design of parking lots, lighting, and signs.

Zoning districts are typically designated with a letter (indicating land-use type) and a number (indicating land-use intensity). An "R-3" district, for example, allows residential development at a medium density (for example, multifamily attached dwellings).

Zoning Overlay Districts

Special "overlay" districts may impose additional development standards, or they may allow greater flexibility in the interpretation of the existing zoning standards. In designated historic districts, for example, design options are restricted to promote the preservation and restoration of buildings with historical significance. For more information on standards and guidelines for protecting historic places, see *Canada's Historic Places* (www.historicplaces.ca/) or the *National Trust for Historic Preservation* (www.nationaltrust.org/) in the United States.

Other special overlay districts, such as major highway corridors or central business districts, may require new construction to conform to specific design guidelines. These special districts are often intended to maintain (or create) a unique identity of a neighborhood, commercial district, or other urban area. "Incentive zoning" may be used to further the public interest in these targeted areas. Incentives may be granted, for example, to encourage development that incorporates public amenities like parks, atriums, plazas, or second-story skywalks (Garvin, 1996).

Subdivision Ordinances

Land development often involves the subdivision of one parcel of land into two or more parcels. This is especially common when land is developed for single-family housing where each house sits on an individual parcel or lot. Land subdivision is a legal process requiring subdivision plat approval. The final plat records the legal boundaries of individual parcels, public easements, streets, and street rights-of-way (Owen, 1994). Upon approval, the final plat is recorded with the local register of deeds (or other appropriate land records office).

This process generally begins with a pre-application meeting where the developer or designer and planning staff member discuss the proposed development and relevant legal requirements. Subdivision controls regulate site development, including: "street widths and design; requirements for sidewalks, shapes of lots and blocks; specifications for street lights, street trees, bus stops, and other amenities; and requirements for the installation of public utilities and other services for new development" (Meck et al., 2006, p. 2–2).

Building Codes

Building codes are concerned with the structural integrity of buildings subjected to various stresses or "loads" from occupants, seismic activity, wind and snow, and the buildings' own weight (Owen, 1994). Building codes also address other health and safety issues associated with building design, including fire safety, plumbing, electrical power, and sanitation. Published national design and construction standards, such as the Uniform Building Code (UBC), are often adopted by municipalities and supplemented with local standards (Owen, 1994).

Unified Development Codes

Unified development codes attempt to eliminate the arbitrary distinctions between the regulation of subdivisions and other forms of development (Meck et al., 2006). These standards apply to all development proposals, whether or not they require the subdivision of land parcels. In the American Planning Association's "Model Smart Land Development Regulations" (Meck et al., 2006, p. 2–3), the best-unified development codes are as follows:

> ...blend the use and intensity review process (typically a part of the zoning process) with design review (traditionally part of subdivision review). The

integrated review process allows citizens and neighbors of the proposed development to get a clearer picture of what is being proposed on the site.

Unified development codes are also easier to comprehend, and provide greater predictability and fewer regulatory contradictions for developers and their consultants.

Rigid zoning codes and subdivision ordinances have contributed to urban sprawl in the United States by separating residential uses from commercial, recreational, and civic uses, and by imposing design standards that essentially mandate inefficient, inconvenient, and grossly out-of-scale development (Duany et al., 2001; Ben-Joseph and Szold, 2005). "Form-based" codes are a more effective approach to reducing development impacts and creating higher density, yet more livable and sustainable communities. These recognize the importance of the built environment's design—in all three-dimensions—to community health, safety, and welfare. Higher density development, if well designed and accompanied by open space, landscaping, and other amenities, creates attractive lifestyle options that appeal to significant segments of the housing market.

Typically, local development codes must be revised to allow, if not encourage, more sustainable forms of planned development. Depending on the context, higher density development could even entail single-family detached housing on small lots. The necessary code revisions may include the following (Wolcott, 2004, p. 3):

☐ Minimizing right-of-way and pavement width requirements (reduces impervious surfaces and stormwater runoff impacts)

☐ Reducing building setback restrictions (allows housing on smaller sites)

☐ Allowing required open spaces to include wetlands, woodlands, and other ecologically significant natural areas (allows higher densities on the site's "net" developable area)

☐ Encouraging rain gardens to help manage stormwater runoff from driveway, parking lots, and rooftops (reduces off-site runoff and the need for large detention ponds)

☐ Allowing smaller dwelling units—about 1,000 square feet or 93 square meters—with single-car garages (recognizes a diverse market segment that does not want or need large houses and lawns)

11.5.2   Site Plan and Design Review

Objectives

In the site plan and development review process, municipalities analyze the impacts of development proposals, including the resulting need for facilities and services (Table 11-1). Site plan review is a systematic assessment of a development proposal's compliance with applicable codes, standards, and accepted site design practices (Sanford and Farley, 2004).

Site plan review can ensure that the site's development will meet basic standards, including the following (Wyckoff, 2003):

TABLE 11-1 Development reviews seek to protect public health and safety and promote the public interest in multiple ways.

Goal	Specific Focus of the Review
PUBLIC HEALTH AND SAFETY	Natural and human-made hazards Excessive light and noise Building ventilation and daylight Pedestrian and bicycle circulation Recreational opportunities Visual quality
CONVENIENCE AND EFFICIENCY	Traffic flow, ingress, and egress Parking capacity Building deliveries and waste removal Land use juxtapositions and intensities
ENVIRONMENTAL QUALITY	Air and water quality Erosion and sediment control Endangered and threatened species habitats Energy conservation
MUNICIPAL SERVICES CAPACITY	Schools Police, fire, and medical protection Utilities (wastewater, electricity, water) Social services
SOCIAL EQUITY	Access to education, recreation, medical care, jobs, and affordable housing Equal participation in political decision making Stabilization of property values

Source: Adapted, in part, from Chapin and Kaiser (1985), Sanford and Farley (2004), and Wyckoff (2003).

□ Protection of sensitive natural environments

□ Prevention of environmental harm

□ Minimal impacts on surrounding properties

□ Efficiency and convenience

□ Proper relationships to public services

□ Adequate consideration to expansion options

Yet, development can—and should—exceed these basic standards. Two critical attributes of sustainable and livable neighborhoods and communities are as follows:

1. Buildings that are human-scaled in their massing and articulation and are responsive to physical and cultural site and contextual conditions.

2. Outdoor open spaces that are human-scaled, appropriately lighted and furnished, and connected with similarly designed and landscaped pedestrian circulation systems.

Achieving the basic as well as the higher-design standards requires the collaboration of multiple disciplines, especially architects, landscape architects, and urban planners. Engineers and ecologists have important roles to play as well. Collaboration among these professions is not only necessary but also synergistic—and can lead to better built environments. Equally important are formal design review processes that benefit from the experience of experts in these allied fields (Box 11-1).

Information Required for Site Plan Review

Site plan review is typically required for development proposals involving new or enlarged buildings, or changes in the size and/or circulation pattern of parking lots, or the appearance or function of a site. Determining whether a proposed development complies with the applicable development regulations requires explicit project information about the following:

☐ Existing conditions

☐ Proposed development activities

☐ Impacts of the proposed development activities

Prior to the formal site plan submittal, a pre-application conference is usually set up with the planning office staff to discuss the applicant's ideas for the site, the relevant development regulations, and the information required. Site-plan review requirements vary among local jurisdictions. An increasing number of communities require the submission of a site analysis to help reviewers assess whether the proposed development fits in with the existing site and contextual conditions, and to determine the proposed development's impacts on the community. Although not yet widely practiced in the United States, this requirement is a significant step toward long-term community sustainability.

Submission requirements for the site plan review typically include most, if not all, of the following:

1. Completed application form

   • Includes a written description of the intended uses.

2. Filing fee

   • May be a prorated fee computed on the basis of the site's area (for example, acres/hectares); dwelling units; or building floor area.

3. Proof of ownership and a current legal description of the property

4. Location map

   • Shows the subject property, zoning classification, and nearby streets.

5. Site analysis

- Depicts cultural and natural features on the site, including existing trees, water courses, topography, and rare or endangered plants

6. Site plan

- Title block, date, north arrow, graphic scale, and legal description of the property
- Legend with data on lot area, floor area, FAR, impervious surface area, impervious surface area ratio, and building height
- Property lines and existing and proposed right-of-way lines; existing and proposed easements
- Existing and proposed building footprints and heights
- Other existing and proposed structures and paved areas
- Signage and lighting
- Existing and proposed drainage facilities
- Location and type of permanently protected green space

7. Landscape or planting plan

- Required buffer plantings
- Required parking lot plantings
- Plant species and sizes, fencing types and heights, and berm heights

8. Site engineering/earthwork plans

- Grading and erosion control
- Stormwater management
- Site utilities

9. Building plans

- Finished exterior treatment, including materials, textures, and colors
- Preliminary ground floor plan

10. Impact assessments

- Environmental impacts
- Economic impacts
- Traffic impacts, including traffic demand management
- Sediment and erosion control
- Stormwater runoff
- Tree protection
- Lighting and noise impacts

11. Schedule for project completion

Public Hearings

Owners of private property typically enjoy specific development rights. Yet, property ownership also comes with responsibilities to the community. A property's development rights are not limitless and depend on the property's physical conditions and location within the community, or context. Land development proposals may generate opposition from neighbors, non-profit advocacy groups, and other stakeholders. The site plan and development review process provides an opportunity for the public to review and comment on the development proposals.

Public meetings are an important part of the site plan and design review process. Municipal planning staff reviews the proposal and may briefly explain it to the appropriate review body (for example, Planning Commission, Design Review Panel, Urban Design Commission). The client or the client's agent (for example, architect and landscape architect) usually explain the project and answer any questions from the review committee.

When evaluating any development proposal, the potential impacts on public health, safety, and welfare must be considered. The criteria for evaluating development plans vary among different project types, sites, and applicable development regulations. Project approval may hinge on the actions that will be taken to avoid or mitigate negative development impacts. To protect public health, safety, and welfare, municipalities may impose conditions for the approval of a development proposal (Box 11-2).

Impact Assessment

If a project is expected to have "significant" environmental impacts, an environmental impact statement (EIS) may be required to explain the adverse impacts and describe the steps that will be taken to mitigate those impacts (Owen, 1994). Compliance with the state or federal Environmental Policy Acts is required if, for example, the project has state or federal funding. State and federal agencies may become involved in reviewing a development proposal if certain natural or cultural resources might be impacted. A site plan is approved when all of its components are found to be in compliance with all zoning and land development requirements. Building permits are not issued for construction until the development has received site plan approval.

Exactions are payments of money or land, in lieu of fees, to compensate local jurisdictions for the costs of off-site improvements to public infrastructure—particularly transportation and utility systems. Necessary improvements may include widening street intersections, adding traffic signals, and extending water distribution or sanitary sewer lines. Development impact fees also may be used for improved fire and police protection, new schools, or purchases of land for parks and playgrounds (Altshuler and Gomez Ibanez, 1993).

Legal challenges to land use regulations in the United States typically address either questions of "due process" or of "constitutionality" (Owen, 1994). Due process challenges may assert that the city council did not comply with the city's own ordinances. Constitutionality challenges assert that one or more of the city's ordinances are in conflict with the Fifth Amendment of the U.S. Constitution. The court may determine, for example, that the restrictions denied the property owner "reasonable" economic use of the land. This would then constitute a "taking" of private property, and it would warrant "just compensation." In evaluating these claims, the courts take into consideration many factors, including the nature of the property and its inherent suitability for the proposed uses.

11.6 CONCLUSION

Smart growth and other related planning and design paradigms are responses to unsustainable forms of development. As human populations continue to grow and the quality of the built environment becomes more widely appreciated, land development proposals will also likely be more closely scrutinized. Increasingly, as part of the development review process, communities are evaluating how well a development plan "fits" the site and its surroundings.

Because site planning and architectural design are explicitly three-dimensional, graphic communication plays a critical role in the development review process. Elevation and section drawings can help explain the intended vertical and horizontal relationships among buildings and other site elements. Other illustrative materials include physical models, axonometric and isometric drawings, and perspective renderings—either from an eye-level or aerial view. Photo-simulations and three-dimensional "fly-through" imaging are also feasible using CAD, GIS, and other specialized computer software. Yet, no matter how skillfully these illustrative materials are prepared, if the proposed development is *inappropriate for the site*, the plan should not be implemented. An *appropriate* site plan not only satisfies program requirements but also is responsive to the site's physical, biological, and cultural attributes. Moreover, evaluating whether a proposed development is appropriate for a site requires supporting evidence. A thorough site- and contextual- analysis must, therefore, be at the heart of any development, redevelopment, or restoration proposal. Justifying a project's design rationale—including its design determinants and mitigated impacts—is an essential step in creating more livable and sustainable built environments.

BOX 11.1   In Practice

DESIGN REVIEW

Scotland

The following selected comments are from meeting minutes of the formal design reviews for three urban infill and redevelopment projects in Scotland. Conducting design reviews is one of the roles of Architecture+Design Scotland (www.ads.org.uk), as indicated by the following mission statement:

> Architecture and Design Scotland (A+DS) is a nondepartmental public body, established by the Scottish Executive in April 2005 as the national champion for good architecture, design, and planning in the built environment.... Our main aim is to inspire better quality in design and architecture in the public and private sectors so that Scotland's built environment contributes in a positive way to our quality of life and our built heritage.

The design review process—as the following comments attest—focus great attention on site and contextual conditions, and on preventing and mitigating negative development impacts. Notably, however, the design review process also encourages improvements in the built environment through the redevelopment and restoration of previously developed sites.

PROJECT 1: RESIDENTIAL AND LEISURE DEVELOPMENT

Site: Former fabrication yard

Location: Whiteness Head, Ardersier, Scotland

Design Review: January 24, 2006

- ☐ The Panel is supportive of the project in principle . . . The way in which nature is being incorporated into the designs is particularly exciting.

- ☐ Increased permeability to the south, and a stronger relationship with the boulevard, could also add enrichment to the waterfront experience.

- ☐ Discussions with neighboring landowners should continue to ensure that the integrity of the forest's edge to the south is maintained.

- ☐ The long, central boulevard could be more broken up along its length, to create more particular and clearly defined spaces.

PROJECT 2: RESIDENTIAL DEVELOPMENT

Site: Former swimming pool site with prominent riverside frontage and a location within a conservation area

Location: Inverness, Scotland

Project Review: January 24, 2006

- ☐ The current proposals would benefit from reworking based on further contextual analysis and awareness of how buildings present to the river.

BOX 11.1   In Practice (continued)

☐ Further work is required to analyze the "grain" of the area and identify how buildings, or building groups, presented and related to the river in a composed manner...the stepped height and curving roof of the major block are incongruous in this setting...this analysis could help to provide a design that is rooted in the riverside townscape of Inverness.

☐ The stepping form of the buildings to the river seems to emphasize their bulk and the separate four-storey block does not best relate to the adjacent development.

☐ The panel does not support the view that an iconic (architectural) statement is merited in this location. Instead the development should seek to reinforce the street pattern and contribute to the backdrop of the wider townscape.

PROJECT 3: MIXED-USE DEVELOPMENT INCLUDING A SUPERMARKET

Site: Inner city site fronting onto Beith Street, located on the north bank of the River Kelvin and close to Patrick Cross.

Location: Glasgow, Scotland

Project Review: February 7, 2006

☐ The wider area is undergoing change and the proposal should be considered in that changing context. This is particularly relevant in relation to the opportunity for creating high quality pedestrian links to Glasgow Harbor and the new Museum of Transport.

☐ The particular qualities of the site offer potential for extremely interesting design solutions that could integrate successfully with its context.

☐ An integrated mixed-use development has not been achieved. Individual uses are separated out and the different elements have not been used to mutual benefit. For example, residential or other uses might have been wrapped around the blank façades of the supermarket to enliven the frontages to the streets and reduce the bulk of development.

☐ The development is not permeable...the unrelenting wall and mass of the development would dominate Beith Street.

☐ How unwelcoming the pedestrian experience would be for anyone passing along either Beith Street or the west of the building. The river-side walkway would be particularly hostile and potentially dangerous.

☐ Problems appear to stem from the application of an overly large retail footprint on a single level...there is scope to reduce the store footprint by splitting retail uses onto separate levels.

☐ As the river is a precious asset, it seemed curious that the store blocked this off; yet, the suggested housing layout for the adjacent site allowed views to the railway embankment...the store could screen the embankment and an attractive, permeable, and inviting residential environment could be created along the river's edge.

BOX 11.2   In Practice

URBAN INFILL

Northwestern Memorial Hospital, Chicago, Illinois

Owner/Developer: Northwestern University

Site Planning: The HOK Planning Group, St. Louis, Missouri

Architecure: Ellerbe Becket, Minneapolis, Minnesota

OVERVIEW

Northwestern Memorial Hospital, in cooperation with Northwestern University and its medical school, commissioned the joint venture team of Ellerbe Becket/The HOK Planning Group to design a new, inpatient pavilion and ambulatory care facility in downtown Chicago. Accommodating the dramatic growth in outpatient care while providing more cost-effective hospital operations, the new medical complex consolidates services previously housed in aging ambulatory facilities located throughout a six-block area. The new complex is more convenient for patients, physicians, employees, and visitors. Construction of the new hospital took place without disrupting patient care at the existing medical facilities on the site.

SITE ANALYSIS

The site for the medical center is in the heart of downtown Chicago, one of the largest cities in the United States. The planning process for this project included the identification and comparative analysis of three potential sites (Figure 11-15). Five different development options for these three sites were compared (Figure 11-16). Several criteria

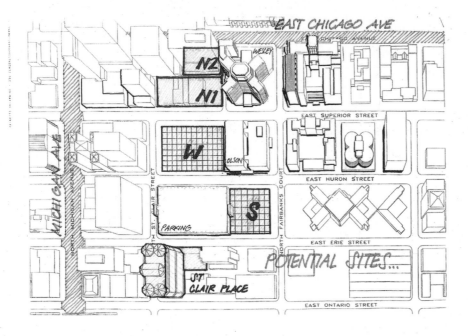

Figure 11-15   Map showing potential hospital sites.
Source: The HOK Planning Group.

BOX 11.2   In Practice (continued)

were evaluated in making the final site selection decision, including each site's effects on the medical center's cost, image, and growth potential. Access and parking were among the other important site selection criteria.

The site inventory and analysis addressed a wide variety of physical, social, and legal issues. These studies also spanned a wide range in scale. For example, studies of vehicle circulation addressed arrival and departure patterns within a radius of several miles or kilometers (Figure 11-17). Other studies of vehicle circulation and access focused on potential arrival and entry sequences within a city block or two of the medical center site (Figure 11-18). Other factors that were considered in the analysis included pedestrian circulation patterns, microclimate, visual character of the surrounding architecture, and land-use regulations for the site.

The planning process for the new medical center also involved extensive negotiations with the building's future occupants, municipal planning staff, and other community stakeholders. For example, the project's programming phase involved verification of the current program (for existing facilities), as well as reprogramming specific components of the existing facilities. One of the spaces designated for reprogramming was the clinical laboratory. The design team chose to develop an on-site core lab, with the majority of the laboratory space located off-site. Community stakeholders also played a significant role in identifying issues that ultimately influenced the design of the medical center (Figure 11-19).

DESIGN FEATURES

The new medical complex includes a 526-bed, one-million-square-foot hospital and a one-million-square-foot ambulatory care facility. The ambulatory care facility includes offices and clinical space for the 400 physicians in the Northwestern Medical Faculty Foundation group practice and 200 additional staff physicians. Special features of the complex include 96 intensive-care-unit beds, all new diagnostic and treatment facilities, integration of inpatient and outpatient services, and parking facilities for 2100 cars in a multistory parking structure.

The design of the medical center building reflects, in many ways, sensitivity to context (Figure 11-20). For example, the key guiding principles for the placement and design of the medical center included the following:

☐ Reduced bulk by "stepping down" the building toward Lake Michigan

☐ Break up of the "super-block" by creating separate towers

☐ Creation of ground-level east/west pedestrian "malls"

☐ Creation of a "gateway" to the medical center

These and other design decisions were made to achieve specific functional and/or aesthetic objectives. Two of these objectives were to reinforce the urban streetwall and to continue the Chicago tradition of designing buildings with distinctive tops.

A project of this complexity requires creativity, negotiation, and a willingness to be responsive to the concerns of community stakeholders. To provide greater flexibility in how the project was designed, the consultants gained a zoning amendment to reclassify the site as a planned development area (Figures 11-21 and 11-22). The conditions for rezoning included no net increase in density and a shift in building mass away from Lake Michigan. Other requirements included improvements to the local pedestrian and vehicle circulation systems (Figure 11-23).

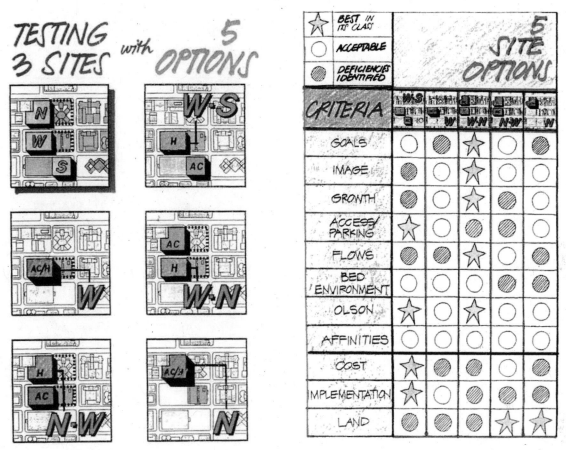

Figure 11-16   Matrix of site selection criteria. The matrix summarizes ratings for five site options and eleven selection criteria. Source: The HOK Planning Group.

Figure 11-17 Inventory and assessment of vehicle arrival and departure patterns. Source: The HOK Planning Group.

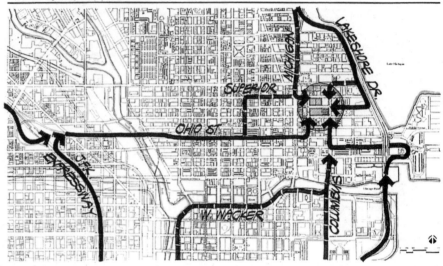

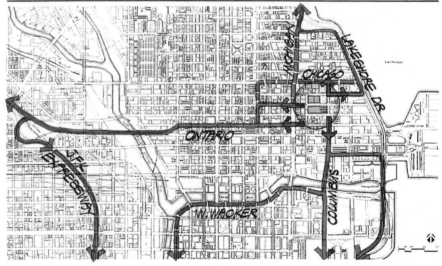

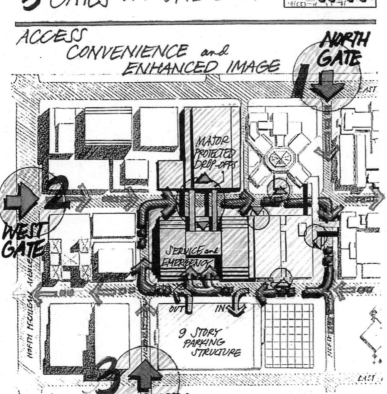

VEHICULAR FLOW and ENTRY ISSUES

3 GATES and ONE LOOP

ACCESS CONVENIENCE and ENHANCED IMAGE

NORTH GATE

WEST GATE

SOUTH GATE

MAJOR PROTECTED DROP-OFFS

SERVICE and EMERGENCY

9 STORY PARKING STRUCTURE

Figure 11-18 Diagram addressing vehicular circulation, entry, and parking issues. Source: The HOK Planning Group.

Figure 11-19 Community input on the planning and design of the proposed building, streetscape, and emergency room entrance. Source: The HOK Planning Group.

Community Input

ISSUES	INITIAL SUBMITTAL	NU/NMH DESIGN RESPONSE
BUILDING	Superblock	GOAL: Consolidate Services and Express the NMH Mission CONTEXTUALLY • Upper Level Setbacks ARTICULATE the ACC and Hospital...Higher Building Toward Michigan Ave. • Integrated Internally, but Visually Separated • Materials and Forms Similar to NU/NMH Campus
STREETSCAPE	No Setback	GOAL: Provide a Walkable Environment of Usable Open Space 10 Areas of Landscape Improvements: 1. 15' Setback @ St. Clair 2. 15' Setback @ Fairbanks 3. Create/Redevelop Setback @ VA 4. Redevelop Setback East of Health Science Bldg. with NU. 5. Pedestrian Way West of Health Science Bldg. 6. Pedestrian Way West of Erie/Fairbanks Garage 7. Landscape CTA Turnaround 8. Landscape West of Wesley 9. Contribute to Eli Schulman Park Development 10. Contribute to Lakeshore Park Development • NMH 9000 s.f. Open Space • Link to Michigan Ave. • Develop Streetscape that Exceeds City Requirements @ Huron and Erie • Open to the Community
EMERGENCY ROOM	Located at Erie and St. Clair	GOAL: Design Clear, Highly Accessible Entry Minimize Congestion at Street • Locate @ Erie and Fairbanks • All Vehicle Movements INSIDE Bldg. • Dedicated Ambulance/Police and Private Vehicle Parking Areas • Trauma and "Fast Track" Service

Ellerbe Becket/HOK   13-MAY-93

Guiding Principles

BUILDING FORM AND CONTEXT

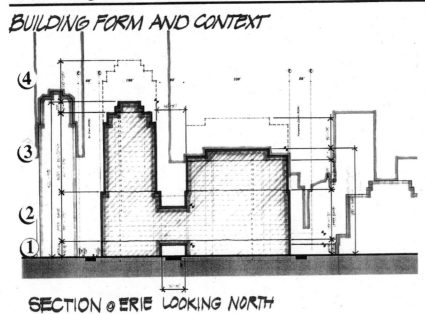

SECTION @ ERIE LOOKING NORTH

(1) PUBLIC BASE
- ENTRY LOCATIONS
- ENGAGE STREETSCAPE and PEDESTRIAN ACTIVITIES
- RECIEVE BRIDGES
- HOUSE ACTIVE and/or
  PUBLIC USES
- CONTAIN DRIVE-THRU/AUTO DROP-OFF

(2) UPPER BASE
- ARTICULATES MASS
- RELATE TO SURROUNDING BUILDINGS
- RECIEVE TOWERS
- SUBTLE EXPRESSION OF ACC

(3) BODY of BUILDING
- SEPARATION BETWEEN ACC & I.P. TOWERS
- TWO TOWERS:
  - DIFFERENT FUNCTIONS/EXPRESSION
  - DIFFERENT CONTEXTS:
    - ACC ADJACENT TO HIGHRISE "CANYON"
    - INPATIENT OPEN TOWARD LAKE MICH.
- ARTICULATION REDUCES MASS/PROVIDES SCALE, RELATES TO CONTEXT

(4) TOP
- TERMINUS to an IDENTIFIABLE PROFILE
- MECHANICAL SHIELD
- FUTURE EXPANSION CAPABILITY

Ellerbe Becket/HOK

Figure 11-20 Section communicates main design principles for building massing. Source: The HOK Planning Group.

Figure 11-21 Proposed zoning amendment proposes a planned-unit development (PUD). FARs are provided by subareas. Source: The HOK Planning Group.

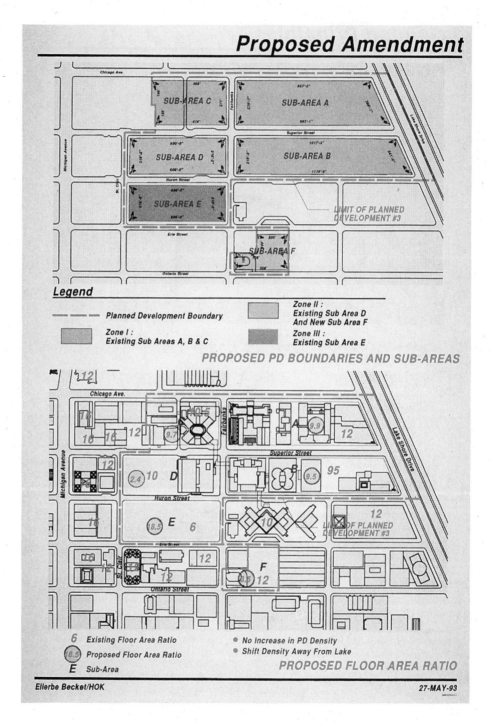

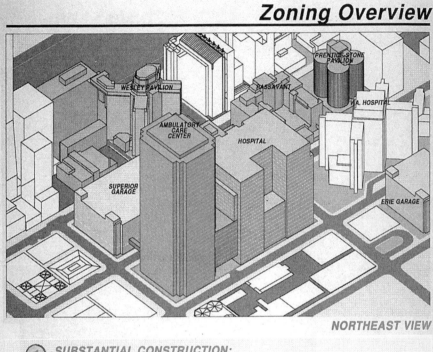

Figure 11-22   Summary table of zoning issues. Source: The HOK Planning Group.

Figure 11-23 Summary table (continued) of zoing issues. Source: The HOK Planning Group.

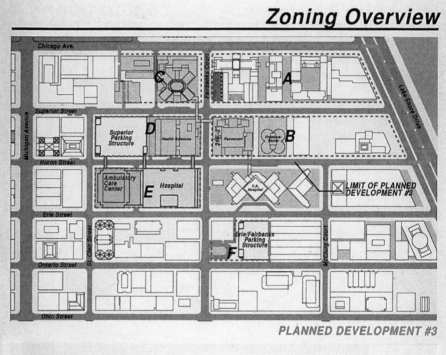

Zoning Overview

PLANNED DEVELOPMENT #3

⑦ LANDSCAPING:
- ST. CLAIR STREET SETBACK
- FAIRBANKS STREET SETBACK
- V.A. HOSPITAL
- UPGRADE EAST OF HEALTH SCIENCES BUILDING
- PEDESTRIAN CONNECTION AT SUB-AREA D
- PEDESTRIAN CONNECTION AT SUB-AREA F
- CTA BUS TURNAROUND

⑧ CIRCULATION:
- ONE CURB CUT ALLOWED ON ST. CLAIR (SERVICE DOCK)
- THREE CURB CUTS ALLOWED FOR E.R. ACCESS ON ERIE
- ONE MID BLOCK DRIVE THRU/DROPOFF ON ERIE & HURON
- CURB CUTS FOR SUPERIOR AND ERIE/FAIRBANKS GARAGES
- ERIE NOT CHANGED TO TWO-WAY CIRCULATION AT THIS TIME

⑨ TRAFFIC MANAGEMENT PLAN:
- NU/NMH RESPONSIBLE FOR IMPLEMENTING OF THE TRAFFIC MANAGEMENT PLAN AS SUBMITTED TO THE CITY.
- EFFECTIVE AFTER ISSUANCE OF THE FIRST CERTIFICATE OF OCCUPANCY FOR THE PARKING GARAGE.
- INSTALLATION OF TRAFFIC CONTROL SIGNALS AT HURON & ST. CLAIR AND FAIRBANKS & ERIE. PAID BY NU/NMH
- REVIEW BY CDOT UPON REQUEST AND ALTERED IF NEEDED

⑩ SITE PLAN APPROVAL PROCESS:
- SITE PLAN REVIEW (SUB-AREA E) NEEDS TO GO TO THE COMMISSIONER FOR APPROVAL
- NO PART II APPROVAL (ADMINISTRATIVE REVIEW) UPON ZONE III (SUB-AREA E) SHALL BE GRANTED UNTIL AN APPLICABLE SITE PLAN HAS BEEN APPROVED
- 30 DAY REVIEW PERIOD

ZONING OBLIGATIONS

Ellerbe Becket/HOK

01-JUN-93

Resources

INTRODUCTION

This appendix includes a variety of interesting Internet sites that were functional in the summer of 2007. This listing of resources is far from exhaustive. Just a small sample of the vast network of websites pertaining to sustainable and context-sensitive site planning and design are included in this list.

FEDERAL AGENCIES (UNITED STATES)

Census Bureau—TIGER

Topologically Integrated Geographic Encoding and Referencing (TIGER) system

URL: www.census.gov/ftp/pub/geo/www/tiger

Resources: Digital database of geographic features such as roads, railroads, rivers, lakes, political boundaries, and census statistical boundaries for the entire United States.

Council on Environmental Quality (CEQ)

URL: http://ceq.eh.doe.gov/nepa/nepanet.htm

Resources: NEPAnet includes information about where and how to file an environmental impact analysis, source of the National Environmental Policy Act, and other federal legislation.

Environmental Protection Agency (EPA)—Office of Water

URL: www.epa.gov/OWOW/NPS

Resources: Information on low-impact development and stormwater management practices; online source of environmental legislation.

Fish and Wildlife Service (FWS)

URL: www.fws.gov

Resources: National wetlands inventory maps and data; information on endangered species, ecosystem management, and other environmental programs.

National Geospatial Program Office (NGPO)

URL: http://www.usgs.gov/ngpo

Resources: Online source of metadata and maps of topography and geology, biological resources, and water resources; Internet links to The National Map, Geospatial One-Stop, and other nodes of the National Spatial Data Infrastructure (NSDI).

National Climatic Data Center
National Oceanic and Atmospheric Administration (NOAA)

URL: http://www.ncdc.noaa.gov

Resources: Climate archives and statistical tables for weather observation stations nationwide; weather summaries for cities and states.

National Weather Service
National Oceanic and Atmospheric Administration (NOAA)

URL: http:/www.nws.noaa.gov

Resources: Statistics on fatalities, injuries, and damages caused by weather related hazards; general information on weather-related topics.

FEDERAL SOURCES (INTERNATIONAL)

Centre for Topographic Information (Canada)

URL: http://maps.nrcan.gc.ca/

Resources: Archive of topographic maps (1:50,000 and 1:250,000 scale).

Department of the Environment and Waters (Australia)

URL: www.environment.gov.au

Resources: Online databases for biodiversity, cultural heritage, marine and water, parks and reserves, and other resources; publications and online courses on sustainability and environmental education; federal environmental and cultural heritage legislation.

National Air Photo Library (Canada)

URL: http://airphotos.nrcan.gc.ca

Resources: Archive of more than six million aerial photographs.

National Geospatial Data Framework (United Kingdom)

URL: http://www.gigateway.org.uk

Resources: Online directory and clearinghouse for providers and users of geospatial data, including standards for spatial data and metadata.

STATE SOURCES (UNITED STATES)

MassGIS
Office of Geographic and Environmental Information (Massachusetts)

URL: www.state.ma.us/mgis

Resources: Online digital orthophotos and GIS metadata and datalayers for political boundaries, infrastructure, topography, coastal and marine features, demographics, and much more.

California Land Use Planning Information Network (LUPIN)

URL: www.ceres.ca.gov/planning/index.html

Resources: Information about federal, state, and local land-use regulations and technical information on various aspects of the built environment, including brownfields, infrastructure, planning and design, permitting, and pollution.

NONPROFIT ORGANIZATIONS

1,000 Friends of Oregon

URL: www.friends.org

Resources: One of several "1,000 Friends" organizations (others include Connecticut, Florida, Iowa, Maryland, and Wisconsin) providing information and advocacy to protect environmental quality and create more sustainable and livable communities.

Center for Liveable Communities

URL: http://www.lgc.org/center

Resources: Bibliographies, studies, reports, and model ordinances pertaining to pedestrian and transit-oriented land use planning across the United States.

Center for Watershed Protection

URL: www.cwp.org

Resources: Information about effective techniques to protect and restore urban watersheds; assists local and state governments in developing effective urban stormwater and watershed protection programs.

Congress for the New Urbanism

URL: www.cnu.org

Resources: News, events, and educational materials related to new urbanism.

Cornell University Legal Information Institute—Land Use Library

URL: www.law.cornell.edu/wex/index.php/Land_use

Resources: Extensive database of federal, state, and local land-use legislation and case law; links to other related websites.

Cyburbia—The Planning Community

URL: http://www.cyburbia.org

Resources: Clearinghouse for information on community development, environment, historic preservation, land-use regulation, transportation, new urbanism, and much more.

Low-impact Development Center

URL: http://lowimpactdevelopment.org

Resources: Information about site design techniques to protect environmental quality by replicating preexisting hydrologic site conditions.

National Center for Bicycling and Walking

URL: http://www.bikewalk.org

Resources: Online library, newsletter, meeting information, and other resources dedicated to creating bicycle-friendly and walkable communities.

National Main Street Center
National Trust for Historic Preservation

URL: www.mainstreet.org

Resources: Books and other resources on urban revitalization and rehabilitating historic buildings.

Smart Communities Network

URL: www.smartcommunities.ncat.org

Resources: Online database of planned developments, communities, and subdivisions; guiding principles, financing, and more.

Smart Growth America

URL: http://www.smartgrowthamerica.org

Resources: Reports, news summaries, meeting information, and assorted other information provided by a coalition of national, state and local organizations concerned with planning and design of cities, suburbs, and metropolitan areas.

Smart Growth Network

URL: www.smartgrowth.org

Resources: Bibliographies, reports, and other information on brownfield redevelopment, infill development, "green" building, and other Smart Growth issues.

U.S. Green Building Council (USGBC)

URL: www.usgbc.org

Resources: Information about the LEED Green Building Rating System, energy and resource efficient building policies, programs, technologies, standards, and design practices.

PROFESSIONAL ASSOCIATIONS

American Institute of Architects (AIA)

URL: www.aia.org

Resources: Online source for books and reports on architectural design, news on government affairs and other related issues, and conference announcements.

American Real Estate and Urban Economics Association (AREUEA)

URL: www.areuea.org

Resources: Research and news about current and emerging real estate issues.

American Planning Association

URL: www.planning.org

Resources: Online catalog of books and reports on community planning and development, conferences and educational opportunities, and online planning advisory service.

American Society of Landscape Architects (ASLA)

URL: www.asla.org

Resources: Online catalog of books and reports on site planning and design, online database of CAD details, and news and conference announcements.

Institute of Transportation Engineers (ITE)

URL: www.ite.org/css

Resources: Tools and information for context-sensitive solutions (CSS) in transportation planning and design.

National Association of Home Builders (NAHB)

URL: www.nahb.com

Resources: Project examples of traditional neighborhood development (TND), "green" building/cluster development, and urban infill development; news on trends in housing construction and costs in the United States.

Urban Land Institute (ULI)

URL: www.uli.org

Resources: Books and other sources of information on urban planning, land use, and real estate development; project reference files summarize lessons learned, development challenges, and project data (including photos and site plans).

COMMERCIAL SITES

CoreNet Global

URL: www2.corenetglobal.org/home/index.vsp

Resources: Corporate real estate news and management strategies, site selection database, and online bookstore.

DevelopmentAlliance

URL: www.developmentalliance.com

Resources: Online site selection database, including community demographics and information on available buildings and sites, research parks, and closed military bases.

Environmental Systems Research Institute (ESRI)

URL: www.esri.com

Resources: Catalog of PC-based GIS and mapping software, including ARC/INFO and ArcView, online bookstore, GIS news and conferences, and GIS education and training opportunities.

GIS Data Depot

URL: http://data.geocomm.com

Resources: Online clearinghouse for a wide range of biophysical and cultural GIS data for counties and states in the United States and for other countries; source of GIS-related news and events.

SunAngle

URL: http://www.susdesign.com/sunangle

Resources: Online tool to calculate solar angle data based on date, time, and location.

Terraserver

URL: www.terraserver.com

Resources: Very high-resolution (less than two meters) satellite imagery (panchromatic digital imagery is ortho-rectified and geo-referenced).

Glossary

Accuracy. The closeness of observations, computations, or estimates to the true values or to values accepted as being true.

Aerial. Of, pertaining to, or occurring in the air or atmosphere.

Aerial Photograph, Oblique. An aerial photograph taken with the camera axis directed between the horizontal and the vertical. (1) high oblique—an oblique photograph in which the horizon is shown; (2) low oblique—an oblique photograph in which the horizon is not shown.

Aerial Photograph, Vertical. An aerial photograph made with the optical axis of the camera approximately perpendicular to the earth's surface and with the film as nearly horizontal as is practical.

Algorithm. A statement of the steps to be followed in the solution of a problem; an algorithm may be in the form of a word description, an explanatory note, or a labeled diagram or flowchart.

Alluvium. Any material deposited by running water; the soil material of floodplains and alluvial fans.

Altitude. Elevation above or below a reference datum; the datum is usually the mean sea level.

Analog. A form of data display in which values are shown in graphic form, such as curves.

Aquifer. Any subsurface material that holds a relatively large quantity of groundwater and is able to transmit that water readily.

Area. A generic term for a bounded, continuous, two-dimensional object that may or may not include its boundary.

Aspect. The horizontal direction in which a slope faces, commonly expressed as compass direction (for example, North, Northeast); degrees clockwise from the North.

Attribute. A defined characteristic of an entity (for example, topographic slope).

Attribute Value. A specific quality or quantity assigned to an attribute (for example, 15 percent slope).

Band. A specific frequency or range of frequencies in the electromagnetic spectrum.

Baseflow. The portion of streamflow contributed by groundwater; it is a steady flow that is slow to change even during rainless periods.

Berm. A low, linear mound of earth and soil.

Buffer. (1) The zone around the perimeter of a wetland or lake where land-use activities are limited to protect the water features; (2) a zone of a specified distance around any map feature in a GIS layer.

Cadastre. A parcel-based land information system.

Carrying Capacity. The level of development density or use that an environment is able to support without suffering undesirable or irreversible degradation.

Characterization. The delineation or representation of the essential features or qualities existing at a site.

Chloropleth Map. A map comprised of areas of any size or shape representing qualitative phenomena (for example, soil fertility) or quantitative phenomena (for example, elevation); often has a mosaic appearance.

Climate. The general or representative conditions of the atmosphere at a place on earth.

Clustering. A land development concept in which buildings and infrastructures are grouped together, and large contiguous areas of open space remain undeveloped.

Coefficient of Runoff. A number given to a type of ground surface representing the proportion of rainfall converted to overland or surface flow.

Color-Infrared Film. Photographic film sensitive to energy in the visible and near-infrared wavelengths of the electromagnetic spectrum (usually from 0.4 to 0.9 mm).

Concentration Time. The time taken for a drop of rain falling on the perimeter of a drainage basin to pass through the basin to the outlet.

Constraint. Any feature or condition of the built or natural environment that poses an obstacle to proposed land uses.

Contour. An imaginary line on the ground, all points of which are at the same elevation above or below a specific datum.

Contour Interval. The difference in elevation between two adjacent contours.

Control Point. Any station in a horizontal or vertical control system that is identified on a photograph and used for correlating the data shown on the photograph.

Coordinate System. A reference system for uniquely defining the location of any point on earth.

Crown Diameter, Visible. The apparent diameter of a tree crown imaged on a vertical aerial photograph.

Data Set. A file or files that contain related geometric and attribute information; a collection of related data.

Datum. A reference system for measuring another attribute, such as horizontal or vertical location.

Decibel. A unit of measurement for the loudness of sound based on the pressure produced in air by a noise; denoted as dB.

DEM (Digital Elevation Model). A topographic surface arranged in a data file as a set of regularly spaced x, y, z coordinates, in which z represents elevation.

Design Storm. A rainstorm of a given intensity and frequency of recurrence that is used as the basis for stormwater management.

Detention. A strategy used in stormwater management in which runoff is detained on-site to be released later at some prescribed rate.

Development Density. A measure of intensity of development or land use; defined, for example, on the basis of area covered by dwelling units, impervious surfaces, or building floor area.

Digitization. The process of converting a photograph, map, or other image into numerical format.

Discharge. The rate of water flow in a stream channel or from a site; measured as the volume of water passing through a cross-section of a stream or swale per unit of time, commonly expressed as cubic feet (or meters) per second.

Discharge Zone. An area where groundwater seepage and springs are concentrated.

Disturbance. An impact on the environment, such as forest clearing, characterized by physical or biological change.

DLG (Digital Line Graph). A digital representation of cartographic information; digital vectors converted from maps and related sources.

DOQ (Digital Orthophotoquadrangle). A digital image with the properties of an orthographic projection; derived from a digitized vertical aerial photograph so that image displacement caused by camera tilt and relief of terrain are removed, or rectified. Orthophotos combine the image characteristics of a photograph with the geometric qualities of a map.

Drainage Network. A system of stream channels usually connected in a hierarchical fashion.

Drainage Basin. The area that contributes runoff to a stream, river, or lake.

Easement. A right-of-way granted, but not dedicated, for limited use of private land for a public or quasi-public purpose.

Ecosystem. A group of organisms linked together by a flow of energy; it is also a community of organisms and their environment.

Ecotone. The transition zone between two groups, or zones, of vegetation.

Electromagnetic Radiation (EMR). Energy propagated through space in the form of an advancing interaction between electric and magnetic fields. EMR is also called electromagnetic energy.

Elevation. Vertical distance from a datum point, such as mean sea level, to a point or object on the earth's surface; not to be confused with altitude, which refers to points or objects above the earth's surface.

Endangered Species. According to the U.S. Endangered species Act, a species in imminent danger of extinction in all or a significant portion of its range.

Environment. The aggregate conditions that affect the existence or development of properties intrinsic to a site.

Environmental Site Characterization. The delineation or representation of the essential features or qualities, including all of the conditions, influences, and circumstance, existing at a place or location designated for a specific use, function, or study.

Environmental Assessment. A preliminary study or review of a proposed action (project) and the influence it could have on the environment; often conducted to determine the need for more detailed environmental impact analysis.

Ephemeral Stream. A stream without base flow; one that flows only during or after rainstorms or snowmelt events.

Erosion. The removal of rock debris by moving water, wind, or another agent; generally, the sculpting or wearing down of the land by erosional agents.

Eutrophication. The increase of biomass of a water body leading to infilling of the basin and the eventual disappearance of open water.

Evapotranspiration. The loss of water from the soil through evaporation and transpiration.

Feasibility Study. A type of planning aimed at identifying the most appropriate use of a site.

Filtration. A term generally applied to the removal of pollutants, such as sediment, with the passage of water through a soil, organic, and/or fabric medium.

Floodway Fringe. The zone designated by U.S. federal flood policy as the area in a river valley that would be lightly inundated by the hundred-year flood.

Floor Area. The area of all floors of a building or structure.

Footprint. Area covered by a building.

Geocoding. A coding process in which a digital map feature is assigned an attribute value (for example, vertical or horizontal location).

Geographic Information System (GIS). A mapping system designed for analysis, planning, and management applications involving overlapping and complex distributional patterns. Two classes of GIS are vector and raster.

Geomorphology. A science that deals with the land and submarine relief features of the earth's surface, or the comparable features of a celestial body, and seeks a genetic interpretation of them.

Georeference. To establish the relationship between coordinates on a planar map and real-world coordinates.

Geospatial Data. Information identifying the geographic location and characteristics of natural or constructed features and boundaries on the earth; geospatial data may be derived from, among other things, remote sensing, mapping, and surveying technologies.

Geostationary Satellite. A satellite placed in orbit above the earth; it rotates with the earth and, thus, remains fixed over the same area.

Global Positioning System (GPS). The Navigation Satellite Timing and Ranging (NAVSTAR) GPS is a passive, satellite-based, navigation system operated and maintained by the Department of Defense (DOD).

Global Coordinate System. The network of east–west and north–south lines (parallels and meridians) used to measure locations on earth; this system uses degrees, minutes, and seconds as the units of measurement.

Gradient. The inclination or slope of the land, often applied to systems such as streams and highways.

Ground Truth (jargon). The term coined for data and information obtained on surface or subsurface features to aid in interpretation of remotely sensed data; ground data and ground information are the preferred terms.

Ground Resolution. The area on the terrain that is covered by the instantaneous field of view of a detector; ground resolution is determined by the altitude of the remote-sensing system and the instantaneous field of view of the detector.

Ground Data. Data collected on the ground, and information derived there from, as an aid to the interpretation of remotely recorded surveys, such as airborne imagery; generally, this should be performed concurrently with the airborne surveys; data collected on weather, soils, and vegetation types and conditions are typical.

Groundwater. The mass of water that occupies the subsoil and upper bedrock zone; the water occupying the zone of saturation below the soil-water zone.

Habitat. The local environment from which an organism gains its resources; habitat is often variable in size, content, and location, changing with the phases in an organism's life cycle.

Hardpan. A hardened soil layer characterized by the accumulation of colloids and ions.

Hazard Assessment. An evaluation of the dangers to land use and people from environmental threats such as floods, tornadoes, and earthquakes.

Horizon. A layer in the soil that originates from the differentiation of particles and chemicals due to moisture movement within the soil column.

Hydric Soil. Soil characterized by wet conditions, or saturation, most of the year—often organic in composition.

Hydrograph. A streamflow graph that shows the change in discharge over time, usually hours or days.

Hydrologic Cycle. The planet's water system, described by the movement of water from the oceans to the atmosphere to the continents and back to the sea.

Impervious Cover. Any hard surface material, such as asphalt or concrete, that limits stormwater infiltration and induces high runoff rates.

Infiltration Capacity. The rate at which a ground material takes in water through the surface; measured in inches or centimeters per minute or hour.

Infrared Image. An image acquired within the wavelength from about 0.7 mm to an indefinite upper boundary, sometimes set at 2.6 mm. Photographic infrared is 0.7 mm to about 2.6 mm; thermal infrared is between 2.6 mm and 13.5 mm.

Infrared Film. Photographic film capable of recording near-infrared radiation (just beyond the visible to a wavelength of 0.9 micrometer), but not capable of recording thermal infrared wavelengths.

Infrared Radiation. Mainly long wave radiation of wavelengths between 3.0–4.0 and 100 micrometers; it includes near-infrared radiation, which occurs at wavelengths between 0.7 and 3.0–4.0 micrometers.

Isopleth Map. A map comprised of lines (isolines) that connect points of equal attribute value.

Lacustrine Wetland. A wetland associated with standing water bodies such as ponds, lakes, and reservoirs.

Land Cover. The materials such as vegetation and concrete that cover the ground. See also Land Use.

Land Use. The human activities occurring within an area of the landscape; for example, agricultural, industrial, and residential uses.

Layer. In a geographic information system, spatial data of a common type or theme.

Legend. An explanation of the symbols, colors, and styles used on a map or plan, usually in a box next to the map or plan.

Lithosphere. The solid part of the earth or other spatial body, distinguished from the atmosphere and the hydrosphere.

Lot. A parcel, tract, or area of land established by a plat or otherwise as permitted by law.

Lot Frontage. The portion of a lot adjacent to a street.

Magnetic Declination. The deviation in degrees east or west between magnetic north and true north.

Map. A graphical representation of a portion of the earth's surface, drawn to scale, on a specific projection, showing natural and manmade features.

Map Projection. An orderly system of lines on a plane representing a corresponding system of imaginary lines on a datum surface.

Metadata. "Data about data" describe the content, quality, condition, and other characteristics of data; for example, the date and source from which field data were collected.

Monochromatic. Pertaining to a single wavelength or, more commonly, to a narrow band of wavelengths.

Microclimate. The climate of small spaces, such as an inner city, a residential area, or a mountain valley.

Mitigation. A measure used to lessen the impact of an action on the natural or human environment.

Mitigation Banking. In wetland mitigation planning, the practice of building surplus acreage of compensation credits through replacement, enhancement, restoration, and/ or preservation of wetlands.

Moraine. The material deposited directly by a glacier; the material (load) is also carried in or on a glacier; as landforms, moraines usually have either hilly or rolling topography.

Mosaic. A term used in landscape ecology to describe the patchy character of habitat as a result of fragmentation through land use; an assemblage of overlapping aerial or space photographs or images whose edges have been matched to form a continuous pictorial representation of a portion of the earth's surface.

Nonpoint Source. Water pollution from a spatially diffuse source such as the atmosphere or agricultural land.

Palustrine Wetland. Wetlands associated with inland sites that are not dependent on streams, lakes, or oceanic water.

Panchromatic. A term used for films that are sensitive to broadband (that is, the entire visible part of the electromagnetic spectrum).

Parent Material. The particulate material in which a soil forms; the two types of parent material are residual and transported.

Peak Discharge. The maximum flow of a stream or a river in response to an event such as a rainstorm, or over a period of time such as a year.

Percolation Rate. The rate at which water moves into soil through the walls of a test pit; used to determine soil suitability for wastewater disposal and treatment.

Percolation Test. A soil-permeability test performed in the field to determine the suitability of a material for wastewater disposal and treatment.

Permeability. The rate at which soil or rock transmits groundwater (or gravity water in the area above the water table).

Photogrammetry. The art or science of obtaining reliable measurements by means of photography.

Photosynthesis. The process by which green plants synthesize water and carbon dioxide and, with the energy from absorbed light, convert it into plant materials in the form of sugar and carbohydrates.

Physiography. A term from physical geography that is traditionally used to describe the composite character of the landscape over large regions.

Planned Unit Development (PUD). An area planned, developed, operated, and maintained as a single entity containing one or more structures and common areas; it may include multiple land uses (for example, commercial or residential).

Plat. A map or maps of a subdivision or site plan.

Point Source. Water pollution that emanates from a single source such as a sewage plant or stormwater outfall.

Projection. See Map Projection

PUD. See Planned Unit Development

Radiation. The process by which radiant (electromagnetic) energy is transmitted through free space; the term used to describe electromagnetic energy, as in infrared radiation or short-wave radiation.

Rainfall Intensity. The rate of rainfall measured in inches or centimeters of water deposited on the surface per hour or minute.

Rational Method. A method of computing the discharge from a small drainage basin in response to a given rainstorm; computation is based on the coefficient runoff, rainfall intensity, and basin area.

Recharge Zone. An area where groundwater recharge is concentrated.

Recharge. The replenishment of groundwater with water from the surface.

Relief. The range of topographic elevation within a prescribed area.

Retention. A strategy used for stormwater management in which runoff is retained on-site in basins, underground, or released into the soil.

Right-of-Way. A strip of land occupied or intended to be occupied by a street, one or more walkways, utility lines, or other special uses.

Riparian Wetland. Wetlands that form on the edge of a water feature such as a lake or stream.

Riparian. The environment along the banks of a stream, often more broadly applied to the larger lowland corridor on the stream valley floor.

Risk Management. An area of planning that involves preparation and response to hazards such as floods, hurricanes, and toxic waste accidents.

Rubber Sheet. A procedure to adjust features of a digital GIS layer in a nonuniform manner; representing "from" and "to" locations are used to define the adjustment.

Runoff. The flow of water from the land as both surface and subsurface discharge; in the more restricted and common use, surface discharge is in the form of overland flow and channel flow.

Scale. The relationship between a distance on a map, chart, or photograph and the corresponding distance on the earth.

Septic System. A sewage system that relies on a septic tank to store and/or treat wastewater; generally, an on-site (small-scale) sewage disposal system that depends on the soil for wastewater treatment.

Setback. The minimum distance that a structure or facility should be separated from an edge, such as a property line.

Siltation. The deposition of sediment in water due to soil erosion and stormwater runoff.

Soil Profile. The sequence of horizons, or layers, of a soil.

Solar Heating. The process of generating heat from absorbed solar radiation.

Solar Gain. The amount of solar radiation absorbed by a surface or setting in the landscape.

Solstice. The dates when the declination of the sun is at 23.27 degree north latitude (the Tropic of Cancer) and 23.27 degrees south latitude (Tropic of Capricorn)—June 21–22 and December 21–22, respectively.

Spatial Data. Data or information with implicit or explicit information about location.

Stream Order. The relative position, or rank, of a stream in a drainage network. Streams without tributaries, usually the small ones, are first order; streams with two or more first-order tributaries are second order, and so on.

Subdivision. The division of a lot, tract, or parcel of land into two or more lots, tracts, or parcels for sale or development.

Sun Angle. The angle formed between the beam of incoming solar radiation and a plane at the earth's surface.

Surge. A large and often destructive wave caused by intensive atmospheric pressure and strong winds.

Threatened Species. According to the U.S. Endangered Species Act, a species with a rapidly declining population that is likely to become endangered.

TIN. Triangulated irregular network. A surface representation derived from irregularly spaced points and breakline features. Each sample point has an x, y coordinate and a z (surface) value.

Topsoil. The uppermost layer of the soil, characterized by a high organic content.

Water Table. The upper boundary of the zone of groundwater. In fine-textured materials it is usually a transition zone rather than a boundary line. The configuration of the water table often approximates that of the overlying terrain.

Wellhead Protection. Land-use planning and management to control contaminant sources in the area contributing recharge water to community wells.

Wetland. An area where the ground is permanently wet or wet most of the year and is occupied by water-loving (or tolerant) vegetation, such as cattails, mangrove, or cypress.

Zenith. For any location on earth, the point that is directly overhead to an observer.

This glossary was compiled, in part, from these sources:

Caliper Corporation. 1994–95. *Maptitude 3.0 User's Guide.* Massachusetts: Caliper Corporation.

Listokin, D., and C. Walker. 1989. *The Subdivision and Site Plan Handbook.* New Jersey: Center for Urban Policy Research.

Marsh, W. M. 1998. *Landscape Planning.* 3d ed. New York: John Wiley & Sons.

References

Abler, R., D. Janelle, A. Philbrick, and J. Sommer. 1975. *Human Geography in a Shrinking World*. Duxbury Press, North Scituate, Massachusetts.

Ackoff, R. L., 1989. From Data to Wisdom. *Journal of Applied Systems Analysis* 16:3–9.

Ahern, J. 1991. Planning for an Extensive Open Space System: Linking Landscape Structure and Function. *Landscape and Urban Planning* 21:131–145.

Alaska Department of Education. 1997. *Site Selection Criteria and Evaluation Handbook*. Juneau, Alaska: Alaska Department of Education.

Alexander, C., S. Ishikawa, and M. Silverstein. 1977. *A Pattern Language: Towns, Buildings, Construction*. New York: Oxford University Press.

Altshuler, A. A., and J. A. Gomez-Ibanez. 1993. *Regulation for Revenue: The Political Economy of Land Use Exactions*. Washington, D.C.: The Brookings Institution.

American Society of Civil Engineers. 1996. *Environmental Site Investigation Guidance Manual*. American Society of Civil Engineers, New York.

American Society of Golf Course Architects. 2000. *Handbook: New Development Steps*. [Online: www. golfdesign.org/regular/hand/dvlpmnt.htm]

Ames, D.L. and L.F. McClelland. 2002. *Historic Residential Suburbs: Guidelines for Evaluation and Documentation for the National Register of Historic Places*. Washington, D.C.: U.S. Department of Interior, National Park Service.

Ammons, D. N., R. W. Campbell, and S. L. Somoza. 1992. *Selecting Prison Sites: State Processes, Site-Selection Criteria, and Local Initiatives*. Carl Vinson Institute of Government, Athens, Georgia: The University of Georgia.

Anderson, J. R., E. E. Hardy, J. T. Roach, and R. E. Witmer. 1976. A Land Use and Land Cover Classification System for Use with Remote Sensor Data, Geological Survey Professional Paper 964. Washington, D.C.: U.S. Government Printing Office.

Anderson, P. F. 1980. *Regional Landscape Analysis*. Reston, Virginia: Environmental Design Press.

Applied Ecological Services. 2000. Cost of Native vs. Non-Native Species for Landscaping. Unpublished fact sheet. Applied Ecological Services, Brodhead, Wisconsin.

Arendt, R. 1999. Crossroads Hamlet, Village Town: Design Characteristics of Traditional Neighbor-hoods, Old and New. Planning Advisory Service Report 487–488. Chicago: American Planning Association.

Arendt, R. 1999. *Growing Greener: Putting Conservation into Local Plans and Ordinances*. Washington, D.C.: Island Press.

Arlinghaus, S. L., ed. 1994. *Practical Handbook of Digital Mapping: Terms and Concepts.* Florida: CRC Press.

Arnold, C. L., Jr., and C. J. Gibbons. 1996. Impervious Surface Coverage: The Emergence of a Key Environmental Indicator. *Journal of the American Planning Association* 62(2):243–258.

Bacon, E. 1974. *Design of Cities.* New York: Penguin Books.

Bacow, A.F. 1995. *Designing the City: A Guide for Advocates and Public Officials.* Washington, D.C.: Island Press.

Beatley, T., and K. Manning. 1997. *The Ecology of Place: Planning for Environment, Economy, and Community.* Washington, D.C.: Island Press.

Beck, E.C. 1979. The Love Canal Tragedy. *EPA Journal* (January). http://www.epa.gov/history/topics/lovecanal/01.htm

Becker, B. and E. Kelly. 2000. *Community Planning: An Introduction to the Comprehensive Plan.* Washington, D.C.: Island Press.

Beer, A. R. 1990. *Environmental Planning for Site Development.* London: E&F.N. Spon.

Bellinger, G., D. Castro, and A. Mills. 2004. *Data, Information, Knowledge, and Wisdom.* [Online: www.systems-thinking.org/dikw/dikw.htm]

Ben-Joseph, E., and T. Szold, eds. 2005. *Regulating Place: Standards and the Shaping of Urban America.* New York: Routledge.

Bloom, A. L. 1978. *Geomorphology: A Systematic Analysis of Late Cenozoic Landforms.* New Jersey: Prentice-Hall, Inc.

Bookout, L. W. 1994. *Value by Design: Landscape, Site Planning, and Amenities.* Washington, D.C.: The Urban Land Institute.

Booth, N. K. 1983. *Basic Elements of Landscape Architectural Design.* Illinois: Waveland Press.

Bosselman, F. P., and D. Callies. 1972. *The Quiet Revolution in Land Use Control.* Prepared for the Council on Environmental Quality. Washington, D.C.: U.S. Government Printing Office.

Brooks, K. R. 1994. Landscape Architecture: Process and Palette. pp. 221–230 in T. J. Bartuska and G. L. Young, eds. *The Built Environment: A Creative Inquiry Into Design & Planning.* California: Crisp Publications, Inc.

Broughton, J., and S. Apfelbaum. 1999. Using Ecological Systems for Alternative Stormwater Management. *Land and Water* (September/October): 10–13.

Brown, C. R., and T. K. Scarborough. 1993. Applying the Problem-Seeking Approach to Engineering Programming, pp. 47–64 in W. F. E. Preiser, ed. *Professional Practice in Facility Programming.* New York: Van Nostrand Reinhold.

Brown, R. D., and T. J. Gillespie. 1995. *Microclimatic Landscape Design.* New York: John Wiley & Sons.

Buss, T.F. 2001. The effect of state tax incentives on economic growth and firm location decisions: an overview of the literature. *Economic Development Quarterly,* 15(1): 90–105.

Burch, R. 2001. Determinants in moving business schools toward sustainability. Assessing Progress Toward Sustainability in Higher Education consultation presentation paper. Washington. D.C.

Burchell, R. and S. Mukherji. 2003. Conventional development versus managed growth: The cost of sprawl. *American Journal of Public Health,* 93(9): 1534–1540.

Carpenter, P., T. Walker, and F. Lanphear. 1975. *Plants in the Landscape.* San Francisco: W.H. Freeman and Company.

Castle, G. H. III, ed. 1998. *GIS in Real Estate: Integrating, Analyzing, and Presenting Locational Information.* Illinois: Appraisal Institute.

Cathey, H. M. 1990. USDA Plant Hardiness Zone Map. USDA Miscellaneous Publication No. 1475. United States Department of Agriculture, Washington, D.C.

Centers for Disease Control and Prevention. 2002. Web-based Injury Statistics Query and Reporting System (WISQARS) Fatal injury reports. National Center for Injury Prevention and Control, Centers for Disease Control and Prevention. [Online: www.cdc.gov/ncipc/wisqars].

Chapin, F. S., Jr., and E. J. Kaiser. 1985. *Urban Land Use Planning. 3d ed.* Illinois: University of Illinois Press.

Chrisman, N. 1997. *Exploring Geographic Information Systems.* New York: John Wiley & Sons.

City of Aberdeen. 2004. Chapter 8 (Community Appearance), in *City of Aberdeen Comprehensive Plan.* City of Aberdeen, South Dakota.

City of Livermore. 1999. *South Livermore Valley Specific Plan* (adopted November 17, 1997; amended January 25, 1999). City of Livermore, California.

City of Madison. 2006. *City of Madison Comprehensive Plan.* City of Madison Department of Planning and Development. Madison, Wisconsin.

City of Seattle Department of Planning and Development. 2005. *Wallingford Neighborhood Design Guidelines.* City of Seattle, Washington.

CLARB, 1998. *Study of the Profession of Landscape Architecture Now Complete.* CLARB (Council of Landscape Architecture Registration Boards) News 13:1–8.

Clark, R., and M. Pause. 2005. *Precedents in Architecture: Analytic Diagrams, Formative Ideas, and Partis.* New York: John Wiley and Sons.

Clark, W. W., and B. A. Bohne. 1999. Effects of Noise on Hearing. *Journal of the American Medical Association* 281:1658–1659.

Computer Terrain Mapping. 1997. *Visual Landform Analysis.* Colorado: CTM, Inc. [Online: www.ctmap.com/ctm/landform.html]

Cooper-Marcus, C. and M. Barnes. 1999. *Healing Gardens: Therapeutic Benefits and Design Recommendations.* New York: John Wiley & Sons.

Cooper-Marcus, C., and C. Francis, eds. 1998. *People Places: Design Guidelines for Urban Open Space.* 2nd ed. New York: Van Nostrand Reinhold.

Cowardin, L. M., V. Carter, F. C. Golet, and E. T. LaRoe. 1979. *Classification of Wetlands and Deepwater Habitats of the United States.* U.S. Department of the Interior, Fish and Wildlife Service Report FWS/OBS–79/31.

Dahl, T. E. 1990. *Wetland Losses in the United States 1780s to 1980s.* U.S. Department of Interior, Fish and Wildlife Service. U.S. Government Printing Office, Washington, D.C.

Daniels, T. 1999. *When City and Country Collide: Managing Growth in the Metropolitan Fringe.* Washington, D.C.: Island Press.

Davis, S. and J. Ogden. 1994. *Everglades: The Ecosystem and Its Restoration.* Delray Beach, Florida: St. Lucie Press.

Dean, A. O. 1997. Listening to Landscape Architects: What Do They Think of Architects? *Architectural Record* 8:44–49, 160.

deGroot, R. S. 1992. *Functions of Nature: Evaluation of Nature in Environmental Planning, Management and Decision Making.* The Netherlands: Wolters-Nordhoff.

Diamond, H. L., and P. F. Noonan. 1996. *Land Use in America.* Washington, D.C.: Island Press.

Dowrick, D. 1991. *Earthquake Resistant Design: For Engineers and Architects,* 2nd ed. New York: John Wiley & Sons.

Dramstad, W. E., J. D. Olson, and R. T. T. Forman. 1996. *Landscape Ecology Principles in Landscape Architecture and Land-Use Planning.* Washington, D.C.: Island Press.

Duany, A., E. Plater-Zyberk, and J. Speck. 2001. *Suburban Nation: The Rise of Sprawl and the Decline of the American Dream.* New York: North Point Press.

Edelman, S., J. Gaman, and R. Reid. 2006. *What Not to Build: Do's and Don'ts of Home Exterior Design.* Upper Saddle River, New Jersey: Creative Homeowner.

Erdey, C. 2007. *Earthquake Engineering: Application to Design.* New York: John Wiley & Sons.

Ewing, R. 2001. Using a Visual Preference Survey in Transit Design. *Public Works Management & Policy* 5(4): 270–280.

Ewing, R. 1999. *Pedestrian and Transit-Friendly Design: A Primer for Smart Growth.* Washington, D.C.: Smart Growth Network. [Online: www.SmartGrowth.org].

Fabos, J. G., G. T. Milde, and V. M. Weinmayr. 1968. *Frederick Law Olmsted, Sr.: Founder of Landscape Architecture in America.* Massachusetts: The University of Massachusetts Press.

Ferguson, B. K. 1999. The Alluvial History and Environmental Legacy of the Abandoned Scull Shoals Mill. *Landscape Journal* 18(2):147–156.

Ferguson, B.K. 2000. *Porous Pavements.* Florida: Taylor & Francis.

Fisher, H. T. 1982. *Mapping Information: The Graphic Display of Quantitative Information.* Cambridge, Massachusetts: Abt Books.

Florida, R. 2002. *The Rise of the Creative Class: And How its Transforming Work, Leisure, Community, and Everyday Life.* New York: Basic Books.

Forman, R. T. T. 1995. *Land Mosaics: The Ecology of Landscapes and Regions.* New York: Cambridge University Press.

Forman, R. T. T., and M. Godron. 1986. *Landscape Ecology.* New York: John Wiley & Sons.

Franklin, C. 1997. Fostering Living Landscapes, in G. F. Thompson and F. R. Steiner, eds. *Ecological Design and Planning.* New York: John Wiley & Sons.

Franklin, C. 1997. Fostering Living Landscapes, p.263–292 in *Ecological Design and Planning.* G.F. Thompson and F.R. Steiner, eds. New York: John Wiley & Sons

Frumkin, H., L. Frank, and R. Jackson. 2004. *Urban Sprawl and Public Health: Designing, Planning, and Building Healthy Communities.* Washington, D.C.: Island Press.

Gale, D. E. 1992. Eight State-Sponsored Growth Management Programs: A Comparative Analysis. *Journal of the American Planning Association* 58: 425–439.

Garvin, A. 1996. *The American City: What Works, What Doesn't.* New York: McGraw-Hill.

Gehl, J. 2003. *Life Between Buildings: Using Public Space.* The Danish Architectural Press.

Glatting Jackson Kercher Anglin Lopez Rinehart, Inc. 20xx. *Principles of Transit Supportive Development.*

Goldman, M., and F. D. Petross. 1993. Planning for a Captive Audience: Approaches and Problems in Programming Correctional Facilities, pp. 357–380, in W. F. E. Preiser, ed., *Professional Practice in Facility Programming.* New York: Van Nostrand Reinhold.

Goodman, W. I., and E. C. Freund, eds. 1968. *Principles and Practice of Urban Planning.* International City Managers' Association. Washington, D.C.

Guskind, R. 1989. Games cities play. *National Journal,* 21: 634–640.

Gutheim, F. 1977. *Worthy of a Nation: The History of Planning for the National Capital.* Washington, D.C.: National Capital Planning Commission and Smithsonian Institution Press.

Hall, E.T. 1966. *The Hidden Dimension.* Garden City, New York: Doubleday.

H. John Heinz Center for Science, Economics and the Environment. 2000. *The Hidden Costs of Coastal Hazards: Implications for Risk Assessment and Mitigation.* Washington, D.C.: Island Press.

Hammond, S. D., and M. Roberts. 1999. Smart Growth Livermore: California Preserves Ag Lands through Careful Planning. *Government West* (July/August): 15–17.

Haresign, D. T. 1999. Is a Corporate Campus Right for Your Business? *Site Selection* (January): 1118–1120.

Heinz Center. 2000. *The Hidden Costs of Coastal Hazards: Implications for Risk Assessment and Mitigation.* Covelo, CA: Island Press.

Heinz Center, 2002. *Human Links to Coastal Disasters.* Washington, D.C.: The H. John Heinz III Center for Science, Economics and the Environment.

Hendrick, B. 1997. Loud Noise Can Delay Language Skills in Children, Research Finds. *The Atlanta Journal* (May 1997): 3G.

Hertzberger, H. 1991. *Lessons for Students in Architecture.* Rotterdam: Uitgeverij 010.

Herz-Fischler, R. 1998. *A Mathematical History of the Golden Number.* Mineola, New York: Dover Publications.

Hilty, J., W. Lidicker, and A. Merenlender. 2006. *Corridor Ecology: The Science and Practice of Linking Landscapes for Biodiversity Conservation.* Washington, D.C.: Island Press.

Hinshaw, M. L. 1995. *Design Review.* American Planning Association. Chicago, Illinois.

Hopkins, L. D. 1977. Methods of Generating Land Suitability Maps: A Comparative Evaluation. *American Institute of Planners Journal* 43: 386–400.

Hough, M. 1990. *Out of Place: Restoring Identity to the Regional Landscape.* Connecticut: Yale University Press.

Hurn, Jeff. 1993. *Differential GPS Explained.* California: Trimble Navigation.

International City/County Management Association. 2002. *Getting to Smart Growth: 100 Policies for Implementation.* [Online: www.smartgrowth.org]

Jakle, J. 1987. *The Visual Elements of Landscape.* Massachusetts: The University of Massachusetts Press.

Jenks, G. F. 1976. Contemporary Statistical Maps—Evidence of Spatial and Graphic Ignorance. *The American Cartographer* 3(1):11–19.

Johnston, R. J. 1980. *Multivariate Statistical Analysis in Geography: A Primer on the General Linear Model.* Essex, England: Longman Scientific and Technical.

Joyce, M. D. 1982. *Site Investigation Practice.* E and F.N. Spon, London.

Kaplan, S. J., and E. Kivy-Rosenberg, eds. 1973. *Ecology and the Quality of Life.* Illinois: Charles C. Thomas.

Kline, J. 2006. Public Demand for Preserving Local Open Space. *Society and Natural Resources* 19:645–659.

Kline, J., and D. Wichelns. 1998. Measuring Heterogeneous Preferences for Preserving Farmland and Open Space. *Ecological Economics* 26(2): 211–224.

Klosterman, R.E. 1999. The What If? Collaborative Planning Support System. *Environment and Planning B: Planning and Design* 26:393–408.

Kmitch, J.H. and B.E. Baker. 2000. State and local government fiscal position in 1999. *Survey of Current Business,* May 2000.

Kneller, G.F. 1965. *The Art and Science of Creativity.* New York: Holt, Rinehart and Winston.

Kolm, K. E. 1996. Conceptualization and Characterization of Ground-Water Systems Using Geographic Information Systems, pp.131–145, in V.H. Singhroy, D.D. Nebert, and A.I. Johnson, eds., *Remote Sensing and GIS for Site Characterization: Applications and Stands, ASTM STP 1279.* American Society of Testing and Materials, West Conshohocken, Pennsylvania.

Kotkin, J. 2000. *The New Geography: How the Digital Revolution is Reshaping the American Landscape.* New York: Random House.

Krasnow, P. C. 1998. *Correctional Facility Design and Detailing.* New York: McGraw-Hill.

Kulash, W.M. 2001. *Residential Streets,* 3rd ed. Washington, D.C.: Urban Land Institute.

Kunstler, J. H. 1993. *The Geography of Nowhere: the Rise and Decline of America's Man-Made Landscape.* New York: Simon and Schuster.

Kunstler, J. H. 1998. *Home From Nowhere: Remaking Our Everyday World for the 21st Century.* New York: Touchstone.

Kvashney, A. 1982. Enhancing Creativity in Landscape Architectural Education. *Landscape Journal* 1(2): 104–111.

Kwon, H.Y. 2000. *Better Site Design—An Assessment of the Better Site Design Principles for Communities Implementing the Chesapeake Bay Preservation Act.* Center for Watershed Protection. Ellicott City, Maryland.

LaGro, J. A., Jr. 1996. Designing Without Nature: Unsewered Residential Development in Rural Wisconsin. *Landscape and Urban Planning* 35: 1–9.

Lawson, B. 2004. *What Designers Know.* Oxford: Architectural Press and Elsevier.

Lawson, B.R. 2006. *How Designers Think: The Design Process Demystified.* 4th ed. Oxford: Elsevier.

Laxton, M. 1969. Design Education in Practice. In Attitudes in *Design Education,* K. Baynes, ed. London: Lund Humphries.

Lewis, P. H., Jr. 1996. *Tomorrow by Design: A Regional Design Process of Sustainability.* New York: John Wiley & Sons.

Libby, G., S. Hinkley and K. Tallman. 2000. *Another Way Sprawl Happens: Economic Development Subsidies in a Twin Cities Suburb.* Good Jobs First, Washington, D.C.

Lillesand, T. and R. Kiefer. 2000. *Remote Sensing and Image Interpretation.* 4th ed. New York: Jhon Wiley & Sons.

Linn, M. W. 1993. *Drawing and Designing with Confidence: A Step-By-Step Guide.* New York: Van Nostrand Reinhold.

Listokin, D., and C. Walker. 1989. *The Subdivision and Site Plan Handbook.* Center for Urban Policy Research, New Brunswick, New Jersey.

Site and Project Planning Group. 2002. *LANL Sustainable Design Guide.* Los Alamos National Laboratory, Office of Energy Efficiency and Renewable Energy, U.S. Department of Energy. [Online: www.eere. energy.gov/buildings/highperformance/lanl_sustainable_guide.html]

Lothian, A. 1999. Landscape and the Philosophy of Aesthetics: Is Landscape Quality Inherent in the Landscape or in the Eye of the Beholder? *Landscape and Urban Planning* 44: 177–198.

Lynch, K. 1960. *The Image of the City.* Cambridge, Massachusetts: MIT Press.

Lynch, K. 1961. *Site Planning.* Cambridge, Massachusetts: MIT Press.

Lynch, K. 1971. *Site Planning.* 2d ed. Cambridge, Massachusetts: MIT Press.

Malloy, N. B. and J. A. Pressley. 1994. LESA: The Next Decade, pp. 262–273, in Steiner, F. R., J. R. Pease, and R. E. Coughlin, eds. *A Decade with LESA: The Evolution of Land Evaluation and Site Assessment.* The Soil and Water Conservation Society, Ankeney, Iowa.

Marks, C. 1997. Seattle's Environmentally Critical Areas Policies, pp. 227–240, in Miller, D., and G. De Roo, eds. *Urban Environmental Planning: Policies, Instruments and Methods in an International Perspective.* Ashgate, Brookfield, Vermont.

Marsh, W. M. 1998. *Landscape Planning: Environmental Applications*. 3d ed. New York: John Wiley & Sons.

Maslow, A. H. 1954. *Motivation and Personality*. New York: Harper.

Maxwell, C. E., and D. R. Brown. 1993. Programming Processes for Military Health Care Facilities, pp. 249–278, in W. F. E. Preiser, ed. *Professional Practice in Facility Programming*. New York: Van Nostrand Reinhold.

McCullough, D., ed. 1996. *Metapopulations and Wildlife Conservation*. Washington, D.C.: Island Press.

McHarg, I. L. 1969. *Design with Nature*. Published for the Natural History Press. Pennsylvania: Falcon Press.

McKibbon, B. 1989. *The End of Nature*. New York: Random House.

Meck, S., M. Morris, K. Bishop, and E.D. Kelly. 2006. *Model Smart Land Development Regulations*. Interim PAS Report. American Planning Association, Chicago, Illinois.

Meinig, D. W., ed. 1979. *The Interpretation of Ordinary Landscapes*. New York: Oxford University Press.

Mileti, D. S. 1999. *Disasters by Design: A Reassessment of Natural Hazards in the United States*. Washington, D.C.: Joseph Henry Press.

Miller, G. A. 1956. The Magical Number Seven Plus or Minus Two: Some Limits on Our Capacity for Processing Information. *Psychological Review* 63:81–97.

Miller, P. A. 1997. A Profession in Peril? *Landscape Architecture* 87(8): 66–88.

Moore, D. G. 1998. Tips for Siting New Plastics Plants. *Site Selection* September: 804–819.

Morata, T. C., D. E. Dunn, L.W. Kretschmer, G. K. Lemasters, and R.W. Keith. 1993. Effects of Occupational Exposures to Organic Solvents and Noise on Hearing. *Scand J Work Environ Health* 19: 245–254.

Morrish, W., and C. Brown. 2000. *Planning to Stay: Learning to See the Physical Features of Your Neighborhood*. Minnesota: Milkweed Editions.

Motloch, J.L. 2001. *Introduction to Landscape Design*, 2nd ed. New York: John Wiley & Sons.

Muller, J. C. 1976. Numbers of Classes and Chloropleth Pattern Characteristics. *The American Cartographer* 3(2):169–175.

Myers, N. 1979. *The Sinking Ark: A New Look at the Problem of Disappearing Species*. New York: Pergamon Press.

National Association of Home Builders (NAHB). 1991. *Tree Preservation Ordinances*. [Online at www.nahb.org. Accessed July 12, 2006.]

National Center for Complementary and Alternative Medicine (NCCAM). 2005. *Mind-Body Medicine: An Overview*. NCCAM Publication No. D239. U.S. National Institutes of Health, Bethesda, Maryland.

National Governors Association. 2000. *Where Do We Grow From Here? New Mission for Brownfields: Attacking Sprawl By Revitalizing Older Communities*. National Governors Association, Washington, D.C. http://www.nga.org/Files/pdf/REPORT200010BROWNFIELDS.pdf

National Main Street Center. 1995. *Keeping Up Appearances*. National Trust for Historic Preservation, Washington, D.C.

National Park Service. 1995. *Economic Impacts of Protecting Rivers, Trails, and Greenway Corridors*, 4th ed. U.S. National Park Service, Washington, D.C.

National Park Service. 1994. Site Design. Chapter 5, in *Guiding Principles of Sustainable Design*. U.S. National Park Service, Washington, D.C. [Online: www.nps.gov/dsc/dsgncnstr/gpsd/toc.html]

Naveh, Z., and A. S. Lieberman. 1984. *Landscape Ecology: Theory and Application*. New York: Springer-Verlag.

NCARB. 2005. *ARE Guidelines Version 3.1*. Washington, D.C.: National Architectural Registration Boards (NCARB).

Nelessen, A. C. 1994. *Visions for a New American Dream: Process, Principles, and an Ordinance to Plan and Design Small Communities*. 2d ed. Chicago: Planners Press, American Planning Association.

Newman, P., and J. Kenworthy. 1999. *Sustainability and Cities*. Washington, D.C.: Island Press.

Newton, N. 1971. *Design on the Land: The Development of Landscape Architecture*. Cambridge, Massachusetts: Harvard University Press.

Nivola, P. S. 1999. *Laws of the Landscape: How Policies Shape Cities in Europe and America*. Washington, D.C.: Brookings Institute.

Odum, E. P. 1959. *Fundamentals of Ecology*. 2d ed. Pennsylvania: Saunders.

Ohm, Brian W. 1999. *Guide to Community Planning*. Madison: University of Wisconsin Board of Regents.

Otak, Inc. 1999. *The Infill and Redevelopment Code Handbook*. Prepared for the Oregon Transportation and Growth Management Program.

Owen, M. S. 1994. Urban Planning and Design, pp. 289–298, in T. J. Bartuska and G. L. Young, eds. *The Built Environment: A Creative Inquiry into Design & Planning*. Menlo Park, California: Crisp Publications.

Paine, D. and J. Kiser. 2003. *Aerial Photography and Image Interpretation*. 2nd ed. New York: John Wiley & Sons.

Pease, J. R., and A. P. Sussman. 1994. A Five-Point Approach for Evaluating LESA Models, pp. 94–105, in Steiner, F. R., J. R. Pease, and R. E. Coughlin, eds. *A Decade with LESA: The Evolution of Land Evaluation and Site Assessment*. The Soil and Water Conservation Society, Ankeny, Iowa.

Peiser, R. B. 1992. *Professional Real Estate Development*. Washington, D.C.: Urban Land Institute.

Perry, E. 1999. *Trees and other Landscape Plants Have Great Monetary Value*. California: University of California Cooperative Extension. [Online: http://www.cnr.berkeley.edu/ucce50/horticulture/6 hlt010.htm]

Petit, J., D.L. Bassert and C. Kollin. 2004. *Building Greener Neighborhoods: Trees as Part of the Plan*, 2nd ed. Washington, D.C.: American Forests and Home Builders Press.

Pimentel, D., L. Lach, R. Zuniga, and D. Morrison. 2000. Environmental and Economic Costs of Non-indigenous Species in the United States. *Bioscience* 50(1): 53–65.

Pine, B.J. II, and J.H. Gilmore. 1999. *The Experience Economy: Work is Theater and Every Business a Stage*. Cambridge, Massachusetts: Harvard Business School Press.

Platt, K., and P. Curran. 2003. *Green Land Planning*. Washington, D.C.: Urban Land Institute.

Platt, R.H. 2004. *Land Use and Society: Geography, Law, and Public Policy*. 2nd ed. Washington, D.C.: Island Press.

Pregliasco, J. 1988. *Developing Downtown Design Guidelines*. California Main Street Program. Department of Commerce, Sacramento.

Preiser, W. F. E. 1985. *Programming the Built Environment*. New York: Van Nostrand Reinhold.

Preiser, W. F. E., H. Z. Rabinowitz, and E. T. White. 1988. *Post-Occupancy Evaluation*. New York: Van Nostrand Reinhold.

Prince George's County. 2000. *Low-Impact Development: An Integrated Design Approach*. Prince George's County Department of Environmental Resources, Programs and Planning Division, Largo, Maryland.

Quraishi, A., Donahue M., Cody B. 2005. *Child Pedestrians at Risk: A Ranking of U.S. Metropolitan Areas*. Washington, D.C.: Safe Kids Worldwide, October 2005.

Rabinowitz, P.M. 2000. Noise Induced Hearing Loss. *American Family Physician* 61 (9): 2749–2757.

Reese, A. 2004. What's your stormwater paradigm? *Land and Water Magazine*, May–June 2004: 22–28.

Robertson, H. 1924. *The Principles of Architectural Composition*. London: The Architectural Press.

Robinson, A. H., J. L. Morrison, P. C. Muehrcke, A. J. Kimerling, and S. C. Guptill. 1995. *Elements of Cartography*, 6th ed. New York: John Wiley and Sons.

Romm, J.J., 1995. *Lean and Clean Management*. New York: Kodansha.

Rowe, D. 2002. *Environmental Literacy and Sustainability as Core Requirements: Success Stories and Models*, in *Teaching Sustainability at Universities*, Filho, W.L., ed. New York: Peter Lang

Russell, J. S. 1997. How Design Hits the Bottom Line: An Overview of the 1997 Awards. *Architectural Record* (October): 54–55.

Saaty, T. L., and L. Vargas. 1982. *The Logic of Priorities*. Massachusetts: Kluver Nijhoff.

Sadava, D., C. Heller, G. Orians, W. Purves, and D. Hillis. 2006. *Life: The Science of Biology*, 8th ed. Massachusetts: Sinauer.

San Francisco Recreation and Park Department. 2006. *Recreation and Park Acquisition Policy*: San Francisco: City and County of San Francisco Recreation and Park Department.

Sanborn. 1999. *Traditional Mapping*. New York: The Sanborn Map Company, Inc. [Online: www.sanbornmap.com]

Sanford, R.M., and D.H. Farley. 2004. *Site Plan and Development Review: A Guide for Northern New England*. Vermont: Putney Press.

Santos, R.L. 1997. *The Eucalyptus of California: Seeds of Good or Seeds of Evil?*. Denair, California: Alley-Cass Publications.

Sauter, D. 2005. *Landscape Construction*. 2d ed. New York: Thomson Delmar Learning.

Schilling, J. and L. Linton. 2005. The public health roots of zoning: In search of active living's legal genealogy. *American Journal of Preventive Medicine*, 28, 2 (S2): 96–104.

Schoen, D. 1987. *Educating the Reflective Practitioner: Toward a New Design for Teaching and Learning in the Professions*. San Francisco: Jossey-Bass Publishers.

Schulze, F. 1994. *Philip Johnson: Life and Work*. Chicago: The University of Chicago Press.

Schwartz, M., and C. Eichhorn. 1997. Collaborative Decision Making: Using Multiattribute Utility Analysis to Involve Stakeholders in Resolution of Controversial Transportation Issues. *Transportation Research Record* 1606:142–148.

Simiu, E. and Miyata. 2006. *Design of Buildings and Bridges for Wind: A Practical Guide for ASCE 7 Users and Designers of Special Structures*. New York: John Wiley & Sons.

Simon, H. 1976. *The Sciences of the Artificial*. Cambridge: The MIT Press.

Simonds, J.O. 1961. *Landscape Architecture: The Shaping of Man's Natural Environment*. New York: McGraw-Hill.

Sobel, L.S., E. Greenberg, and S. Bodzin. 2002. *Greyfields into Goldfields: Dead Malls Become Living Neighborhoods*. Washington, D.C.: Urban Land Institute.

Stein, K. D. 1997. Good Design Is Good Business. *Architectural Records* (October): 54–55.

Steiner, F. 1991. *The Living Landscape: An Ecological Approach to Landscape Planning*. New York: McGraw-Hill.

Steiner, F. R., J. R. Pease, and R. E. Coughlin, eds. 1994. *A Decade with LESA: The Evolution of Land Evaluation and Site Assessment*. Soil and Water Conservation Society, Ankeny, Iowa.

Steiner, F. and K. Butler. 2006. *Planning and Urban Design Standards*. Student Edition. New York: John Wiley & Sons.

Stenberg, K. J., K. O. Richter, D. McNamara, and L. Vicknair. 1997. A Wildlife Habitat Network for Community Planning Using GIS Technology, pp. 241–254, in Miller, D. and G. De Roo, eds. *Urban Environmental Planning: Policies, Instruments and Methods in an International Perspective*. Ashgate, Brookfield, Vermont.

Strom, S., K. Nathan, J. Woland and D. Lamm. 2004. *Site Engineering for Landscape Architects*, 4th ed. New York: John Wiley & Sons.

Talarico, W. 1998. Evaluating Hidden Site Conditions. *Architectural Record* (May): 247–250, 390–392.

Teed, J., P. Condon, S. Muir, and C. Midgley. 2002. *Sustainable Urban Landscapes Neighborhood Pattern Typology*. The Sustainable Research Institute. University of British Columbia. [Online: www.sustainable-communities.agsci.ubc.ca/projects/SDRI/typ.pdf]

Teller County Planning Department. 2002. Chapter 7, Site Evaluation, Teller County, Colorado, Heavy Services Solid Waste Management Plan, 1998–2017.

Thompson, W. and K. Sorvig. 2000. *Sustainable Landscape Construction: A Guide to Green Building Outdoors*. Washington, D.C.: Island Press.

Tiner, R. W. 1997. Technical Aspects of Wetlands Wetland Definitions and Classifications in the United States, in *National Water Summary on Wetland Resources*. United States Geological Survey Water Supply Paper 2425. [Online: http://water.usgs.gov/nwsum/WSP2425/definitions.html]

Trancik, R. 1986. *Finding Lost Space: Theories of Urban Design*. New York: John Wiley and Sons.

Triad Associates. 2001. *Feasibility Studies: An Informed Buyer is a Smart Buyer*. Triad TIPS. [Online: www.triadassoc.com. Accessed July 5, 2006.]

Triad Associates. 2005. *School District Impact Fees*. Triad TIPS. [Online: www.triadassoc.com. Accessed July 5, 2006.]

Trust for Public Land. 2005. *LandVote Database*. Boston: Trust for Public Land. [Online: www.tpl.org. Accessed August 17, 2005.]

Turner, M.G., R. H. Gardner and R. V. O'Neill, R.V. 2001. *Landscape Ecology in Theory and Practice*. New York: Springer-Verlag.

Tusler, W. H., F. Zilm, J. T. Hannon, and M. A. Newman. 1993. Programming: The Third Dimension, pp. 227–247, in W. F. E. Preiser, ed. *Professional Practice in Facility Programming*. New York: Van Nostrand Reinhold.

U.S. Department of Housing and Urban Development. 2006. *Affordable Housing Design Advisor*. [Online: www.designadvisor.org]

U.S. National Park Service. 1993. *Guiding Principles of Sustainable Design*. United States Department of the Interior, National Park Service, and Denver Service Center.

United Nations Environment Programme. 2003. *Sustainble Cities and Local Agenda 21*. Move Forward at 2003 Global Meeting in Alexandria. INSIGHT, December 2003 edition.

United States Department of Agriculture. 1990. *USDA Plant Hardiness Zone Map*. USDA Miscellaneous Publication No. 1475.

United States Environmental Protection Agency. 1993. *Guidance Specifying Management Measures for Sources of Nonpoint Pollution in Coastal Waters*. EPA840B93001c. (Revised January 21, 1997.)

United States Geological Survey. 2000. National Geologic Map Database.

United States National Oceanic and Atmospheric Agency. 2000. *Heat Wave*. National Weather Service Internet Weather Source. (Revised June 27, 2000.)

United States National Oceanic and Atmospheric Agency. 2000b. *Coastal Zone Management Act of 1972* (as amended through P.L. 104150, The Coastal Zone Protection Act of 1996). (Revised April 5, 2000.)

Urban Design Associates. 2003. *The Urban Design Handbook: Techniques and Working Methods*. New York: W.W. Norton & Company.

Venturi, R., D. Scott Brown, and S. Izenour. 1972. *Learning from Las Vegas: The Forgotten Symbolism of Architectural Form*, rev. ed. Cambridge, Massachusetts: MIT Press.

Wackernagel, M. and W. Rees. 1996. *Our Ecological Footprint: Reducing Human Impact on the Earth*. Canada: New Society Publishers.

Washington State Department of Transportation. 2005. *Hood Canal Bridge Site Selection Report: A Summary of 18 Proposed Sites for New Graving Dock Facilities*. Olympia, Washington: Washington State Department of Transportation.

Way, D. S. 1978. *Terrain Analysis: A Guide to Site Selection Using Aerial Photographic Interpretation*. 2d ed. Pennsylvania: Dowden, Hutchinson & Ross.

Wester, L. M. 1990. *Design Communication for Landscape Architects*. New York: Van Nostrand Reinhold.

Western Australian Planning Commission. 2000. *Liveable Neighborhoods*. 2d ed. Western Australian Planning Commission, Perth, Australia.

White, E. T. 1983. *Site Analysis: Diagramming Information for Architectural Design*. Arizona: Architectural Media.

Whyte. W. H. 1980. *The Social Life of Small Urban Spaces*. Washington, D.C.: Conservation Foundation.

Wike, L.D. and J.A. Bowers. 1995. *Facility Siting as a Decision Process at the Savannah River Site*. WSRC-RP-95-664, Rev. 1. U.S. Department of Energy, Office of Scientific and Technical Information.

Wilcove, D. S., D. Rothstein, J. Dubow, A. Phillips, and E. Losos. 1998. Quantifying Threats to Imperiled Species in the United States. *BioScience* 48: 607–615.

Wilson, E. O., ed. 1988. *Biodiversity*. Washington, D.C.: National Academy Press.

Wolcott, J. 2004. Home developers seek well-developed PRD rules. *Snohomish County Business Journal*, April 2004: 1–3. [Online: www.snohomishcountybusinessjournal.com/archive/apr04/prdrules–apr04.htm]

World Commission on Environment and Development. 1987. *Our Common Future*. Oxford: Oxford University Press.

Wyckoff, M.A. 2003. *Site Plan Review: A Guidebook for Planning and Zoning Commissions*. Michigan: Michigan Society of Planning.

Yeang, K. 1995. *Designing with Nature: The Ecological Basis for Architectural Design*. New York: McGraw-Hill.

Zeisel, J. and M. A. Maxwell. 1993. Programming Office Space: Adaptive Re-Use of the H-E-B Arsenal Headquarters, pp.153–184, in W. F. E. Preiser, ed. *Professional Practice in Facility Programming*. New York: Van Nostrand Reinhold.

Index

WILEY BOOKS ON Sustainable Design

For these and other Wiley books on sustainable design, visit www.wiley.com/go/sustainabledesign

Environmental Benefits Statement